BIOG SFO

Lev, Elizabeth.

The tigress of Forl`i

**Please check all items for damages
before leaving the Library.
Thereafter you will be held
responsible for all injuries
to items beyond reasonable wear.**

Keep 3/17

Helen M. Plum Memorial Library

Lombard, Illinois

A daily fine will be charged for
overdue materials.

NOV 2011

THE TIGRESS OF FORLÌ

· THE ·
TIGRESS OF FORLÌ

Renaissance Italy's Most
Courageous and Notorious Countess,
Caterina Riario Sforza de' Medici

ELIZABETH LEV

HOUGHTON MIFFLIN HARCOURT
BOSTON   NEW YORK
2011

Library of Congress Cataloging-in-Publication Data
Lev, Elizabeth.
The tigress of Forlì: Renaissance Italy's most courageous and notorious countess,
Caterina Riario Sforza de' Medici / Elizabeth Lev.
p. cm.
Includes bibliographical references and index.
ISBN 978-0-15-101299-2
1. Sforza, Caterina, 1463–1509. 2. Countesses—Italy—Forlì—Biography. 3. Forlì
(Italy)—Biography. 4. Forlì (Italy)—History—Exhibitions. 5. Renaissance—
Italy—Biography. 6. Italy—History—1492–1559—Biography. I. Title.
DG537.8.S3L48 2011
945'.4805092—dc22
[B]
2011016053

Book design by Victoria Hartman
Map by Jeffrey Ward

Printed in the United States of America
DOC 10 9 8 7 6 5 4 3 2 1

Photo credits appear on page 289.

Contents

Author's Note

MY FIRST ENCOUNTER with Caterina Riario Sforza de' Medici took place during a sort of personal exile. After twenty-odd years of city life, I had moved to the countryside of Emilia-Romagna in northern Italy with my three children, to complete my graduate degree in art history. After a lifetime in Boston, Chicago, New York, and the university town of Bologna, I had settled in the plains of Imola. Although warm and welcoming to families, this quiet little town, with its dearth of museums, theaters, and ethnic restaurants, left me feeling as if the world had left me behind.

Caterina Sforza became my first friend there. The daughter of the duke of Milan, the denizen of a glittering papal court in Renaissance Rome, she too had been transplanted to the countryside, where she ruled as countess of Imola and Forlì for eleven years. The Imolesi, proud of their local heroine, named streets after her, organized conferences in her honor, and recounted her story at every opportunity. For rural lore, it was remarkably dramatic: a young woman who had to fend off her husband's assassins, the French army, and even the infamous Cesare Borgia.

During an afternoon visit to the Civic Museum of Bologna I first encountered an artifact directly related to Caterina: a small steel breastplate, modeled to fit a petite woman, stood alone among the hulking armor of Renaissance warriors. In this battle gear, a diminutive beauty had squared off against the most dangerous men of her age—how had such a heroine gone unnoticed? Why did no films, websites, or Halloween costumes pay tribute to her? Generations had sung of Achilles and Darius and Alexander, so where was the glorious ballad of Caterina? My studies thus far had focused on fifteenth-century art, a male-dominated world; Caterina's extraordinary life gave me a fresh perspective on the Renaissance.

Fate then brought me to Rome, where I assumed that my discoveries concerning Caterina would come to an end. But over the course of many hours spent in the Vatican Museums, I saw her image again and again, proudly striding amid courtiers in group portraits, present at all the most important moments of Rome's fifteenth-century rebirth.

As I delved into her life, it became clear that Caterina's story was not straightforward. She was a figure of controversy. Local authors from Emilia-Romagna tended to wax romantic about her adventures while glossing over her more problematic episodes; other historians dismissed her as a tyrant, propelled by greed for power and an insatiable sexual appetite.

Tracing back from recent studies and biographies to older records, I arrived at the two principal contemporary sources for the more lurid legends of Caterina, the Venetian diarist Marino Sanuto and the Florentine politician Niccolò Machiavelli. Reading Sanuto was like perusing a celebrity gossip blog; tales of sex and scandal flow, page after page, in what is clearly not the most reliable source. Machiavelli, never particularly respectful of women, wrote especially insidiously about her. As a young man he had had direct dealings with Caterina and had not come out the better. His assessment seemed more than a little tinged with vindictiveness.

Caterina's life as it played out in Imola and Forlì was recorded by two local chroniclers, Leone Cobelli and Andrea Bernardi, eyewitnesses to many events in which she played a part. This proximity in time and place does not, however, make them reliable witnesses in every way. Each had his own reasons for emphasizing certain points and obscuring others.

The racy legend and historical record were masterfully distilled by Count Pier Desiderio Pasolini in his three-volume biography of

Caterina, published in 1893. His meticulous assemblage of documents assisted my own research tremendously. Two problems overshadow his work, however: first, writing in post-unification Italy after the hostile takeover of papal Rome, Pasolini's vision of the papal court was colored with late-nineteenth-century anticlerical sentiment, which obscured Caterina's relationship with her first husband's uncle Pope Sixtus IV; and second, Pasolini's fawning admiration for Caterina actually draws attention away from the documented accomplishments and failings of this exceptional woman.

Reconstructing this story anew has been very rewarding. The journey has taken me to the archives of Milan, Rome, and Florence, with the texts of Bernardi and Cobelli as well as many other accounts as my ever-present travel companions. Dozens of Caterina's letters are extant, several excerpted here for the first time in English. Also, the past few years have witnessed a tidal wave of scholarship that has changed how we understand Renaissance clothing, furnishings, and everyday life; researching the "set design" for certain episodes in Caterina's life has helped me place her firmly in her own world and thereby analyze some of her actions with greater acuity. As an art historian, it was particularly gratifying to find her portrait among the panels of the Sistine Chapel, rendered by none other than Sandro Botticelli.

Indeed, Caterina's life brought her into contact with the greatest artists of her age. Her uncle, the duke of Milan, employed Leonardo da Vinci for seventeen years, and Caterina met him. A modern theorist has even proposed her as the model for the *Mona Lisa*! She posed for one of Leonardo's finest disciples, Lorenzo di Credi, and she was present in Florence as Michelangelo's sculpture *David* was hauled into place. I would like to think that readers of this book will enjoy, as I did, pausing to consider the impression these masterpieces might have made on Caterina and her contemporaries.

Although Caterina Sforza died half a millennium ago, she was a remarkably modern woman. As a bearer of many qualities and virtues that we admire today, Caterina is an ideal guide to the Renaissance world, especially for women. On the one hand, she was a renowned beauty who cared a great deal about fashion and her appearance, and on the other she functioned as a tough-minded CEO, who in addition could handle a weapon. Caterina lived the modern balance of loving mother and successful career woman in tougher times than ours, with both dramatic successes and failures.

But most of all she was a woman who made mistakes. Colossal, horrific, public ones. She dedicated the same passion and energy to her noble undertakings and her wicked ones. Perhaps Caterina's greatest ability was her determination to get up after a disastrous fall. She never gave up, not even when her worst enemy was herself. For Caterina, the show had to go on.

THE FOUR-YEAR PROJECT of writing this book owes thanks to the heroic efforts of many friends and collaborators. George Weigel, who first suggested the book project, introduced me to Cathy Hemming, my agent, who was instrumental in shaping the proposal for this story. John Cabot University gave me a grant that enabled me to visit archives and study materials essential to this work, while Michael Wright and Duquesne University granted me the flexibility to devote long stretches of time to it. Gregory DiPippo helped me wade through the Latin text of numerous documents. David and Ann Wilkins offered precious advice and art history wisdom, and Thomas Williams was invaluable in shaping the storytelling. Alan Droste and Rajia Kahlil read the manuscript and contributed insightful commentary.

Without Andrea Schulz and Thomas Bouman, this manuscript would never have seen the light of day; I am particularly grateful for their expertise, patience, and kindness. Their lessons in taking library data and turning it into a living story will always be remembered when I work in the classroom and at the keyboard.

Like many of the works produced during the Renaissance era, my twenty-first-century project was very much a family undertaking. My gratitude to my mother and father knows no bounds; they read every line and generously lent their wisdom and experience as I developed this manuscript; my sisters, Sarah and Katie, offered encouragement and advice. My greatest debt of gratitude, however, is to my children—Claire, Giulia, and Joshua—who were unflaggingly supportive and loving despite their mother's frequent distractions.

Prologue: Christmas Cannons

AS THE GREAT Jubilee Year of 1500 approached, a mood of unusual festivity prevailed in Europe. At the stroke of midnight on Christmas Eve, amid great pomp and solemnity, Pope Alexander VI Borgia had thrown open the Holy Door he had specially installed in Saint Peter's Basilica to mark the occasion. From the Atlantic Ocean to the Danube River, kings, clergy, and peasants were all celebrating the birth of Christ the Savior. Bells rang out in each town and feasts were laid on every table. In the ancient jubilee tradition of forgiveness of debts, thousands of pilgrims commenced the trek to Rome seeking a plenary indulgence, a chance to wipe clean the slate of the soul and begin again.

But on Christmas morning, 1499, the tiny Italian village of Forlì awoke not to the merry peal of church bells, but to pounding artillery and cursing soldiers. A force of fifteen thousand, composed of Italian, Swiss, and French soldiers, had gathered at the base of the fortress of Ravaldino, overlooking the town of Forlì, and were hammering away at its defensive walls. The bulk of the troops were on loan from the king of France, Louis XII. Commanding those seasoned troops was Cesare Borgia, the most feared warrior in Italy. Cesare's personal bravery and cruelty were as widely known as his powerful connections—he was duke of Valentinois in southern France and the illegitimate son of Pope Alexander VI. Even as the pope was offering salvation to everyone in Christendom, his second-born son was bent on eradicating the ruler of Forlì. If any of his soldiers found this situation ironic or morally troubling, they doubtless kept their perplexity to themselves, for the Borgia commander was known to treat disloyal friends as ruthlessly as he did his enemies.

The soldiers knew that their mission had been approved by the pope himself, who had deposed all the rulers in the northern Italian region of Romagna by decreeing them guilty of tyranny as well as derelict in paying their tributes to Rome. The delinquent states were given to Cesare, who lost no time in collecting his new possessions. Many of the towns had capitulated without a fight, some even hailing Cesare as their liberator. But there had been resistance in Imola, about twelve miles from Forlì, where the fortress keeper, Dionigio Naldi, had held out for almost a month, claiming the town for its rightful lord, Ottaviano Riario. Few stood by him and he was defeated on December 11. After eight days of celebrating that victory, Cesare's army arrived at Forlì. In this tiny town, hardly more than a village, they expected a few perfunctory hours of negotiations before they ousted the present ruler and took control.

At first, all seemed to go according to plan for Cesare. The inhabitants opened the gates, welcoming the troops into the city. Several noblemen even offered hospitality to the captains of the various regiments. Above the town, however, loomed the seemingly impenetrable fortress of Ravaldino, reminding the army that Forlì would never be theirs while the defenders occupied the fort. No easy capitulation was forthcoming from behind those high stone walls. A week after their confident entry, the huge force representing the combined power of the papacy and the king of France was still arrayed at the foot of the fortress, held at bay by a paltry band of nine hundred.

Day and night, the ruler of Forlì patrolled the fortress ramparts, eyes alert for weak spots or changes in the invading enemy's formation. The defending soldiers leapt at every order, unquestioningly loyal to a commander every bit as determined as Cesare. No wonder he was offering an extravagant reward to whoever could capture or kill the indefatigable general, Caterina Riario Sforza de' Medici, the countess of Forlì. Five thousand ducats was a tempting sum. To many, no doubt, it was an amount worth murdering for. Yet no soldiers at Forlì had taken the bait, driven as they were not only by loyalty to their commander but by an ingrained sense of chivalry.

In the preceding days, the attacking soldiers had caught occasional glimpses of Caterina on the ramparts of her fortress. At five feet, four inches, she was noticeably shorter than the men fighting by her side, though she stood at a respectable height for Italian women of her day. Her figure, beneath a steel cuirass engraved with the image of Saint Catherine of Alexandria, was remarkably slim, despite the fact that she had borne six children. When her long, light brown hair occasionally escaped its restraints and flowed around her face and neck, she looked even younger than her thirty-eight years. As she walked with sure, determined steps around her fortress, her enemies strained to see the woman who had challenged the College of Cardinals, single-handedly put down a revolt after the murder of her husband, seduced and married the handsomest member of the Medici clan, and was now locking horns with the formidable Cesare Borgia.

The bleakness of Caterina's Christmas morning was relieved only by the knowledge that her children were safely ensconced with their Medici relatives in Florence. She knew that while she defended their birthright, their day would begin with worship in that city's beautiful churches; perhaps their anxious spirits would be lifted for a while by the glorious music of the choirs. Later they would feast in grand halls by blazing fires, while their mother shared a frugal meal in the guardhouse with the cadre of faithful followers who remained in Ravaldino.

There, Christmas morning had begun with the traditional Mass at dawn. After leaving the chill of the stone fortress chapel, the countess set about ensuring double rations for her men, listening to their personal stories, writing letters of commendation for bravery, and otherwise alleviating the dismal mood. For a time, silence in the enemy camp suggested that those soldiers too might be observing this holiest of days, but soon a barrage of cannon fire shattered the calm.

Cesare's father, Pope Alexander VI, had made great plans for the Jubilee Year. The construction of new buildings and the offering of special prayers were intended to draw the whole Christian world to Rome to make a fresh start. Caterina had been planning to go to Rome as well, for she too had reasons to seek forgiveness. For five years she had waited, with much on her conscience, knowing that the jubilee offered a singular opportunity to erase terrible spiritual scars. Now the pope's own son had become the greatest obstacle in Caterina's path. She could give up her lands and her children's inheritance, allow Cesare to become the prince of Romagna, and move in with her Medici relatives. That would secure her life and her freedom. Or she could defend town and title, risking death or imprisonment. Although many other rulers of Romagna had ceded their towns and taken the paltry papal compensation for their noble titles and their lands, Caterina had no intention of stepping aside quietly so that Cesare's father could award him her state as a twenty-fifth-birthday gift. He would have to win it from her the same way her family had won their lands—with blood and steel.

Now the usurping army was quartered in her town, looting her palace and the homes of her followers. The townspeople who had given up the town to the invaders, preferring to place their fate at the mercy of the Borgias rather than join the seemingly hopeless cause of the Riarios, had received little clemency. The soldiers sacked their homes and raided the convents, looking for young women of Forlì to provide them with "entertainment." On Christmas Day, the occupiers were drinking wine stolen from the cellars of the Forlivesi and wearing the warm wool clothing belonging to their "hosts," while even the elderly and sick were left to shiver in the winter cold. Caterina, who knew from experience that the weakest were always the first victims of war, had begged her people to stand with her. Now she stood helplessly above the town, watching its devastation.

Caterina's mind revolted at the thought of Cesare and his entourage devouring her people's food and celebrating the capture of her lands. No stranger to the daring bluff, she formed a plan. Perhaps she could not rid Forlì of Cesare for Christmas, but she could render his holiday as unpleasant as hers. She ordered her men to find the flag of the powerful Republic of Venice and to raise the Venetian lion high above the ramparts of Ravaldino. Venice was the wild card in the politics of Renaissance Italy. A fierce defender of its lands, with an extensive fleet and skilled sailors at its disposal, the Most Serene Republic had many known political bedfellows. What worried every state on the peninsula was the unknown number of its secret allies. Had Caterina put her state under the protection of Venice? Was the Venetian army already marching toward Forlì?

Caterina didn't have to wait long to see her plan bear fruit: the mere sight of the golden lion of Venice galvanized the enemy. From the ramparts Caterina could see the soldiers on watch running to the palace where Cesare and his cousin were lodged. Cesare, upon seeing the scarlet and gold standard, called an emergency council to evaluate the possibility of a hitherto unknown alliance between Venice and Forlì, which could extend the Venetian sphere of influence farther inland from the Adriatic and closer to the border of the Florentine Republic. Cesare knew that Caterina had previously sought assistance from Florence and been refused. Had she avenged the rebuff by offering Venice a gateway into Tuscan lands?

Riders left the city at a gallop to seek confirmation of the disturbing news, while scouts were placed on vigil to look for approaching troops. Festivities were interrupted as soldiers reorganized the camp for a potential attack from outside Forlì. There was no more time to raid homes and abduct women as the men nervously prepared for battle.

Caterina knew it would take just a few short hours to verify that no Venetian army was en route to Forlì, but she returned to her room in the keep, content in the knowledge that she had secured a little Christmas peace for the people of Forlì. Once again she had acted with ingenuity and boldness, qualities that made her an object of fascination throughout Italy. Admirers saw her as an inspired warrior along the lines of Joan of Arc, whereas malicious tongues compared her to the lascivious manipulator Cleopatra; all the people, whatever their opinion of her, wondered where such an extraordinary woman had come from. The outrageous gambles, astute strategies, and iron determination of Caterina Riario Sforza de' Medici had drawn Europe's attention to the siege of Forlì.

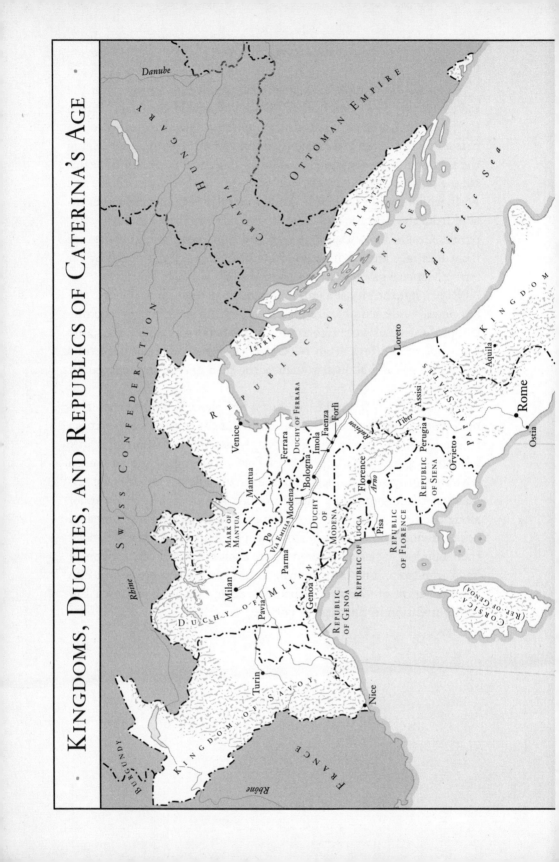

KINGDOMS, DUCHIES, AND REPUBLICS OF CATERINA'S AGE

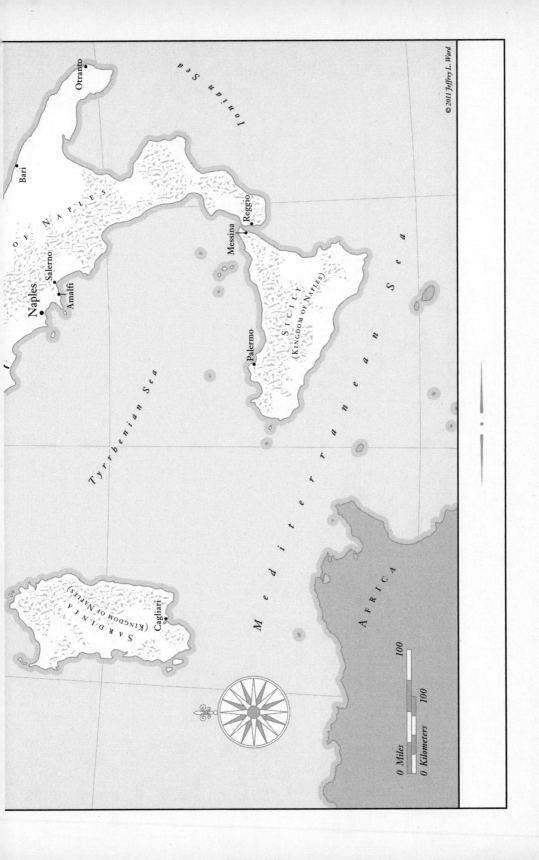

© 2011 Jeffrey L. Ward

Ionian Sea

Otranto

Bari

OF NAPLES

Reggio

Messina

Naples
Salerno
Amalfi

SICILY
(KINGDOM OF NAPLES)

Palermo

Tyrrhenian Sea

Mediterranean Sea

SARDINIA
(KINGDOM OF NAPLES)

Cagliari

AFRICA

0 Miles   100
0 Kilometers   100

THE TIGRESS OF FORLÌ

THE EDUCATION OF AN AMAZON

ATERINA WAS BORN in Milan in 1463, the illegitimate daughter of Galeazzo Maria Sforza, heir to the Duchy of Milan, and the beautiful Lucrezia Landriani, who, for Galeazzo's convenience, had been married off to a compliant palace courtier. In almost any other realm in Europe, illegitimacy was a stigma that effectively prevented a person from attaining a respectable social standing, but in Italy, bastard children were the norm—especially in the ruling house of Milan. Custom held that natural children would be raised in the house of the father, side by side with the rightful heirs, and thus Caterina grew up in the ducal household. She carried her Sforza surname with such pride that even after three marriages she would still retain it.

The Sforza family had risen from peasantry to nobility by sword and skirmish. Muzio Attendolo, the founder of the Sforza line and Caterina's great-grandfather, had run away from his family farm in the 1390s to fight as a mercenary soldier, a *condottiere*. Fourteenth-century Italy was a mosaic of separate principalities characterized by complex military alliances and shifting borders. From the kingdom of Sicily to the free Republic of Venice, young warriors looking for fame and fortune were well accommodated with battles to fight. Muzio Attendolo's courageous exploits on the battlefield had earned him the nickname "Sforza," meaning "strength." After fighting for the papacy, the Republic of Florence, and the kingdom of Naples, he settled into regular service with the duke of Milan, Filippo Maria Visconti. The Viscontis, who had been vested with the dukedom of Milan in 1395 by the Holy Roman Emperor Wenceslaus, had turned Milan into a wealthy state and one of the most politically significant territories in Italy. Muzio's illegitimate son Francesco carried on the new family name, Sforza, and its mercenary enterprise, earning increasing fame through his valor in Italy's ceaseless wars and military disputes. Francesco Sforza married the illegitimate daughter of Filippo Maria Visconti, Bianca Maria, and when Duke Filippo died without a male heir in 1447, Sforza was poised to claim the duchy.

Francesco's plan was foiled by the Milanese nobility, who on the day of Filippo's death declared the city a republic, destroyed the Visconti castle of Porta Giovia, and occupied all the public buildings. The newly formed republic soon faced formidable enemies including Venice, which exploited the weakened city by plucking away its territories. The embattled republic had no choice but to hire the Sforza army to repel these foreign foes, and in a swift campaign, Francesco recaptured the subject cities. In 1448, Francesco signed a treaty with Venice and then turned to retake his own city. After a couple of months of siege, Milan finally capitulated and opened its gates to Francesco, the de facto duke of Milan, confirming one of the many shrewd statements of the political theorist Niccolò Machiavelli: even a tenuous hereditary claim to a throne is an advantage in regaining power.

The Holy Roman Emperor never officially recognized Francesco and Bianca Maria, but they ruled Milan as grandly as any duke and duchess the city had ever known. Boasting one of the largest urban populations in fifteenth-century Europe—about 200,000 inhabitants—the city enjoyed the products of its fertile farmlands as well as thriving commerce, particularly in the production of silk and armor.

Under Francesco Sforza, Milan set up one of the first printing presses in Europe and became world famous for its sophisticated technical advances in myriad industries.[1] Nonetheless, a constant undercurrent of violence rippled beneath this busy surface. The first architectural project of the Sforza rule was the rebuilding of the defensive castle of Porta Giovia, which would later be renamed Castello Sforzesco. Francesco devoted particular attention to reinforcing the battlements facing the city, reflecting his belief that the greater danger to the Sforza family lurked within, not outside, the city walls. Despite internal tensions, Milan flourished. Francesco built the innovative and highly effective Maggiore hospital and the magnificent Certosa di Pavia, a monastery at the customary burial site of the Visconti dukes.

Francesco's son Galeazzo Maria continued the tradition of emphasizing municipal development along with military prowess during his ten-year reign. Assuming the leadership of Milan upon Francesco's death in 1466, he enacted Milan's most lavish displays of luxury and extravagance. He was superbly instructed in the arts befitting a prince, but Galeazzo Maria's streak of self-indulgence would earn him many enemies within his own boundaries. Caterina was three when her father, Galeazzo, became duke of Milan, and along with her father's court she took up residence in the renovated castle of Porta Giovia. Surrounded by every luxury produced by nature and man, she received a first-rate education alongside the duke's four legitimate children. Little difference was drawn between male and female offspring. The children spent long hours with their tutor, Francesco Filefo, a humanist and poet of the court. Filefo had authored *Sforzinda*, an epic poem inspired by Homer's *Iliad*, memorializing the grand deeds of Francesco Sforza's conquest of Milan. Under his tutelage, the Sforza children learned to read Latin, particularly the works of Virgil, Cicero, and Seneca. The vast ducal library contained over one thousand books, some exquisitely illuminated with brilliantly colored scenes and fine tendrils of gold leaf highlighting the borders; others were transcribed in the innovative, easy-to-read Florentine script. To complement their study of the classics, the young Sforzas read the stories of the saints. From the legend of her namesake, Catherine of Alexandria, Caterina learned that faith can make a young girl wiser than fifty philosophers. The family's immense book collection was also liberally sprinkled with French chivalric romances of the type that Cervantes would satirize a century later in *Don Quixote*. For Caterina and other young aristocrats, however, they were useful manuals, initiating them into the duties and ideals of their station through captivating tales of noble deeds and adventures.

Like many noblewomen of the Renaissance, young Caterina spent many an hour immersed in Boccaccio's popular *De Mulieribus Claris (Illustrious Women)*. The first collection of women's biographies written in the West, *Illustrious Women* recounted with earthy detail 104 stories of the most famous female figures of all time, from Eve in the Garden of Eden to Joanna, queen of Jerusalem and Sicily. Joanna had been a contemporary of Boccaccio, and she had not only hired Caterina's great-grandfather Muzio Attendolo as her personal bodyguard but was also rumored to have been his lover. Within those vellum pages Caterina found the glorious histories of the virtuous Zenobia, queen of Palmyra, and the decadent Semiramis, queen of the Assyrians—to whom Caterina would later be likened by detractors. The stories were worldly and sexually explicit, often touting grand deeds rather than strict morals. Little did Caterina suspect that by the time she was thirty-three years old, she herself would be named as an illustrious woman in Jacopo Filippo Foresti's similar collection, *De Plurimis Claris Selectisque Mulieribus*.

The muscles of the Sforza scions were as well trained as their minds. The children passed hour upon hour learning to bear and wield arms in the tradition of their warrior family. Duke Galeazzo Maria Sforza, a passionate and frequent hunter, acquired the best weapons and the finest horses, dogs, falcons, and hunters for the family's huge park at Pavia. Hunting was an age-old tradition in the training of young knights and princes. King Alfonso of Castile in the fourteenth century had sung its praises: "A knight should always engage in anything to do with arms and chivalry and, if he cannot do so in war then he should do so in activities that resemble war. And the chase is most similar to war."[2] The hunt required alert minds, toned bodies, and the occasional forgoing of sleep, food, and other creature comforts. Most important, it taught children at an early age to overcome fear.

Unlike the nobility of most other European courts, the Sforzas emphasized training the female children alongside the males in the use of weapons, riding, and the chase. Thus Caterina gained an unusual advantage over her peers: her education developed both the intellect and the fundamentals of military leadership. Isabella of Castile, Caterina's contemporary in Spain, would also learn to hunt and ride, but she would be little schooled in the arts and letters because

her indoor hours would be spent in the chapel. Closer to home, Isabella d'Este, the daughter of the illustrious duke of Ferrara, would
hone her literary skills and develop an art connoisseur's eye, but she
would be kept from activities that required the physical exertion that
is essential to the hunt. These young women, who would all serve as
marital bargaining chips in the contest for political power in Europe,
received an upbringing that fit the character of their court of origin.
As *condottieri*, the Sforzas had fought their way to the throne and considered strength and discipline to be their greatest assets. Hunting
instilled in their women the ability to master their emotions, which
would serve them well as they left home at a youthful age to venture
to strange lands with new husbands. It also taught children to take
swift and decisive action tempered with patience. Caterina frequently
set out alongside her stepmother and grandmother, both formidable hunters, to the well-stocked Pavia hunting grounds. Carrying a
child-size hunting knife with fine gold chasing or a falcon sporting a
tooled-leather hood decorated with gilt, Caterina chased stag, boar,
hare, and even ostrich alongside her male kin.

Most of Caterina's early life was spent at the Sforza castle in Pavia and the Milanese fortress of Porta Giovia. The high stone walls
that surrounded her from infancy offered a sense of protection and
security. War, and all the devastation that came with it, was a constant in Renaissance Italy. Caterina's world was a microcosm of peace
and privilege, and for the moment the powerful ramparts shielded her
from poverty, unrest, and danger.

Fifteenth-century Milan was already an international center for
luxury clothes and high-tech armor. Agents throughout the world
flocked to the Via dei Spadari, "Street of the Swordsmiths." Early
in the morning they would line up outside the large palace marked
MY, the symbol of the Missaglia family, the most famous armor-
ers in Europe.[3] Tommaso Missaglia's development of asymmetrical
plates, allowing warriors greater freedom of movement, had revolu-
tionized fighting. From France to Naples, kings sported the distinctive rounded armor bearing the MY logo. The design of this state-of-
the-art equipment took into account recent improvements in firearms
as well as in defense; special auxiliary plates at the back of the helmet and the center of the breastplate offered greater protection from

projectiles. To fill the massive orders, Milanese manufacturers set up primitive assembly lines to mass-produce the suits. Watching her brothers being fitted for Missaglia armor, Caterina would learn to appreciate a well-made cuirass.

Even more opulent than the specialized armor was Milan's fashionable clothing. The city's long association with France inspired its designers to create more elaborate, intricately constructed costumes than anything previously seen in Italy. Milan's primacy in silk production kept Milanese men and women shimmering in brilliant-hued robes. The nobles wore form-fitting garments covered by long overdresses called *pallande*. Sporting lengthy trains and voluminous sleeves, each robe was made from more than eighteen feet of cloth; the most extravagant incorporated gold brocade. The gowns were embroidered with jewels or pearls and also boasted a distinctive trim called "dagging," specially cut and twisted strips of cloth. This finery would later prompt Leonardo da Vinci to write, "I remember having seen them in my childhood, grown men and young boys going about with every single edge of their clothing dagged, from head to toe and down the right and left sides. At the time it seemed such a wonderful invention that they even dagged the dags."[4]

Although over the course of her life, many people would admire Caterina for her beauty and style, none would ever doubt the mettle beneath the elegance. Throughout her childhood, Caterina had been surrounded by strong-willed women. During her first years at court, she was raised by her grandmother, Bianca Maria Visconti, aunt of the king of France, Louis XI. Bianca, a beloved leader of her city, co-ruled with her son for the first few years of his reign, until Galeazzo Maria felt himself dwarfed by his mother, complaining that she treated him "as if he were a boy of little intelligence." Upon his marriage in 1468 to Bona of Savoy, he sent Bianca Maria to her dowry city of Cremona, where she died shortly after. The people of Milan mourned Bianca, praising her warm, caring treatment of her subjects as well as her courage in fighting by her husband's side in battle. After the death of her grandmother, Caterina was welcomed by Galeazzo Maria's new wife, who treated the five-year-old girl as her own daughter. Sister to the queen of France, Bona was renowned as a beauty. The Milanese ambassador who had negotiated the match with Galeazzo promised that the duke would be "much pleased with so beautiful a lady,"[5] and when the court painter Bonifacio Bembo returned from France bearing a portrait of Bona to be shown to her intended, a smitten Galeazzo kept the work, claiming that he could not bear to part with it. Bona was a marvelous horsewoman and enthusiastically accompanied her husband on hunts. But beneath the beautiful and fun-loving demeanor of this fashionable lady there lay political savvy and a will of steel.

Caterina's first foray outside the confines of her family and court came in 1471, when her father embarked on a series of state visits to the neighboring territories. Galeazzo had been officially elected ruler of Milan in 1469, the same year that Lorenzo de' Medici assumed the rule of Florence. Ostensibly to fulfill a vow that he had made with his wife to visit the Church of Santissima Annunziata in Florence, Galeazzo began planning the most elaborate cavalcade in living memory for a tour through the cities of Mantua, Ferrara, and Florence, intending to impress his peers, allies, and rivals.

Eight-year-old Caterina and her siblings were outfitted with new clothes, more elaborate than anything they had ever worn. In March 1471 the family set out in a flamboyant show of wealth that left onlookers marveling. Fourteen carriages decorated in gold and silver and drawn by horses draped in cloth-of-gold accompanied the ladies. The family escort comprised two thousand cavalrymen and five hundred infantrymen wearing silk costumes in the Sforza colors, red and white. To enliven the journey, the duke brought a thousand dogs and innumerable hawks and falcons as well as dwarfs, jesters, and musicians.

The ducal family spent the first few days in Mantua as guests of the Gonzaga court. Ludovico Gonzaga, marquis of Mantua, had much in common with Galeazzo Maria. His family had also risen from the status of *condottiere* to rule the wealthy and fertile lands of Mantua. The Gonzagas loved hunting, and Mantua bred the best hunting dogs and horses in Europe. The duke also found an outlet for his bawdy humor with the marquis. But for all the roughness, the Gonzaga court also embraced elegant refinement. Its choir was the finest in Italy, surpassing the pope's own singers. Assembled from all over the world, these musicians sang traditional liturgical music but also composed lively songs for the court's illustrious guests. Within the gloomy stone ramparts of the Gonzaga fortress lay chamber after chamber adorned with marvelous paintings, including those recently executed by the ingenious court painter Andrea Mantegna. It was here that Caterina was first exposed to the power of art. Galeazzo Maria spent hours studying the nearly complete Camera Picta, a room whose murals depicted the Gonzaga clan receiving guests and relatives. Grand architectural structures framed many of the scenes, proclaiming Mantua's urban renewal; others were set in lavish landscapes to underscore the fertile lands and generous spirit of the ruling house. The ceiling was a masterful demonstration of Mantegna's skill in trompe l'oeil: the medallions depicting the great caesars of Rome seemed to be carved of marble instead of painted. The vault was crowned with a painted aperture through which one seemed to view the sky. An illusionist dome, intended to resemble the Roman Pantheon, alluded to a connection between the Gonzaga court and imperial Rome. In Mantua, under Gonzaga dominion for over 150 years, art celebrated the success of kingship, not republican rule.

What the Sforza family saw in Mantua showed them that Italians valued more than displays of opulence, and nowhere was this more true than in the Republic of Florence, where Caterina and her family were greeted by Lorenzo de' Medici and welcomed into his home on the Via Larga. Although the Medicis were not officially the rulers of Florence, they were the de facto leaders of the powerful city-state. Florence, unlike Milan or Mantua, had succeeded in winning its independence during the wars between the papacy and Holy Roman Empire in the twelfth and thirteenth centuries. Together with Siena, Pisa, and Bologna, Florence was one of a handful of little Italian city-states with a fledgling form of representational government. Milan had twice attempted to throw off its feudal shackles (most recently before the reign of Galeazzo's father), but its proximity to France, the oldest monarchy in Europe, and its weak grounding in the principles of humanism seemed to destine all bids for freedom to failure.

Lorenzo de' Medici was neither prince nor duke, yet his people called him "the Magnificent" in recognition of his leadership and his generosity. He did not live in a castle, protected by high walls and moats, but in a palace similar to those of other wealthy Florentine families. Its exterior did not boast state-of-the-art battlements or other defenses. Instead, hand-tooled stones were arranged in decorative, orderly patterns, and large windows illuminated the interior, bathing the rooms with light.

The house contained a library even richer than that of the Sforzas, and the Medicis took great interest in its contents. Lorenzo kept among his household an academy of scholars who discussed the works of the ancient authors, particularly Plato, and who wrote copiously themselves. Lorenzo often spent time with them, composing poems. Less exuberant than his handsome younger brother Giuliano, Lorenzo the Magnificent was nonetheless never considered a weakling. Still very young, Caterina was captivated by this ruler, who fought his enemies valiantly, discussed Plato knowledgeably, and wrote poetry passionately. Her love for Florence and particularly the Medici family would long remain with her.

The Medicis were grateful for the friendship of the Sforzas. Less than one hundred years earlier, under the Viscontis, Milan had been Florence's bitterest enemy. As soon as Francesco Sforza assumed the rule of Milan, Cosimo the Elder, grandfather of Lorenzo, had offered his friendship and considerable banking power, opening a Medici bank in Milan and transforming adversary into ally. Lorenzo was a gracious host and staged various entertainments for his noble guests, even commissioning one of his favorite artists, Piero del Pollaiuolo, to paint Galeazzo's portrait. Nonetheless, the austerity of the Florentines must have surprised the Sforza entourage. The Republic of Florence had adopted strict sumptuary laws, which prohibited luxuries in dress and accessories for both men and women. The pearl embroidery, horned headdresses, and lengthy trains typical in Milan were strictly forbidden in Florence. Although Tuscany produced the finest dyed luxury cloths in Europe, its citizens wore simple attire, more often made of wool than silk or gold brocade. Though the women of Florence chafed under these rules, they were nevertheless scandalized by the extravagance of the Milanesi. Some even considered the company from Milan to be a negative influence on the city's youth. Machiavelli would later lament that if Duke Galeazzo had found the city with a tendency toward "courtly finery and customs contrary to any well-ordered society, he left it even more so."[6]

The wealth of Florence was displayed in its streets. The mighty cupola of the cathedral of Florence, Brunelleschi's astonishing architectural feat, dominated the city. The guild building of Orsanmichele, a few steps from the cathedral, was a proud showcase of sculpture commissioned by the Florentines. Donatello's *Saint Mark* was carved with a gravitas alien to the gothic-style sculptures of Milan, and *Saint John the Baptist* by Ghiberti was the first bronze life-size sculpture to be cast in a single piece since antiquity. Newly unveiled and the pride of the city were Ghiberti's doors to the Baptistery of Florence, with ten gilt-bronze panels in relief, which an admiring Michelangelo would later dub "the gates of Paradise."

The greatest Florentine riches, however, lay in the ingenuity and the creativity of its free citizens. The Florentines tried to outdo one another in inventiveness and novelty, not lavish display. For example, the Sforza family arrived in time for the Feast of the Annunciation. This holiday, celebrated on March 25, recalls the day the angel Gabriel told the Virgin Mary that she would bear a child, the Son of God, and it marked the first day of the New Year in Florence. Their Medici hosts took the duke and his family to see miracle plays at the churches of Florence, including the most beloved production of the year, the "Ascension of Christ" at the Church of Santa Maria del Carmine. This breathtaking spectacle included arrays of flying angels played by local children, who descended from the skies to welcome Jesus as he rose on clouds into Paradise. Engineers had built machines to lift and move people, props, and scenery. The Florentines likewise excelled in games, from boxing to tennis, but always favored strategy over force. Even in jousts, they prided themselves on overcoming brute strength through intellectual superiority.

The Sforzas, expecting to overwhelm their Tuscan neighbors with their obvious military might and dazzling demonstration of wealth, found themselves gently rebuked by these practical, hardworking people. What the Milanesi had perceived as glamorous the Florentines derided as gaudy. And although not a single person in Florence — not even Lorenzo the Magnificent — vaguely approached Galeazzo Maria in rank and stature, it seemed that the people of this proud republic, ennobled by their intellectual achievements, were looking down on him and his entourage. The Milanese party returned home, sober but enlightened.

2

CHILDHOOD'S END

As Caterina's travels came to a close, her childhood too was drawing to an end. The wide-eyed ten-year-old was about to become a pawn in political maneuvers that lay beyond her ken.

At the end of October, shortly after his return to Milan, Duke Galeazzo Maria fell deathly ill with smallpox, plunging the ducal household into panic. The fatalism with which the duke viewed his illness alarmed his dependents, and an emergency alert spread throughout the court. No situation was trickier than the death of a sovereign while his heirs were still too young to rule. Galeazzo himself, who was an adult at the time of his father's death, had been first ambushed and then besieged as he tried to reach Milan—despite having disguised himself as a Frenchman's servant in a vain effort to avoid detection. Raised amid court intrigue in France, Caterina's stepmother, Bona, knew well what was at stake. Paradoxically, widowhood could be a woman's path to power in the Renaissance, through regency for an underage heir. While women could not gain the rule of a city by inheritance, with enough support a widow with a very young son could assume the position of regent until he came of age. Because this was a frequent occurrence, especially in turbulent states, a wise woman learned the art of statecraft early. Like riding an unruly animal, controlling a realm, whether large or small, was a difficult and complicated challenge, especially for a woman. Threats external and internal abounded. Widows were commonly obliged to remarry in the interests of peacekeeping. Noble mothers of infant sons often had to fight off usurping relatives or foreign claimants to protect their filial inheritance. The demise of many a young widow and child heir had followed hard upon the death of a ruler. The risks were particularly high in Milan, where popular uprisings were still a part of living memory, and several adult brothers of Galeazzo were hungry for the ducal throne.

As powerless doctors hovered over her father's bedside and a steady stream of notaries, couriers, and confessors flowed in and out of the castle, young Caterina learned much about the transfer of power. Bona took action immediately to protect the dukedom for her son, Gian Galeazzo, an infant of just two years. She wrote to her brother-in-law, Louis IX, king of France, requesting that the powerful monarch support her child's claim. For more immediate military support, in case it proved necessary, she contacted the Gonzaga family of Mantua, allies with a strong army a few hours' march away.

The tense atmosphere in the castle dissipated, however, when to everyone's surprise Galeazzo Maria regained his strength. His recovery from a brush with death seemed to infuse him with renewed vigor, for he proceeded to set Milan on a course of transformation that would enable it to compete with the great courts of Italy. Art, architecture, and especially music flourished over the following years. Milan's crude warrior princes acquired a patina of Renaissance humanism. Caterina herself reaped many benefits from these stimulating developments: she learned to compose and recite Latin verse and to appreciate fine art. She also saw how a realm could be enriched through intelligent, far-sighted building programs. Galeazzo fostered a printing industry, and in short order Milan emerged as an energetic rival to intellectual Florence. Galeazzo Maria had been deeply impressed with the Gonzaga castle in Mantua, which demonstrated that a well-fortified defensive structure could also make a magnificent residence. The duke had been especially taken with Andrea Mantegna's monumental Camera Picta, the lavishly painted chamber that Galeazzo dubbed "the most beautiful room in the world." The four walls presented the family, friends, and allies of the Gonzagas in colorful procession against a richly detailed landscape. One aspect of that work, however, was highly displeasing to Galeazzo Maria: his own portrait had been left out of the array of political notables.

In 1472, the duke commenced work on his own cycle of decorative paintings in the Porta Giovia castle. One-upping the single chamber of the Gonzaga palace, Galeazzo's program would cover two halls. For this ambitious undertaking, he commandeered the services of the best Lombard painters, Bonifacio Bembo and Vincenzo Foppa. The project was never completed, perhaps because the duke fretted excessively over its planning, demanding endless modifications as his family grew and his political affiliations changed.

The great hall was to boast a hunting scene featuring the duke, his brothers, and court intimates, including a spoof of the poor riding skills of one of the duke's favorites, a certain Alessio Piccinino from Albania, who was depicted in an embarrassing position after "a stag has thrown him from his horse and he is raising his legs to the sky in as attractive a manner as possible."[1] The purpose of the decoration was to underscore the rightful succession from Visconti to Sforza rule. In an unusual yet poignant touch, the two-year-old heir, Gian Galeazzo Sforza, was represented holding the hand of his father. Galeazzo Maria also intended to use the fresco cycle as a retort to the perceived insult from the Gonzagas. The marquis of Mantua—of the Gonzaga family—would be included, but he was placed next to the marquis of Monserrat, a tiny, insignificant state.

Galeazzo also planned an even grander project during this period, an equestrian monument to his father, Francesco Sforza. If the Gonzagas could adapt the Pantheon to their Camera Picta, the Sforzas could commission a statue to rival that of Emperor Marcus Aurelius in Rome, the sole surviving bronze equestrian monument from antiquity. This ambitious commission would eventually draw Leonardo da Vinci to Milan in 1482.

Closer to Galeazzo Maria's heart than any statue or painting, however, was the dream of amassing the grandest choir in Europe, for music delighted him more than any other art. To this end, the duke sent agents to many different Italian states, often upsetting diplomatic relations as he hired away the best singers and other musicians. An especially awkward situation arose when Galeazzo lured several performers away from King Ferdinand of Naples shortly after they had negotiated a long-awaited and precarious alliance. Peace was maintained, but King Ferdinand was left *cum la bocca molto amara*—"with a very bitter taste in his mouth." The duke's extraordinary choir soon achieved the preeminence Galeazzo had sought. The forty musicians, from both Italy and abroad, transformed Milan into the most exciting city in Europe for choral music.

ALONGSIDE THESE CULTURAL endeavors, intended to lend magnificence to his rule, Galeazzo Maria also embarked upon several political maneuvers that would irrevocably shape the course of Caterina's life. In Romagna, a region bordering Milanese territory, the little fiefdom of Imola had been in a state of political unrest due to revolts against the ruling family of Taddeo Manfredi. A constantly shifting pawn on the political landscape, Imola had been ruled by both Milan and the pope, as part of the Papal States; both Venice and Florence were eager to acquire it. Imola had fertile soil for growing wheat as well as other crops and held a strategic position between northern and southern Italy. It was well placed on the roads to the Adriatic coast, the launching point for the rich commercial trade with the East.

Using the unstable Manfredi rule as a pretext, Galeazzo Maria took Imola by force in 1471, adding it to his own territories. Many neighboring rulers were enraged by this bold and undiplomatic maneuver, none more so than Lorenzo the Magnificent. To placate the powerful Florentine, the duke promised to sell him the town, but as subsequent events revealed, Galeazzo had other ideas in mind.

Another upheaval occurred that same year, with the death of Pope Paul II Barbo. After the funeral ceremonies for the Venetian pope, the College of Cardinals entered into conclave and on August 9 elected Francesco della Rovere from Savona as Pope Sixtus IV. The new pope was well aware that the principal promoter of his election had been the duke of Milan, and Sixtus IV wasted no time in making overtures to his new friend and ally, with a view to cementing their relationship. The currents set in motion by the ascension of a della Rovere to the papacy and the conquest of Imola by Galeazzo would soon converge on the young Caterina.

The Milanese Christmas celebration in 1472 was the most lavish Caterina had ever witnessed. An array of noble guests attended court festivities that were hailed as the finest in Christendom. The preparations began as early as October, as guest lists were drawn up and lodgings found for visiting heads of state. Along with everyone at court, Caterina was given a splendid new wardrobe. Hundreds of yards of red and black velvet were procured and trimmed with silver and gold brocade. A widespread search was undertaken for material the "color of lion skin" to dress the thirty-two singers of the choir. Stores were laid up for the two hundred people expected at the ducal celebration.

At last the much-anticipated holiday arrived. At sunset on December 24, Caterina and her three brothers and sisters gathered in a large hall of the castle while a kind of yule log known as the *ciocco*, a piece of pinewood adorned with juniper and laurel, was burned in the fireplace amid much merriment. Intimates of the family at this private celebration included Ludovico Gonzaga, marquis of Mantua; Pino Ordelaffi, lord of Forlì; Giovanni Bentivoglio of Bologna; and a new guest to the court, Girolamo Riario, a dissolute nephew of Pope Sixtus IV who had recently been made the count of Bosco.

As Caterina sang along with her family, enjoying the spicy fragrance of the smoldering *ciocco* like everyone else, she may have been dreaming of a new year of health and happiness. Her father and Girolamo Riario, however, were interested in another portent of the yule log: prosperity. Thirty-year-old Girolamo Riario was the son of the pope's sister Bianca and a shoemaker; several contemporaries sneered at his lineage. Having received a cursory education, Girolamo had been pursuing a lowly career as a customs official in Savona when his uncle was elected pope. This turn of events had brought about his promotion to captain of the papal armies. Machiavelli would later refer to Girolamo as springing from a "very base and vile condition,"[2] an opinion shared by many in the Milanese court.

Melozzo da Forlì's idealized portrait of Girolamo in the Vatican Museums shows a trim, handsome man with large gray eyes and golden-brown hair falling in fashionable tresses above his shoulders. This popular hairstyle among Renaissance men framed the face with fair curls, like a luminous halo. Although he was portrayed with regular, even noble features, contemporaries described him quite differently. His detractors saw him as fat, with a heavy peasantlike appearance, pale skin, and a sickly disposition. Neither innately bright nor well read, Girolamo clearly owed his title and position to his illustrious uncle.

Duke Galeazzo celebrated the Feast of the Nativity with great pomp for reasons that were not entirely driven by personal piety. Cloaked in a long robe of crimson damask, the duke dutifully attended three Christmas Masses with his family and court. But he was also exploiting the holiday gathering to consolidate his rule, mend feuds, ennoble faithful retainers, and grant pardons.

Galeazzo was also planning a marriage. His hope during the Christmas season of 1472 was to unite the papal family to the Duchy of Milan, thus enlisting papal support to reinforce the legitimacy of Sforza rule. The question of legitimate rule had been a thorn in his side from the beginning of his reign. While the Milanese population accepted him as their de facto ruler, the Holy Roman Emperor refused to recognize him as the duke of Milan and had even avoided passing through Milanese territory during his last visit to Italy. Over the preceding three centuries, numerous claimants had fought their way onto the thrones of many Italian territories, but the larger, more powerful states often did not deign to recognize their authority. During the long years of war between the Guelphs (papal factions) and Ghibellines (supporters of the Holy Roman Empire), the Holy Roman Emperor, as successor to Charlemagne, claimed feudal rights over the northern Italian territories, particularly Milan. Therefore only Emperor Frederick III could officially confer the sovereign title of duke on Galeazzo, but he appeared to have no intention of doing so. Sforza agents at the emperor's court were authorized to pay virtually any price to obtain the title, but the emperor preferred to keep the Sforzas on a tight leash. Pope Sixtus, on the other hand, was interested in securing the protection of the strongest state in Italy, for he himself was of humble origins and lacked a powerful family to back him. Accordingly, Girolamo's visit was part of a plan to formally establish the betrothal of a member of the Sforza clan to the pope's nephew. The girl selected was eleven-year-old Costanza Fogliani, daughter of Duke Galeazzo's uncle Corrado Fogliani and Gabriella Gonzaga, the natural daughter of Ludovico Gonzaga of Mantua.

By the time the holiday festivities were underway, however, the engagement plans had soured. While Gabriella originally had agreed to the written terms of her daughter's marriage contract, the prospective groom arrived in Milan with one additional, and unacceptable, demand—to have sexual relations with the future bride upon formalizing the engagement.

Gabriella Gonzaga flatly refused to allow the debauched Riario—of inferior rank, to boot—to deflower her daughter, insisting that he await the legal of age of consummation, fourteen. Infuriated at this roadblock, Galeazzo railed and threatened, but the mother held out staunchly.

On January 6, 1473, the marquis of Mantua wrote to propose a compromise that would be satisfactory to his daughter Gabriella and (he hoped) the count of Bosco. To consider the marriage legally and bindingly consummated, Gabriella would allow her child to be "put to bed" with Riario, with herself and several noblewomen present, as well as any other witnesses the groom might choose to include.[3] This ceremony alone would be considered equivalent to consummation, though no actual carnal intercourse would take place. Girolamo refused and threatened to leave Milan. Galeazzo, watching his plans unravel, needed to placate Girolamo immediately.

As Caterina sat at her father's table, enjoying the lavish holiday fare, she would have heard melodious singing and the clatter of dishes, but not the hurried and desperate negotiations in which her fate was being settled by her father, the marquis of Mantua, and the count of Bosco. Finally, Galeazzo offered to substitute his own ten-year-old Caterina as bride in Costanza's stead. Girolamo accepted and on January 17, 1473, the wedding contract was stipulated in a tiny ceremony, with only the duke, the duchess, and the court doctor present.

In the Renaissance world of arranged marriages, there were no romantic proposals on bended knee—only notaries and contracts. The process consisted of three stages. The first was the negotiation between the parents of both parties regarding dowry and any arrangement of alliances or transfer of lands. The second was the betrothal ceremony, at which the bride and groom would be presented to each other, often for the first time. Before a series of witnesses, a notary asked if they wished to be married, and the couple responded "*Volo*," "I do." The contract would be signed and the agreement sealed with a ring and a kiss. If the new husband and wife were of age, meaning about fourteen, the marriage could then be consummated, but this was not usually done until the third stage, the actual transfer of the bride to her new husband's house. Consummation, or carnal intercourse, was the point of no return in a Renaissance marriage. After having been "possessed" by her husband, the young woman could no longer back out of the marriage without grave scandal accruing to herself and to her family. Reaching this last stage could take up to a year for most families; with nobles, it could take much longer.[4]

Caterina's voice was never heard or solicited during this period, nor would she have expected anyone to ask her opinion. Like all noble girls of her age in this era, she expected to be married in a year or two and to be producing children soon after. Although the sudden marriage and premature intercourse would indeed have been traumatic for ten-year-old Caterina, she had been raised to do her part to maintain the family fortunes. A lucky child like Costanza might have a determined parent with enough connections to impose her will, but in Caterina's household, her father's word was law. Children in the Sforza clan would have understood that they existed to be bartered for the greater good of the Sforza name and Sforza claims. Raised in a worldly court, where mistresses were the norm and bawdy humor preempted erudite conversation, Caterina probably knew what awaited her on the wedding night.[5] Although her first sexual experience was probably painful and unpleasant, Caterina got over her psychological and physical wounds quickly. She never wavered in her affection for her father, even after his death, and later in life she would be known as a woman who enjoyed sex to an "unseemly" degree.

That Caterina's father was satisfied with the arrangement is well documented in the proud missives he sent to Pope Sixtus IV, recounting the successful outcome of the negotiations, as well as in the retaliatory letters the duke sent to Gabriella Gonzaga. Pondering her last-minute refusal, the duke professed himself mystified. "To tell the truth, Lady Gabriella seems strange and wild to us," he wrote to his ambassador in Rome on the day of Caterina's wedding. "We have been considerate of her because she is a woman and, this being the nature of women, we don't want to argue with them."[6]

A week later, the duke reported that "Count Girolamo leaves this morning from here to return to his Holiness the Pope and to His Eminent brother. We welcomed him gladly and affectionately while he was here, because we liked him a great deal. And he slept with his wife another time and he is very happy and content. Please relate this to His above-mentioned Holiness and His Eminent brother, adding that we accepted him wholeheartedly not just as a son-in-law, but as a son, and thus we want to keep and consider him."[7]

The hasty consummation did not please the pope, however, who was obliged to issue a papal bull within a matter of weeks to clear up the irregularities in the marriage. The document, signed on February 26, 1473, declared the last-minute switch in bride valid and absolved all parties involved in the illegal intercourse.[8] And so Caterina, the child who had watched the yule log crackle on Christmas, was a wife by the time the ashes had cooled.

Once the two families were united through marriage, it was time to get down to business. Caterina brought with her a hefty dowry of ten thousand ducats, while Girolamo presented expensive gifts of jewels, dresses embroidered with pearls, and silk and brocade capes, meant for whichever wife he obtained.[9] But the real objective was Imola. On September 12, 1473, Girolamo's brother Cardinal Pietro Riario arrived in Milan to close the deal. Though two years younger than Girolamo, Pietro was the smarter of the two and served the pope as his most trustworthy delegate. Handsome, witty, and well educated, he had been appointed cardinal at the age of twenty-six and oversaw international affairs for his uncle.

Rumors of Pietro's far-from-ascetic tastes reached Milan long before he did, and the duke went out of his way to welcome the cardinal in grand style. Dozens of trumpets greeted the churchman and his retinue of 220 (Girolamo had, by contrast, traveled with an entourage of 60). Rooms were enlarged and repainted, and the vaulted ceiling of one reception room was lined with expensive red velvet. Sumptuous parties followed upon lavish hunts, and the honored guest did not shy away from these worldly entertainments. Smiling, charming, and notoriously successful with women, Pietro Riario delighted the Sforza court, especially his new sister-in-law Caterina. Upon his arrival, Caterina recited verses of welcome in Latin, and the cardinal flattered her profusely, admiring both her beauty and her education. But as easily distracted by games, feasts, and local beauties as he may have been, Pietro never forgot why he was there. By October 23, Pietro Riario had completed the purchase of Imola from Milan for the steep price of forty thousand ducats. Although the pope reeled from sticker shock, he soon recovered and set about procuring loans from

Florentine banks. As part of the deal, he nominated Girolamo—"for his noble blood, wealth of merits, and distinctive valor"—as count of Imola, a title to be passed on to his heirs.

With the negotiations concluded and the festivities over, Pietro Riario left Milan, only to die three short months later at the age of twenty-seven. Contemporary chronicles relate that the "whole world wept" at the passing of this worldly and luxury-loving cardinal, and that the pope especially was heartbroken. Girolamo wasted no time laying claim to his brother's vast fortune as well as his high position at the papal court. Meanwhile, Caterina, the eleven-year-old countess of Imola, waited quietly in Milan for word from her husband.

3

THE COUNTESS-IN-WAITING

WITH THE LEGALITIES of the marriage settled and familial alliances consolidated, the oddly matched couple parted company for three years. Caterina was left to her father's care in Milan, to continue her studies until she turned fourteen, when she would join her husband in Rome. Girolamo, for his part, was not pining for his child bride. Not one letter was exchanged between the spouses between the hasty ceremony of winter 1473 and Caterina's departure for Rome in 1476. Girolamo, in fact, was consoling himself with several mistresses during those years and had produced an illegitimate son, Scipione.

Caterina, meanwhile, was pursuing more innocent pastimes, alternating between schoolroom lessons and long hunting expeditions. She learned to play *palla*, a precursor to tennis, which had become the rage among the Milanese aristocracy. The duke was so enamored of the game that he outfitted his castle in Milan with its own indoor *palla* court, where the family could play, rain or shine. Caterina competed with her siblings, hitting the ball back and forth with her round racquet. The Sforza family practiced and promoted the sport to encourage good coordination, agility, and use of strategy. As months turned to years, Caterina grew from a pretty little girl into a slim, refined young woman, favored with fair hair, graceful limbs, and elegant features.

Girolamo, meanwhile, was consolidating his authority in Rome, playing old family rivalries against each other. He gathered titles from his papal uncle but demonstrated little sense of the customary reciprocal relations of protection and loyalty between ruler and ruled. When he was named count of Imola, Girolamo didn't even bother to visit his latest acquisition—the possession ceremony took place by proxy. The sharp tongues of the rebellious Trastevere area of Rome began to call him the "Archpope," a sign that dislike for the arrogant upstart was growing every day.

While Caterina's husband was making enemies in Rome, her father, Galeazzo, was alienating some of his own long-standing allies. The duke of Milan had thrown his military support behind the duke of Bourgogne, known as Charles the Bold, the mortal enemy of King Louis XI of France. This rash decision to turn against King Louis, his own cousin and brother-in-law, soon proved a mistake and Galeazzo swiftly returned his allegiance to France. At the same time, the marriage of Alfonso of Aragon, duke of Calabria, to Galeazzo's sister Ippolita Sforza had sealed an alliance between Milan and King Ferdinand of Naples, the father of the groom. Yet when Ferdinand confidently called on the duke to aid him in claiming the island of Cyprus for his son, he discovered, to his surprise, that the duke intended to support his rival, Venice. Galeazzo's decision was practical—he did not want to risk hostilities with the maritime republic that bordered his state—but the Neapolitan king, already furious with Galeazzo for pilfering his best singers, caustically rebuked his former ally. To be a good ruler, he warned, "it's not enough to declare 'I'm the duke of Milan, young, prosperous, rich, with a thriving state and strong soldiers.' The reputation and the dignity of a lord rest on his good government."[1] The duke shrugged off this wise counsel.

On the domestic front, the duke's ardor for civic improvement in Milan was cooling. The program of frescoes for the Porta Giovia castle was abandoned, the plan for the equestrian statue became a mere memory, and no new projects were undertaken. The economic toll of civic improvement was beginning to strain the ducal finances. His faithful secretary of state, Cicco Simonetta, dealt with day-to-day business loyally and efficiently but, subservient to the duke, proposed no initiatives for saving or making money.

In the spring of 1474, fresh hopes for the establishment of a republic were aroused among the Milanesi when word spread that the duke had summoned the Council of Nine Hundred, a group of representatives elected throughout the duchy, to a special session. Except to swear loyalty to Galeazzo as duke in 1469, the council had not been convened for twenty-five years. The people of Milan interpreted the news as a sign that the duke had decided to adopt a more representational form of government, perhaps similar to that of their Savoyard neighbors. On April 13, the sense of anticipation was palpable as the councilors assembled in the Court of Arengo, the duke's official Milanese palace.

The representatives were bitterly disappointed. They were separated into sections, so no deputy from the outlying areas could speak with those from the city. They were not invited to discuss legislation, although two of the duke's brothers were present, should any deputy choose to make a private petition. Instead, they were handed a series of ducal decrees to be ratified without modification. The duke's real intentions were soon apparent. Most of these decrees were financial in nature and imposed, not in name but in fact, the most onerous and loathed tax of all, the *inquinto*—a fifth part added to existing taxes on the most basic staples: meat, bread, and wine.[2]

The duke needed money to support his extravagant court and lifestyle. Always a self-indulgent man, Galeazzo made less and less effort to hide his excesses from his people and his family. He loved fine clothes and armor and had endless outfits made up for himself and his courtiers from the most costly materials. His hunts in the gardens of Pavia, specially stocked for each event, were also ruinously expensive. One year, the duke spent forty thousand ducats, the cost of the town of Imola, on jewels alone.[3]

The Venetian ducat was the principal currency of the Renaissance era. Six to seven lire made up a ducat; each lira was composed of twenty soldi. A fifteenth-century laborer considered himself fortunate if he earned one ducat a year. As the citizens of Milan struggled to pay this heavy tax on their daily necessities out of such meager earnings, they came to resent Galeazzo's profligate spending.

Besides inciting indignation and envy with his display of sumptuous possessions, certain of the duke's personal excesses were becoming more audacious. He had once boasted that his greatest sin was lust and that he possessed it "in full perfection, for I have employed it in all the fashions and forms that one can do."[4] Wives, daughters, and sisters of other men were not safe from the duke's advances, and part of his private purse dealt with "personal affairs" (*certi nostri segreti*)—payoffs to mistresses and dishonored girls.

In 1474, however, the thirty-year-old duke developed an all-consuming infatuation with Lucia Marliani, a noble nineteen-year-old deemed the "most beautiful woman in Milan." Lucia became Galeazzo's new mistress with the complicity of her husband, Ambrogio Raverti, a Milanese merchant who knew a good business opportunity when he saw it. Raverti received four thousand ducats in hush money from the duke and another four thousand to dower Lucia's sisters; Lucia herself was awarded a yearly allowance plus an expensive residence. The besotted duke made just one contractual stipulation: Lucia must not "intermingle herself with her husband in carnal bond without our special permission, nor to have it with any other man except our person."[5]

At first the duke tried to keep this affair secret. But as he made extravagant outlays for his mistress, such as twelve thousand ducats for a single brooch, word was bound to get out. By 1475, Lucia had been made a countess, and consequently the duke's donations to her were legally protected against any future attempt at recoupment that the duke's wife or his successor might make.

As Galeazzo's behavior became increasingly despotic and depraved, dissatisfaction mounted in the public square and hostility grew abroad, casting a shadow over the ducal household. The atmosphere of Christmastide 1476 was very different from the festive events preceding Caterina's marriage.

To make matters worse, that December the plague had erupted in neighboring Pavia, which meant quarantine for the city, panic in all the neighboring towns, and a shortened list of Christmas guests. Far from dampening Galeazzo's holiday spirit, the reduced numbers relieved him. Not without reason, he was beginning to suspect plots against his life. In November, he sent two of his own brothers, Ludovico (called "the Moor") and Sforza Maria, to France for the entire Christmas season, owing to the disagreeable fact that the duke could not be sure that they were still loyal to him. Bona of Savoy was tormented by nightmares. And the citizens of Milan were remarking on ominous portents—mysterious comets, hovering ravens, and ghostly flames enveloping the duke's chambers.

Caterina, now old enough to sense the uneasy atmosphere around her, would have wondered why her uncles were not present for the burning of the *ciocco*. Perhaps she was struck by the contrast between her father's relentless mirth and the grave and worried expressions of his courtiers. On Christmas Day, a jovial Galeazzo Maria attended his usual three Masses and enjoyed a long hunt. His foreign enemies were far away, intimates of dubious loyalty were at a safe distance, and the little coterie that remained was composed of faithful retainers. Convinced he had suppressed any enthusiasm for revolt in Milan, he rejoiced in the good fortunes of the house of Sforza.

As the Milanesi celebrated the Lord's birth, however, three citizens were busily plotting their lord's demise. Behind the walls of the monastery of Saint Ambrogio, Andrea Lampugnano, Carlo Visconti, and Girolamo Olgiati were beseeching the patron saint of Milan to help them rid the city of its tyrannical ruler and restore freedom. At least that was the prayer of nineteen-year-old Olgiati, the youngest of the conspirators. A poet and gentleman of the court, he owed his superb classical education in part to the ducal library. Having read of Brutus, Cassius, and the tyrannicide of Julius Caesar, he dreamed of republican liberty, eventually hatching the plot against the duke. Lampugnano, another courtier, would not have objected had such high motives been ascribed to him as well, but the true reasons for his involvement were rather more pedestrian. Having invested and lost substantial sums in unfortunate real estate deals, he hoped that the civil unrest following the duke's death would wipe clean his numerous debts. As for Carlo Visconti, the duke would have been shocked to see him among the conspirators. Visconti was the ducal chancellor, had been a trusted member of the duke's Council of Justice since 1474, and handled the delicate negotiations and correspondence with the Holy Roman Emperor when Galeazzo tried to gain recognition as the duke of Milan. Galeazzo would have been even more taken aback to hear of Carlo's motive: he was bent on avenging his sister, who had been seduced by Galeazzo. In a milieu where many husbands were happy to sell their wives to curry a little ducal favor, few would have thought that an outraged brother would become the instrument of the duke's end.

December 26, the Feast of Saint Stephen, was a cold, gray day in Milan. Icy winds from the Alps had brought enough snow to blanket the roads, and the duke was reconsidering his plan to hear Mass in the Church of Saint Stephen. Anxiously Bona begged him to remain in the castle, but the choir had already been sent ahead, and Galeazzo decided to maintain his yearly tradition of honoring the first Christian martyr. In his favorite room of the castle — decorated with golden sunbursts surrounding a dove against a red ground and Bona's motto, À BON DROIT, inscribed in gold — Galeazzo's children gathered to see their father off. His armorer brought the steel breastplate that he usually wore under his clothes for protection, but the duke, fearing that the metal would ruin the line of his new ermine-trimmed silk robe, decided to go without it. He embraced his two eldest sons and mounted his horse, riding off with his usual entourage of twenty courtiers.

At the church, Galeazzo dismounted and entered the ancient marble portal. Throngs of subjects surrounded their ruler, offering him good wishes. The lackeys, in livery of bright red and white, cleared a path as Galeazzo made his way down the nave, returning the greetings of the Milanesi. Then Andrea Lampugnano, assuming the subservient pose of a petitioner, approached the duke. Galeazzo, accustomed to frequent requests from Lampugnano, raised a preemptory hand as the conspirator knelt, sweeping his cap off his head. What the duke took to be a pleading gesture was in reality the secret signal to the assassins. Lampugnano struck first, plunging his knife into the duke's chest, and in a matter of moments the assassins rained fourteen blows on their victim. Thirty-two-year-old Galeazzo Maria fell, with barely enough time to gasp "I am dead." He expired on the cold floor of the basilica, his new scarlet suit stained with the deeper crimson of his own blood.

The conspirators had assumed that the people of Milan would rejoice at the assassination and rally to them in the expectation of greater freedom. They had miscalculated. Several horrified Milanesi moved forward to avenge their duke. Olgiati and Visconti escaped, but Lampugnano was found hiding among the skirts of the women and was killed instantly. The vengeful crowd dragged his corpse through the streets until it was mangled beyond recognition. Visconti was turned in by his own family, and Olgiati was apprehended almost immediately. Both men were publicly quartered, but Olgiati's stoicism earned him the admiration of the onlookers. His last words were *Mors acerba, fama perpetua*—"Death is bitter, but fame is eternal."[6] When the news reached the palace, there was no time for grieving. Everyone in Caterina's world sprang into action. Fearing a popular uprising in the wake of the duke's death, Galeazzo's trusted secretatary of state, Cicco Simonetta, raised all the drawbridges of the Porta Giovia castle, rendering the building secure. He then announced that six-year-old Gian Galeazzo was the new duke of Milan. Bona and Cicco both suspected that the duke's brothers, in league with the king of France, had a hand in the murder, but to avoid precipitating a coup d'état they chose not to publicly implicate them and instead declared that the assassins had acted alone, under the spell of ancient Roman ideology. This served to reassure their Florentine allies that the state was stable.

Bona then declared herself regent for her young son. Gathering the men-at-arms, she put them under the command of Robert Sanseverino, who had served the duchy for thirty-seven years. To placate the people of Milan, the duchess abolished the odious *inquinto* as well as several other taxes on basic necessities. Caterina witnessed Bona's transformation from quiet, patient wife and mother, enjoying leisurely days in her cottage on the castle grounds, to a dynamic and competent head of state, managing her responsibilities to the populace and dealing with rival claimants and external threats. The metamorphosis of Bona must have been a great lesson to the young countess, who knew that one day she might well find herself in a similar position.

Archived amid businesslike correspondence establishing her son's rule and issuing decrees, an extant letter from Bona of Savoy to Pope Sixtus IV provides an interesting glimpse into the private fears and thoughts of the newly widowed duchess. Frightened that her despotic, unfaithful husband Galeazzo had died suddenly and in a state of sin, she asked the pope if there was any way of obtaining absolution for him after death. Aware of Saint Francis's harsh dictum—"Woe to those who die in mortal sin!"—Bona was trying to save her husband's soul. Bona confessed for him, declaring that Galeazzo was "versed in warfare, both lawful and unlawful; in pillage, robbery, and devastation of the country" as well as "in carnal vices; in notorious and scandalous simony and in various and innumerable other crimes." Yet despite the duke's overwhelming sins, the duchess desired to free "that unhappy soul from the pains of Purgatory" because, as she wrote, "after God" she "loved [him] above all else."[7]

Sixtus IV was more than willing to use his papal authority to absolve the duke and even went so far as to declare that with Galeazzo's death, "peace itself died in Italy." Bona, in return, repaid the sums her husband had extorted and donated a conspicuous amount of money to the papal fund for the defense of Christendom against the Turks.

Nor did Bona forget Caterina. In the first weeks of 1476, a month after Galeazzo's death, she wrote to Girolamo, confirming all the marital arrangements and declaring Caterina, now thirteen, old enough to join her husband in Rome. Her haste was probably dictated by concern for Caterina's safety in case a coup was attempted in Milan and as a preemptive move before the pope or Girolamo chose to repudiate the bride, now that her powerful father was dead. Cardinal Mellini, papal legate of Sixtus IV, traveled from Rome to celebrate the wedding, the last step in finalizing the marriage. Bona and all the court were present at the ceremony in Milan, which was simple and without pomp because the state was in mourning. In a bizarre turn of events, the one person who didn't appear was the bridegroom, Girolamo, for reasons that remain unclear. The count claimed that urgent business in Rome kept him from attending his own wedding; its nature remains unknown. Perhaps the sickly Girolamo was too ill to face the journey. At any rate, his behavior stood in sharp contrast to that of the eager and amorous suitor of 1473.

The simplicity of Caterina's wedding by proxy paralleled that of Galeazzo's burial. After the morning of December 26, when her father rode to his death at Saint Stephen's, Caterina never saw him again. As the assassins were hunted and captured, the duke's corpse lay unattended on the basilica floor. During the night, Bona had sent three hundred ducats' worth of jewels and a new robe to clothe her husband's body. After this small concession to Galeazzo's love of finery, the earthly remains of the duke of Milan were unceremoniously dumped into his father's sarcophagus in the cathedral; not even an inscription of his own name was added. The magnificent choir, which had delighted him so much in life, did not sing at his funeral, for no public Mass was offered, in fear that it might stir up rebellion. None of the pageantry so dear to Galeazzo graced his farewell to life, and Caterina's goodbye to her childhood home was equally unremarkable.

Christmastide, once the most blissful time of year for young Caterina, had now been twice tainted: by her premature deflowering and by her father's murder. In later years, when Caterina would have to fight for her life instead of celebrate around the *ciocco*, she would be more than ready.

· 4 ·

THE TRIUMPHAL PARADE TO ROME

"TODAY I ARRIVED safe and sound in Parma, but nonetheless inconsolable."[1] Writing to her sister Chiara, on April 27, 1477, Caterina admitted that she keenly felt the separation from her family. Only three days into her journey to join her husband in Rome, Caterina's thoughts turned often and fondly to her stepmother, Bona, to whom she owed "all the honors paid her from land to land." On the same day, Caterina also wrote to Bona directly, using more formal tones as befitting her new rank but expressing the same message: the thirteen-year-old girl was holding up well but was already homesick.

Anyone who witnessed the lavish parade winding its way through Lombardy would never have guessed that the elegant young countess with the extravagant escort was feeling such lonely nostalgia. Count Girolamo had added his own retainers to Caterina's Milanese entourage of 40 relatives and servants, swelling their numbers to 150 or more. The glamorous retinue included the archbishop of Cesena and his escort of 13, the governor of Imola with 12 men, plus local nobles, musicians, and ladies in waiting. Caterina's procession coursed like a bright ribbon through the low-lying green plains of Lombardy. The scarlet and white flags emblazoned with the Sforza viper were followed by the silver and black livery of Cesena and the reds and blues of Imola; the vermilion rose of the Riario family blossomed among them. Before the era of mass media, such processions reinforced a family's status, announced political events, and provided entertainment. Village women gawked at the latest fashions, men discussed the suits of armor, and children scampered to find some souvenir of the passage of a contemporary celebrity. In the spring of 1477, the sound of trumpets echoing through the countryside announced the arrival of the new countess of Imola, bride of the pope's favorite nephew and sister to Gian Galeazzo Sforza, the new duke of Milan.

A day later, another member joined the party: Gian Luigi Bossi, counselor to the duke of Milan. Bossi, carrying specific instructions from Bona of Savoy, was to accompany the party all the way to Rome. His special task was to watch over Caterina, ensuring that the young countess "conduct herself well and honorably and that she not become ill either from riding or the heat."[2] Bona's dual concerns reflected her twin roles: a head of state dealing with a delicate political situation and a loving stepmother whose daughter was traveling far from home for the first time.

Bona had done everything she could to prepare the way for Caterina, writing ahead to each town, alerting its people to offer a proper welcome to their noble guest. Only in the little town of Reggio was there no one to greet the cavalcade, but that was only because the group had arrived earlier than expected. On that evening, the aristocratic retinue stayed in relatively humble accommodations, which Caterina, unruffled, described as "a pleasant inn." In Modena and Piacenza, however, local nobles opened their homes and hearts to Caterina. Not only was she "affectionately and enthusiastically" received in Bologna, but she also stayed as a guest in the palace of the ruling family, the Bentivoglios. Caterina politely expressed much delight in being so honored, but in letters to her sister, she modestly acknowledged that the pomp and glory could not be ascribed to her own merits, but to "the grace of Her Ladyship, my mother." Like many an adolescent, Caterina was more energized than fatigued by her busy social calendar of visits, feasts, and parties, enabling Bossi to write to the duchess that he had found Caterina "healthy, beautiful, and well-mannered."[3] Her childhood amid the elaborate rituals of her father's court had prepared her well for long hours of banquets, speeches, and spectacles: not once did anyone catch the young countess looking impatient or weary.

The homage she received in towns along the route paled by comparison with Caterina's reception in her new dominion. On May 1, she left Bologna to travel the twenty miles to Imola. She arrived in the late afternoon to find the entire city turned out to greet her. As Caterina gushed in her letter to Chiara, "The people of Imola don't usually celebrate much, but it seemed that even the very stones were delighted by my arrival."[4]

The curious onlookers were not disappointed by the first appearance of the young countess. Teenager though she was, Caterina knew how to walk the red carpet. She requested a pause in the journey as soon as the town came into view in order to bathe, change her clothes, and groom herself elegantly. She rode into Imola not dusty and travel worn, but splendidly attired, a young woman with a regal bearing. The Milanese sense of style was ingrained in Caterina, and high fashion delighted her.

Countess Caterina Riario wore the most magnificent of her wedding gifts from her husband: a gold brocade dress embroidered with almost a thousand tiny pearls. Several strands of pearls of varying sizes encircled her long fair neck, while from her straight, slim shoulders hung a heavy cape of black silk trimmed with gems. There were nevertheless some incongruities in her appearance. Her heavy veil and jeweled hair net, appropriate for a matron, seemed cumbersome framing such a youthful face.

The elders of Imola greeted her at the gate and presented her with the keys to the city. This gesture was followed by a ceremony during which odes and orations honored the new rulers. The most spectacular blooms of May had been gathered and woven into garlands to line Caterina's path along the straight main street. The heady scent of lilies and roses mingled with the sweet trilling voices of the Imolese children, who ran alongside the countess, serenading her. In the central square, a grand pavilion had been erected for the occasion and here Caterina took her place on a podium, which was swathed in luxurious green velvet, and met the nobles of the city.

Girolamo's sister Violante Riario Ricci, the wife of the governor of Imola, was there to welcome Caterina and introduce her to the other noblewomen. In a short time they were all happily acquainted. After the formalities and presentations were concluded, the banquets began. The main hall of the governor's palace had been specially decorated for the occasion, and even the Milanesi, world famous for their silks and brocades, were stunned by the dazzling panels of turquoise cloth lining the ceiling and the exquisite tapestries adorning the walls. One section of the room was taken up by a broad cabinet groaning under the weight of the gold and silver dinnerware arrayed on its shelves.

Five hundred years ago, Emilia-Romagna was already the food capital of Italy, and its denizens put great stock in meals and feasts. The Imolesi brought Caterina foodstuffs as gifts: golden wheat from the fertile plains of Romagna, fragrant sausages and cured meats made from the well-fed pigs of the region, and numerous delectable cheeses, some aged to sharp perfection and others still fresh and soft. Caterina invited her many well-wishers to remain for dinner and the party went on far later than expected; candelabras were brought into the dining chamber to keep the festivities going until late at night.

For several days, Caterina's life was a constant celebration. Morning Mass in the chapel was followed by picnics in the countryside, visits to the marketplace, and of course, many meals, which were wonderful not only for "the variety and the delicacy of the foods but also for the abundance." Caterina was installed in quarters appropriate to her state. Her suite of rooms was lavishly appointed with white damask silk panels highlighted with gold embroidery. Dozens of soft cushions covered the velvet chairs, and a crimson coverlet lay upon her bed.

Outside, however, the town of Imola appeared starkly rustic. Gian Luigi Bossi, Caterina's protector, reported that Imola was small and the houses poor looking, although he admired the fortress (recently rebuilt by Galeazzo Maria), which was strong and well fortified. While he had much to comment on concerning the customs of Imola, especially the dancing, he understood that his mission was not to observe the food, fashions, or footwork of the townspeople, but rather to assess the political stability of the city and its usefulness to Milan. He also had orders from Bona to inform the elders of Imola of the Sforza position on the question of Taddeo Manfredi.

He had been the lord of Imola until 1471, when it became apparent to all interested parties that he was losing his grip on the reins of power. With Taddeo enmeshed in quarrels with the branch of the Manfredi family in Faenza and threatened by his own immediate relatives, Imola had been ripe for the plucking. Venice and Florence were already extending exploratory tentacles into the city when Galeazzo Maria abruptly intervened. The Sforzas had ousted the Manfredi family gently: first, they invited Taddeo to Milan; then, after wining and dining him, they offered him a hefty pension if he would give up the city. In 1477, though Taddeo was safely ensconced within Milanese territory with his son, he was ever present in the minds of troublemakers in Imola. After the assassination of Caterina's father, word began circulating that there were plans to restore the Manfredi rule there. These rumors had reached Bona, who dispatched a message via Bossi to the leading families of Imola, stating that Count Girolamo Riario had the full support and trust of the duke of Milan. She warned any supporters of Manfredi that they would find themselves with more enemies than they bargained for if they made a move on Imola. At the same time, Bona assured the townspeople that she fervently wished them prosperous years of "peace and quiet" with their new lords.

Caterina's letters from her voyage reveal a dutiful daughter who knew that her childhood years were over and that she must now embark on adult life. Snippets of youthful emotion flash in her excitement over her popularity or in her wistful greeting to an old nursemaid, but she was trained to temper sentiment with obedience. Nonetheless, faint stirrings of an intuitive and impulsive nature do emerge. Despite all the splendor and amusements surrounding her, Caterina knew something was wrong. The countess had no count, the bride no groom. Girolamo had not been heard from. He had not met her in Milan nor was he here to share the honors with her in Imola. Caterina eagerly awaited the moment when she would be summoned to Rome to begin married life, but each day came and went with no news. On May 4, a rumor spread through Imola that Count Girolamo was coming to escort his bride personally to Rome. Caterina's impatience to continue her journey was noted by Gian Luigi Bossi, who wrote to the duchess of Milan that Caterina was "so desirous to find herself in the presence of his Holiness and to see her Count Girolamo that it seems to me her principal care and concern."[5] Although Caterina had supposed she would spend only a short time in Imola, she found herself delayed yet another ten days.

Bona of Savoy knew why. Letters from the Milanese ambassador at the papal court had apprised her of an attempt on Girolamo's life. The pope's favorite had already displayed a gift for making enemies, one of whom was his own cousin Giuliano della Rovere, cardinal of the Church of Saint Peter in Chains and another nephew to Sixtus IV. In Rome, two men had been captured and imprisoned for plotting to murder the count. They confessed that they had been approached by a bishop, the patriarch of Venice, in the name of Cardinal Giuliano and offered a large reward for the assassination of Girolamo. Interrogated further, however, they admitted that they had never received any such orders directly from the cardinal's lips. Anxious for Girolamo's well-being and alarmed by the rampant treachery within the very walls of the Vatican palace, the pope thought it best that the count avoid travel for a while. As an added precaution, Sixtus replaced Girolamo's personal bodyguard with the trusted Giovanni Battista da Montesecco, prized for his discretion.

The pontiff likewise deemed Rome unsafe for the young Caterina and offered the anxious young bride a number of plausible excuses for the wait. In one letter to the countess, he expressed concern for her health and offered an alternative means by which the young couple could be reunited. "The extreme heat which has arrived early this year and the natural bad air [malaria] in Rome, . . . and the suspicion of plague" made it unwise to bring the "beloved" Caterina to Rome. As she had grown up in the "good air" of Milan, she would not be used to hot Roman summers. The pope feared that her voyage to Rome would end in people saying that he "had brought her here to kill her," and he suggested that she remain in Imola until the cooler season began in September. The wily pontiff also appealed to the countess's love of glamour and pageantry, pointing out that because it was so soon after her father's death, he would not be able to put on a lavish reception for her at this time, out of respect for the memory of the fallen duke. To relieve Caterina's worries about her husband's absence, the pope offered to send Girolamo to Imola at the beginning of June.[6]

The pontiff's missive expressed a view of marriage more romantic than that of Girolamo. He too had sent a letter—not to Caterina, but to Bona and the child duke Gian Galeazzo—two days after Caterina's arrival in Imola. He too cited the poor health conditions of Rome as the reason to delay Caterina's journey, but he made only the most perfunctory allusions to his love for his wife and his recognition of her merits.

But Caterina never saw either letter. Before they could arrive, she took the initiative and left Imola for the twelve-day journey to Rome. Each night, the huge entourage was feted as it stopped along the route, until May 24, when she finally arrived at Castel Novo fourteen miles from the city.

The news of the imminent arrival of the countess galvanized the papal court. Courtiers were summoned, gifts were prepared, and grand halls decorated to pay homage to the union of the Sforza and Riario lines. The next morning, Caterina embarked on the last leg of the journey into Rome. At seven miles from the city gates, the Milanesi were met by a large party of horsemen arrayed in black silk and velvet, despite the hot May sun. As the elegant coterie grew nearer, the standard of the Riario rose came into view. After four years, the bride and groom would finally set eyes on each other once more. Onlookers were delighted to see that when the count and countess descended from their horses, they "took each other by the hand and kissed and embraced."[7] Caterina must have seemed much changed to Girolamo, who had last seen her as the ten-year-old hastily packaged for his bed in 1473.

Girolamo, now thirty-four, was aging fast. Ill health, a self-indulgent lifestyle, and several sleepless nights due to the conspiracies against his life made the count seem even more sallow. But Caterina evinced only delight at being reunited with her husband as they moved out of the blazing sunshine into a grove of shady trees, where Girolamo presented his Roman escort to the Milanese envoys. Numerous soldiers accompanied Girolamo, but Caterina, unaware of the plots against her husband, would have taken their presence as an indication of his powerful position rather than protection against assassins.

After traveling a few miles farther, the princely cavalcade stopped for a lunch arranged by the Riario clan, and after the hottest hours of the day had passed, they continued toward Rome. More and more city notables appeared to greet the papal favorite and his wife as they approached. The prefect, or mayor, of Rome, Leonardo Riario, another papal nephew, met them at the three-mile point. Shortly thereafter, when they crossed the last bridge, the Ponte Molle, to enter the city, they were joined by members of the papal court. The coterie of dignitaries grew, numbering among them cardinals and ambassadors, and the enormous train made its way up the Monte Mario, a high hill just north of Rome, boasting a spectacular view of the city. There they stopped at the villa of the cardinal of Urbino. After a sumptuous dinner, Girolamo took Caterina to her chambers and presented her with a magnificent pearl necklace. Pearls were the most prized jewels of the Renaissance. The matching spheres of unblemished white were symbols of perfection and purity. The finest oyster beds lay in the Red Sea and Persian Gulf, both dominated by hostile Turkish fleets, which made obtaining the "Queen of Gems" extremely difficult. Girolamo's gift was probably meant as a token of apology for his long and silent absence. He did not, however, spend the night with his wife. He had been expressly ordered by the pope to return to the papal apartments that same evening. This time he was under instructions from his uncle to wait until the union had been formally blessed.

The next morning the sun rose on Pentecost Sunday, one of the most glorious holidays of the year. While the Romans were donning their best clothes and adornments to celebrate the coming of the Holy Spirit and the birth of the church, Caterina was readying herself to see the Eternal City for the first time. Her slender frame was enveloped in a mantle of gold brocade and dark silk, which opened to reveal a voluminous crimson skirt. Her sleeves picked up the motif of the brocade, and sapphires, emeralds, and rubies from distant India, cut into myriad shapes and sizes, hung from her neck and bedecked her graceful fingers. These trappings were so heavy that they slowed her pace. In truth, the gem-encrusted costume was designed less for flattering the female form than for displaying the combined wealth of the Sforza and Riario families.

At the Roman gates, an astounding sight awaited her. Six thousand horsemen appeared from all sides and fell in with Caterina as she made her way to Saint Peter's Basilica. She was shown to a place of honor there as the pope entered in procession with the College of

Cardinals to celebrate the solemn Mass of Pentecost, which lasted a full three hours. Afterward, Cardinal Giuliano della Rovere, back in papal favor, and Count Girolamo conducted Caterina, Gian Luigi Bossi, and the dignitaries of her escort to Sixtus. Meeting the Vicar of Christ for the first time, Caterina did as she had been taught to do: she knelt before him and kissed the toe of his red velvet slipper. The other dignitaries followed suit, and Gian Luigi Bossi launched into a long, elegant, well-prepared speech bearing the greetings of the duke of Milan and extolling the virtues and modesty of Caterina. He spoke passionately and eloquently. The delighted pope honored Bossi with knighthood on the spot.

But Sixtus had a more important task at hand. He commanded that Girolamo and Caterina be brought before him and that their marriage ceremony be repeated. No hasty consummation after a financial contract, no ceremony by proxy here: what the pope joined together, no one could cut asunder. The pontiff then presented a gift of his own to the bride. He removed the pearl necklace given to her by Girolamo the evening before and replaced it with another considerably more precious one, with larger, perfectly round pearls of the purest white from his own treasury at the Castel Sant'Angelo.

On being presented to the College of Cardinals, Caterina kissed each eminent hand dutifully, as she had been instructed. The newlyweds then took their leave of the papal court and started off to their new home in Campo dei Fiori. The short trip across the river took the couple through streets rendered fragrant with incense and embellished with bright cloth and floral arrangements bearing the coats of arms of the pope, the Sforzas, and the Riarios.

Nothing that Caterina had seen in Florence or Milan prepared her for the vastness and splendor of her new residence in Rome. At the heart of the palace was a large courtyard hung with festive tapestries for the arrival of the new inhabitants. Dozens of superbly decorated rooms looked out onto a central courtyard in what the Milanese ambassador described as "earthly paradise." Two hundred guests vied for the countess's attention, and gifts worth over twelve thousand ducats were piled high before the stunned and overjoyed young woman. Her wedding banquet was the sort of spectacle that only a city with a two-thousand-year love of theater could produce. Each course was preceded by a child dressed as an angel, who was borne into the room upon a triumphal chariot and then recited a few verses from famous Greek myths. The exotic treats included sugarcoated oranges, and fish encrusted with silver and gold shimmered on the tables. Two calves were roasted whole in their skins and were presented to the countess by two more "angels" holding hunting spears and reciting poetic accolades. An edible tableau of life-size figures sculpted in sugar astonished the guests as it was unveiled for dessert.

At her father's court, Caterina had experienced plenty of extravagance and taken part in costly feasts, but the magnificence of Rome was overwhelming. The sumptuous food and lavish gifts were rendered more awe-inspiring by the presence of the pope and his religious authority. Sacred and profane intertwined to make Caterina's wedding feast a unique event.

Now that Caterina had delighted the papal court and taken her place in her new home, the time was ripe for Bossi to attend to his last commission from Bona of Savoy. Using the goodwill garnered by Caterina, Bossi negotiated with Girolamo to obtain a cardinal's hat for her twenty-two-year-old uncle, Ascanio Sforza. Even though Caterina slept peacefully in her Roman palazzo, her new position and influence were already at work.

5

COURTIERS AND CONSPIRACIES

THE CEREMONIAL PROCESSION arranged for Caterina's arrival displayed Rome's most glorious finery, but the tapestries and garlands along the streets had hidden dirty, unpaved alleys and the façades of rickety buildings. The incense burned in her honor had disguised the smell of rotting animal corpses and the other fetid odors of a city lacking a sewer system. As Caterina's new life there began, she soon discovered that the unclean roads were merely the most visible sign of decay in Rome. The papal court, the citizens, and even her own home were rife with corruption.

The Romans were a different breed from the diligent, serious Milanesi. Caterina found herself in a much more claustrophobic environment. Fifteenth-century Rome was also a far cry from the city that had been lauded in antiquity as the *caput mundi*, the "head of the world." The Florentine humanist Leonardo Bruni had once contemptuously referred to its latter-day denizens as Romans "of whom nothing remains but empty boasting."[1] The sixty thousand inhabitants didn't produce costly silks or exquisitely worked armor, nor did they harvest huge surpluses of crops to sell to other regions. Like parasites, they lived off the traffic of pilgrims and the presence of the papal court. They were reputed to be envious and rumormongering, with a violent temper too. Courtiers whispered and intrigued. Cardinals and princes vied to put on the most luxurious parties and the most grandiose public pageants, while the populace, watching these extravagances from their ramshackle abodes, harbored resentment that could escalate into riots at any moment.

Caterina's first Roman home was a palace situated in the heart of the city, near the Campo dei Fiori, its main market. Since Pope Sixtus had recently moved the other major market from the Capitoline Hill to the Piazza Navona a few short blocks away, the young countess found herself in the busiest part of town. Artisans rubbed elbows with the highest prelates; exotic wares sat side by side with spelt flour and onions.

Every time she left her house, Caterina experienced firsthand the tensions and contradictions of Rome. As she and her retinue strolled through the markets, she witnessed some of the immense changes wrought by her visionary patron, the pope. The bustling Via Mercatoria, which stretched from the banking section of town by the river through the Campo dei Fiori market to the Piazza Venezia, flourished with commercial activity. The pope had widened the road and cleared it of overhanging balconies, transforming it into a well-lit, clean path where Roman shops could display their wares to advantage.

Sixtus's restoration of the road did not spring purely from aesthetic taste or a desire to help local merchants. He had acted in response to friendly advice from King Ferdinand of Naples, who had commented that Sixtus would "never be the Lord of Rome as long as women dropping stones from overhead can crush your best soldiers or make them turn tail and run."[2] Falling rocks were not the only hazard related to these architectural protuberances. A passerby had to be alert to the possibility that almost anything might be tossed out of Roman windows—from dead cats to the contents of chamber pots.

Although Caterina was used to seeing her father armed and wearing a cuirass when he traveled, she would have been taken aback by the sight of several small armies marching about in the city streets, each in the pay of a noble family. Caterina and her husband were always escorted by armed guards who resembled thugs and were nothing like the elegant Swiss Guard of the modern papacy. Carrying swords and daggers, and quick to draw them, they shoved a path clear for the noble couple as they passed through town. All the important families in Rome employed them, mostly out of necessity. For example, the death of a pope, whether sudden or expected, would unleash anarchy: mobs attacked the houses of the wealthy, and crime infested the streets. Hence, during this period, referred to as *sede vacante*—"the vacant throne"—private armies were essential protection for home and property. Order would be restored with the election of a new pontiff, after a few final throes of violence. As soon as the name of the new successor to Saint Peter was announced from the Vatican loggia, Romans would rush to the man's family palace and loot it. Once crowned, the new pope would make a foray into the city, taking the processional route from the Basilica of Saint Peter to the Basilica of Saint John Lateran and back again. To the rest of the world this symbolized the pope's possession of his cathedral and his regal rule of Rome, but for the inhabitants of the Eternal City it was a ritual gauntlet to be braved by the newly elected pontiff. He rode on the Via Papalis, which twisted and turned through the heart of the city, passing by anti-papal strongholds and the homes of families that had ruled Rome for centuries despite the presence of the papacy. The road skirted the foot of the Capitoline Hill, the great Roman stronghold of the republican age, where certain of Rome's citizens expressed their hostility to papal rule. During Sixtus IV's possession ceremony, stones were thrown at his carriage as he traveled past its slopes.[3]

Caterina certainly recognized that the presence of so many private armies meant that her new family did not control its city as firmly as her father had ruled Milan. Yet rather than stay locked indoors, she spent most of her time outside her home, getting to know the members of her new family: the Riarios, the Basso della Roveres, and particularly her husband's cousin, Giuliano della Rovere, the striking cardinal of the Church of Saint Peter in Vincoli.

An endless round of parties began in the afternoon and lasted well into the night. These four-course feasts often boasted forty different dishes. Like a theatrical production, each course was heralded by a master of ceremonies, who changed his clothes and jewels to match the theme of the course. These Renaissance galas entertained the noblest families, greatest thinkers, richest bankers, and loveliest women. Caterina, the crown princess of this luxurious realm, played her part to the full. Roman diarists waxed eloquent about her fair tresses, rare in raven-haired Rome, and gushed over her dresses,

which, unlike the high-necked Roman style, displayed daring décol-
letage. Her intelligence, manners, and sense of fashion were so widely
admired that a later chronicler, Fabio Oliva, wrote that "in popular
opinion she was the most beautiful and gracious woman of her time."
Like many young girls, Caterina delighted in exquisite dresses and
sumptuous parties. Much of her day was absorbed by her toilette; out
late, she rose late and began the slow process of dressing. Using pow-
ders and cosmetic paints, Caterina transformed her teenage features.
During her first forays into public life, Caterina found that her stepmother, having once been her mentor in social graces, now acted as
her greatest source of fashionable accessories. Bona frequently sent
gifts of ribbons, jeweled belts, and beaded hairnets, allowing Caterina
to flaunt the latest northern styles. More than these items, however,
Caterina appreciated the affection that permeated Bona's letters. In a
note dated November 9, 1477, Bona tells Caterina that "hearing you
are well fills us with joy as it is with every mother toward a beloved
daughter as you are to me,"[4] while in another she describes the only
consolation "of being deprived of your sweet conversation . . . is the
thought of your happy circumstances."[5]

In her return letters to her stepmother, Caterina revealed that her
delight in riding and hunting had not diminished. When Bona sent
Caterina and Girolamo a fine pair of hunting dogs in January 1478,
Caterina was particularly effusive in her thanks. Departing from the
stiff formal epistolary tone that characterized her obligatory courtly
letters home, Caterina wrote that the dogs were "very dear to me and
even more so to my husband . . . he was delighted to see them and
played with the dogs for hours." Still enamored of the chase, Caterina's happiest moments occurred during equestrian adventures outside the city limits. A few blocks away from her house, Sixtus had
built a new bridge, the first since antiquity to span the Tiber. The
Ponte Sisto, as it was called, cut traveling time to the Vatican for prelates and pilgrims alike, but for Caterina it was the route to the lush
gardens and forests of the Janiculum Hill, where she could breathe
freely, away from the stuffy halls and crowded streets of the city. On
these days she could leave behind the pounds of silk and brocade and
the weighty jewels that even for a fashion maven could sometimes be
burdensome. In a light woolen gown, with her hair loosely tied, she
would set off on horseback with her dogs to race up and down the

hills of Rome. Exploring the thick forests of Lazio was a refreshing change from picking her way through the labyrinth of alleys in the city center, and the fierce boar was a more straightforward foe than the scheming flatterers at court.

Caterina's correspondence home, however, was not all shopping lists and personal news. As soon as she settled into her new home, the young countess went to work. Stacks of letters requesting promotions for courtiers, merciful treatment for an arrested retainer, or parishes for clerics kept her busy for hours every day. The sister of a duke and now the niece of a pope, Caterina was a powerful intercessor, and both her old family and her new one called upon her to exercise this role. In her first two years in Rome, Caterina wrote dozens of personal and official dispatches, and although her tone remained invariably cheery, her life was not without cares and concerns.

The pontiff was eagerly awaiting news of a Riario heir. Given that Caterina would eventually bear her husband six children, the twenty-six-month wait for their first child suggests that Girolamo was more occupied with his plots and schemes than with his lovely and charming bride. Only a few short months after Caterina's arrival in Rome, Girolamo began to consort with two men who shared an implacable hatred of the Medici family of Florence. Thus began the plot that would notoriously go down in history as the Pazzi conspiracy.

Relations between Florence and the papacy had begun auspiciously, but by the time Caterina arrived in Rome, Lorenzo de' Medici, leader of the Medici clan, had earned the displeasure of the pope and his family. Following the election of Sixtus IV, the Medicis had held the lucrative position of papal bankers, and Lorenzo was angling for a cardinal's hat for his brother Giuliano, still a teenager. The relationship soured at the time of Girolamo's betrothal to Caterina, when the sale of Imola, the principal part of the Sforza bargain, almost fell through as a result of Lorenzo de' Medici's refusal to underwrite a loan for the pope. The infuriated pontiff turned to the other great banking family, the Pazzis, who promptly produced three quarters of the price. Both the pope and Girolamo realized that Lorenzo would be an obstacle to Girolamo's plan to form a state in Romagna, a region bordering on Tuscany. To thwart this expansion, Lorenzo further stoked the papal ire by providing armies to towns resisting Girolamo's mercenaries in that region.

From Caterina's first days in the Riario household, Francesco de' Pazzi had been a familiar face in the master's apartments. The head of the Roman branch of the Pazzi bank, "Franceschino," as he was called, and his aristocratic family held a long-standing grudge against the Medicis. Envious of this upstart family, with no ancient nobility lending importance to their name, the Pazzis competed with the Medicis at every turn. By 1478, the Pazzis had convinced themselves, not without grounds, that Lorenzo was using his authority to block their endeavors. Franceschino was certain that if only the Medici brothers could be eliminated, Florence would turn to the Pazzi family for leadership. To that end, he had allied himself with an even more arriviste family, the Riarios, probably assuming that his new ally's power would disappear as soon as Girolamo's papal patron was deceased; therefore Riario would not be a serious menace for long.

The third and most unsavory member of this conspiratorial trio was Archbishop Francesco Salviati. He also loathed the Medicis, and Salviati offered himself as a willing participant in any scheme that would undermine their rule. Pope Sixtus had appointed Salviati as archbishop of Pisa, home to a flourishing new university, despite numerous protests from the Florentines. At Pisa, the corrupt prelate would be able to foster anti-Medici support among impressionable students. The crafty Florentines, however, accepted the inevitable appointment but then invented enough obstacles to prevent the new archbishop from taking possession of his diocese for three years. Salviati spent that time in Rome, nursing his resentment, indulging his vices, and poisoning the papal court against the Medicis. Through his efforts, Giuliano's hopes for becoming a cardinal were definitively shelved.

By early 1478, the plot was organized. The Pazzis would see to the assassination of the Medici brothers, and Girolamo would muster an army in Imola to put down any insurrection against the rule of the Pazzis. The plan now needed one final approval: that of the Pazzi family members in Florence. The go-ahead was slow in coming, for Jacopo de' Pazzi, head of the clan, was decidedly against the scheme. His son Guglielmo had married Lorenzo's sister Bianca and he thus had hopes of defeating the Medici family from within.

The conspirators faced yet another stumbling block: their quarry. It was one thing to talk of killing Lorenzo and his brother, another to do so. Although Lorenzo was given to intellectual rather than physically robust pastimes, everyone in Florence remembered that he had single-handedly fought off an ambush and that his swift reflexes rendered him deadly with a sword. It would take a true professional to do away with him.

The very man was already in Girolamo's retinue. Giovanni Battista da Montesecco, whom Pope Sixtus had assigned to protect the count, was invaluable for both his fighting skills and his good judgment. But when the trio approached Montesecco with their plot, the honorable soldier demurred, unwilling to believe that the pope would sanction such a drastic solution to his political woes. To persuade Montesecco, Girolamo escorted him to the papal chambers. Though it was conducted behind locked doors and closed windows, the ensuing conversation has nonetheless reached modern ears through an account left by Montesecco himself.

While Sixtus IV confirmed that he "much desired a change in the government of Florence," deploring Lorenzo as a "villain who had treated us badly," the pope also adamantly stated that he did not want anyone killed. A realist, Montesecco pointed out that to overthrow the Medici government without bloodshed would be very difficult, if not impossible. Girolamo, never one for subtlety, interjected that they weren't deliberately planning to murder anyone, but should the unthinkable happen, he was certain that "His Holiness would pardon whatever [Montesecco] did." This crude response drove the pope into a rage. Bellowing at Girolamo, Sixtus called his nephew "a beast" and forcefully reiterated his point: "I do not want the death of anyone, just a change in government."[6]

When Girolamo spoke to Montesecco alone a few minutes later, he interpreted the pope's equivocating statements as a tacit acceptance of the plan, and Montesecco reluctantly joined the conspiracy.

Caterina had barely arrived in Rome and was still getting to know the man she had married. While she was undoubtedly aware of furtive conversations between her husband and Franceschino, the last thing she would have imagined was that they were scheming to assassinate the man who had made such a great impression on her when she was a seven-year-old guest at the Medici court. Nonetheless, the worried scowls of her husband's bodyguard and the discomfiting unctuous manner of Archbishop Salviati cast a shadow over her first months as a bride.

The papal "consent" at last convinced Jacopo de' Pazzi, and by March the plan was fully formulated. The only problem left was how to ambush the two brothers together and unprotected. The conspirators' eyes fell upon sixteen-year-old Cardinal Raffaello Riario, Girolamo's nephew, who was to attend the University of Pisa under the tutelage of Salviati. The adolescent had been elevated to the highest rank in the papal court in December just as the plot was taking shape. If the Pazzis were to invite Raffaello to Florence, the Medicis would not fail to entertain such a distinguished visitor.

As planned, the young cardinal arrived in Florence, and everything looked promising for the fulfillment of the plot. Then, unexpectedly, Giuliano de' Medici suffered an attack of sciatica and was bedridden, so the plan had to be postponed.

Cardinal Riario wittingly or unwittingly provided the occasion for the next attempt. The young prelate was fascinated by Roman antiquities and knew that a famous collection of cameos and coins from the imperial age, formerly belonging to Pope Paul II Barbo, had been sold to Lorenzo the Magnificent upon that pope's death in 1471. Lorenzo proudly informed the eager young man that his city palace in Florence contained not only the celebrated collection but also recently excavated ancient statues, including a particularly fine marble Venus whose "smile was enchanting." Enthralled, Raffaello pleaded with Lorenzo to allow him to see it, and they finally agreed that the young cardinal would come to Florence on April 26, 1478, and visit the Medici treasures before they all attended Mass together. It was settled. The murder would take place in the Cathedral of Santa Maria del Fiore, renowned as the largest church in the world and crowned by the glory of Florence, the gigantic dome designed by Brunelleschi. This imposing structure, visible for miles, was the very symbol of Florence.

When Montesecco received word of the date and venue for the assassination, he stubbornly refused to participate in a murder taking place inside a church. The desperate conspirators reassigned Montesecco to the city gates, where he would guarantee the entry of Girolamo's army, and they recruited two priests, angry with the Medicis, as assassins in his stead. The plotters hoped that what these men lacked in skill and experience would be made up in greed and vindictiveness.

That Sunday morning, the dignitaries made their way the few blocks from the Medici palace to the Duomo. Although Giuliano was still feeling unwell and felt inclined to remain at home, Franceschino and his cousin took him by either arm and, feigning good-humored laughter, practically dragged him to the cathedral. As Salviati and Jacopo de' Pazzi waited for the word to seize the town hall, Girolamo was marching his army from Imola to Florence. Everyone was in place. As if a murder in a house of worship wasn't blasphemous enough, the signal for the assassins was the elevation of the host, the most solemn moment of the Mass. As the heads of the assembly bowed in reverence, Franceschino delivered a fatal blow to the top of Giuliano's head and continued to stab him, even after he fell to the ground. Nineteen blows mutilated the body of the handsome and charming Medici scion. The two priests assigned to murder Lorenzo were not so efficient. Antonio Maffei managed only a glancing blow to the neck as Lorenzo leapt through the choir and across the high altar to safety.

The grossest miscalculation on the part of the conspirators was to underestimate the Florentines' acceptance of Medici rule. As with the death of Caterina's father, Galeazzo Maria, no citizens rallied to the cries of "People and Liberty!" Instead, they instigated a widespread manhunt to track down anyone involved with the conspiracy. The archbishop and the killers were apprehended and executed almost immediately. The Florentines hung the corpses above public squares, as examples of the fate of traitors. Sandro Botticelli, then just starting his career, painted the dangling bodies as a grisly reminder for posterity. Montesecco and Jacopo de' Pazzi attempted to flee but were captured a few miles outside Florence. Montesecco was tortured and confessed—his words on the eve of his execution give the most complete account of the conspiracy from the inside and thoroughly implicated Girolamo and, by association, the pope.

Cardinal Raffaello Riario was seized moments after the assassination. The Medicis behaved as if the boy cardinal had been an unknowing pawn, yet they kept him as a "guest," or hostage, to forestall any reprisals in Rome against Florentine citizens in the wake of the execution of the archbishop of Pisa. Cardinal Raffaello was detained almost six weeks and witnessed the bloody vengeance of the Florentines. According to contemporary accounts, when the cardinal finally returned to Rome, he appeared ashen and exhausted.

Innocent or not, Raffaello was well compensated for his troubles. Three days after the cardinal's release from Florence, Caterina wrote a letter to Bona of Savoy at the instigation of the pope and Count Girolamo. In her missive, she requested that the generous income from the Abbey of Chiaravalle near Milan be turned over to Cardinal Riario.

Some historians have envisioned fifteen-year-old Caterina at her husband's side, encouraging him in his role in the scandalous conspiracy, but it seems highly unlikely that the teenage girl was privy to the machinations of her husband and his co-conspirators. Moreover, Caterina always held Lorenzo in high esteem, and when he died in 1492, she grieved the loss of such a great man, whose memory she cherished. Over the course of Caterina's life, her ties to Florence would grow much stronger than her connection to Milan and Rome.

Girolamo's clumsy and impious plot had publicly humiliated her and their family. After Montesecco's confession, Girolamo's role in the most disgraceful event of his time became public knowledge. The pope was infuriated, and the people of Rome viewed Count Riario with a mixture of repulsion and ridicule. At sixteen Caterina found herself bound to an inept murderer and the butt of Roman humor. She never complained, not even to her beloved Bona, but something had changed for Caterina. This would be the last time she passively stood by to watch events that so deeply affected her life.

6

THE GROWTH OF THE
RIARIO DYNASTY

THE SHOCKING NEWS of the slaughter in the cathedral of Florence spread quickly throughout Europe, and it soon became common knowledge that Pope Sixtus had been party to the sacrilegious plot.

To save face, Sixtus struck back at the Florentines. He blamed them for the abduction of Cardinal Riario and the murder of Archbishop Salviati. In a renewed effort to undo the Medicis, Sixtus approached Ferdinand I, the king of Naples, and easily secured his support in taking Florence from them, a plan that would neatly fall in with the king's expansionist designs on northern Italy. Siena was also recruited to lend a hand in the downfall of Florence, its ancient enemy. While the papal troops were mobilizing to bring this about, Sienese and Neapolitan soldiers were dispatched to join them. Florence's allies backed away one by one, and the city found itself alone, facing a powerful pincer action.

During this tumult, Girolamo revealed the vicious side of his character. As captain of the papal armies, he was privy to his uncle's maneuvers to wrest Florence from the Medicis. Yet every step that Girolamo took exposed his lack of political wisdom. As soon as he learned of the arrest and confession of Montesecco, Girolamo stormed the house of the Florentine ambassador, Donato Acciajuoli, and arrested the elderly gentleman, with the aim of exacting retribution. Only the discovery of Cardinal Raffaello Riario's detention at the hands of the Medicis saved the life of the respected Florentine. Then, stubbornly continuing in his attempt to assassinate Lorenzo, Girolamo turned to more disreputable associates and bribed an Imolese priest to enter a scheme whereby he would offer himself to Lorenzo as an assassin eager to rid the world of the pope's troublesome nephew Girolamo. The priest would then convince Lorenzo to supply him with a poison. That accomplished, the cleric would denounce the Florentine ruler for attempted murder and produce the poison as proof. The crude ploy did not fool Lorenzo, who promptly expelled the priest from Florence.

As he masterminded these desperate and haphazard plans, Girolamo incurred the displeasure of the entire papal court and the permanent enmity of his cousin Cardinal Giuliano della Rovere. The cardinal had argued against the Pazzi conspiracy, but he had been overruled. Now, in the wake of the disaster, the pope heeded Cardinal Giuliano's vehement protest against Girolamo's fruitless actions. The count desisted, but the rift within the papal family was already widening. Girolamo realized that it was time to regain the pope's favor by producing an heir.

After over two years of waiting, Caterina became pregnant with her first child over the Christmas holidays of 1478. Girolamo, in his new spirit of dedication to hearth and family, purchased a new family palace, tucked behind the Piazza Navona, in early 1479. The building needed a considerable amount of work, so between the arrival of the firstborn and the departure from the first home, there was much to prepare.

Whatever private disappointments Caterina may have felt regarding her husband's character and political failures were put aside as she dedicated herself to the role of devoted wife, whose first and foremost duty was to produce a male heir to carry on the family line. Caterina's life altered radically in the months of her pregnancy. Her long horseback rides and hunts ceased, and she spent more time in chapels, praying for a safe delivery and the arrival of a baby boy. Every year at Easter, the wax from the Paschal candle, a symbol of Christ's resurrection, was molded into little cakes, each called "Agnus Dei," or

"Lamb of God," and stamped with a sacred image. The most precious of these would be personally blessed by the pope and kept in a special gold box. Almost every expectant mother would be given one, as it was believed to help protect women in childbirth. Pope Urban VI (1378–1389) had sanctioned this practice, declaring a century earlier that this object of devotion "preserves the pregnant woman and delivers her of her child."[1]

Caterina received her Agnus Dei from Pope Sixtus, along with his blessing. Over the next months it would provide spiritual solace as she faced the fears related to childbirth. In Caterina's age, painkillers were few, and one of every ten women died from complications of delivery.

On August 31, 1479, Caterina and Girolamo's first son was born. Caterina sent a letter, marked by joy and relief, to Bona the very next day: "It being pleasing to the great Creator and His glorious Mother on the last day of August at about the sixth hour of the night [midnight], I gave birth to a beautiful male child: God be praised."[2]

Indeed, her prayers had been answered: it was a boy and she was already recovering. The celebrations began, as relatives and well-wishers lined up outside the Riarios' house, bearing gifts. For Caterina they brought fruits and sweets piled high on beautifully crafted "birth trays." After the perishables were consumed, the family could keep the brightly painted platters, some of wood, some of ceramic, some painted with the family coat of arms, and some decorated with a plump and cheery image of the infant John the Baptist, cousin to Jesus and born safely to the aged Elizabeth. The proud parents hung the trays on the walls. The new mother, proud, radiant, and arrayed in special robes, welcomed her visitors while sitting up in her maternity bed, now covered with sumptuous cloths. Musicians, discreetly tucked into a corner of the room, played soothing airs on pipes and lyres to accompany the murmurs of Caterina's guests. The infant, laid like a precious pearl in his cradle, received luxurious swaddling linens and coral amulets, which were worn as protective talismans.

For families of this era, however, delivery was only the first hurdle. Half of all children died before the age of two, and another half of those remaining died before they reached sixteen years. The fear of infant death made baptism a pressing concern. More than a gift-giving party or the official entry into society, baptism offered the assurance that whatever happened during the uncertain years of childhood, the infant's soul would live forever in Heaven. The baptism of Girolamo and Caterina's firstborn was a grand affair, celebrated by the pope himself. The child was given the name Ottaviano, the birth name of the heir of Julius Caesar who became the emperor Augustus, ruled the Roman Empire, and brought peace to war-torn Rome. This auspicious name proclaimed the design of Sixtus and Girolamo to create a Riario empire.

Among the many high-ranking Romans present at the baptism, the most celebrated of all was Cardinal Roderigo Borgia, who stood as godfather to the infant Ottaviano. Born in Spain in 1431, he was made a cardinal in 1456 by his uncle Pope Callistus III, and he had been climbing curial ladders ever since. Roderigo had obtained the most lucrative position in the church, that of papal vice chancellor, and thus he headed the office responding to requests for papal favors. Any person looking for work, references, or recommendations from the pope had to apply to Cardinal Borgia, with a "gift" in hand. In this coveted role, Roderigo had amassed an enormous amount of money, much of which he spent building the most splendid palace in Rome, likened by contemporaries to the legendary Domus Aurea, the Golden House of the emperor Nero.

Roderigo's similarities to Nero did not end with domestic architecture. The handsome Borgia cardinal also fueled Rome's gossip mills. With his dark, flashing eyes and hawklike features, he was fascinating to women and made no attempt to restrain his sexual appetite. Roderigo's successes with the most beautiful women of his age were attributed to his "honeyed and choice eloquence" as well as his massive personal fortune. Already the self-indulgent cardinal had been rebuked by Pope Pius II, no stranger to excess himself, for a garden party he hosted in Siena, which, according to reports that had reached the pope's ears, could only be called an orgy. At the time of Ottaviano's baptism Roderigo already had six or seven children, and his mistress Vanozza de' Cattanei was pregnant and would give birth to a daughter, Lucrezia. This scheming, sensual prelate had great ambitions for his own offspring. The hands that tenderly cradled Caterina's son at the baptismal font would eventually work against him.

Caterina recovered quickly from the birth of her first child, due in part to her youthful good health and also to her desire to show off her firstborn to her stepmother. But her plans to visit Bona unexpectedly came to a halt. Her sunny news from Rome was met by chill winds from Milan.

Caterina's stepmother had been efficiently ruling Milan as regent for her young son, Gian Galeazzo, helped by her deceased husband's loyal secretary of state, Cicco Simonetta. Cicco had given a lifetime of service to the Sforza family, weathering the challenges posed by revolution and assassination. It would take a different sort of entanglement to end Bona and Cicco's administration.

In 1479, palace voices whispered that the thirty-year-old widowed duchess had taken a lover. His name was Antonio Tassino, a handsome young footman in her household. The infatuated duchess shared the secret deliberations of her court and other sensitive information with her new favorite, earning him the resentment of the faithful Cicco, who refused to discuss matters of state in the presence of the upstart. Soon the duchess found herself at the center of a bitter rivalry within her own intimate circle. Her brothers-in-law, especially Ludovico, known as "the Moor" because of his dark complexion, had been waiting for such a golden opportunity to reintroduce themselves into court. Their ambition and dubious loyalty had led Galeazzo Maria to keep them at arm's length, a policy followed by the regent Bona. They seized upon the naive Tassino as a path to Bona. Professing a sincere desire to make peace with his sister-in-law, Ludovico implored Tassino to convince Bona to speak with him. Under Tassino's influence, the duchess relented and agreed to meet him on September 7, 1479. The moment Cicco heard of the encounter, he solemnly foretold that because of it, he would "lose his head and the illustrious duchess would lose her reign."[3] Three days later, Cicco was imprisoned for treason.

These machinations surprised Caterina, who had delivered her first child two weeks earlier. Bona's letter of congratulations was followed two days later by the news of Cicco's arrest. For the modern reader, Caterina's perfunctory letters of congratulations to Bona and to the duke's secretary upon hearing the news of Cicco's arrest are hard to interpret at first glance. Although the letter to Bona is more guarded in content, promising prayers for a peaceful reign, Caterina wrote in buoyant tones to the secretary of Duke Gian Galeazzo and his new guardian, Ludovico the Moor, claiming that "short of raising her father from the dead," nothing could please her more than the news of the arrest of the "nefarious Cicco."[4] While undoubtedly the papal courtiers had explained to her that Cicco had betrayed her family and was even complicit in the murder of her father, she must have wondered how a mainstay of her childhood household, whom she had seen continually at her father's side, could have turned traitor. A further detail sheds more light on Caterina's approach to this situation. Her letters were sent on September 18, 1479, on the same day and in the same mail pouch as Pope Sixtus's response to the news. The pontiff was delighted at this change of affairs, hoping to establish an alliance with a more powerful ruler in Milan and perhaps form a league against Florence, a goal that was still foremost in his mind. Caterina's letters, echoing papal sentiments, show that she was learning the ways of diplomacy. Caterina adapted quickly, and two months after the upheaval in Milan, she was already writing Bona to ask for new hunting dogs and lamenting that Roman hounds "were no good."[5] Returning to her riding regimen soothed her spirits.

Within a year, Cicco's dire prophecy came true: the man who had served three dukes of Milan was beheaded, and Bona lost her political authority. Ludovico the Moor took over the rule of Milan as regent for the young duke Gian Galeazzo.

Caterina had little time to enjoy the hunt or concern herself with Milanese affairs since by Christmas 1479 she was pregnant again, just three months after the birth of Ottaviano. Renaissance noblewomen were discouraged from breastfeeding their own children, and consequently they could become pregnant again soon after childbirth. Caterina prepared to put aside her hunting gear once more and to don the garb of an expectant mother. This time, however, sixteen-year-old Caterina's days were packed with increased responsibilities. The new palace was nearing completion, and the Riarios had to see to its decoration. Girolamo, nouveau riche that he was, had a taste for conspicuous consumption. He hired Sixtus IV's court painter, Melozzo da Forlì, to create most of the murals, and Luca Pacioli, the famous mathematician, to serve as architect. These two men had worked in many important courts and could recognize that Girolamo, unlike their more cultured patrons, knew nothing about art. He equated the most expensive and complicated with the best, and so the two men amused themselves at Girolamo's expense. As the last pilasters of the courtyard were put into place, Pacioli and Melozzo vied to invent the most intricate designs possible for the capitals. The two practical jokers plied Girolamo with the names of famous aristocratic patrons who employed this decoration, then watched as Girolamo seized upon the idea and browbeat the poor master carver into fashioning the gaudy stonework. Yet despite Girolamo's lack of taste, the Riario palace, like all those constructed for the family of Sixtus IV, grew into a magnificent structure.

Caterina's front door was situated one block from the new market in the Piazza Navona. As she and her attendants returned from the daily shopping and crossed the narrow stone entrance, the guards stationed in a room to the right leapt to attention. Her servants veered to the left to deposit the day's purchases in the kitchen while Caterina herself entered the columned courtyard at the center of the house. This area was a beehive of activity. All the little rooms facing onto it were filled with the Riarios' dependents, who were hard at work. The muffled scratch of quills on parchment came from one office, where secretaries huddled over the count's correspondence and accountants toted up the domestic expenses. Footmen were dispatched to bring staple goods from storage cellars, and a few off-duty servants would be chatting while sharing a quick snack. Under the tower, the horses were groomed in the stable and carriages received their regular maintenance. A little garden peeked through an archway, offering an oasis of fresh air and greenery in the heart of the city.

As she climbed the wide stone stair to the *piano nobile*, the most elegant story where the family lived and received guests, the clatter and buzz of cooking and talking would fade. A few steps from the landing, Caterina entered the relative quiet of her own apartments. Her rooms were comfortably furnished, and because the dowry of a Sforza noblewoman traditionally included magnificent textiles, expensive tapestries adorned the walls, and plush silk and velvet cushions padded the furniture. Her clothes and accessories were kept in large wooden chests called *cassone*, storage solutions for an era without bureaus or closets. Caterina had accumulated many such chests since her childhood, and several boasted painted panels portraying heroines of chastity, models for a young bride. Young Ottaviano's nursery was close to her room; the child was constantly tended by a servant there. Girolamo's rooms were separate but easily reached, and they were decorated with equal splendor. His courtiers occupied the outer rooms, and the count's inner sanctum consisted of three rooms and a study. A long hall with a large carved fireplace stood between the two sets of living quarters and served as a reception space for the numerous noble visitors that the nephew of the reigning pope was expected to entertain.

Melozzo da Forlì, still receiving accolades for his stunning murals in Sixtus IV's new Vatican library, executed the decorative painting for the public areas of the palace. Only one fragment survives today, but the faded fresco offers an interesting glimpse of the owner's tastes. Melozzo was renowned as a master of the avant-garde one-point-linear perspective, the technique of making a three-dimensional image on a two-dimensional surface. For the Riarios he painted an illusionistic cupboard against an elaborate tapestry background. Arrayed along the wooden shelves, he depicted an elaborate silver service, with scalloped plates and bowls. This display of finery perfectly matched the description of the arrangement of Caterina and Girolamo's wedding gifts at their marriage banquet three years earlier. It is unlikely that Caterina would have approved the commission. Though she had been raised in an extravagant court, the duke of Milan would never dream of decorating his public rooms with paintings of his possessions. But Caterina did admire the skill of the artist. Years later, when she would finally commission her own paintings, she too would hire Melozzo da Forlì.

The new year brought the dawn of a new era, both for the Riario family and for Rome. On January 8, 1480, Sixtus IV announced his ambitious plans to restore the Eternal City to its former grandeur. After the popes had abandoned Rome for most of the fourteenth century, taking up residence in the French town of Avignon, the poverty-stricken city had suffered from rampant illness and lack of clean water. The churches that had been the glory of Rome were falling to pieces. Since the papacy had returned to Rome in 1417, little had been done to alleviate the suffering of most of the inhabitants. From the moment of his election, Pope Sixtus IV had thrown himself headlong into repairs and renovations. One of his first acts was to donate five ancient Roman bronze statues to the people of Rome, housing them in the Conservator's Palace on the Capitoline Hill. When Caterina first arrived, she too had admired the colossal head of Constantine as well as the archaic bronze sculpture of the famous she-wolf—which, according to myth, had suckled Romulus and Remus, the legendary founders of Rome.

Careful study had informed the new projects aimed to return Rome to its former status as *caput mundi*. Sixtus demanded a complete rejuvenation of the city's once-famed engineering. The Acqua Vergine, a thirteen-mile aqueduct that had once brought fresh, pure water to Rome, was built by Emperor Augustus's heir, Agrippa, in 19 B.C.; northern invaders had destroyed it in the sixth century A.D. Sixtus rebuilt this conduit, returning clean water to a city that had long made do with the polluted flow of the Tiber River. Sixtus also rebuilt the hospital of Santo Spirito, still functioning today, a few short blocks from Saint Peter's. With its modern structure and large wards, Santo Spirito became a model for other hospitals in Italy and beyond. Wider roads and grander palaces appeared just as the Sistine Chapel, a pet project of the pope that was to replace a dilapidated structure, was nearing completion.

Through these public works, Pope Sixtus cast himself in the role of a Christian Emperor Augustus. Just as the first Roman emperor had boasted that he had "found Rome a city of brick and left it a city of marble," so Sixtus intended to transform the capital of Christendom into a center worthy of its illustrious past. "For if any city should be clean and beautiful," Sixtus declared, "it should indeed be the one which is capital of the world and holds primacy among all others because of the throne of Saint Peter."[6]

In the course of her daily social calls, Caterina saw busy teams of workers everywhere and witnessed the Romans' delight in these civic improvements. Although her father had also embarked on a plan to renovate Milan, Galeazzo's efforts had been erratic and mostly aimed at improving mercantile productivity. Sixtus's concern for clean water and healthful living conditions for all Romans taught Caterina that demonstrable interest in the well-being of average citizens could serve as a valuable political tool.

New churches built in an innovative yet austere style were cropping up all over town. The monumental Church of Saint Augustine was underway next door to Caterina's palace. Up on the Janiculum Hill, Sixtus built a stately church on the site where, according to contemporary belief, Saint Peter had died. But the Church of Santa Maria del Popolo, at the end of the Via Flaminia, stood out as the pope's most cherished ecclesiastical project. Situated at the northern gate of the city, through which most pilgrims entered Rome, Saint Mary of the People was the first building visitors would see in the city. The broad travertine façade recalled the great temple fronts that had adorned the Rome of old. Saint Mary of the People also served as the family church. Three of Sixtus's nephews endowed side chapels, and a steady stream of important painters and sculptors enhanced the structure with imaginative decorations in the family name. Girolamo was appointed chief warden of the newly completed church in 1480, meaning that Caterina and her family attended Mass there regularly. Every Saturday, the pope himself would cross the Tiber River to spend a little time in prayer there. Indeed, every major event of this pontificate — war, victory, thanksgiving — would see the della Roveres and the Riarios gathered at this site. This single building not only brought the diverse members of Sixtus's family together under one spiritual roof (even Caterina's uncle Cardinal Ascanio Sforza would be buried there) but also proclaimed the pope's grand dreams for the Eternal City. The art historian Lisa Passaglia Bauman has written that in this edifice, for the first time in papal history, "one pope and his family had melded an ideology of power with the rhetoric of art to create a vision of dynasty."[7]

The Riario-Sforza dominions were growing as fast as the family. On August 23, 1480, Pope Sixtus IV formally conferred upon Girolamo the territory of Forlì, a little town slightly less than ten miles south of Imola, thereby doubling the Riarios' realm. The papal bull of investiture lauded the count's "learned experience, circumspect wisdom, and his shining faith," charging him to "nurture concord, treat his subjects kindly, and administer justice to all persons without exception."[8]

On the following day Caterina gave birth to her second son, named Cesare (Caesar) for the Roman statesman who had so fatefully crossed the Rubicon River just a few short miles from Forlì. As in the case of Ottaviano, the choice of name illustrated the grand hopes of the Riario family: the count and countess of Forlì and Imola were well on their way to creating both a state and a dynasty.

Caterina wrote to her beloved stepmother, Bona of Savoy, to proudly announce the arrival of a *"bellissimo figlio maschio,"*[9] little realizing that the rapidly changing situation in Milan was about to deprive her of regular communication with the woman who had been so important to her. Ludovico the Moor had already usurped Bona's role as regent, but he still feared her ability to influence her young son, Gian Galeazzo. One month after Caterina's letter arrived, he transferred Bona to the Abbey of Abbiategrasso, where she died twenty-three years later, never having seen any of Caterina's children. With the sequestering of Bona of Savoy, Caterina's last bond of affection to the Sforza court was severed. Caterina was fond of her brothers and sisters there, but Bona was what made Milan a home to her. Ludovico now occupied the ducal throne, and he would think of Caterina as a pawn, to be used and sacrificed at will. She would have to commit her future fortunes entirely to the Riario clan.

The close of 1480 brought an end to hostilities with Florence. On November 25, twelve Florentine ambassadors from the most famous families of the republic—the Tornabuonis (who were papal bankers), the Vespuccis (one of whom would soon make a trip of discovery to America), the Guicciardinis (one of whom would author the history of Florence), and the Soderinis (who would employ Michelangelo to sculpt the *David*)—came to the portico of Saint Peter's Basilica. Before the enthroned Sixtus, the noblemen dropped to their knees. The pontiff, his angular features set in his sternest expression, "with most binding words and admonitions finally absolved them and admitted them to the kissing of the feet."[10] All offenses forgiven, the pope and the ambassadors entered the church together for a Mass of thanksgiving. For the time being, blessed peace settled over Italy.

The Riario clan had much to celebrate this Christmas: the Florentine feud had formally ceased, two hale and hearty baby boys ensured the continuation of the family name, and plans were in the air to visit the new Riario lands in the upcoming year. Any sadness that Caterina felt over the alienation of her stepmother would not be shared by Girolamo or his kin, nor would they indulge any dampening of the jovial mood. Caterina's only outlet for these feelings took place during whispered prayers in her chapel or vigorous rides in the Roman woods. Girolamo was confident that as long the pope stayed healthy, the run of good fortune would continue. As the yule log burned in the new Riario palace, the sweet smell of success filled the air.

7

THE FAIREST IN THE REALM

WHILE IN ROME the count and countess were enjoying a respite from political strife, trouble was already brewing in their new lands. In 1480, the little town of Forlì in the heart of Romagna had a slightly larger population than nearby Imola—about ten thousand people, including both residents within the walls and country dwellers.[1] The two Riario states, Forlì and Imola, were separated only by the tiny village of Faenza. Any hope the count had of consolidating his two lands would require possession of Faenza, but the Manfredis who ruled the town were backed by the military might of the Este family in Ferrara. For half a millennium, Forlì had known little stability, bouncing back and forth between church possession and domination by a succession of petty tyrants. The town's turbulent history, marked by bloody battles and destruction, had rendered its inhabitants highly suspicious of any new regime, including that of the Riarios.

For almost fifty years, Forlì had been governed by a local family, the Ordelaffis. In defiance of Duke Francesco Sforza, Caterina's grandfather, Antonio Ordelaffi seized power in 1438, largely through the help of the Venetians. Antonio's son Francesco, or "Cecco," had succeeded his father, but he was soon murdered by his brother Pino, who stabbed him to death after failing to kill him with poison. In a rare gesture of clemency, Pino refrained from killing Cecco's sons and merely sent them into exile. Pino then claimed the rule of Forlì in 1466, taking the name Pino III Ordelaffi. Following the scandalous fratricide, Pino went on to become a sort of Renaissance Bluebeard. He poisoned his first wife, Barbara Manfredi from neighboring Faenza, out of jealousy. Then, in a dramatic show of public grief, he commissioned an exquisite marble tomb, still in the Abbey of San Mercuriale today, one of the first Renaissance works of sculpture to grace Forlì. Within a few years, Pino's second spouse, Zaffira Manfredi (from the Imola branch of the family), also died of poisoning, along with her mother. This time Pino didn't bother with a fancy tomb. According to a local diarist, his next bride, the beautiful Lucrezia Pico della Mirandola, "was very cautious about what she ate."[2]

Despite his numerous wives, Pino never managed to produce a legitimate heir. He finally settled upon his bastard son Sinibaldo and formally recognized him. When Pino fell fatally ill in 1480, shortly after fighting for the pope against Florence, he was so detested that the people of Forlì rose up to speed his demise. He was dragged down the stairs of his house and into the central piazza, where he expired as the Forlivesi spat on him, kicking and beating him into the next world.

The newly widowed Lucrezia didn't waste time. She assumed the regency for fourteen-year-old Sinibaldo only moments before Cecco's three exiled sons, Antonio Maria, Francesco, and Ludovico, stormed into Forlì with a contingent of troops from Ravenna to reclaim the town. But unlike Bona of Savoy, who had marshaled powerful allies to stave off her brothers-in-law, Lucrezia found herself alone. Her only recourse was to close herself up in the strongest fortress of Forlì, Ravaldino, and wait out the siege. With things seemingly at an impasse, events suddenly took a surprising turn: the new lord of Faenza, Sinibaldo, mysteriously died in the fortress.

Meanwhile, Sixtus IV and Girolamo had been circling like vultures as the struggle of the Ordelaffis played out. When Sinibaldo died, they seized their opportunity. Declaring the Ordelaffis' claim invalid, they sent a contingent of soldiers to take possession of Forlì and turn it over to Girolamo.

Lucrezia, however, proved herself a gifted negotiator. She left the fortress with 130,000 ducats and a baggage train of thirty-two carts, and moved into a new castle given to her by the pope. Shortly thereafter, the clever widow remarried. The three sons of Cecco, on the other hand, retreated empty-handed to Faenza to await their next opportunity.

Girolamo did not visit his new lands immediately. Instead, he sent his extremely able and trusted *condottiere* Gian Francesco Maruzzi, known as "Il Tolentino," to serve as governor. Speculation was rife over Girolamo's reluctance to leave Rome. Some thought the pope was ill and Girolamo was afraid to leave lest Sixtus should die; others suspected he was relying on the advice of astrologers, who were counseling him as to the most propitious time to arrive in Forlì.[3] Most likely, Girolamo was so busy scheming to garner power in Rome that Forlì seemed unimportant by comparison. After a time, a delegation of notables of Forlì came to Rome to take stock of their new ruler. Girolamo made a good first impression, welcoming them graciously and sending them back to Forlì with promises of lucrative positions and good news for the citizens: they could expect a certain amount of tax relief.

The Ordelaffi brothers, for their part, were seething with anger at being deprived of what they regarded as their rightful inheritance. Upon their return to Faenza, they had immediately begun plotting against the new count of Forlì. On October 13, 1480, they struck, sending sixty men with orders to take control of the fortress of Ravaldino. The band, abetted by two local priests, was to assassinate the keeper and occupy the castle. Fortunately for the Riarios, Il Tolentino had a nose for conspiracies. The loyal governor discovered the plot, rounded up the rebel band, hanged the two puppet priests, and exiled the remaining soldiers. The Ordelaffi brothers licked their wounds and awaited another chance. Tranquility returned, but the incident gave the Riarios a taste of intrigues to come.

Finally, in the spring of 1481, Girolamo and Caterina began preparations to visit Imola and Forlì. An immense baggage train, piled high with the finest possessions of the Riario household, departed under a heavily armed escort, accompanied by the Riario children, Ottaviano and Cesare. Caterina was pregnant again, and the servants packed an array of the latest and costliest fashions in different sizes to accommodate their mistress's expanding figure. The party traveled at a leisurely pace, putting in few hours on the road and stopping every evening at aristocratic estates or humble inns along the way. Two weeks later, the Riarios arrived two miles outside Forlì and for the first time laid eyes on the town that would be their new home. The territory of Forlì sprawled over eighty-eight square miles of Romagna, but the town center was enclosed by an irregular brick wall, 3.3 miles long. This thick shell was punctured by eight gateways, where merchandise passing through was tallied and taxed and foreign visitors were registered. The town was dwarfed by the fortress of Ravaldino, which dominated the southern roads leading to the Apennines. Its crenellated walls, towering over a wide moat, were the first thing the Riarios saw as they approached.[4]

The new rulers paused at the house of a local landowner, Marino degli Orcioli, to determine, in counsel with the count's astrologers, the most propitious hour of arrival. During the wait, however, a fire broke out in the palace destined to be home to the new count and countess—an inauspicious omen. A local friar, who sympathized with the Ordelaffi brothers, attempted to stir up sentiment against the Riarios by declaring that "the Ordelaffis had entered the city with a mighty wind; now the new lord was entering with fire." To the more superstitious of the Forlivesi, wind was associated with the Holy Spirit, and fire with Hell.

Those grim portents were dispelled, however, by the well-planned first appearance of the Riarios. At sunset, the party rode past Ravaldino to enter the Porta Cotogni. One of Forlì's largest gates and the site of the principal customs office, the Porta Cotogni opened onto the main thoroughfare of the town, the Strada Petrosa (the paved street). The arrival of the Riarios was the grandest procession in the history of Forlì. Nobles carrying banners and lances marched at the head, as brass horns announced their passage through the narrow streets. Clergymen decked in richly embroidered liturgical robes walked in stately order; their white-gloved hands bore jeweled reliquaries, and one held high a golden crucifix that glinted in the last rays of sunlight. Acolytes waved palm fronds, as had the people of Jerusalem upon Jesus' triumphant entry on what came to be celebrated as Palm Sunday. Myriad pennants proudly proclaimed the artisan trades, and the leading citizen of each of the four neighborhoods of Forlì marched in the throng.

Caterina, Girolamo, and their children were resplendent in multicolored silks. The count's soldiers wore silver cloaks over their armor, while the knights of his escort were dressed in gold brocade. The people of Forlì crowded the alleys and climbed onto balconies to catch a glimpse of the splendid retinue, which included members of the ancient noble Roman houses of Orsini, Colonna, and Savelli. Decked head to toe in fine pearls, rare jewels, and sumptuous fabrics, the rainbow of courtiers looked more than worthy of their renowned heritage.

The aristocratic assemblage rode under a triumphal arch—similar to those still visible among the ruins of the Roman Forum—and entered the main square of Forlì, where the count and countess would reside. Here they encountered a group of actors masquerading as the great citizens of old, striking dignified poses on a victory chariot: the legendary founder of the town, Claudius Livy; the celebrated Roman playwright Titus Maccius Plautus; and the town's first bishop, Saint Mercuriale, joined other native heroes in welcoming Girolamo into their midst, with odes and hymns. Guido Peppo, the local classicist and philosopher reputed as being "well-versed in Latin, Greek, and Hebrew," acted as keynote speaker, delivering an elegant laudatory oration.[5]

The party rode up the few steps to their new palace. Although five months pregnant, Caterina dismounted gracefully and watched serenely as the young men who had gathered to see the famous beauty scuffled over the privilege of taking the bridle and leading her horse away. Several gentlemen of Forlì stepped forward for the honor of carrying the countess up the stairs to her new palace. Unlike Girolamo, who was nervous when crowds pressed in on him, Caterina touched the outstretched hands and appeared delighted by the attention. She smilingly promised the gentlemen who had taken charge of her horse that if it was returned to her well tended, she would give them the jeweled overdress she was wearing—a promise that she duly kept.

Upstairs in the reception room of the palace, the people of Forlì were awed by the array of silver and other wares arranged in large open cabinets. For eight days the townspeople had watched mules and carts delivering huge trunks and crates to the house, as the residence was prepared for the arrival of the new lords. When at last they were allowed to see the treasures of the pope's nephew, the display did not disappoint. Finely wrought silver ewers and plates and gold vases were stacked on shelves that stretched from floor to ceiling. A major purpose of this display, worth some hundred thousand ducats, was to reassure the people of Forlì that the Riarios would not need to squeeze their land for revenue, but indeed would bring riches to this little town of artisans and farmers. Every day the objects on the shelves were changed so that the people could admire the seemingly endless resources of Count Girolamo. Even Antonio Appiani, the sophisticated and well-traveled ambassador to the duke of Milan, conceded that the count "had made an astounding display." Appiani was particularly impressed by Caterina, writing that although "she had had two children and was pregnant with her third," she looked "beautiful and lively and was well-furnished with jewels."[6]

In provincial Forlì, men, women, and children jostled for a glimpse of the famous young countess who dazzled the Forlivesi with the latest fashions. Every detail of her dress was noted by the town's noblewomen, who would soon be striving to achieve the same look. On the evening of the welcoming banquet, she wore a turban that framed her radiant youthful face. Trailing from the headdress was a long veil of woven silver threads embroidered with pearls. The border featured a pattern of a rising sun, with rays penetrating a cloud underscored by her personal motto, DIVERSORUM OPERUM, "manifold works." As with the finest couture, her unique robe was months in the making. During her four weeks in Forlì, locals noted that she never wore the same dress twice. Her wardrobe and gems served their purpose: the people of Forlì were enchanted by their new countess.

Flame-colored silks draped the banqueting hall where Girolamo accepted more homages of poetry by the town's literati. Caterina and Girolamo then greeted the farmers from the countryside, who presented them with gifts of livestock and chickens, beeswax, wheat, and jams as well as fruit from the local orchards.

At the height of this display of affection and jubilation, Girolamo rose to address his new subjects. "People of Forlì," he began, "I promise that I will be a good son of this city and father to the people." He then went on to confirm the promise he had made to the delegation in Rome. The *dazi*, the taxes levied on entering the city and on purchasing grain for personal use, would be removed. Girolamo solemnly vowed that he would "maintain that promise in perpetuity," stating that "neither I nor my children shall repeal it or even remember it."[7] This munificent but shortsighted policy met with wild applause and cheering but was in fact a time bomb. On that evening, July 15, 1481, Girolamo still enjoyed his position as the pope's favorite nephew, who could dip his hands into the papal coffers as often as he liked. This largesse, however, would last only as long as his uncle lived.

No concerns about an uncertain future were evident as the noble company danced and dined. To one local diarist, it seemed like the beginning of a golden age. Leone Cobelli, born and raised in Forlì, was a dancer, teacher, musician, and painter, and he was enthralled by Caterina from the moment he first laid eyes on her. Cobelli was playing the *baldosa*, an instrument similar to a guitar but with thirty copper strings, for the gala. In the musicians' gallery, the scent of Caterina's perfume wafted over him as she danced and her fair skin and hair glowed golden in the torchlight. That night he wrote his first lines describing Caterina and "the most beautiful dance I have ever seen or think I ever will."[8] Not of a station that made him eligible as a confidant of the aristocratic countess, Cobelli would vent his passionate interest in Caterina by studying every aspect of her life during her years in Forlì. Beginning on that magical evening, Cobelli appointed himself as Caterina's personal historian. (Mostly he would watch her from afar; his one substantial personal encounter with her proved unpleasant.) His *Chronicles of Forlì* remains one of the most interesting sources for the stories, scandals, and fashions of Caterina's time in Forlì.

The next morning, Caterina appeared at Girolamo's side on the palace balcony, and together they tossed coins into the crowd below. They then took their seats to watch a spectacle created specifically in their honor. A large wooden castle resembling a fortified town had been constructed in the center of the main piazza. Forty young nobles and a priest took their places within the four towers, representing the citizens of Otranto on the Adriatic coast of southern Italy, defenders of their land. On August 2, 1480, Otranto had been captured by the Ottoman Turkish fleet of Sultan Mehmed II. The attack was sudden and unexpected, and many feared that "if God had not intervened, we would have been in their hands in short order."[9] This event had so shocked Italy that it put an end to the war between the Florentines and the pope, who united to face a common enemy. Although the sultan had died two months earlier, in May, which caused rejoicing throughout Italy, Otranto still remained in the hands of the invaders. Fear of the Turks forged a bond among the people of the Italian peninsula. Thus, the re-creation of the Otranto siege held vital meaning.

Two hundred young men posed as the attackers, eagerly storming the castle to win the prize of five yards of precious velvet and four gold ducats. After a violent struggle lasting about an hour and a half, during which many people were wounded, a certain Francesco da Caravaggio claimed his reward as the first to enter the fortress, but at the cost of his eye. The afternoon ended with a joust between the Roman nobles Paolo Orsini and Giovanni Colonna, with the new governor, Il Tolentino, joining in. Although the riding was superb and the arms and weapons of the latest models, the crowds were disappointed that no winner was declared. Yet they soon forgot their displeasure as music began for a dance and food appeared for a feast.

The couple remained for a month of festivities in Forlì, but while the countess, heavily pregnant during the hot summer months, made the effort to visit and socialize with her new people, Girolamo closed himself up in his apartments.[10] Despite the smiles the two evinced in public, the first signs of a rift between Caterina and her diffident husband began to show during this sojourn. Caterina actively engaged the citizens, unafraid to walk among her subjects; Girolamo, always wary of strangers, shied away from social situations. Even in mid-August, when they moved on to Imola, Girolamo kept to his rooms after attending the initial banquets and festivities. Yet after ten years of his rule, the Imolesi had every reason to love the count. Although he had barely visited the town, Girolamo had made numerous improvements. Inspired by his uncle's precedent in Rome (and subsidized by the papal purse), Count Riario strove to foster goodwill among his new subjects. The city wherein the Milanese orator Gian Luigi Bossi had disdainfully taken note of small houses and unpaved streets was now a jewel in the crown of Romagna. Girolamo had lured the builder Giorgio Fiorentino from Tuscany to construct houses in the style of the Medici family's properties, with expensive rusticated stone bases and elegantly arched windows. High arcades of loggias spanned façades throughout the town, sheltering the people of Imola from the elements and lending a lofty mien to the city squares. Over the course of four years, paved roads had replaced muddy streets.

Nonetheless, Girolamo was never to be seen. Soon enough the Imolesi were murmuring. What was the new count afraid of? Was he ill? What was wrong with him? Appiani suspected that Girolamo was too weak to govern the two cities. The insightful ambassador rightly guessed that the count was afraid of assassins, particularly in Forlì. When in Romagna, he preferred to remain in Imola, since unlike the Forlivesi, the Imolesi were not prone to violent action and confined their rebellions to lively chatter over a bottle of Sangiovese wine.[11]

Girolamo's distrust apparently extended to Caterina as well. Ludovico the Moor, the acting duke of Milan while he served as regent for Caterina's brother, extended an invitation to Caterina through his ambassador, Antonio Appiani, to come to Milan and visit her family for a month. The countess told Appiani that she yearned to visit Milan, but when she had mentioned the possibility to her husband he had brusquely denied her request, and "not without anger," as she put it. When Appiani suggested that he might speak to Girolamo himself on behalf of the duke, the worried wife begged him not to, for fear that Girolamo would think that she had engineered his intervention, and it would all end in a messy fight.

Appiani, however, had his orders from the duke and sought an audience with the count, explaining that Caterina's family had not seen her in several years and would like to meet their nephews. Girolamo could not be moved. In his first response, a false one, he stated that he "wouldn't know how to live without her"; this was belied immediately when he mentioned his intention of leaving Caterina in Romagna when he returned to Rome. When Caterina heard that Girolamo intended to leave her behind, she made plans to go to Milan as soon as he departed. Nevertheless, Appiani was left with the distinct impression that the count would neither come to Milan nor allow Caterina to do so. It was not uncommon for Renaissance wives to travel to see their families even during pregnancy, and Milan was a relatively short journey on even terrain. But ever since Ludovico the Moor had been crafty enough to come between Bona of Savoy and Cicco Simonetta, Girolamo had good reason to worry that the duke would lure Caterina into serving the interests of Milan instead of those of Rome.

For the time being, Caterina would have to remain in her home in Forlì.

Disappointed that peace with Florence had been achieved, Girolamo was already stirring up more trouble. No sooner had the pope declared the reconciliation with Florence than Girolamo had cast his eye on Faenza, the little town that stood between his two holdings in Romagna. The count schemed to close the gap between Forlì and Imola by taking control of that little Manfredi state. But to conquer the Manfredis, he would have to first weaken their powerful protectors, the Este family of Ferrara.

Ferrara was a flourishing duchy neighboring the most important states of northern Italy: Florence, Bologna, Milan, and Venice. Ercole d'Este, the warlike and powerful ruler of the prosperous city, had wheeled and dealt with both the papacy and the Holy Roman Emperor to amass a wide swath of land from Modena to Reggio as well as the town of Ferrara. A handsome man with soft graying hair, he had also contracted a brilliant marriage with Eleanora of Aragon, the daughter of King Ferdinand of Naples. During the conflict between Florence and the papacy, Ercole, as papal *condottiere*, should have fought in the interests of the papacy. But he had decided instead to defend his neighbor, Florence, thus incurring the enmity of Pope Sixtus and Girolamo. During the nine months that Caterina was carrying their third child, plans for vengeance were gestating in Girolamo's mind.

In early September, Girolamo and Caterina, now in her eighth month, set out on a voyage to the Republic of Venice. A mighty baggage train of thirty-six mules and twenty-one carts announced the arrival of the couple in Ravenna, and on September 8 they cruised into Venice on special gondolas constructed for the arrival of exalted guests. The ruler of Venice, Doge Giovanni Moecenigo, accompanied by 115 members of the nobility, sailed out to meet them. Sleek black gondolas glided silently across the Grand Canal as the sun sparkled on the ripples in their wake. The doge, from his golden barge, greeted Girolamo effusively, heralding him as "a true son of Mars." One might wonder if he was wryly alluding to the count's penchant for causing bloodshed rather than his martial abilities and courage.

Venice, with its dark and winding canals, was a breeding ground for intrigue. Lorenzo de' Medici knew Girolamo's trip meant more than the ostensible excuse of recruiting the Venetian navy to free Otranto from the Turks. He correctly suspected that the real plan was to ally with Venice against Ercole d'Este. In the name of Pope Sixtus, Girolamo offered to carve up Ercole's territories, giving Reggio to Venice while keeping Faenza for himself.

But the crude cunning of the count was no match for the sly tactics of the Venetians. As one report to Lorenzo the Magnificent said, Girolamo "saw more things that provoked displeasure than gratitude."[12] The doge honored him with fabulous balls and banquets and lavished empty titles on him, but Girolamo never got what he came for. The Venetians did not want to risk war with the powerful father-in-law of the duke of Ferrara, King Ferdinand of Naples.

It is doubtful that Caterina found the Venetians congenial. Straightforward herself, she probably sensed their duplicity as she dined on the tiny, sweet Adriatic shrimp scented with heady spices, which had been obtained through Venice's questionable dealings with the Turks. Florentine ambassadors, always attentive to relations among their restive neighbors, wrote reports alluding to how the Venetian ladies feigned friendship, but behind the Riarios' back they sneered at the provincial manners of the Romans.[13]

Girolamo feared that Caterina might speak indiscreetly, and it appears that her husband did not confide his plans to her. On August 16, shortly before the trip to Venice, Caterina wrote a cheery little missive to the wife of Ercole d'Este, Eleanora of Aragon, asking for new hunting dogs. Clearly a connoisseur, Caterina requested "a singular and special gift of a pair of greyhounds that were great runners and capable of running down the hares of the Roman countryside, which are very fast, and a pair of good bloodhounds" for following scents and trails. She also asked for a pack of retrievers to work with her falcons "so well trained and valiant that I hope to be able to say when they catch a wild animal, 'Those are the dogs given to me by the illustrious duchess of Ferrara.'" She wrote engagingly, recognizing their common love of hunting and Ferrara's supremacy in the matter of hunting dogs; she seemed unaware that her husband was plotting to usurp her new friend's realm.

On their return from Venice, the couple took a longer route to avoid passing through Ferrara. They stopped in the tiny village of Cotignola, where Caterina's great-grandfather, Muzio Attendolo, had been born. There the villagers poured into the dusty streets to see Caterina, raising the cry of "Sforza! Sforza!" and welcoming her to "her home."[14] To Caterina, it must have been heartening to hear her proud family name echoing in the streets, after the pain of being refused a visit to her home and family. Soon enough that name would be honored in a far greater setting than Cotignola.

The Riarios' second arrival in Forlì was not as felicitous as the first. Already sparks of discontent were igniting among the Forlivesi, and Lorenzo de' Medici was attempting to fan them into flames. The powerful Florentine had not forgotten the murder of his brother, and now that Girolamo was near at hand, it was time to strike. Ercole of Ferrara was only too glad to help, given Girolamo's attempts to usurp his rule. It was easy enough for them to find some discontented tradesmen of Forlì whose work brought them to Florence and Ferrara. The so-called Artisan conspiracy was thus hatched in late September to kill both Girolamo and Caterina along the road between Imola and Forlì on the last leg of their return from Venice. Il Tolentino, the faithful factotum whose ear was always to the ground, discovered the plot in time to save the count and countess. But when Girolamo heard of it, he flew into a rage. "How can it be that people of Forlì want to kill me and restore Ordelaffi?" he cried. "Is this the thanks I receive for getting rid of their taxes?" As he railed against the people of Forlì, he overlooked his real predicament. He had antagonized two of the most powerful men in northern Italy, whose families had ruled for several generations. As a newcomer from a foreign family, he would always be at a disadvantage. He instructed Il Tolentino, however, not to say a word about the conspiracy, lest his authority appear to be in jeopardy.

The next day, Girolamo went to Mass at San Mercuriale, unaccompanied by his family and friends but surrounded by three hundred armed soldiers. This show of strength was meant to remind the Forlivesi that the pope's nephew could, as he desired, bring riches to the town or summon an army. No parties or dances attended Girolamo's last days in town, and when the count set off on October 14, he took several citizens of Forlì as guests to Rome, with the announced intention of entertaining them in the Eternal City. In reality they were hostages.

In the wake of the Artisan conspiracy Caterina traveled a different route to Rome, with an escort of fifty horsemen and ten female attendants. Stopping in Imola, the safer of the two cities in the Riarios' realm, she left the children and a conspicuous portion of the family treasures, along with their summer clothes. She met up with her husband in Rimini and together they embarked on the road to Rome. Caterina was riding on a mule in a sort of carriage made of two baskets, as she was now nine months pregnant. For most expectant noblewomen of the Renaissance era, the ninth month was generally treated as a "lying-in period," during which they would wait in their chambers for labor to begin. Caterina displayed strength of both body and mind in making this trip, as certainly everyone, including her husband, would have tried to dissuade her from doing so. Willing to risk a haphazard roadside delivery, Caterina obviously had no intention of leaving her husband in Rome alone. On October 26, only a few days after her arrival, Caterina gave birth to her first girl, Bianca. The child was named for Caterina's grandmother, who with Bona of Savoy had helped raise her. The delivery was uncomplicated and her husband surprisingly solicitous, hurrying to her bedside and declaring himself "more pleased with a girl than a boy."[15]

Girolamo waited until November, the month of the dead, to exact justice for the Artisan conspiracy. When he and his family had resumed their life in Rome, Il Tolentino hanged five men in the main square of Forlì and exiled many others. A few months later, however, the count recalled several of the exiles in an effort to instill a spirit of forgiveness and restore goodwill in the town.

Throughout the Italian peninsula, a quiet mood masked undercurrents of war. Despite Venice's refusal to assist Girolamo in obtaining Ferrara, the Most Serene Republic picked a fight of its own with Ercole d'Este. The subject of the dispute was salt. In the ages before refrigeration, salt was a precious commodity, necessary for preserving food. Ancient Rome had grown wealthy by controlling the salt mines to the north, and in Renaissance Italy salt was so precious it could be used as currency. Venice controlled huge salt marshes on the Adriatic coast and therefore almost all the salt production and distribution.[16] Ferrara coveted this million-ducat business and started extracting salt from Comacchio, a territory it leased from Venice. The Venetians, still "official" owners of that land, forbade this undertaking, but Ercole ignored them. War began in the spring of 1482.

The northern Italian powers, Milan and Florence, always distrustful of Venice, leapt to the aid of Ferrara. Genoa, on the other hand, assisted its fellow maritime republic. Yet the costliest battle of the Salt War would play out in Rome.

King Ferdinand of Naples, father-in-law to Ercole, dispatched his son Alfonso, duke of Calabria, to relieve beleaguered Ferrara. The troops were well trained and seasoned after having finally freed Otranto from the Turks the preceding autumn. On April 23, 1482, Alfonso approached the borders of the Papal States with three thousand infantrymen and twenty squadrons of cavalry and asked permission to pass through papal territory to assist his brother-in-law at Ferrara. Although the duke had been the only leader to answer Sixtus's plea to save Otranto while Girolamo had been scheming in Venice, the pope refused him. Indignant, Alfonso, with the help of his Roman allies, entered the Papal States anyway and proceeded to devastate the countryside.

As captain of the papal armies, Girolamo was summoned to defend Rome. He assembled his infantry and set up camp by the southern gate on the Via Appia, steps away from the cathedral of Rome, Saint John Lateran. But instead of seeking out Duke Alfonso, he and his men waited inside the city walls. Girolamo claimed that he was ensuring that the Romans themselves would not revolt, but in fact Girolamo, though quick to order that others be assassinated, was circumspect when he himself faced actual combat.

Caterina, whose father, grandfather, and great-grandfather had won their fame and their lands through boldness in battle, must have found the conduct of her husband disgraceful. The Sforza name had never before been associated with cowardice. Adding to her woes, scandalous stories were coursing back to the Vatican palaces from the camp. Girolamo Riario, captain of the papal army, whiled away the days playing dice with his soldiers on the high altar of the cathedral, above the very table where Saint Peter and the first popes had celebrated Mass in the first century A.D. Horrified clerics reported that the soldiers sat on cases and boxes containing the most famous collection of relics in the world as they swapped obscene tales.[17] The nave of the church, once fragrant with incense and filled with harmonious chant, now echoed with blasphemies. Caterina no doubt burned with shame. Her father, with all his failings, had always shown respect for the sacred, and Bona, despite Duke Galeazzo's many betrayals, had made the soul of her murdered husband her foremost concern. At the beginning of these tensions, Caterina had offered to go to Milan with her husband to "calm and pacify these issues,"[18] but nothing came of it. From that letter in January 1482, Caterina wrote nothing more until the final battle of the Salt War played out in August of that year.

Caterina, barred by gender from negotiating for her husband among the temporal powers, became his advocate before God. Like many other women of her age unable to intervene in earthly affairs, she invoked divine assistance. And because Caterina always threw herself wholeheartedly into her endeavors, she did more than light a few candles. According to her eighteenth-century biographer Antonio Burriel, her pale figure, emaciated from fasting, knelt for hours in a penitent's robes at the altar or distributed alms to the poor. She certainly prayed for peace, but probably also that her husband would desist from destroying the last shreds of respectability he enjoyed in Rome.

Spurred by complaints from the peasants around Saint John Lateran, whose lands had been raided by Girolamo's soldiers, Pope Sixtus appealed to the Venetians in the hope that new forces would break the stalemate. The Venetians sent a *condottiere* from Rimini, Roberto Malatesta, who arrived in Rome with his own well-trained troops to the relief of the Roman people, who now believed that the destructive impasse between Alfonso, the duke of Calabria, and Girolamo, the count of Forlì, would be broken. On August 15, Malatesta and Girolamo marched their troops in review before the pope. Nine thousand infantry paraded through the city before heading out to meet Duke Alfonso's army, now swelled with followers of the Colonna and Savelli families.

After a few skirmishes, the day of the decisive battle came. The question would be settled on August 20 at Campo Morto. The very name of the battleground, "the field of death," presaged what would be the most violent conflict of the decade. Generally, wars among the Italian states resulted in few casualties; the mercenary soldiers who fought them tended to circle one another, with only an occasional clash of arms, while the overlords negotiated. This day would be different. The battle began at 4 P.M., when the brutally hot summer sun began to wane, and continued ferociously until 11 P.M., two hours after darkness had fallen. The papal troops were victorious. Caterina, waiting anxiously in Rome, was among the first to receive the good news. From the moment the rider burst into the papal apartments to inform Sixtus, Caterina was already writing letters announcing that "with maximum honor and our victory they had broken and dispersed"[19] the troops of the duke of Calabria. Two thousand lay dead on the field, while many more succumbed to the "bad air" of the marshes in Campo Morto—one of the highest death tolls of any battle fought on Italian soil in the fifteenth century. Stagnant water and rampant malaria made the area a lethal trap. Meanwhile, 360 of the enemy's noblemen were led to Rome, where they were imprisoned in the papal fort of Castel Sant'Angelo to await trial.

Sadly, Caterina saw little improvement in her husband's behavior. While Roberto Malatesta led his troops in the battle, fearlessly throwing himself into the fray, Girolamo stayed at his camp to "guard the tents." Although he tried to take credit for the victory, too many people knew of his cowardice; therefore Pope Sixtus ceded the honors of war to Malatesta. Like the great generals of antiquity, Roberto triumphantly entered Rome on the same road Scipio Africanus had taken after conquering Hannibal. One cardinal walked before the victor, holding the bridle of his warhorse, while the rest of the College of Cardinals marched behind him in a scarlet train. The streets of the city resounded with the cries of Romans hailing their liberator. The pope came out on the steps of Saint Peter's to meet Malatesta and personally accompanied him into the basilica for a Mass of thanksgiving.

With Girolamo exposed as a coward, Caterina, humiliated, retired in disappointment. Instead of seeing her consort parading through the streets like a caesar of old, she now saw him relegated to the retinue. And the worst was yet to come. Nine days after the battle, Roberto Malatesta, hero of Campo Morto, died of dysentery. The pope himself came rushing to administer last rites to the dying man and ultimately erected a monument to him in Saint Peter's. Most people thought that Roberto had contracted the illness on the battleground, but malignant voices insisted it was poison, administered by the envious Girolamo. Theories of foul play gained credence when Girolamo galloped to Rimini in a vain and shameful attempt to usurp the dead warrior's state from his infant son. Florence moved quickly to block this attempt, and the thwarted count returned empty-handed yet again. In fact the pope himself, knowing nothing of Girolamo's plans, had already confirmed the rights of Malatesta's son Pandolfo the day after the warrior's death.

The Battle of Campo Morto temporarily dulled the appetite for conflict among the states of Italy. By November, Milan, Florence, Ferrara, Naples, and the Papal States had agreed to an armistice, and on December 13, 1482, the return to tranquility was celebrated in the pope's new church, Santa Maria della Pace—Saint Mary of Peace—built to commemorate the end of this war.

By Christmas 1482, Caterina realized that despite her husband's high position and ornately trimmed garments, nothing of substance existed within.

THE BIRTH OF ATHENA

IN 1484, THE ROMAN CHRONICLER Stefano Infessura recorded
that a local painter was arrested for a peculiar offense. While living on retainer in the Orsini stronghold in Montegiordano, the
artist had executed a large mural portraying the military exploits of
Count Girolamo and the papal armies. Brightly colored camps and
vivid depictions of combat made the work a visual treat. The pope,
however, took such umbrage at the painting that he ordered the
young man to be apprehended and executed. Some observers maintained that the pontiff was offended by the fact that the papal armies
appeared ineffectual in the clashes. Others more maliciously suggested that the papal ire had been provoked by what was going on inside the commander's tent: a woman was being amorously embraced
by a man who wore the tonsure and brown robe of a Franciscan friar.[1]
Ultimately, the offending artist was freed after ten strokes of the *corda*
because, as everyone knew, "he was a little crazy."

Infessura slipped this little anecdote into his diaries to foment
damaging gossip about the family he hated most in Rome, the Riarios. Pope Sixtus was of the Franciscan order, and Caterina was the
wife of the commander of the papal armies; some would interpret the
suggestive little vignette as alluding to an affair between the pope and

his nephew's wife. Many contemporaries noted that the elderly pope enjoyed the young woman's company, and small wonder, for she was the most accomplished and interesting of all his nieces-in-law. Stories of the special favor that Caterina had won at the papal court even reached the ears of people who never came to Rome, one of whom noted that the most powerful princes of Europe soon learned to voice their requests through the young girl sitting by the pope's feet, for "he could deny her nothing."[2] While no evidence whatsoever suggests that an affair ever transpired between nineteen-year-old Caterina and her sixty-eight-year-old uncle-in-law, the idea of the austere Franciscan friar seduced by his nephew's youthful bride was bandied about in the kind of titillating whispers that still feed gossip columns today.

The storyteller Infessura, however, had much more than amusement in mind. A staunch promoter of a republic in Rome, he despised the papacy. By hinting at and later openly making accusations of sexual misbehavior, he was making use of an ancient theme familiar to all Romans: the kidnapping of the ruler Menelaus's wife, Helen, started the Trojan War; the rape of the Roman matron Lucretia spelled doom for the Etruscan kings; and the host of Christian virgins who chose death over dishonor played a part in the downfall of the Roman Empire. Sexual scandal could topple kingdoms and almost invariably left an indelible mark. That Sixtus would come in for more than his fair share of salacious rumors was part of what it meant to sit on a throne. It didn't help that he came from an unknown family, and was scorned for it. Born Francesco della Rovere in 1414, Sixtus IV was a rarity in the Renaissance papacy: a self-made man. Malicious courtiers and political enemies would maintain that he was the son of a Ligurian fisherman. In fact he was born of a fairly well-to-do merchant family in Savona, a town on the border of the Republic of Genoa and the Duchy of Milan. The second of seven children, Francesco was destined for the church from birth, and from the moment he joined the Franciscan order in 1428, he flourished in his vocation. By the age of twenty-five, he had already acquired a reputation as a passionate and persuasive speaker. Five years later, he earned his doctorate at the prestigious University of Padua. His debating skills and excellence in teaching soon brought him to the attention of the erudite Cardinal Giovanni Bessarion, a dynamic Greek prelate who served as the right-hand man of Pope Paul II. Bessarion transferred the brilliant young

Franciscan to the archbishopric of Perugia, where he served as the cardinal's personal confessor.

At the age of fifty, Francesco was made superior general of the Franciscan order. In 1467, again through the offices of Cardinal Bessarion, Pope Paul II appointed him a cardinal. Unlike many scions of noble families or wealthy merchants, Francesco did not win his red hat in exchange for cash or lands; he earned it through his abilities as a theologian and administrator. Four years after he moved to Rome, Francesco della Rovere was elected pope in 1471 and took the name Sixtus IV. Vatican pundits were amazed that an unknown Franciscan from Liguria could have risen above the numerous cardinals attached by birth and rank to the Italian nobility or those who had years of curial service under their scarlet sashes. Envious conjecture attributed his success to bribery or bizarre sexual favors—anything but merit. But Sixtus, a frugal man of austere personal habits, was guilty of neither. Many cardinal-electors seemed impressed by his abilities. Among Sixtus's strongest and most influential supporters was Caterina's father, Galeazzo Maria Sforza, the duke of Milan. In a certain sense Caterina's destiny was decided on August 9, 1471, the day of the papal coronation.

The new pope chose his name in honor of an illustrious predecessor, Saint Sixtus III, the fifth-century pope and theologian who had triumphed over the Nestorian heresy at the Council of Ephesus. Sixtus III was also a builder who constructed Rome's most elegant basilica, Saint Mary Major, and an able administrator who labored to reunite a church torn apart by heresies.

Having lived in Rome for only four years before his election, Sixtus IV found himself at a grave disadvantage. He was unacquainted with most of the ecclesiastics in Rome and knew little of the political alliances that linked local clans. To remedy this, Sixtus brought down members of his own family from Savona and raised them to high political and curial offices. Of the thirty-four clerics whom he elevated as cardinals during his reign, six were his own nephews. The important positions of governor of Rome and captain of the papal armies, moreover, were given to other family members. Most of his cardinal nephews revealed themselves to be profligate spenders, however, scandalizing Rome with lavish banquets and retinues. Pietro Riario spent 300,000 ducats in two years as cardinal—more than the amount budgeted by Sixtus for the war against the Turks! Others, like Girolamo, not only spent extravagantly but also used papal protection to bully and extort the Romans. Only Cardinal Giuliano della Rovere appeared worthy of his newfound eminence, serving his uncle as legate to Avignon and attempting to dissuade Girolamo from his plots to assassinate Lorenzo de' Medici.

Unlike most of the pope's relatives, Girolamo's young and beautiful wife lived up to expectations. Well educated, Caterina could appreciate the efforts the pope put into creating the Vatican library. After nine years of Sixtus's pontificate, the collection boasted thirty-five hundred volumes, triple the size of even the celebrated Medici library.[3] Caterina read voraciously and was particularly interested in historical and devotional literature. Stories of heroes strengthened her will, while stories of saints sustained her spirit. She managed to find time for reading among her duties to her family and the court, where her principal job was to intercede with one relative or another as requested by various parties. Her intervention saved several Milanese men from capital punishment in Rome and gained important positions for Romans in Milan. On one occasion she was even able to overturn Count Girolamo's decision to hang a member of the Manfredi clan.[4] Numerous letters from this period testify to the influence of the busy countess.

During most of her years in Rome, Caterina was either pregnant or recovering from childbirth. These confinements often kept her from her beloved outdoor pastimes. Particularly from 1479 to 1481, when she had three children in two years, she spent hours in the papal palace. During this period, Sixtus was working on his most ambitious decorative projects. The Sistine Chapel had just been completed, and within the forbidding fortresslike brick walls Sixtus envisioned a cycle of the most beautiful murals in the world.

Fulfillment of that dream came from a surprising quarter. In 1481, despite Girolamo's botched assassination attempt and Sixtus's warmongering, Lorenzo de' Medici offered a remarkable olive branch to his old nemesis: the finest painters from his own circle to decorate the pope's chapel. Rome was abuzz with exhilaration awaiting the arrival of the dream team of Florentine art. The elite group included Sandro Botticelli, painter of the celebrated *Birth of Venus;* Domenico Ghirlandaio, who would soon receive the young Michelangelo as an apprentice; and Pietro Perugino, the creator of solemn and dignified altarpieces throughout central Italy, and destined to tutor to greatness the as yet unborn Raphael. The great masters prepared their drawings and set about creating frescoes in the chapel.

The Florentine painters began with three panels around the altar in 1481. By the time the cycle was complete in late 1482, it included fourteen scenes drawn from the Old Testament, known collectively as *The Stories of Moses*, which were paralleled by the New Testament series, *The Life of Christ*; they would delight the papal court as well as future generations. Above these panels, the same artists depicted the first thirty-two Roman pontiffs, the sainted predecessors of Sixtus IV. The vault boasted golden stars against a lapis sky; twenty-eight years later, Michelangelo would transform it into *The Stories of Genesis*. The lowest level of the chapel was painted to resemble tapestries interwoven with the coat of arms of the della Rovere family: an oak tree and acorns. The sumptuous gilding around the rich crimson and cornflower hues echoed the magnificent liturgical vestments of the court. Other panels celebrated the achievements of Sixtus IV.

As the artists worked, this solemn liturgical space was transformed into the hottest social scene in Rome. Courtiers vied to be immortalized in one of the frescoes. From crowned heads to the endless series of Riario relatives, notables flowed through the papal chapel, eager to be included, and many were. Numerous sovereigns grace the walls of the chapel. King Ferdinand of Naples (an ally at the moment) and the papal *condottiere* Federico di Montefeltro have pride of place in *Christ Delivers the Keys to Saint Peter*, while Charlotte, queen of Cyprus, whose island state had been taken by the Turkish fleet and who was living in exile in Rome, listens to Christ in *The Sermon on the Mount*. Members of the Italian intelligentsia are also showcased, from the papal secretary Andrea de Trebizond to Francesco Filefo, the former tutor of Caterina and her brothers. Even the canines of the court found a place in these splendid masterworks. One courtier managed to get his lapdog depicted in *The Last Supper*. The little terrier frolicking on its hind legs in Cosimo Rosselli's panel was the beloved pet of one of Sixtus's nobles.

Few visitors to the chapel would have overlooked the Turkish costume worn by the pharaoh in *The Crossing of the Red Sea*, placed to the left of the papal throne. Terror of the Ottoman Turks and their invincible fleet had salved political rifts throughout Europe. Since the rise of Mehmed II and his expansionist policies in the mid-fifteenth century, the Turks had snatched the Holy Land, Cyprus, and, most fatefully, Constantinople from the Christians. In this dramatic image, the waters of the Red Sea engulf soldiers in Turkish attire, while men in armor stand around Moses, representing the knights who fought to defend Otranto in the terrible battle that cost twelve thousand lives. Sixtus also paid homage to the man who had helped put him on the throne of Saint Peter; he had a posthumous portrait of Cardinal Bessarion added to the picture. The snowy-bearded prelate carries a reliquary in memory of his own triumphal arrival in 1462 bearing the relic of Saint Andrew's head to Rome.

The most significant panels of the series were entrusted to the two most gifted painters, Botticelli and Perugino. *The Delivery of the Keys*, the image symbolizing Jesus' institution of the papacy, was assigned to Perugino, famous for the stateliness and dignity of his work. Botticelli was awarded the commission to paint the panel dearest to the pope, the one facing his throne. Although only two years earlier Botticelli had portrayed the members of the Pazzi conspiracy, including Archbishop Salviati, hanging indecently above the piazza after their execution, Sixtus now wanted the brilliant Florentine to execute the scene that would be peopled with members of his own family.

The Purification of the Leper and *The Temptation of Christ* was among the first four panels executed in the summer of 1481. In the background, Botticelli rendered several miniature scenes from the temptation of Christ; the foreground features the high priest accepting the sacrifice offered by the leper whom Christ had healed. This is the only panel of the series where Jesus is absent from the principal scene. The priest's deep lapis robe laced with gold and his high tiara-like hat, with a single acorn on the summit, associate this noble figure with the pope and his authority to judge whether one is cleansed of sin. Santo Spirito, the hospital complex recently completed by Sixtus, dominates the image. This great gift to the city cared for both pilgrims to Rome and Romans themselves, all spiritual children of the pope. The striking fresco alludes to the pope's desire to heal the ills of both body and soul. By including this distinctively Roman building, Botticelli transported the scene out of first-century Galilee and placed it squarely in the Eternal City. Facing the papal throne stands Cardinal Giuliano della Rovere, holding a white handkerchief to symbolize his elevated authority in the papal court. Directly behind the high priest Botticelli then placed Girolamo Riario, wearing the heavy gold chain that marked his important civic status. In this portrait, the count's fleshy face droops into the scowl fast becoming his most characteristic expression. The two papal nephews, already great rivals, face each other on either side of the high priest.[5] On the right, however, Botticelli inserted a single graceful female figure. Painted in the style of his Flora of *The Primavera*, she approaches like a gentle breeze. This figure can be recognized as Caterina, entering the sixth month of her pregnancy with her third child, Bianca. The lovely woman of the fresco wears her swollen belly easily, walking with a light step as her golden hair trails behind her. At the time the panel was painted, Caterina was busily preparing for her trip to Forlì. Botticelli seems taken not only with the beauty of the countess but also with her vibrant energy. The figure in the painting effortlessly carries firewood over her shoulder, perhaps an allusion to Caterina's industriousness despite the summer heat and her advanced pregnancy. At her feet, an infant bearing grapes recoils as a viper winds itself around his leg. Since the viper is the symbol of the Sforzas, this child could be Cesare, the one-year-old son of the Riarios.

Botticelli and Caterina may indeed have spent more time together during his stay in Rome. Several art historians have recognized Caterina in his portrait of Saint Catherine kept in the Altenburg Staatliches Museum.[6] The golden-haired woman in sharp profile represents Caterina's high position as well as her modesty as the wife of one of the most powerful men in Europe. This early portrayal of Caterina, noble, beautiful, yet turned away from the viewer, captures a young woman still dominated by her household and circumstances. Soon that phase of her life would come to an end.

Although their images in the Sistine Chapel suggest a glittering world free of cares and strife, the days of Riario glory were numbered. Sixtus was growing weaker. As the Romans realized that his papacy was drawing to a close, plans were laid to avenge Girolamo's extortions and outrages. The armed guards surrounding Caterina and her husband grew to a cumbersome and unruly number as Girolamo's fear of going out in public grew.

Girolamo exploited every minute of the waning papacy to extract as much money as possible from the College of Cardinals. Many of the churchmen capitulated to the count's demands. Joining forces with his nephew, Cardinal Raffaello Riario, who only a few years earlier had been the terrified Florentine prisoner in the wake of the Pazzi conspiracy, Girolamo ruled Rome from behind the now weak and aged pontiff. The Sienese ambassador Lorenzo Lanti warned his home republic that "the pope had put all the government in the hands of the count [Girolamo] and San Giorgio [Raffaello Riario]: temporal, spiritual, money, and everything." Lanti also noted that almost every judge in Rome was "ready to uphold their sentences."[7] Girolamo sold church offices, demanded immediate payments of up to a thousand ducats from papal employees to allow them to keep their jobs, and imposed random taxes. He had torn down and burned numerous houses in the course of his extortions, and stole reliquaries and missals. Girolamo's own relative Antonio Basso della Rovere had denounced the count from his deathbed before witnesses, accusing him of having "committed crimes that had scandalized the universe" and warning that "God's justice, which no human being can escape, would soon be on him."[8]

Although most of Girolamo's accomplices were street thugs and ruffians, a few were brave, intelligent, and surprisingly loyal. Il Tolentino, the trusted governor of Forlì, had been recalled to Girolamo's side shortly after the Riarios returned to Rome. The count needed his acute ability to sniff out danger in the Curia, the governing body of prelates at the Vatican. A substitute for Il Tolentino in Forlì had been hastily chosen in the archbishop of Imola, a cruel and inept man who wrongfully punished the entire city for a supposed conspiracy by detaining all the citizens inside the city walls and forbidding the harvesting of grapes for wine, a major source of income to the town. The keeper of the citadel, Tommaso Feo, fearful of a full-scale revolt, sent word to Rome of the excesses of the archbishop. Il Tolentino leapt into the saddle and in three days and three nights of ceaseless riding returned to Forlì, where he was greeted with tears of joy from the grateful populace.

Girolamo's other trusted henchman was Innocenzo Codronchi, keeper of the Castel Sant'Angelo, the papal fortress of Rome. A citizen of Imola, Codronchi had proven his worth during the Battle of Campo Morto. In return, Girolamo gave him control of the most imposing building in Rome. The Castel Sant'Angelo had been built by the emperor Hadrian in the second century A.D. as a burial site for himself and future emperors. It didn't take long for the medieval Romans to realize that the building, a solid round drum of bricks and stone blocks, would make an impregnable fortress. Its strategic position across the Tiber from downtown Rome and its close proximity to the Vatican made its location decisive: the person who controlled the castle controlled Rome. The Castel Sant'Angelo (so named after the miraculous apparition of the archangel Michael in A.D. 590) protected the citizens of Rome until the eleventh century, when it was first used to detain political prisoners. In 1400, when the popes returned from Avignon, they assumed direct control of the fortress. With its high, thick walls, and its cannons trained on every part of the city, the Castel Sant'Angelo underwrote the papal insurance policy against internal revolt.

While Il Tolentino governed in Forlì and Codronchi resided in the castle, a new crony of Girolamo's appeared on Caterina's doorstep—Virgilio, lord of Bracciano, head of the power-hungry Orsini clan. The new partnership between Girolamo and Virgilio would drag Rome into civil war.

Although an international peace of sorts had been gained by 1480, in Rome the perennial tensions between the Orsini and the Colonna families—age-old rivals of the Roman aristocracy who had been feuding for centuries—were reaching the boiling point. Entire networks of Romans were tied to one or the other tribe, while the papacy teetered on a tightrope between the two. The hostilities between the Orsini and Colonna clans was one of the spurs that had goaded the popes to Avignon. Girolamo foolishly thought himself crafty enough to maneuver the situation to his advantage. In reality, Virgilio Orsini saw in the rapacious papal nephew a chance to bring about the downfall of his ancient enemy.

During the Salt War of 1482, when the duke of Calabria appeared outside Rome with his army, Sixtus called all of his Roman knights to his service. Virgilio Orsini hastened to obey but the Colonna, Savelli, and della Valle families refused, joining the duke and exploiting his military force to expropriate Orsini lands and expand Colonna holdings.

Although most of the noncombatant members of the Colonna

clan took cover safely in their country estates, their allies were left to fend for themselves within the city walls. On April 3, 1482, the Santa Croce family, supporters of the Orsinis, spurred by Virgilio and assisted by Girolamo Riario's own soldiers, attacked the palace of the della Valles, staunch Colonna allies, with two hundred men. In the resulting fracas, a Colonna was killed.

Sixtus, desperately trying to restore calm, exiled the Santa Croce clan despite Girolamo's protection. He then razed their houses, hoping to eradicate the cancerous hatred of these clans by uprooting the family enclave. But Girolamo was implacable. On June 2, the count turned on members of the pope's cabinet, accusing Cardinal Giovanni Colonna, half brother to the murdered Colonna, as well as Cardinal Giovanni Battista Savelli of attempting to have him assassinated. Despite their high office as princes of the church, Girolamo insisted on their arrest. The first night of their imprisonment, they were housed in comfortable accommodations, which was Girolamo's sop to Sixtus, who protested the arrest; but as soon as the elderly pope was distracted, the count transferred his prisoners to the dank cells of the Castel Sant'Angelo.

Now when Caterina walked through the papal apartments, she no longer heard the lilting Tuscan accents of the Florentine painters, the giggles of women posing for frescoes, and the spirited discourse of theologians and philosophers. Instead, the clang of armor resounded in the halls, as did the voices of the mercenary soldiers, speaking in mixed languages. At the door of the papal palace, as the diarist Sigismondo dei Conti described it, "soldiers stood with their swords unsheathed ready for battle. All the court was filled with pain and anguish and the exasperation of the people was kept in check by force of arms."[9] All of Caterina's intercessory powers were rendered useless, as the pope, failing in health, was no longer able to control his rampaging nephew. Sixtus's golden age of renewal was over. Girolamo was ushering in an age of iron.

Anticipating the pope's death and frantic to ensure the continued prosperity of his family, Girolamo purchased another house in 1483. Called "The Garden," it was deeded in the name of his four-year-old son, Ottaviano. This maneuver, Girolamo hoped, would protect the property from the many eager to retaliate once the count had lost his powerful benefactor.

In February 1483, Caterina and Girolamo hosted exceptionally flamboyant festivities for the Roman carnival. Together, she and Girolamo frequented the dances, races, and other amusements. Wine ran from fountains and tables groaned with food as the Riarios employed the ancient technique of bread and circuses to win favor in Rome. When the week of carousing was over, Caterina and Girolamo received ceremonial ashes and prepared to suffer the forty penitential days of Lent alongside their fellow Romans.

During the first sobering weeks of the season, Sixtus fell seriously ill. Convinced of the pope's imminent death, the College of Cardinals prepared to expropriate all of the Riario properties and titles while vengeful Romans made ready to sack and destroy Girolamo's home, erasing his decadelong stranglehold on the city.

The pope recovered, but Caterina and Girolamo had seen what awaited them in the absence of papal protection. Facing a formidable list of enemies, Caterina and her husband put aside their differences and stood united to protect their children's inheritance. In March, Sixtus appointed Caterina's uncle Ascanio Sforza as cardinal, giving the Sforzas another friend in the Curia. In June they left for Forlì once again, most likely bringing the rest of the most valuable Riario possessions with them. Cart after cart transported children, furniture, and cash far from the hands of the vindictive Romans and into the well-protected fortresses of their own dominions. They returned in November and Girolamo set about making his last play in Roman politics. A month later Caterina was again with child.

Despite the pope's precarious health and the Riarios' concerns for their future, Girolamo, instead of shoring up alliances, continued to provoke difficulties and divisions. In 1484 he began open war with the Colonna family, ostensibly for their treason during the Battle of Campo Morto. With the assistance of Virgilio Orsini, he occupied Colonna lands surrounding Rome, but his sights were set on Paliano and Marino, the largest of the Colonna fortresses. To that end, Girolamo demanded that the pope summon Lorenzo Colonna, lord of Marino and protonotary of the church, to answer the accusations against him. On May 30, Girolamo brought two hundred men to the Colonna house near the Piazza Venezia, where a brutal skirmish ensued, lasting two hours and leaving several dead. Wounded in the hand, Lorenzo Colonna wisely surrendered to Virgilio. According to Infessura, Girolamo, half mad with rage, tried repeatedly to stab the protonotary as he was taken to the Castel Sant'Angelo and threatened him: "Oh you traitor, you traitor, I'll hang you as soon as we get there."[10] The only obstacle separating Lorenzo from Girolamo and his dagger was Virgilio Orsini, who kept the crazed count at bay.

The Colonna houses were sacked and pulled down, together with the palaces of the Savellis. Books, artworks, and other treasures of the family that had produced Pope Martin V and returned the papacy to Rome were stolen or destroyed. Dust and smoke arose at the foot of the Capitoline Hill, where the buildings lay in ruin.

An ambassador for the Colonna family sought an audience with the count to beg for the release of Lorenzo, offering in return the strongholds of Marino and Ardea. Girolamo's greed, however, would no longer be sated with only two of their properties. "I will take all of their fortresses by storm!" he declared before putting the hapless messenger to death.[11]

Cardinal Giuliano della Rovere, a neighbor of the Colonna family, pleaded during a family council for the pope to end this persecution. Girolamo, he warned, would "burn down God's church, and completely ruin it" by causing this strife and turmoil. Girolamo turned on his cousin, shouting that "rebels and enemies of the church are in his house!" and accusing him of treason. Cardinal Giuliano protested to their uncle, but there was nothing the ailing pope could do to keep Girolamo in check. "I'll burn you in your own house!"[12] Girolamo said, threatening Giuliano before the entire court and vowing that Giuliano's property would meet the same end as that of his friends. Count Riario thus succeeded in alienating the most powerful member of his own family.

Girolamo Riario completed his revenge against the Colonnas on Rome's most important feast day, June 29, the solemnity of Saints Peter and Paul. Lorenzo Colonna, unrecognizable after a month's imprisonment, was dragged out into the courtyard of the Castel Sant'Angelo. Wrapped in a tattered cape, he nonetheless maintained his noble mien as he repudiated the confession extracted from him under torture, expressing more concern for his friends than for his own reputation. Lorenzo sent his blessings to Pope Sixtus before approaching the executioner's tripod and laying his head upon it. Then the blow was struck. Lorenzo Colonna was no more.

When his body was returned to the family, they opened the coffin and discovered the extent of Girolamo's cruelty. Lorenzo's severed head was crowned with a red beret, a cruel joke. During imprisonment he had been suspended with weights attached to his feet until his arms became dislocated, and his feet had been ripped and cut. His thighs had been sliced and his knees sprained. Girolamo had ensured that every moment of the last month of this man's life had been excruciatingly painful.

The next day Girolamo sent his henchmen to destroy the Colonna vineyard behind the wrecked palace. While the trellises were being pulled up, several beams were taken out of Cardinal Giuliano's veranda, no doubt an act of petty vengeance on the part of the count.

Although numerous chroniclers recount the horrific actions of Girolamo, they remain silent regarding the countess. Sidelined by her husband's madness and her papal protector's weakness, she remained by the side of the aged pontiff, comforting him as he helplessly watched Girolamo cast a shadow over his pontificate.

Rome suffered through the summer of 1484. Girolamo and the Orsinis were devastating the countryside, besieging all the Colonna lands. Within the city, Girolamo's reign of terror had everyone from cardinals to cobblers trembling behind closed doors. On August 7, word reached Rome of a new treaty involving Naples, Florence, Milan, Ferrara, and Venice but excluding Pope Sixtus. In response to this political humiliation, Sixtus failed fast. On August 11, the articles of the agreement were brought to Rome and the pope read with pain that not one of the stipulations he presented to the negotiators was included. The next day he died. Upon Sixtus's death, thirteen years of pent-up rage exploded. Roman mobs raced to the Riarios' house and tore it down. The elegant columns with the intricate capitals, the delicate frescoes, the wooden furniture, and even the door and shutters were removed and shattered. The rioters even took out the lead water pipes and troughs in the stables, crying, "Colonna, Colonna!" The protonotary Lorenzo was avenged. The Romans then sacked the Riarios' farmhouse at the Castel Jubileo, about ten miles outside the city, and their supplies and livestock—a hundred cows, a hundred goats, several pigs and chickens, the stock of Parmesan cheese, and a supply of Greek wine—swelled the local pantries.

Caterina was with Girolamo at the Orsini camp near Paliano. She had been moved out of the city in July to ensure her safety, should the pope die. Despite her popularity among the Romans, their wrath against Girolamo made her a potential target for revenge. But instead of cowering behind her husband's soldiers, Caterina responded to the news of Sixtus's death and the resulting reprisals with daring action. Girolamo, ostensibly obeying the order of the College of Cardinals to cease hostilities with the Colonnas at once, left Paliano and with Virgilio Orsini made his way toward the Ponte Molle, just outside Rome. The Colonnas and Savellis were pouring back into the city, and soon it would be a deathtrap for the hated Riario count. With the Colonnas influencing the College of Cardinals and Girolamo unable to enter Rome to demand his rights, the Riario family stood to lose everything gained during Sixtus's pontificate. Caterina leapt into the saddle and rode toward Rome, accompanied only by Paolo Orsini. A seven-month-pregnant noblewoman, she had a better chance of being let through the city defenses than any other member of the Riario faction. Caterina didn't go to the papal palace to find the cardinals, however. She headed straight to the papal fort of Castel Sant'Angelo. As dusk fell on August 14, Caterina marched up the ramp to the castle and assumed control of it, and thereby the city. Pointing the cannons toward all access roads to the Vatican, she cut the cardinals off from the ecclesiastical nerve center. Caterina's decisive action threw the College of Cardinals into an uproar. While they debated moving their meetings to another palace out of the reach of the castle's artillery and argued over who should talk to the countess, Caterina was girding herself for war by dismissing all the senior keepers of the castle, including Innocenzo Codronchi, who had been personally appointed by her husband as the lieutenant of the fortress. Although he was devoted to Girolamo, Caterina refused to have him within the castle walls. This gesture has perplexed historians; some speculate that she distrusted everyone and wanted to be the only person in the fort with the authority to give orders, and others surmise that perhaps she had overheard seditious words from this ostensibly faithful retainer. Another possibility is that she wanted to act free of her husband's influence. Innocenzo would have done as the count wished, and Girolamo, without the backing of the pope, might be feeble in pressing his own claims and look for a quick compromise. As things stood, Girolamo was issuing empty threats from the safety of the Orsini camp, claiming that he would intervene with his army if any of the cardinals he hated was elected pope. The cardinals could easily dismiss Girolamo, but Caterina knew they would have to take her cannons seriously. The only hope to save her family's fortunes was to force the cardinals into recognizing the Riarios' titles and properties before they elected a new pope.

On the ramparts of the castle, the vivacious darling of the court showed herself to be a fierce warrior. In response to demands that she turn over the fortress, Caterina declared that Pope Sixtus had made her husband responsible for the castle and that she would turn it over only to the next pope. Electing his successor was easier said than done, however, since Caterina's cannons kept the cardinals from crossing the bridge to reach the Sistine Chapel, the designated site of the conclave.

On August 17, a lonely funeral took place for Sixtus IV. Only eleven cardinals attended, since many of the others, including Cardinal Giuliano della Rovere, were terrified of approaching the Vatican precinct while the castle remained in Caterina's hands. As was the case when her father died, Caterina never had the chance to bid farewell to the remains of this man who had welcomed her so warmly and cherished her during her years in Rome.

The day after the funeral, a messenger came to the fort bearing a letter from Girolamo's nephew Cardinal Raffaello Riario. The frightened rabbit of the Pazzi conspiracy now held the position of camerlengo, which meant he was in charge of organizing the conclave to elect Sixtus's successor. As a close relative, he took it upon himself to soothe the feisty countess. Distrustful, Caterina allowed only one person to accompany Cardinal Riario's envoy inside to present the missive. When the go-between balked at Caterina's conditions for the meeting, she fixed her interlocutors with a fiery eye and declared, "So he wants a battle of wits with me, does he? What he doesn't understand is that I have the brains of Duke Galeazzo and I am as brilliant as he!"[13] Caterina's first recorded spoken words, unlike those found in her dutiful epistles, reveal the proud Sforza warrior spirit that had long lay dormant in the Riario household. Stunned by her audacity, the cardinals retreated once again.

Anarchy was always a danger during the interregnum, the period between the death of a pope and the election of his successor. Without a reigning head of state, rioting, looting, and the settling of old scores were the norm. Adding to the general chaos of the *sede vacante* was the Colonna family back in Rome with two hundred soldiers and more grievances. The Orsinis were stationed near the Vatican. With the Castel Sant'Angelo in the hands of the Riarios, Rome became a battleground.

Desperate, on August 23 the College of Cardinals came to an agreement with Girolamo, offering him eight thousand ducats to pay his soldiers, provided he retreat immediately from Rome. They promised an indemnity for his lost property, an ongoing role as captain of the papal armies, and the continued lordship of Forlì and Imola. Girolamo, content with the cardinals' promises, made ready to leave. Caterina did not.

The next night, Caterina smuggled 150 more soldiers into the castle. After all her years at court she had little faith in the promises of men like Roderigo Borgia or Raffaello Riario. She planned to wait out the conclave and then deal directly with the next pope. The cardinals were infuriated by this new development and put pressure on Girolamo to end the trouble, threatening to revoke their agreement. Girolamo, having received cash and a few promises, was getting ready to leave Rome, and Caterina found herself publicly abandoned and humiliated by the husband whose property she had just saved.[14] In the heat of August in the swampy area of the castle, Caterina was feeling the weight of her pregnancy and was frequently unwell. Bribes and threats could not move her, but a husband's betrayal and an impending delivery did.

On the evening of August 25, Caterina's uncle Cardinal Ascanio Sforza came to the castle accompanied by eight cardinals. They treated her with the utmost respect, promising to care for her and her family and allowing her to keep her escort of 150 men as she left Rome. They also confirmed in writing and before witnesses that the lands of Imola and Forlì belonged to the Riario family.

The next morning, the drawbridge of the Castel Sant'Angelo was lowered and Romans and visitors alike crowded around to see this extraordinary woman, who had held the College of Cardinals at bay for eleven days. The pretty little favorite of Pope Sixtus had commandeered a castle to defend her family's rights, something worthy of legend and song. Although she was pale from illness and exhaustion, and heavily pregnant, her beauty still impressed the onlookers. She wore a brown silk dress with a long train and a feathered black velvet cap. But she had added a new touch to her elegant attire. A man's belt, heavy with a coin purse and sword, hung from her hips. Surrounded by foot soldiers and cavalry and framed by a forest of lances, "she was feared, because that woman with the weapons in her hands was proud and cruel."[15] Riding off to her new life in Forlì, she resembled less the delicate subject of Botticelli's portraits and more the powerful women who would appear in Michelangelo's painting in the Sistine Chapel.

THE LEAN YEARS

THE RETURN OF the Riario family to Forlì was a far cry from their triumphant arrival three years earlier. Although the Forlivesi put on elaborate shows of welcome and organized a multitude of festivities, Count Riario's "return was very bitter for him, his wife, and his children, and . . . those days were filled with great sadness," according to the local chronicler Andrea Bernardi.[1] Upon the death of Sixtus IV, Girolamo's days as a papal favorite were finished, along with the funding and protection he had enjoyed.

Despite the promises of the College of Cardinals, Girolamo maintained only a tenuous hold on the lands of Imola and Forlì. The new pope, Giovanni Battista Cybo, who had assumed the name Innocent VIII when crowned with the papal tiara, struck contemporaries as a sincere and kind man. But as the Florentine ambassador informed his city, "As cardinal he was no friend to the count."[2] Furthermore, the new pope numbered among his close friends Cardinal Giuliano della Rovere, Girolamo's cousin and nemesis who had opposed him during the Colonna hostilities. Cardinal Giuliano had not forgotten Girolamo's threats and accusations nor the damage inflicted upon his own palace. For his part, Pope Innocent fervently hoped that the conflicts that characterized the era of Sixtus had ended and that his reign would be remembered for its peace and prosperity. The diplomats from the Italian courts, however, had already spotted an indecisive streak in the pontiff, a weakness that Girolamo's enemies were quick to exploit. Cardinal Savelli, embittered by his imprisonment in the Castel Sant'Angelo at the count's hands, had immediately sought and obtained an appointment as legate to Bologna, only a few miles from Girolamo's territories. Lorenzo de' Medici had long been friends with Cardinal Cybo before the latter's election and thus knew that the pope would not impede his long-awaited revenge on the perpetrators of the Pazzi conspiracy. Closer to home, the Manfredis of Faenza nurtured an intense hatred of Count Riario for his designs on their lands; in addition the duke of Ferrara still fumed over the Salt War. Surrounded by hostile neighbors, Girolamo was becoming aware that Caterina's powerful connections could be more instrumental in keeping his enemies at bay than respect for his personal might.

Three days after their arrival in Forlì, a papal bull arrived confirming the agreements Caterina had signed on her last day at the Castel Sant'Angelo. The document relieved some concerns; Forlì and Imola were officially theirs and the title would remain hereditary for their descendants. Girolamo maintained his position as captain of the papal armies, but the pope had relieved him of any obligation to come to Rome in that capacity, making it abundantly clear that the family's close connection to Rome had been truly severed. Caterina and Girolamo were on their own.

In public, the Riarios put on an optimistic face. Two months after their return to Forlì, Caterina's fourth child was born, on October 30, 1484. On a rainy morning two weeks later, Ludovico Orsi, Girolamo's closest friend among the Forlì nobles, cradled the infant in his arms as he walked from the Riarios' palace across the piazza to the Abbey of San Mercuriale. In the chill of the dimly lit church, he was joined by the ambassadors of the marquis of Ferrara, the marquis of Mantua, and the lord of Rimini. This array of northern nobility stood as godparents to the newborn Riario, who was baptized with the name Giovanni Livio, for the legendary founder of Forlì.

Girolamo strove to win the favor of his people during his first year as the resident ruler. He upheld his promise of limiting taxation, even though it became increasingly evident that this system was driving the city into ruin. To save money, he decreased the number of guards on the city gates, discontinued certain public offices, and delayed payment of salaries to public employees. At the same time, terrified of assassination plots, he maintained a heavy personal guard. Although almost as hampered by armed soldiers as she was in Rome, Caterina must have been pleased by the energy and resources Girolamo put into modernizing the fortress of Ravaldino. The family lived in a modest palace overlooking the main square, but the fortress was being equipped with the latest designs in defensive architecture and would eventually serve as a sumptuous residence.

Yet even nature itself seemed to conspire against the new rulers. During their first year in Forlì, drought struck the region of Romagna, destroying the harvest and driving grain prices to the skies. Girolamo struggled on, scraping the bottom of his personal coffers to purchase grain from abroad, which he sold to the citizens of Forlì at the considerable discount of 4.5 soldi per bushel instead of the market rate of 5.7.

But neither Girolamo's gentler public relations strategies nor his belated displays of civic generosity rendered his reign easier. On October 22, less than a week before the birth of Giovanni Livio, the exiled nobleman Hector Zampeschi and his two brothers stormed and occupied three fiefs on the outskirts of Forlì. Pope Paul II had originally transferred these territories to the brothers, but after the Zampeschis fought for Florence against the papacy, Pope Sixtus had reclaimed the lands and donated them to Count Riario. Enraged by the Zampeschis' aggression, Girolamo immediately summoned Il Tolentino to win the fiefs back by force, but Caterina intervened and her wisdom prevailed. She suspected that Pope Innocent had funded the soldiers and weaponry for the assault. Therefore, any retaliation would find no military or legal support from Rome. Thinking practically, Caterina also pointed out that the Zampeschis had crossed through Florentine territory to invade the lands, suggesting the complicity of Lorenzo de' Medici. Moreover, by sending his best soldiers to reconquer the fiefs, Girolamo would be leaving his own family unprotected, providing a golden opportunity for the pope and the Florentines to attack. Caterina counseled patience. This conciliatory approach, so unlike her adamant stand at the Castel Sant'Angelo, was motivated by political expediency, not a sense of forgiveness. The loss of those fiefs could be tolerated until she had time to contemplate the best response and procure the resources to effect it. Nonetheless, this first nibble into the Riario holdings indicated what might lay in store for the count and countess. Once their predatory neighbors smelled blood, would they all take bites out of the Riario lands?

Then, as 1484 drew to a close, Caterina fell deathly ill. The battles in the Roman countryside that summer, Sixtus's death, the commandeering of the Castel Sant'Angelo, the hard ride to Forlì, and the delivery of Livio had taken their toll. Quartan fever, a malarial illness characterized by a high temperature recurring every seventy-two hours, kept her bedridden for a month. She probably contracted malaria during the hot summer at Campo Morto; she had spent the autumn of 1483 sidelined by the same illness, and the malady would sporadically assail Caterina for the rest of her life.

That Christmas, while the *ciocco* smoldered, the young countess burned with fever. Doctors poured down her throat a concoction of mint, vinegar, and opium extract dissolved in wine, but this standard remedy of the time did nothing to improve Caterina's condition. In the end, her strong constitution and fighting spirit likely served her better than medicinal brews. Early in the new year she regained her customary health and vigor, and by the end of January, Caterina was hunting in the Romagnol countryside again. The near loss of his wife evidently increased Girolamo's appreciation for her. By the spring of 1485 Caterina was pregnant with her fifth child.

During the distraction caused by Caterina's illness, the formerly tranquil town of Imola staged its first insurrection. Taddeo Manfredi, the former ruler, possibly abetted by Cardinal Giovanni Battista Savelli in Bologna, came out of retirement in Milan and attempted to organize a coup d'état with several citizens of Imola. Again the loyal Il Tolentino sniffed out and squelched the plot and hanged thirteen of the ringleaders in the town square. Manfredi alone escaped.

Caterina's resilience allowed her not only to recover from illness but also to adapt to her change of station. Cast from the world stage to the backwoods, Caterina was not petulant; rather, she embraced her new life. She took over her duties as countess of Forlì gracefully and with ease. Her court was much reduced; ladies in waiting from the loftiest houses in Italy were replaced by local girls with clumsier manners. Her former entourage of philosophers, poets, and musicians was gone, replaced by the tough soldiers of Girolamo's personal guard.

Her master of court was a local artisan made good, so the fabulous entertainment that had filled many an evening in Rome became a memory. In her letters to family and friends, and according to the writings of the diarists and ambassadors in her court, she never expressed nostalgia for her old life nor impatience with her new one.

The Riarios were not in high demand on the Italian social circuit, but they did welcome a few illustrious visitors over the course of 1485. In the spring, Giovanni Bentivoglio of Bologna spent a few nights in Forlì on his way to the pilgrimage shrine of the Holy House of Loreto in the nearby Marche region. Caterina and Girolamo, eager to show their neighbor that exclusion from Rome had not weakened them in the slightest, lodged him in the palace. During these days Caterina delighted her guests with the beauty, style, and elegance that had endeared her to both Rome and Forlì.

Girolamo's nephew Cardinal Raffaello Riario and his huge retinue also descended on Forlì, bearing news from Rome. In the papal court, he said, plots abounded to remove the despised Girolamo. Despite these concerns, Caterina and Girolamo took full advantage of the presence of their important nephew, putting aside the antagonism of the days of the Castel Sant'Angelo. They paraded the tall figure, wearing his rich red robes, through the city so the people of Forlì could gawk at the prince of the church, flanked by two bishops as he blessed children and accepted marks of obeisance. Girolamo wished everyone to know that he still had powerful relatives. The cardinal presided over a splendid Mass in the cathedral and awed the townspeople with the grandeur of Rome.

Several months later, Duke Alfonso of Calabria also arrived in town, with Girolamo's former ally Virgilio Orsini in tow. Custom held that such exalted company would stay in the palace of the leading citizen, while his entourage would be housed in the homes of various local nobles, but word had spread of the count's straitened finances. To spare Girolamo the expense, Duke Alfonso and the Roman noble rented rooms at local inns. Girolamo showed little gratitude for the duke's tactful gesture. Girolamo and Alfonso had faced each other as enemies at the Battle of Campo Morto and had reconciled the following year. After Alfonso had betrayed Pope Sixtus by allying with Florence in the armistice of 1484, Girolamo was apprehensive about the presence of such a powerful but unreliable figure.

The count declined to greet the two men, pleading illness. To save face, Caterina mustered the diplomatic skills she had learned in her twenty-two years at court and invited the men to dinner. Despite the count's absence, the two aristocrats were impressed by how elegantly Caterina had navigated her reversal of fortune. No music or theatrical performances accompanied their meal, but fresh local food was exquisitely prepared and her lively conversation convinced the two men that the countess was flourishing in her new role.

Caterina lamented little about life in Forlì, but the dearth of good dressmakers dismayed her greatly. After a lifetime in the great centers of Italian fashion, Caterina balked at the prospect of wearing the simple smocks made of plain materials that were available in Forlì and did her best to keep up with what aristocrats were wearing elsewhere. She wrote to her friend Eleanora of Aragon, the duchess of Ferrara, whose style and beauty were much admired. Despite the enmity between Duke Ercole and Count Girolamo, Eleanora maintained easy and friendly relations with the Riarios, and when Caterina explained her sartorial predicament, the duchess sent her own Maestro Tommaso, the cleverest designer in the region. Caterina ordered a new wardrobe and wrote back effusive thanks, well pleased with the new styles.

As in Rome, correspondence filled her days, but Caterina was no longer saving lives and dispensing patronage in the form of high benefices as she had once done at the papal court. Now she could obtain only a few midlevel jobs at smaller courts for her favorites. At eighteen, she had been one of the most powerful women in Europe; now at twenty-two, she was countess of a relative backwater. Nonetheless she persevered, tending to the education of her oldest son, Ottaviano, now five years old. The Riarios' tight budget precluded hiring illustrious tutors, but Caterina found a local pedagogue to begin teaching the heir. The countess personally ensured that he learned to ride and hunt, hoping to shape a bold Sforza from the soft stuff of the Riarios.

Country life brought both pleasures and discomforts. The severe climate of Forlì required some acclimation. Rome was warm most of the year, with hot weather always posing more of a threat than the cold, but in Romagna winters were harsh and long. Caterina bought twenty-five new warm feather beds to ensure the comfort of everyone in her house. Accustomed to foods from her well-stocked farm outside Rome, where she raised her own livestock and vegetables, she may have preferred the simpler foods of her new home to the complicated confections of the city. Forlì was also surrounded by hilly countryside, ideal for hunting, which perfectly suited the athletic countess.

Though the Riario house dominated Forlì from its position in the main square, it was unassuming compared with the Roman palace destroyed by looters. One particular room, the Hall of the Nymphs, was the family favorite. Overlooking the piazza, the large hall had been painted for Pino Ordelaffi by a local artist, Francesco Menzocchi. The walls pictured nymphs dancing while pensive muses struck dignified poses against a light background—a place for pleasure as well as business. The family hosted receptions, took meals, and often simply whiled away the hours in the luminous, airy space.

While Girolamo kept to his rooms and went out only when surrounded by guards, Caterina tried to participate in the public life of the city, particularly in religious events and feast days. In June 1485, the townspeople arranged the most elaborate procession in the city's history to celebrate the Feast of Corpus Christi. Throughout the spring, artisans had constructed nineteen papier-mâché floats, each one representing an allegorical scene. The Battuti Neri (the Black Flagellants), a religious confraternity responsible for collecting the abandoned dead, masterminded the whole procession. Caterina not only attended but made a point of lauding the confraternity effusively for its extraordinary work. Although no dark dreams of death had crossed her mind while chanting psalms, the time would soon come when Caterina would be beholden to these dedicated brothers. The countess's public piety was well supplemented with her private charities. The Riario family never turned away beggars empty-handed, and many religious orders prayed daily for their magnanimous Riario benefactors.

Although their main architectural undertaking in Forlì had been the fortress, Girolamo and Caterina had contemplated leaving a religious legacy of their lordship. After the death of Sixtus IV, the painter Melozzo da Forlì resurfaced in Forlì. Pope Innocent took little interest in the arts, and without friends in the Curia, Melozzo had no chance of landing the few projects available. Having served the count well while designing his Roman palace, Melozzo hoped that Girolamo would find work for him. Like Sixtus, who had rebuilt the Church of

Santa Maria del Popolo as a family shrine, the Riarios commissioned Melozzo to refashion the Church of San Giovanni in Faliceto into a sophisticated Renaissance monument intended to dwarf Pino Ordelaffi's tomb in the cathedral. After he completed a few drawings and models, however, it became clear to the artist that the Riarios could not finance such a project, and Melozzo allowed himself to be lured away by Cardinal Giuliano della Rovere, who had taken charge of reconstructing the shrine of Loreto.

On December 18, 1485, Caterina bore her fifth child, another boy. He was named Galeazzo in honor of the father Caterina idolized. Despite his death eight years earlier, Caterina had Galeazzo Maria in the forefront of her mind when she held the Castel Sant'Angelo, and later in life she would use only his surname, Sforza, as her own. Her father defined her ideal of bravery and elegance. Little Galeazzo was also baptized in San Mercuriale. In their boldest bid for peace yet, Caterina and Girolamo asked a personal representative of Lorenzo the Magnificent to serve as godfather to their fourth son. For a brief moment, the count of Forlì seemed to find serenity in his new land.

But that cold Romagnol winter was only briefly warmed by the new addition to the Riario family. Bordering on bankruptcy, without hope of paying public officials or other duties of seigniorial upkeep, Girolamo desperately needed to raise money to keep his town afloat. During December, he had been deep in counsel with his most trusted advisers, the notary Niccolò Pansechi, Andrea Chelini, and Ludovico Orsi, Girolamo's closest friend. The most acrimonious debates always revolved around the problem of taxation. After five years without sales taxes or gate duties, the count was considering bringing back the *dazi*, as these taxes were called. Pansechi, realistically surveying the terrible financial situation of Forlì, adamantly argued that without sales and customs taxes the city was finished. The Forlivesi had long been the envy of Italy and had for a time enjoyed the opportunity to prosper with few taxes and enormous subsidies from the papal coffers. Now that the generous pope was dead, the city had to bid farewell to privilege and join the ranks of the taxpayers.

Girolamo objected, with the support of Chelini and Orsi. Pansechi scoffed at their objections, exclaiming that "in all of Romagna there is no people more stupid than the Forlivesi!"[3]

Two days after Christmas 1485, the Council of Forty, the representative body of Forlì, met with Pansechi and a sullen Count Riario. The notary began his announcement with a dramatic flourish. "The traitor . . . Pino Ordelaffi ate our hearts and sucked our blood with his heavy gate and sales duties, but Count Girolamo is benign and clement like a gentle lamb. Would the city demand that the Riarios impoverish themselves in order to sustain expenses that rightfully belong to all who live in a city?"[4] Pressing his advantage, Pansechi called on each member by name to vote for or against the dreaded tax. They voted with beans, dropping a white one into the basket for an affirmative vote or a black one to signify a nay. One by one the dazed men walked to the desk and dropped a white bean into the basket. By unanimous vote, on December 27, 1485, the sales tax and gate duties were reinstated in Forlì.

The council dispersed, some sighing, some weeping, but all permanently alienated from their ruler. Pansechi's efforts were well rewarded. Appointed chief collector of the new taxes, he was ensured great wealth as well as the implacable hatred of the city. His sons in turn profited from comfortable city jobs, now that the means had been found to fund them.

Niccolò Machiavelli, commenting on different errors of government concerning taxation, seemed to have had Forlì in mind when he wrote in *The Prince* that while it "would be well always to be considered generous," by dropping taxes too radically the ruler "will consume all his property in such gestures." The result would be that "he will be forced to levy heavy taxes on his subjects . . . Thus he will begin to be regarded with hatred."[5]

Machiavelli's observation was borne out immediately in 1486 when the assassination attempts increased. In March, Girolamo's soldiers apprehended a certain Antonio Butrighelli under the window of the Hall of the Nymphs; he was carrying letters to co-conspirators from Antonio Maria Ordelaffi, one of the ousted heirs to the city. Butrighelli was a known enemy of the Riarios. He had been twice implicated in plots to kill the count and had been twice pardoned. This time the letters were damning: that very afternoon, a group of Ordelaffi supporters were poised to take control of the Porta San Pietro, the northern gate that led to Ravenna. Others were to raid the church, where Girolamo and Caterina would be attending Good Friday services, and murder them both. The spine-chilling similarity

of this plan to Girolamo's Florentine conspiracy eight years earlier
was not lost on the count. Butrighelli was hanged outside the Riarios'
window, but the hydra of hatred that now infested Forlì would spring
more heads.

Then a wave of bubonic plague hit hard in April, giving Girolamo
and Caterina a chance to prove themselves benevolent rulers. Caterina
made forays into the poorest quarters where the death toll was highest and the suffering greatest. There she tended to the ill and brought
food and medicines of her own preparation. Many were shocked that
the young and beautiful countess would be so heedless of her own
health and life, but she dismissed the danger, claiming that she had
seen the plague many times in Rome and had noticed that "those
who die are weak and downtrodden." The people were grateful to the
countess for her personal warmth, bravery, and practical advice. Girolamo, on the other hand, never left his rooms, but he did send for
doctors, priests, and friars, all trained in dealing with the pestilence,
to care for his subjects.

Spring rains washed away the disease and brought a good harvest, and it seemed that secret plots, taxes, famine, and epidemics had
been forgotten. But more setbacks awaited the couple in August when
the trusty Il Tolentino left their service. Skilled, brave, and tactically
brilliant, he couldn't last long in a petty court, watching the back of a
washed-up noble. He was paid only sporadically and no opportunities
for glory would ever arise in this position. Financial tensions weighed
heavily on Caterina and Girolamo and they frequently fought over
expenses. Two Milanese observers in the Riario court witnessed the
conjugal disputes over finances and kept their duke informed.[6] Each
of Il Tolentino's demands for payment ignited another battle between
husband and wife, and these confrontations became increasingly bitter until Il Tolentino left to join the Venetian army in 1486. The soldier of fortune was killed a year later, torn to pieces by angry peasants.

A flurry of correspondence between the Milanese ambassador and
the duke of Milan lifts the veil on one very intimate moment in this
floundering marriage. In November, on behalf of the duke, Francesco Visconti extended an invitation to Caterina to come to Milan
for the wedding of her sister Bianca Maria to Maximilian I, the son
of the Holy Roman Emperor. The sealing of this exalted match was

the most exciting social event of the year and nobles from all over Europe would be attending or sending representatives. Girolamo made Caterina's response for her, by explaining to Visconti that although he would be delighted for her to attend, she herself had refused to go. The count divulged that her gems had all been pawned in Bologna and Ravenna and she was ashamed to appear before her family bereft of the jewels and pearl-speckled robes she had worn when she had last seen them. Girolamo then launched into a long lament about the family finances; they were slowly sinking in a sea of debt. "Clothed or unclothed, bejeweled or not, I would be happy to let her go just to please her," Girolamo told the ambassador, with tears glistening in his eyes, "but she says that she will not go without her jewels!"[7]

Though it would be perfectly normal for a young woman to avoid a major social event if she lacked the proper attire, Girolamo's response nonetheless does not ring true. Borrowing jewels was the norm among noble families, especially for weddings. Silver and gold plate, pearls and gem-encrusted gowns crisscrossed the regions. Certainly Caterina had enough appropriate clothes to make an impressive arrival in Milan, and once there, her brothers and sisters would have supplemented them, if only to maintain the family honor. Appearances concerned Caterina only up to a point. It stretches belief that the woman who had arrived in Rome nine months pregnant and carried in a vehicle made of two baskets, then walked away from the Castel Sant'Angelo wearing a sword and a money belt, would worry about how many strands of pearls she would be wearing. After years of trying to get to Milan to see her mother and her sisters on Sforza soil, Caterina would not likely have been deterred by considerations of dress and adornment.

It seems that the duke of Milan had a similar impression and wanted to change Caterina's mind, because the next letter startles for its sudden vehemence. Visconti affirms that Caterina burst into his rooms in a state of great anxiety and revealed the tragic situation of her marriage in an uncharacteristic torrent of words. "You don't know how awful things are between my husband and me," she confided. "The way he treats me is so bad that I envy those who have died by him."[8] The discretion and reserve that distinguished Caterina ever since her first journey to Rome crumbled, and she revealed her miserable state as a "derelict, neglected, and abandoned" wife. Visconti was not a close friend or confidant; he was the eyes and ears of the duke, yet Caterina revealed to him her situation. As Visconti's role was simply to record what happened, Caterina knew that her tearful outburst would be on the duke's desk in a few days. Then she quickly regained her composure and reported that the duke's regard for her over the past few days had slightly improved her husband's behavior. More inclined to solve problems than bemoan them, she enlisted her family's help to sell a few of her properties in Milan in the hopes of solving their economic problems at least temporarily.

Marital discord was not the only threat to Girolamo and Caterina. For the first year after the announced change in fiscal policy in Forlì, taxes were not collected until the final month, so for twelve months most people continued to favor the count, perhaps thinking that he might change his mind before it was time to make any payments. When the taxes actually came due, many townspeople flatly refused to pay, and Pansechi received constant death threats. During January 1487 a steady drone of grumbling filled the streets of Forlì. After losing Il Tolentino, Girolamo knew he was vulnerable to violent attack.

In March, the Riarios tried for a change of scenery. Leaving Forlì, they moved to Imola, which they had always considered the safer of the two towns. Domenico Ricci, Girolamo's brother-in-law, was transferred from his post as governor of Imola to act as surrogate ruler of Forlì. Girolamo, relaxing at last, finally conceded and allowed Caterina to take a long-awaited sojourn in Milan, and on April 9, the countess embarked on the Via Emilia toward her childhood home. No extant documents reveal whether the gesture signified a truce between the two, or whether Caterina decided to leave on her own. But she set out, pregnant once again, to at last see her family, almost ten years to the day since she had left in the wake of her father's murder.

When Caterina arrived at the sumptuous court of Milan, it bore little resemblance to the one she had left. Her father had been surrounded by an earthy, fun-loving gang of friends given to unchecked luxury. The Milan of 1487, while as opulent as ever, was more focused on industry and achievement—engineers, architects, doctors, and scientists were all presenting plans and projects for approval and funding. It was a busy, exciting, flourishing environment presided over by Ludovico the Moor, the de facto ruler behind the throne of Gian Galeazzo. While Caterina's father had made a dozen false starts to rebuild his city, Ludovico was accomplishing great things. Milan was now one of the liveliest and most sophisticated cities in Europe.

By far the most fascinating member of Ludovico the Moor's court was a Florentine artist named Leonardo da Vinci. He had come to Milan five years earlier, bearing a gift from Lorenzo the Magnificent: a silver lyre of Leonardo's own construction, in the shape of a horse's head. His talent at playing the instrument and composing songs delighted the music-loving court, and his remarkable abilities as a military engineer, architect, and artist had obtained him a job.

The thirty-five-year-old polymath turned heads with his physical beauty. Boasting long, flowing hair, he was lithe and strong and his every move had the graceful ease of an athlete. After the plump prelates of Rome, Caterina must have delighted in the charm of the artist, who also loved horses as much as she did. Leonardo frequented the duke's innermost circle and Caterina would have heard him entertaining the court with word games or outlining plans for his latest project.

Leonardo had recently finished his first altarpiece in Milan, *The Virgin of the Rocks*, today housed in the Louvre. Caterina viewed this enigmatic painting in its original setting, the Chapel of the Confraternity of the Immaculate Conception. Although she had seen Botticelli at work—he had studied with Leonardo in Verrocchio's Florentine studio—the golden figures emerging from dark, mysterious landscapes were completely new to her.

Leonardo filled the role of court portraitist for Ludovico the Moor, painting images of his succession of mistresses. In 1487, Leonardo had just completed his portrait of Cecilia Gallerani, the duke's seventeen-year-old paramour. Stiff portraits in profile had been the norm in Rome, and the likeness of Cecilia was astoundingly different. She was captured in a three-quarter view, with almost her entire face turned toward the viewer. Although she modestly avoided a direct meeting of eyes, her body filled the space of the canvas. Leonardo had posed his model in a dynamic twist that breathed verve and energy, qualities studiously shunned in earlier female portraits, which were placid in character. The long, thin fingers of the beautiful courtesan stroked an ermine cradled in her arm. The nimble creature seemed to stop momentarily, calmed by Cecilia's soft touch. Leonardo's work introduced an element of sensuality into Italian art. Years later, Caterina would hire Lorenzo di Credi, a follower of Leonardo, to paint her own portrait, remembering the power of Leonardo's images. In 2002, the German art historian Magdalena Soest went so far as to propose that Leonardo's famous portrait of the *Mona Lisa* was indeed an image of Caterina Sforza.[9] Although most likely untrue (at the time *Mona Lisa* was painted, Caterina was not in a position to commission such an expensive work), the comparisons show how Leonardo's style permeates the painting by di Credi.

Fortune favored Caterina: she arrived in Milan during the first stages of Leonardo's most exhilarating project, an equestrian monument to Francesco Sforza. Originally conceived by her father as an homage to the first Sforza duke of Milan, the idea had been revived by Ludovico the Moor and placed in the hands of the brilliant Leonardo. Meant to embody pride in the Sforza name, it would never reach completion.

After many long years, Caterina was reunited with her birth mother, Lucrezia Landriani, and her still-unmarried sisters, Stella and Bianca. Her beloved sister Chiara, recipient of several letters during Caterina's journey to Rome, had since married and left Milan. She also met with her eleven-year-old brother, Duke Gian Galeazzo, and her uncle Ludovico. Certainly Caterina made the most of these encounters, securing their support should death befall Girolamo and clarifying the policies toward neighboring states.

This idyllic time was interrupted by news of Girolamo's sudden life-threatening illness. Caterina departed for Imola immediately and by May 31 she was at Girolamo's side. Locals were touched by the solicitousness of the count's wife, who brought doctors in from Bologna, Ferrara, and Milan, but Caterina's concerns were more practical than sentimental. Ottaviano was only eight and many eyes were gazing hungrily at Imola and Forlì. Situated on an open plain, Imola was difficult to defend, and its fortress, although recently restored, still had many vulnerabilities. As Bona of Savoy had once done, Caterina anxiously prepared for an uncertain future while she sat by her husband's bedside, willing him to live although the doctors had despaired.

Girolamo slowly recovered, but he had lost the upper hand forever. Caterina saw that his lack of physical vigor and weak moral character made him unfit to rule. She installed her mother and sisters in her home in Imola and prepared to take the reins of her life and her realm.

· 10 ·

TAKING CENTER STAGE

W HILE GIROLAMO'S CONVALESCENCE kept him bedridden, Countess Caterina governed in his stead, honing her
strategic skills as she confronted numerous new situations,
both domestic and international. Her political maneuvers no longer
took place in the shelter of the chancery—now she confronted her
adversaries face to face.

Caterina's first solo venture upon the stormy seas of politics fell
hard on the heels of her return from Milan. During the worst of Girolamo's illness, Caterina laid careful plans to secure her dominions
should her husband not survive. She had renewed her alliance with
Milan and successfully courted the Bentivoglio family of Bologna,
but she would need to be able to protect her claims until reinforcements from those quarters arrived. Without Ravaldino, the most important fortress of Forlì, under her direct control, Caterina and her
children would be easy prey for usurpers and assassins. Caterina distrusted the present castellan, Melchiorre Zaccheo, a distant relative
from Girolamo's hometown of Savona. A brutish man, he regularly
scandalized the citizens by spouting blasphemies. Rumors hinted that
in the past he had been a pirate who had enslaved many a Christian
soul and skinned alive or drowned those who defied him. Returning

to Italy with money to spare, Zaccheo had materialized in Forlì just as Girolamo was most desperate for cash. In return for making loans to the count, Zaccheo demanded to be installed as commander of the fortress of Ravaldino. Girolamo dismissed the trusted Innocenzo Codronchi from the post he had held since the Riarios had returned from Rome. Now this man of dubious loyalty held the means of controlling the city.

Caterina, as countess of Forlì, made it her first order of business to clean out her castle. Using surprise tactics to catch Zaccheo off-guard, Caterina, in her eighth month of pregnancy, mounted her horse at nightfall and rode the ten miles to Ravaldino. The trip took well over the usual time because she had to negotiate a longer and more hazardous route around hostile Faenza. At the foot of the ramparts she dismounted and called to Zaccheo, requesting that he release the castle to her. The coarse sailor turned soldier rudely refused, claiming that the count had given him his commission and only the count could take it away. Prepared for this objection, Caterina brandished a letter of authorization signed by Girolamo, but Zaccheo sneered, saying that he had heard that Girolamo was already dead. That being the case, he would turn the castle over only to five-year-old Ottaviano upon payment of Girolamo's debt and added that he would vacate the fortress only when he "was good and ready." Insulted, exhausted, and lacking a clear idea of the next step to take, Caterina left.

Dawn was stretching over the golden fields of Romagna as Caterina rode back to Imola, assessing the situation at Ravaldino. Until Zaccheo was ousted from the fortress, her family would never be secure. She couldn't use force of arms; the defenses were too solid. Starving him was out of the question; the castle held enough supplies to last for years. She couldn't afford to wait out Zaccheo either. By the time she reached the Riario palace in Imola, her scattered thoughts were beginning to weave into a plan.

On August 10, Innocenzo Codronchi appeared outside the walls of Ravaldino. Plenty of bad blood ran between Codronchi and Caterina; everyone knew how the countess had expelled him from the Castel Sant'Angelo after Sixtus's death. Girolamo, however, repaid Codronchi's long-standing loyalty by bringing him to Romagna. In what amounted to a rebuke to Caterina, he had made him the castellan of Ravaldino. When Girolamo was forced to give Zaccheo that position, the count then appointed Codronchi as captain of his personal guard. No one, least of all Zaccheo, would ever imagine that Codronchi would abet the countess in her scheme to retake Ravaldino. In fact, Zaccheo and Codronchi had socialized often: playing cards, drinking wine, and reminiscing about their adventures. So when he turned up on this occasion, Zaccheo welcomed him as an old comrade at arms. Codronchi brought dice and refreshments and the two played well into the evening for these stakes: the loser would spring for a fine luncheon the next day. Codronchi lost and left Ravaldino, promising to pay his debt promptly.

The next morning, Moscardino, Codronchi's personal servant, appeared at the gates bearing fowl to cook for lunch. Zaccheo admitted him to prepare the meal, and after the birds had been plucked and roasted and all made ready, Moscardino lingered on in the castle, chatting with the other servants. Codronchi arrived at midday, showing himself to be a good sport eager to settle his obligation. As toasts and jokes enlivened the table, Moscardino positioned himself behind Zaccheo's stool. After the feast, Zaccheo rose. Before he could straighten up, Codronchi grabbed the startled castellan while Moscardino hit him on the head. Then Zaccheo's own slave, a Turkish captive whom Moscardino had bribed, stabbed his master repeatedly in the chest. Codronchi struck the final blow with Zaccheo's own scimitar, an exotic trophy from one of the sailor's raids.

They dropped the body down a well in one of the castle towers, and Codronchi, bloodstained scimitar in hand, offered to serve up Zaccheo's followers as a garnish. The terrified crew fled, leaving Codronchi to raise the drawbridge and wait for events to unfold.

On August 11, Caterina was already preparing to give birth, as her baby was due that week. But the moment her brother-in-law, Governor Domenico Ricci, brought her the news of Zaccheo's murder, she leapt on her horse and took the hard road to Forlì as fast as her unwieldy body would allow. "Pregnant up to her throat" as contemporaries described her, Caterina rode up to the moat and called to Codronchi to explain why he had killed her castle keeper. "Madam," he drawled laconically, "you shouldn't entrust your fortress to drunkards and people with no brains." He did what he did, the soldier added, "because I felt like it." His tough tone melted, however, when he looked over the ramparts and saw Caterina in her riding cloak, as wide as she was tall, physically drained from the long ride. Codronchi relented. He told the countess to get some rest and invited her to come the next day for lunch and negotiations. The canny soldier posed one condition: the countess could bring only one maidservant with her.

For all her self-assured demeanor, Caterina didn't sleep more than a couple of hours that night, worried that her tricky gambit might go wrong. But the next morning, no trace of fear or weariness marred her face as she strode toward the drawbridge with her maid. The servant carried a large basket containing the countess's lunch. She had had her maid prepare the meal, intending to make onlookers think that she was wary about poison. But she evinced no trepidation as she stepped into the castle and disappeared from view into the dark stone passageway. The two met alone, having left their personal servants outside, ostensibly to negotiate the handing over of the castle. The few people remaining inside were allowed only a glimpse of the pair signing a document. The townspeople gathered around the castle, some curious, some anxious, some thrilled by the drama enlivening the lazy days of August. After a few hours, the countess emerged, mounted her horse, and returned to Imola.

The crowd observing these enigmatic comings and goings had no idea what had transpired until three days later when Caterina returned, bringing a new castellan, Tommaso Feo. The countess and her companion entered the castle and a short while later, Caterina came out with Codronchi while Feo remained behind. The countess and Codronchi rode in silence into Forlì, followed by the puzzled Forlivesi. Reaching the threshold of the Riario palace, Caterina turned and addressed her subjects with her customary directness and brevity. "The fortress was lost to me and to you while in the hands of Zaccheo," she called out to the cheering crowd, "but I have regained it and I have left a castle keeper of my own choosing!" Having reasserted her control over the city, she disappeared into the house, with Codronchi in tow. After dinner, he left the city. This was the last appearance of Girolamo's faithful soldier. After his departure from Forlì, Codronchi was never heard from again.

The following morning, Caterina returned to Imola to bring the good news to Girolamo, leaving the Forlivesi to speculate about the real story behind the murder of Zaccheo and the meetings between Codronchi and Caterina. Most suspected that the pair had staged an elaborate scene to murder the problematic sailor while safeguarding the count's reputation for clemency. Wisely, Caterina left friends, family, and subjects in the dark. The sensational story made its way to Rome, however, where Stefano Infessura, the Roman diarist with an ear for scandal, automatically assumed that Caterina herself had given the order for the murder. In this case he was probably right. Girolamo still suffered from illness and, without the papal army behind him, was indecisive even in his most lucid moments. Caterina, on the other hand, had already shown her instinctive drive to control the fortress at any cost.

LEONE COBELLI, CATERINA's self-styled biographer, went digging for inside information on the mysterious affair of Caterina, Codronchi, and the castellan. Part journalist and part stalker, Cobelli drew the story of Zaccheo's murder from the eyewitness Moscardino, probably over a few drinks in the piazza, and then penetrated Caterina's servants' quarters to glean the intimate details of how she slept and ate during her first difficult assignment. He would always be more intrigued than scandalized by Caterina's exploits. By contrast, Niccolò Machiavelli did not take such an approving view of Caterina's capacity for action. In *The Prince*, his handbook of leadership, Machiavelli lauded Cesare Borgia for a similar ruse, praising his deeds as "notable and worthy of imitation."[1] Though Caterina embodied Machiavelli's idea of *virtù*, the boldness and cunning necessary for a Renaissance ruler, the Florentine was repelled by the idea that a woman could possess those qualities. Despite the fine education and the power that regencies vested in them, women in Renaissance Italy were held to very different standards of behavior than men were. Women were trained to compose sweet verses of love, recite pious prayers, and rely on the counsel of their male guardians. Creative thinking and intellectual strategizing were the province of men. And during the Renaissance, when chaste modesty was the most prized of female virtues, Caterina, who engaged her adversaries face to face, flouted the strictest social custom of all.[2]

On August 17, the day after the Codronchi incident, Caterina's sixth child was born. Caterina named the boy Francesco after her illustrious grandfather, the first Sforza duke of Milan and the subject of Leonardo da Vinci's commanding equestrian monument, which

she had seen when it was being created in Milan. The child was nicknamed "Sforzino." To serve as godfather to this child, Caterina's uncle, Ludovico the Moor, sent one of the duke's ambassadors. This
public display of Caterina's close connection to the mighty state of
Milan brought her one step closer to ruling her cities and her life in-
dependently.

Caterina also had to learn to walk the tightrope of international
relations. As de facto ruler of Forlì, Caterina now staged epistolary
showdowns with opponents who were trained to spot any sign of
weakness. Her first battle was with a seasoned veteran, Duke Ercole
of Ferrara. Ever since the Battle of Campo Morto, relations between
Ferrara and Forlì had been precarious. With Girolamo incapacitated,
Caterina's new responsibilities included keeping an eye on her restive
neighbor. Caterina's correspondence with the duchess of Ferrara, Eleanora, invariably expressed warmth and friendship between reports
on Maestro Tommaso and his fashions, exchanges about hunting animals, and letters of recommendation. Her correspondence with Duke
Ercole, however, took quite a different tone. Ercole had been a successful *condottiere* in his youth, fighting loyally in the service of both
his brothers. Despite a persistent limp from a wound to the foot sustained in battle, he was a virile and handsome man prone to seeing
women as playthings rather than peers. He had enjoyed exchanging
lewd jokes and ribald stories with Caterina's father, but his treatment
of the countess often bordered on boorish. Their first clash took place
over a few trinkets—a gold chain and some other baubles—that Caterina had sent to her cousin in Milan. The items were stopped at customs in Modena, Este territory, and appropriated by local officials.
Caterina had first attempted to recoup them through her friendship
with Eleanora but to no avail. Eventually Caterina had no choice but
to call on Girolamo to write to the duke directly. During the duke's
subsequent sojourn with Count and Countess Riario at their palace
in Imola, relations continued to deteriorate. Upon his return home,
Duke Ercole complained that several of his belongings had "gone
missing" during his stay. Ercole chose a moment certain to goad the
countess. Girolamo was hovering between life and death, and Caterina was consumed by worry.

"Your messenger," she shot back in reply, "arrived here with your
letter requesting the return of your chair covering (*spalliera*), which

your Excellency claims was left in Forlì . . . and used incredible rude-ness and insolent words for this." Caterina was uncharacteristically vehement in this letter, repeating how she had been insulted by the ducal messenger and how poorly the Riarios' hospitality had been re-paid. In response to the implication that her husband might have sto-len the object, she haughtily stated that "it is not in our nature to un-duly desire things of others, nor does necessity compel us to have to; through the grace of God, with these and other things we are more than well furnished." She closed her letter by diverting blame to Er-cole's own court, pronouncing that his problems lay in his own house. His courtiers had made a bad impression, she wrote, and likely they resorted to offensive accusations against the Riarios only to "cover their own perfidy and ribaldry."[3]

But the final stroke came two days after Sforzino was born. Ca-terina, suspicious of Ercole, had built a farmhouse on the border be-tween her lands and Ferrara. From Trentino in northern Italy she im-ported thirty fine cows, which grazed peacefully in the pastures, and had filled the yard with sheep and chickens. But the farm served more than agricultural purposes. A contingent of soldiers also lived there, constantly watching Ferrara territory and serving as a first-alert sys-tem should Ercole decide to invade the Riarios' land.

The duke, something of a strategist himself, saw through the trick and incited the peasants of his lands in Massa Lombarda to sack and destroy the *cascina*, as the little farm was called. On August 19, 1487, while Caterina was still confined to her bed after childbirth, the peasants tore down and burned the house, stealing the cattle and other animals. Caterina fired off letters of protest from her bed, but the duke blandly responded that she had built her farm on Ferrarese land and was at fault for overstepping the boundaries. Caterina per-severed, eventually taking the case before a Roman tribunal, but she ultimately lost to the more powerful duke, who had agents situated in every court in Italy.

The embers were still smoldering at the *cascina* when the next di-saster struck. Antonio Maria, the Ordelaffi claimant to Forlì, also raced to exploit the weakened rulers there. In September 1487, his agents Nino Biagio and Domenico Roffi gathered a group of farmers from the village of Rubano and stormed the western gate, the Porta Cotogni, intending to clear a passage for Ordelaffi. His forces took the tower, but Domenico Ricci, the steadfast governor, acted immediately and after a few hours of fighting he regained the gate and apprehended the ringleaders. Ricci hanged five of them on the spot and detained the others in holding cells, then rode to Imola to inform the count. Though Caterina had delivered her sixth child only a month earlier, it was Girolamo who still kept to his bed. There was no question as to who would go. Caterina galloped back to Forlì as the governor labored to keep up with her. She didn't stop until she reached the fortress, where she insisted on interrogating the prisoners herself.

She first interviewed Nino Roffi, one of the ringleaders. Ordelaffi had planned the whole attempt, he claimed, but the real organizer had been another farmer, a man named Passi. He was the real enemy. Caterina got up from her chair and commanded that Passi be brought to her. Within the hour, the police thrust the terrified man, bound hand and foot, into the cell. Caterina watched as the two men faced each other, and she ordered Nino to repeat his accusation. As he listed names, dates, and meetings that allegedly took place at Passi's house, the defamed prisoner jolted in his chair and shouted his defense. He protested that he hadn't spoken to Roffi for eight months because he didn't like the way he lived, talked, or thought, and he certainly wouldn't share the hangman's rope with him. Caterina, intently following this exchange, interrupted the argument by dispatching Roffi to the gallows. Roffi confessed on the way to his death; he had lied about Passi because he knew the man had influential relatives who might have been able to help them.

With the truth revealed, Caterina smiled at the distraught Passi. Taking him by the arm, she led him out of the fortress. Before the gathered crowd, she told him to "go and return to your wife and children; you are a good and faithful subject."[4]

She had freed the innocent; now she had to deal with the guilty. Girolamo's crowd-pleasing policy of giving pardons had only brought characters like the twice-pardoned Antonio Butrighelli (who had planned to assassinate them the previous year on Good Friday) back for more. Out of respect for the nominal ruler of Forlì, Caterina wrote back to Girolamo with her findings. She listed the culpable, the blameless, and those who had just gone along with the crowd. To her query regarding penalties, Girolamo, grateful to have the burden of responsibility lifted from his shoulders, replied that she had leave to do as she wished. Caterina chose the route of exemplary punishment.

She exonerated those who had simply run through the streets invoking the church, Venice, and the Ordelaffis, but she publicly executed the six who assaulted the tower. The culprits were brought to the main square of Forlì and beheaded; their bodies were then quartered. To carry out this sordid task, Caterina summoned an amateur executioner named Barone, the unfortunate watchman responsible for protecting the tower of the Porta Cotogni. Illness had confined him to his bed, allowing the gate to be overrun. Caterina, doubtful as to whether his sickness was due to infection or bribery, awarded him the task of executing his fellow citizens before the gathered townspeople. Barone laid out the mutilated bodies in the square as a warning that the countess was not as malleable as her husband. That night the bodies vanished before the confraternity of the Battuti Neri could see to their burial. The next morning, three of the heads were found impaled on lances at the Porta Cotogni; the bodies hung outside the city wall. Two more cadavers decorated the Porta San Pietro and the last dangled outside the fortress of Ravaldino. Caterina, although not shocked, disapproved of this kind of barbaric spectacle and commanded the miserable Barone to collect the remains for burial. After these trials, the poor man immediately left on a pilgrimage to the shrine of Loreto in the hopes of erasing the bitter memory of his deeds.

Girolamo's mysterious illness remains a puzzle to historians. Some see it as a kind of clinical depression, while others claim that his malady stemmed from his obesity. During his recovery, however, Girolamo returned to some of his old Roman tricks. Once he had reinstated the *dazi*, he seemed to think he had nothing to lose by squeezing the Imolesi a little more. He demanded a tribute from them to pay for a four-hundred-strong mounted guard; they did so, but after a year of having the count in residence, the Imolesi realized that the guard consisted of only one hundred men. Girolamo kept the money for himself. Moreover, he appropriated benefices, claiming the revenues from the churches of Saint Mary of the Regola and Saint Peter for himself. He didn't even balk at stealing the gold embroidered vestments and altar cloths from the convent church of Saint Francis to make new clothes for himself and his family. Several citizens unsuccessfully tried to sue him in the tribunal of Imola after he had forced them to sell their mills to him for pennies. Soon the discontent that had arisen in Forlì permeated Imola, and Girolamo decided to return to Forlì. The near success of the Roffi plot convinced Girolamo that Forlì needed its rulers in residence, and on November 2, 1487, the Riario family was reinstalled in the palace in the piazza.

In the Renaissance era, November was observed as the month of the dead. Nobles and peasants prayed in cemeteries and church crypts and offered Masses for the souls suffering in Purgatory. A somber mood fell over Forlì as the days grew shorter and colder. The penitential spirit was enhanced by the arrival of a young Franciscan preacher from Siena, Giovanni Novello. Looking younger than his twenty-four years, with fair hair and wide blue eyes, the friar had a dramatic flair. A rough white robe (the uniform of the penitent Christian) engulfed his slim frame, while his black hood highlighted his ethereal pallor. His bare feet bore the thick calluses of one who had walked many a mile on sharp stones, and he carried a four-foot iron cross, which seemed to weigh more than he did.

The haggard count, still reeling from his brush with death, was entranced by the holy man and ordered all businesses closed on the day of Father Giovanni's first sermon, so that the whole town could attend. The crowd poured into the main square while Caterina and Girolamo, dressed in clothes made of a plain dark fabric, sat side by side at the window of the Hall of the Nymphs. The Franciscans were famous throughout Europe for their preaching. Saint Francis, the founder of the order, had been a passionate and eloquent preacher, breathing new life into the sacred stories with his direct and colorful speech. For an era without newspapers, cinema, or radio, itinerant preachers provided not only spiritual nourishment but also entertainment. Giovanni's sermon was worthy of his order. Following in his founder's footsteps, his first concern was for the poor of Forlì. He beseeched the town to assist those living in poverty by creating a Monte di Pietà, a fund that would provide low-interest loans for the needy, using pawned objects as collateral. These stirring words and practical solutions so moved Count Girolamo that he leapt to his feet and offered three hundred ducats on the spot, exhorting his fellow citizens to do the same. Determined to assist the young friar, Girolamo even gathered the Council of Forty to put the proposal before them. But the council, on which sat many bankers, still resented the reinstatement of the *dazi:* the black beans dropped into the dish one after another, saying a staccato no to Girolamo's attempt to redeem himself before God and his subjects.

Not long after, most of Italy rejoiced at the wedding of Innocent VIII's son Francescetto to Caterina, the daughter of Lorenzo de' Medici, which took place in January 1488. But to the count and countess of Forlì, the wedding bells sounded like death knells. Two sworn enemies uniting in a formal alliance could only mean disaster for the Riarios. Girolamo feared both Rome and Florence and monitored known sympathizers of the Ordelaffis. Unnerved by the peasant uprising led by the Roffi family, Girolamo began ruffling the feathers of the nobility in an effort to placate the lower classes. In early 1488, a group of farmers petitioned Girolamo to relieve their taxes on land that was actually owned by city dwellers. The count, finding no flaw with their argument, agreed to shift the burden of taxation to the townspeople. As soon as the satisfied delegation departed, Ludovico Orsi, who had been listening to the exchange, reproached Girolamo. The nobleman attempted to convince the count that it was a mistake to pander to peasants at the cost of angering the nobles and artisans. Exasperated at Girolamo's indifference to his rank, Orsi could contain his anger no longer. "They will tear you to shreds and then me!" he shouted.

Girolamo's demeanor went cold. He spat back, "You never were my friend and you lie!" Then, in the menacing tone that many had learned to fear, he asked, "Perhaps you would rather that I die?"

Ludovico fled the count's rooms in terror. He had been part of Girolamo's inner circle for many years and knew him well. Ludovico stormed into the Orsi family palace, a block from the Riarios' house, calling for his brother Checco. He found him in one of the larger halls, taking a dance lesson from Forlì's finest instructor, none other than the diarist Leone Cobelli. Intrigued by the agitation in Ludovico's voice, the curious Cobelli contrived to make himself invisible in order to eavesdrop on the conversation. Ludovico alternated between rage and terror, first railing against the count's obstinacy then speaking in dread of his cruelty. Checco punctuated the tirade with outbursts of his own. Checco had been given the lucrative position of collecting the tax on the sale of meat but now owed the count two hundred ducats, which Girolamo requested daily. His demands for repayment were growing increasingly threatening. The brothers finally agreed that things had taken a definite turn for the worse with the count: *credo che nui arimo piu bon taglieri* ("we won't share the same table anymore"), a Romagnol phrase denoting the end of a friendship.

But the Orsis had more in mind than absenting themselves from the count's guest list. Ludovico, now fearful of Girolamo, remained closeted in the house. On the one occasion when he went out, he tried to disguise himself, but Girolamo, vigilantly watching the piazza from his windows, spotted him. The count's soldiers dragged the petrified man to Girolamo's quarters. Girolamo inquired why Ludovico didn't visit anymore and why his brother Checco had been avoiding the piazza for weeks. Orsi stuttered a few words about money for the count and other soothing phrases, but as Girolamo's soldiers stepped toward him, he panicked. Pushing and screaming wildly, Ludovico stumbled out of the room and raced back to his own house. The break with Girolamo was complete, and everyone in the family was well aware of the fate reserved for enemies of the count. They decided that they would act first. Pooling their knowledge, the Orsis looked for a chink in Girolamo's armor. Ludovico had heard that two of Girolamo's personal guards, Ludovico Pansecho and Giacomo del Ronche, had not been paid in months and were ready to rebel. The Orsi family made plans to murder their enemy, with Pansecho and Ronche as accomplices.

Girolamo habitually took his midday meal in the Hall of the Nymphs, away from his family, and after a little siesta he held audiences in the afternoon. All the assassins needed were a few minutes alone with the count, and they knew how to get it. Girolamo had recently hired Giacomo del Ronche's nephew Gasparino as a court page, and the young man was stationed in the Hall of the Nymphs. It was easy to persuade the unwitting boy that his uncle needed a few minutes alone with the count about a private matter. Gasparino, indebted to his uncle, readily agreed to signal from the window when Girolamo was taking his rest.

Monday, April 14, was a market day. The main square of Forlì was packed with artisans and farmers hawking their goods. The Forlivesi strolled through the square, buying necessities and admiring luxuries. The local barber and diarist Andrea Bernardi was in the middle of the fray, giving shaves and haircuts. Together with Leone Cobelli's, Bernardi's chronicles allow the modern reader to feel present at these events. The steady bustle and chatter of the square died down at lunchtime, and by the time Girolamo was ready for his brief repose, the area had emptied; only those packing up carts and cleaning away debris were left. Caterina and the children were dining in the *tinello*, a room off the kitchen close to the tower of the palace. As Girolamo stretched out on a bench, young Gasparino went to the window and waved his cap. Giacomo del Ronche saw the signal and quickly informed the others. The time had come.

The band of six Orsis, all clad in armor, joined Ludovico Pansecho and Ronche outside the palace. They climbed the main stairs leading to the Hall of the Nymphs. As arranged, Checco entered first, armed with his excuse for the intrusion. Girolamo had awakened and was conversing with his chancellor, Giovanni da Casale, and Corrado Feo, a distant relative. A liveried manservant was preparing the count for his afternoon audiences. Leaning lazily against the windowsill, Girolamo turned as Checco crossed the threshold into the room and asked, "What brings you here, my Checco?"

As if announcing glad tidings, the assassin reached into his pocket as he said, "I want to show you this letter from my friend. Soon I will have the money to pay you." In one smooth gesture, Checco drew a dagger from the folds of his cloak and struck the count on the right side of the chest. Girolamo jerked back with a shout and turned to run toward Caterina's rooms near the safety of the tower. Just then Pansecho and Ronche dashed into the room, seizing Girolamo by the hair and throwing him to the ground. As he lay prone, feebly trying to resist his assailants, they delivered blow after blow, reducing Caterina's plump husband to a mass of ragged flesh. The conspirators' shouts of "Liberty! Liberty!" summoned the Forlivesi, while the entire palace shook with combat. Darting up the main stairs, the Orsis' followers met Andrea Ricci, son of Domenico, who was engaged to Caterina's sister Stella. Andrea tackled Checco's son, Agamenone. Andrea got the better of his adversary, who died of his wounds twelve days later. Ludovico Orsi turned to fight off Andrea as he tried to enter the Hall of the Nymphs. When Andrea da Parma, one of Girolamo's personal guards, poked his head into the room to see what had befallen the count, it was struck and nearly cleaved in two by Checco's sword. The

Forlì chief of police, Antonio da Montecchio, sprinted to the piazza but never made it up the stairs. Not content with killing him, the vicious attackers burned off all his hair, which had been his great pride. Even Caterina's jester Grego got into the fray, poking and jabbing with his dagger, but was no match for the professional men-at-arms and was killed immediately.

The bewildered townspeople crowded into the square, unable to ascertain if their lord was dead or alive. Instead of rallying in support of the Orsis, they argued among themselves, debating whether the count had been killed or wounded or had escaped altogether. Through the palace doors, they could see the fighting. Some yelled from a side street that the countess and her children were at another window, crying for help. Resolving the doubts of the people, three soldiers grasped Girolamo's battered, naked corpse and threw it over the balcony into the square. The horrified Forlivesi circled the barely recognizable body; discerning the facial features of the count, they knew that he was dead. They then raced into the palace.

The frescoed walls of the Riario home were already pockmarked by swords and smeared with blood, but worse was to come as rioters spread through the rooms. The house was ransacked; silver plate, jewels, bedding, and furniture disappeared into the greedy hands of the mob, leaving the denuded palace bereft of its owners and its adornment.

Girolamo lay in the piazza like a piece of meat discarded at the market: the corpse was dragged through the square, then kicked and spat upon. A few fanatics tried to tear the body to shreds, but the slow chant of the confraternity of the Battuti Neri processing into the square dispersed them. No one approached the Battuti Neri in their white hoods and robes as they silently ministered to the lifeless count. Loading the bedraggled remains of Girolamo into their cart, they carried him off, "pissing blood," to the cathedral. But the principal religious authorities of Forlì would not take the body in. They had received great benefits from Girolamo, but they were afraid of provoking a battle inside the church. Thus turned away, the brothers did as they would with the body of a criminal or an unclaimed murder victim found in a field. The Battuti laid the count in the sacristy of their own church, which was dedicated to Saint Francis. Forty-five-year-old Girolamo Riario, lord of Forlì, captain of the papal army, was dead; his tumultuous career ended with a creak as the lid of the cheap wooden coffin was nailed shut.

Caterina, who had been dining with her family in her rooms, assumed the worst when she heard the shouts of "Liberty!" She quickly gathered her family in a defensible room in the tower and dashed to the window with Ottaviano, calling for help for the heir to Forlì. But the palace was in the hands of the Orsis and their henchmen, and no help could reach the Riarios. Caterina looked at the pale, frightened faces gazing up at her. Her six children—from nine-year-old Ottaviano to the infant Sforzino in his nurse's arms—were crying. Scipione, Girolamo's illegitimate son, who was now fourteen, put on a brave face, but he was still absorbing the shock of his father's murder. Caterina's mother, Lucrezia, and her sister Stella were also present, looking to her for guidance. Caterina knew what was at stake. The smartest move for the assassins would be to kill her and Ottaviano next, thus removing the heirs. Caterina barricaded the door to buy herself some precious time. From the window she called out to her loyal followers that it was useless to fight now, since her family was outnumbered and the Orsis had control of the palace. By then, the attackers had reached the inner court and were enraged to find the way blocked. As her words were punctuated by the blows at the door, she hastily issued instructions to a faithful retainer, Ludovico Ercolani, to get word to the Bentivoglios of Bologna and, most important, to her brother, the duke of Milan. The battering continued, marking the seconds she had left before capture. Caterina ordered all those who were loyal to her to meet in the fortress of Ravaldino. Under no circumstances could the castle be surrendered to the rebels. As the door splintered and burst open, Caterina spun away from the window and took her position among her family as the widow of Forlì.

Portrait of Galeazzo Maria Sforza,
Piero del Pollaiuolo, 1471

This portrait of Caterina's father, the duke of
Milan, was painted in 1471 during the duke's
state visit to Lorenzo de' Medici, which was
the first time Caterina saw Florence.

Sixtus IV Appoints Bartolomeo Platina Prefect of the Vatican Library,
Melozzo da Forlì, c. 1477

This, the earliest surviving ceremonial portrait of a papal family, contains
images of the most important members of Sixtus's court. Pope Sixtus is
seated on the right, with Cardinal Raffaello Riario next to him. Facing
the pope is Cardinal Giuliano della Rovere; Platina kneels in the foreground. Girolamo Riario, Caterina's first husband, stands above Platina,
and next to him on the far left is Giovanni della Rovere.

Detail from *The Purification of the Leper*, Sandro Botticelli, 1481

This fresco was painted to face the papal throne in the Sistine Chapel; it features members of Pope Sixtus's family. Caterina is on the far right, pregnant and carrying firewood, while her son Cesare fends off a viper at her feet. The cardinal holding the handkerchief is Giuliano della Rovere, Caterina's cousin by marriage.

Fresco fragment from the *Sala della Piattaia* in the Altemps Palace, Melozzo da Forlì, c. 1479

This image is all that remains of the decoration of the main hall of Girolamo and Caterina's home in Rome. It illustrates the elaborate silver service given to the Riarios at their wedding in 1477.

Etching of the tomb of Hadrian on the Tiber River, Giovanni Antonio Dosio, sixteenth century

The ancient imperial mausoleum was known in Caterina's day as the Castel Sant'Angelo. Used as a fortress and prison since the tenth century, the defenses shown in the drawing were constructed by Pope Alexander VI and his son Cesare Borgia.

Lead medal of Caterina Riario Sforza, Niccolò Fiorentino, c. 1488–1490

This medal was struck during Caterina's first years of ruling Forlì. The recto is a portrait of Caterina, while the obverse bears the motto FAME FOLLOWS VICTORY.

A detail from *The Miracle of Saint James the Elder*, from the Feo Chapel in the church of San Biagio, Marco Palmezzano, 1494–1495

These frescoes were destroyed in 1944, but photographs have preserved the image of Caterina's second husband, Giacomo Feo, standing in the center of the lunette, in front of the column. Ottaviano, her eldest son, is on the right, speaking to a kneeling Caterina. Girolamo, her first husband, kneels in front of Giacomo.

Portrait of Giovanni de' Medici,
Giorgio Vasari, 1555

Cosimo de' Medici commissioned this
portrait of Caterina's third husband,
Giovanni de' Medici Il Popolano, who
died at the age of thirty-one. It was placed
beside her portrait in the hall dedicated
to Cosimo's ancestors in the Palazzo
Vecchio.

Portrait of Caterina Sforza de' Medici,
Giorgio Vasari, 1555

This portrait was commissioned by Cosimo de'
Medici for the hall that he dedicated to Giovanni
dalle Bande Nere in the Palazzo Vecchio in
Florence. Vasari portrays Caterina in a widow's
veil after the death of her third husband,
Giovanni de' Medici.

The fortress of Ravaldino

Caterina defended this fortress both in 1488 and 1500 and lived here for more than
ten years. It later became a prison and after that, a tourist attraction.

Portrait of Isabella d'Este, Marquess of Mantua, Titian, c. 1535

Isabella d'Este, a contemporary of Caterina, was one of the most famous women of her day. Whereas Caterina earned her notoriety through military exploits, Isabella was renowned as an exacting patron of the arts. Nonetheless Isabella expressed admiration for Caterina's courage during her defense of Ravaldino against Cesare Borgia.

Portrait of a Man, Girolamo Marchesi da Cotignola, c. 1500

This portrait, most likely of Cesare Borgia, was painted shortly after his conquest of Forlì. It hangs next to a portrait of Caterina, *The Lady with Jasmine*, in a special section of the municipal art gallery of Forlì.

Portrait of Giovanni dalle Bande Nere, Gian Paolo Pace, c. 1545

This portrait was commissioned by Pietro Aretino after the death of Giovanni, as a gift to Cosimo I of Tuscany. Giovanni, a celebrated *condottiere*, was Caterina's youngest son born from her marriage to a Medici. He died of battle wounds at the age of twenty-eight.

Portrait of Cosimo de' Medici, Bronzino, c. 1545

Caterina's grandson Cosimo by her youngest child, Giovanni di Giovanni de' Medici, became the first grand duke of Tuscany in 1569. It was at his order that a marble tombstone was erected on the simple site of Caterina's grave.

11

THE RETORT AT RAVALDINO

S WORDS DRAWN, GIROLAMO'S assassins crowded into the chamber to find the countess embracing her children protectively; only a few tearstains betrayed her emotions. Snarling orders and spewing threats, the murderous crew lined up the little group of women and children. No one dared touch the countess, but one foolhardy ruffian grabbed Caterina's younger sister Stella and, claiming to search for hidden jewels, began to grope under her dress. She was not Caterina's sister for nothing; a crack echoed through the room as Stella replied with a stinging slap.

Surrounded by this rough escort, the family picked their way through the shambles of their home as more looters poured in. Out in the piazza, a broad crimson stain marked the spot where the body of Girolamo had lain. Mercifully, the corpse had already been removed before Caterina and family arrived there. Within minutes, they had crossed the threshold of the Orsi palace. Away from the eyes of the townspeople, Caterina knew they were completely at their captors' mercy. Yet she comforted her family, praying that the messages she had hastily dictated had arrived at their destinations.

The assassins had also sent riders off in every direction to notify neighbors and allies of their coup, counting on garnering support among the many enemies of the Riarios. The Orsis knew that they possessed neither the clout nor the might to impose their rule on the Forlivesi but hoped that a powerful state, such as Florence or Venice, might intervene to control the town, return the Ordelaffis to rule it, and ultimately reward Ludovico and Checco with high positions. Mere hours after murdering the count, the Orsi brothers convened an extraordinary meeting of the Council of Forty to discuss the next steps for the orphaned town. The representatives of the districts and guilds of Forlì gathered with trepidation in the great hall. Checco Orsi explained the reasons for his deeds, reminding the council that in that very room, Girolamo had broken his promise to abolish the *dazi*. Decrying the count's proclivity to violence and extortion, Checco even dared hint that Pope Innocent himself had blessed their actions, though the assassin wisely refrained from making an outright claim of papal complicity. Checco made no mention of the Ordelaffis, fearing the council might split into two factions: for and against the former ruling family. He did, however, allude repeatedly to both Venice and Florence. Forestalling any suggestion to invite any such greedy neighbors in, Niccolò Tornielli, the leader of the council and an older man who had lived through many years of Pino Ordelaffi's as well as Girolamo's rule, proposed a different course of action. He advised Forlì to put itself under the authority of the church. In this way, it could remain a relatively free ecclesiastical state, with a cardinal governor from Rome. The papal army would guarantee peace while they thrashed out the problem of succession. Tornielli, looking to the good of all the Forlivesi, expressed the hope that this equitable compromise would reduce the tension of the situation and, he added, avoid "breaking the heart of the countess any further."[1]

These prudent words soothed the turbulent spirits of the Forlivesi. By nightfall the council had decided. They dispatched a messenger to Cesena, where the papal governor and protonotary Bishop Giacomo Savelli was installed. The papal stronghold was only thirteen miles south on the Via Emilia and, with a fast rider, the council could expect a response within two hours. Bishop Savelli, a member of the Savelli family of Rome, loathed Girolamo, and for good reason: the count had imprisoned his relatives, torn down their houses, and destroyed their property. Savelli was delighted by the news of his enemy's death, but he viewed the city's decision to submit to papal authority with skepticism. They had, after all, just murdered a former papal nephew. Fearing an uprising from the volatile people of Forlì, Savelli decided to send a trusted set of eyes and ears to the town to report on events. His emissary ascertained that the count was indeed dead, that the Orsis had taken Caterina and her family into custody, and that the council's proposal was serious. Forlì was ready to enter the papal fold.

On April 15, 1488, Bishop Savelli rode into Forlì, accompanied by a contingent of soldiers carrying the broad banner of the Papal States. Seeing that the colorful flags contained no menacing Venetian lion or Milanese viper, the townspeople cheered in relief. Instead, the white and gold standards bore the insignia of a golden tiara above two crossed keys, symbolizing the authority of the pope. Under this ancient standard fluttered Innocent VIII's personal coat of arms: a diagonal blue-and-white-checked band set against a crimson background. Bishop Savelli's first order of business was to ensure the well-being of the sister of the duke of Milan. Whatever Savelli may have thought of Count Riario, he was well aware of Milan's importance to the Papal States. He rode straight to the Orsi palace and spent some time comforting the widowed Caterina with promises that neither she nor her family would be harmed. Before taking his leave, the bishop strictly ordered the countess's captors to treat her and her family with the utmost respect.

Savelli then remounted his horse and rode to the main square, where the excited populace was streaming in from every street and alley. Instead of the flowers, ribbons, and incense usually amassed to greet a new ruler, shards of glass and pieces of wood, plaster, and rubble from the desecrated Riario palace littered the piazza. Nevertheless, the citizens of Forlì, desperate for leadership, shouted their support as Bishop Savelli and his retinue ceremoniously rode three times around the piazza, symbolically taking possession of the town. Forlì was now in the hands of the pope, at least nominally.

The fortresses of Schiavonia and Ravaldino still lay in the hands of supporters of the Riarios; therefore Forlì remained divided. Until those in the main gates and towers submitted to papal authority, peace could not return. Bishop Savelli swiftly turned to the question of securing the defenses of Forlì, starting with the Porta San Pietro, the only tower held by supporters of the Orsis. The prudent prelate immediately dismissed them and substituted his own men, who were certain to follow his orders. He also disbanded the Council of Forty, re-forming it as the much-reduced Council of Eight—all strong supporters of the papacy and, to a lesser degree, the Orsis. This accomplished, Bishop Savelli then turned his attention to the other two strongholds.

The most expedient approach was to bring Caterina to those fortresses and order her to command the castellans to surrender. Eager to be in the forefront of the action, Ludovico Orsi and Giacomo del Ronche rushed to the Orsi palace, where they wrenched the countess away from her family. Caterina hugged her children one by one and set off, stone-faced, with her captors. They marched Caterina to the foot of Ravaldino: the exact spot where she had stood a year earlier with Innocenzo Codronchi. Tommaso Feo, the custodian she herself had conducted to the castle on that occasion, looked down at the countess, his face expressionless. Meanwhile, among the crowd stood the barber Andrea Bernardi, recording the conversation that ensued.

"My lady," Feo asked, "what do you want?"

Caterina took a deep breath and in a rush of words, broken by tears and sobs, implored him to "give the fortress to these men, so they will free me and my children!"[2] Slowly and respectfully, the loyal keeper shook his head. His duty, he explained, was to hold the castle for the heir of Girolamo. Caterina, with much handwringing, wailed that not only would she be killed but all of her little children would be brutally slaughtered by these criminals, who would stop at nothing to control Forlì.

Feo played his part to perfection: his love of the Riario family was well known, he replied, but his orders were to keep the castle for Ottaviano, the son of Girolamo and the nephew of the duke of Milan. The people crowded around the fortress heard the names Sforza of Milan, Bentivoglio of Bologna, and Cardinal Raffaello Riario and realized this was no friendless widow. Caterina's connections could summon huge armies. If her captors were so rash as to hurt one of the children, terrible retribution would fall on the whole town. Watching this exchange, Giacomo del Ronche and Ludovico Orsi began to suspect that the words of the countess and Feo were staged for the benefit of the onlookers and that they had no real plan to surrender the castle. The two men hustled Caterina away.

The day was drawing to a close when Giacomo del Ronche and Ludovico Orsi marched the countess to the smaller watchtower of Schiavonia to repeat her request to give over the stronghold. The keeper, well apprised of Feo and Caterina's theatrical repartee at Ravaldino, replied shortly that he would follow Feo's lead.

Ronche was certain that the countess had tricked them. Incensed that he had wasted a whole day caught in her ruse, he snarled, "My lady Caterina, you could turn over those castles if you wanted, but you don't want to, do you?" Ronche pressed the sharp iron point of his lance against her chest and spat, "If I wanted to, I could just run this spear from one side of you to another and you would fall at my feet, dead."[3] The wailing widow's demeanor abruptly changed. Caterina leaned against the hard blade, thrusting her face inches from Ronche's. "Oh, Giacomo del Ronche," she replied, with no tremor in her voice, "don't you try to frighten me." As if drawing strength from the cold metal of the lance, she locked eyes with the soldier and said, "Certainly, you can hurt me, but you can't scare me, because I am the daughter of a man who knew no fear. Do what you want: you have killed my lord, you can certainly kill me. After all, I'm just a woman!"[4]

The armed men in their cuirasses stepped back. At a loss for how to subdue the countess, they led her back through the streets to the Orsi palace as evening approached.

Once they had returned her to her prison, Caterina's captors thought to use her piety to break her spirit. Bishop Savelli had strictly forbidden anyone, hostile or friendly, to contact Caterina, but the Orsis smuggled a priest into her rooms. Acting as their agent, he confronted the weary Caterina with a list of her own and her husband's sins. Using even more dire threats than Ronche had, he commanded her to give up the fortresses. Count Girolamo, he warned, "was killed for his sins and through the will of Divine Justice." Caterina, who had benefited from "his destruction of churches and persecution of priests and nuns," would face the same fate later. He predicted that the punishment of death by starvation, followed by eternal hellfire, would be meted out to her and her children if she didn't surrender the castles. Horrified, Caterina banged on the door, screaming to have him removed. Later, among her followers, Caterina would confide that hearing these harsh words was more traumatic than losing her husband in a brutal murder.[5]

Bishop Savelli, concerned for Caterina's safety, transferred the Riario family to the tower of the Porta San Pietro, which was wholly under his control. Caterina, the children, their two nursemaids, her mother, and her sister Stella were escorted across town and placed in a small, ill-equipped cell. Soldiers bustled from town to fortress to find a crib for Sforzino, food and toys to distract the crying children, and fresh clothes for the ladies.

The comings and goings at the Porta San Pietro made it easy for Ludovico Ercolani, the trusty Riario partisan who had escaped with Caterina's messages moments before her capture, to slip into the fortress unseen. Ercolani, working with the castellans and the few others who were still loyal to the Riarios, was coordinating the defense of Caterina and her family. The guards on duty outside Caterina's cell, sympathetic to the beautiful and intrepid countess, turned a blind eye to their meeting. In whispers, the two hatched an audacious plan to turn the tables on the Orsis. At the break of dawn, Ercolani sneaked back into the Ravaldino fortress and relayed the scheme to the willing Feo.

On the morning of April 16, Ercolani presented himself before Bishop Savelli with a message from Tommaso Feo. The custodian would surrender the fort on one condition: Countess Riario would have to pay him his back wages and write him a letter of recommendation so future employers would not think that he had succumbed on ignoble terms. The countess would have to come alone, of course, as Feo could not trust the Orsis, known assassins, to accompany her safely. Relieved, Bishop Savelli leapt at such an easy resolution, but when he put the idea to the Orsis, he was astonished by the vehemence with which they rejected it. The conspirators knew that Savelli pitied Caterina as a forlorn widow, but they had seen her iron constitution under the velvet wrappings. If Feo wanted to see her alone, the two were plotting something.

The reluctant Savelli eventually compromised with the brothers and stipulated that the negotiation between the countess and her castle keeper take place in full view; Caterina would remain outside the walls. Again Caterina walked to the ramparts, trying to hide the energy in her step as she prepared for action. She called up to Feo, promising before the whole town as witness that he would have all he asked for. Standing behind the battlements, he insisted that the countess enter the fort to sign the recommendation after he had read it. As was the case with Innocenzo Codronchi, only one person, a servant, would be allowed to accompany her. The Orsi brothers protested violently, but after an impasse of several minutes, Savelli, whose dearest wish was to end these dealings, struck down the objections and sent Caterina into the castle, with a three-hour limit, to conclude her business with Feo. This time she didn't select a gentle maid with a picnic basket to accompany her. She chose a brawny young groom named Luca.[6]

The lances enclosing her parted and Caterina stepped away from her captors toward the drawbridge with her single escort. Having crossed the wooden planks, she paused and turned to the crowd on the bank; framed by the gaping entrance, she raised her hand, with index and ring fingers folded back and thumb tucked between them, before disappearing into the castle. Caterina had just given them the "fig," the Renaissance equivalent of "the finger."

The dumbfounded spectators blinked. Did they just see the elegant countess of Forlì gesture like a common foot soldier? The diarists depicted the scene in different ways. Cobelli gleefully repeated this story, told to him by Caterina's henchman Ludovico Ercolani, but Bernardi mentioned only that the countess entered the castle.[7] In any case, her guards were left to wait out the next three hours, which ticked by slowly as various diplomats composed letters to the foreign courts they represented. Many other people, hearing of the dramatic events taking place at Ravaldino, traveled from nearby towns to witness history in the making. The Orsis tried to maintain a semblance of calm while controlling a mounting fear. Time was not on their side.

Each passing hour brought the duke of Milan and the Bentivoglios of Bologna a step closer to Forlì. Should they arrive while Caterina was still barricaded in the fortress, it would be a simple matter for their armies to reclaim the city for the Riario family. But if the strongholds had passed to the supporters of the Orsis, with papal reinforcements on the way, any aggression on the part of Caterina's relatives would be perceived as an act of war. Caterina recognized the importance of delaying as long as possible. Since the moment of her husband's murder, she had done everything in her power to slow them down, awaiting the arrival of Ludovico the Moor.

The designated three hours came and went, with no sign of the countess. Bishop Savelli called to Caterina, reminding her of the time limit, but his voice echoed ineffectually off the ramparts. To the Orsis and the embarrassed Savelli, the wait seemed interminable until finally Tommaso Feo reappeared at the battlements. He announced that he had taken Caterina captive. The clever keeper raised the stakes by offering to exchange the countess for several noble hostages, all Orsi supporters.

As the bewildered bishop struggled to understand the latest turn of events, the desperate Orsis upped the ante. They knew that Caterina and Feo had cooked up yet another lie, again to waste precious time. The moment had come to play their trump card. Ronche and the Orsis raced back to the Porta San Pietro, fury propelling their every step. They burst into the cell of Caterina's family. They seized Ottaviano, her firstborn and the Riario heir; her mother, Lucrezia; and Stella, her sister. Then Ludovico Orsi grabbed four-year-old Livio, whom he had once cradled at the baptismal font, and thrust him into the arms of his nurse, adding him to the group of hostages. The other children remained behind in their prison cell.

The Orsis led their sacrificial lambs back to Ravaldino. The chronicler Bernardi saw nine-year-old Ottaviano clinging to his grandmother's hand while Livio's nurse clasped the child close to shield him from the sight of the spears and daggers pointed at them. The men roared threats, clanging their steel weapons for emphasis. Caterina's children begged for mercy, and their shrill pleas penetrated the thick walls of the castle, summoning her to the ramparts. The anguished mother had to face her worst fear.

Caterina had hoped that Bishop Savelli would be able to protect her family, yet before she even stepped onto the drawbridge, she had realized that a moment like this one might arrive. She was a woman, and men knew where women were most vulnerable: their first duty was to their children. Tradition, custom, and religion dictated that Caterina must give in at the sight of her endangered offspring. But this descendant of warriors was able to think strategically. As she had boasted at the Castel Sant'Angelo, pregnant with Livio, she not only possessed her father's courage but also his practical reason and imagination. She knew that Bishop Savelli was well aware that her children were the nephews of the duke of Milan. If they came to any harm,

Milan would retaliate with full force against the Papal States. Moreover, they were the cousins of Cardinal Raffaello Riario. Under no circumstances would Pope Innocent countenance any harm befalling these relatives of a highly placed churchman, especially in a public setting.

Also, Caterina would have recognized that surrendering the castle would give her no advantage. She would lose any leverage against the Orsis. Most likely her family would be imprisoned for a lengthy period and then discreetly poisoned to ensure that there would be no future Riario claimants to Forlì. The Orsis would rest easy only when she and her male children were dead. She had a much better chance of saving herself and her family by fighting here, as ambassadors of every major Italian state watched. In captivity, hidden from these powerful witnesses, she would be at the mercy of her enemies. So she held her position.

According to the most well-known version of the story, Caterina strode to the edge of the ramparts. With daggers drawn, the Orsis called to her, promising to kill her children, mother, and sister on the spot. Certain of imminent victory, they taunted her by making the children cry all the harder. In response, Caterina bellowed, "Do it then, you fools! I am already pregnant with another child by Count Riario and I have the means to make more!"[8] Then she turned on her heel and walked back into the castle.

That retort at Ravaldino would define Caterina Sforza throughout history. The Venetian ambassador, floored by her audacity, dubbed her a "tigress," willing to eat her young to gain power.[9] Galeotto Manfredi, whose own sexual proclivities had sent his wife running, passed down a particularly earthy version of the retort at Ravaldino. Writing to Lorenzo de' Medici, Manfredi claimed that Caterina, faced with these murderous threats, had brazenly raised her skirts, pointed to her genitals, and crowed that unlike the men gathered below, she had the equipment for making more.[10] Although no one else included these crude details in descriptions of the spectacle, Niccolò Machiavelli chose to repeat this salacious version in his *Discourses*.[11]

In fact, based on a close analysis of the most reliable historical documents, Caterina's words and actions appear quite different. While no fewer than five letters written at the time[12] and several contemporary accounts have immortalized her outrageous statement spoken from the ramparts, Cobelli and Bernardi, both eyewitnesses, do not mention a word of Caterina's retort. Bernardi claims that "she had gone to rest in a certain room far away from the ramparts"[13] and was unaware of what was happening above. This seems a bit too passive a stance for a woman who certainly knew exactly what was at stake. Both local authors concur that the children were brought to the ramparts and threatened with violence, but they also claim that despite the screams of Ottaviano and Livio, Caterina never came out. Cobelli suggests that Caterina remained below intentionally, perhaps to avoid addressing the Orsis in front of her children, and that Feo, concerned that the cries would weaken Caterina's resolve, ordered several volleys of cannon fire to drown out the sound and to scare the Orsis.[14] Bernardi, in his turn, confirms this discharge of artillery from the castle.

Caterina was roundly condemned by most of Renaissance society, even by the notoriously amoral Machiavelli, for gambling with the lives of her children. She never deigned to reveal the reasoning that informed her actions on that day, but by calling the Orsis' bluff, Caterina succeeded in saving her children. Furthermore, her lifetime of concern and sacrifice for all her offspring is mute testimony to the fact that she was a loving mother whose best option in this instance was to outfox her enemies.

Bishop Savelli realized that his own promise to secure the safety of the children was being undermined by his unstable allies. He reclaimed the family immediately and returned them to the Porta San Pietro under a stronger guard, forbidding anyone but himself to move them again. The Orsis went back to their palace, where Andrea Orsi, the aged sire of Ludovico and Checco, had returned from his country house, eager to hear the outcome of the plot. As Ludovico recounted the events of the past two days, Andrea, though recovering from a severe illness, rose to his feet, shaking with rage. "You have done a bad thing and done it badly," he wheezed. "Once you had killed the count you should have done away with the whole family." He prophesied a terrible end for the entire Orsi clan. Now that Caterina was in the fortress, the old man predicted, "she will fight [you] to the death" and in the end "all of you—even me, old and sick as I am—will have to bear the punishment for your lack of foresight!"

Savelli, realizing that the situation had escaped his control, wrote to Rome, asking for a contingent of soldiers to occupy the city. But

Rome was slow to respond while ambassadors and advisers debated the Forlì question before the pope. The stalemate at Ravaldino had transformed the conquest of Forlì from a battle of strength into a game of endurance.

Lorenzo de' Medici was aware of everything transpiring in Forlì. Noting that Girolamo's murder occurred a few days before the tenth anniversary of the Pazzi conspiracy, which had claimed the life of Lorenzo's beloved brother Giuliano, some contemporaries hinted that the Florentine ruler instigated the assassination. Feverish correspondence poured onto Lorenzo's desk in the wake of the killing, mostly from Lorenzo's agents, but Giovanni Bentivoglio of Bologna wrote as well, repeatedly asking whether he should respond to Caterina's messages and come to the countess's aid. Lorenzo chose not to reply, and even his own ambassadors marveled at how slow Lorenzo was to respond to their correspondence.

The days stretched on. Caterina, to keep the invaders' nerves on edge, had periodic artillery blasts shot at the houses of her enemies, ensuring that property would be damaged without injuring people. Vandals, on the other hand, took advantage of the uncertain situation to steal as much as possible.

On April 18, several townsfolk defected to Ravaldino, seeking safety with the countess behind its mighty walls. First the Jewish pawnbrokers, tired of the unchecked looting of their shops, joined Caterina. Shortly thereafter, the artisans of Forlì, sensing that power was slipping away from the Orsis, smuggled themselves and their wares into the fortress.

The Orsis rounded up the wives and children of the deserters and brought them to the moat, as they had with Caterina's family, hoping to bring to heel the new allies of the Riarios. But Caterina had publicly taken the measure of the Orsis and they had proved weak, so the artisans remained within the walls, sensing it was an idle threat. And indeed, the families were returned to the city unharmed.

Bishop Savelli transferred Caterina's mother and sister to Cesena, out of reach of the Orsis, and reinforced the guard on the children and nurses in the Porta San Pietro prison. But the silence from Rome worried him. Papal armies were stationed nearby at Urbino and Rimini; they should have already arrived. Why, he wondered, was Pope Innocent stalling in sending aid? Forlì was actually at the forefront of the pope's mind, but he couldn't decide what action to take. Meeting with the ambassadors of Florence and Milan, Pope Innocent dithered, expressing concern for the safety of the Riario children, his desire not to offend either Florence or Milan, and the tempting idea of presenting Forlì to his son Francescetto as a wedding gift. Perhaps, the pope optimistically suggested, they could transfer Caterina and her children to Cesena "for their own good,"[15] hoping that clearing out the Riarios would smooth the path to his takeover. But the Milanese ambassadors rushed to dispel this idea: Caterina was already in the fortress; if she was going to leave, shouldn't she retreat to Imola, which was, after all, still Riario territory? Furthermore, if the pope threw his support behind rebels and assassins, what kind of message would he be sending? Would it not incite other townships to do the same? The vacillating pope realized that Milanese troops were close to the city and sending soldiers would mean finding himself at war with a very powerful duke. The question was shelved and no papal armies departed from Rome.

To make matters worse for Savelli, Giovanni Bentivoglio interpreted Lorenzo de' Medici's silence as a green light for Bologna to rescue Forlì. With a force of eight hundred cavalrymen and a thousand infantrymen, he marched to Forlì on April 21 and set up camp outside the city gates. A herald rode into the city in the name of Bentivoglio and informed the people that Milan and Bologna both supported the Riario claim to the city.

Bishop Savelli remained cool, and his measured response calmed the Forlivesi. Forlì was under papal protection. The Riarios had forfeited Forlì by failing to pay tribute to Rome and by their ill use of their own citizens. The Riario family could move to Imola, where there were no signs of rebellion, and withdraw their claim on Forlì. The Orsis, on the other hand, made no effort to enter into diplomatic negotiations. They hurled insults at the messenger and cursed the Bentivoglio family. Two days later, menacing new messages arrived from Giovanni Bentivoglio: invasion was imminent. The townspeople, frightened, began to mutter regrets about asking assistance from the church. As the murmurs swelled into shouts, Savelli sent one of his own relatives to ride into the city with the papal standard. Posing as a messenger, Savelli's cousin bore letters promising papal support. The people saw the golden keys and tiara, heard the words of reassurance, and rebuffed the Bolognese envoy. What they didn't know was that the documents brandished by the "papal" messenger as letters from Pope Innocent himself were forgeries produced by Savelli and his cousin.[16] Emboldened by the conviction that papal support was on the way, the Forlivesi kidnapped and beat the Milanese envoy and his Bolognese companion. Checco Orsi boasted that he had killed the Riario children, hoping word would trickle back to Ravaldino and devastate their worried mother. Two more Bentivoglio agents, trying to get word to Caterina that her brother's troops had arrived, were captured and hanged by the mob.

Still locked out of the fortress, with the Bentivoglio army at the gate, Ludovico and Checco Orsi tried to enlist the aid of Florence. Writing to Lorenzo de' Medici, they claimed that they had avenged not only the wrongs done to their people but also to the house of Medici. Portraying themselves as patriots who had rid Forlì of the tyrant who "sucked the blood of the poor, was untrue to his word and finally, loved no one but himself,"[17] they suggested that their exploit was more "divine than human." They confided that "we hope to start the siege [of Ravaldino] today" and that the complete takeover of the city would follow shortly. Lorenzo ignored this invitation to lend his aid to the conspirators. With his archenemy dead and his brother avenged, he could afford to sit back and watch events unfold.

In the midst of this stalemate, there was one happy event. Caterina's sister Stella Landriani and Andrea Ricci, Girolamo's nephew, were married. Stella, who with a bold spirit had resisted the count's killers, and Andrea, who had been among the first to draw his sword in the defense of the Riarios, were well matched. Wounded in the fray, Andrea had been nursed back to health by the solicitous Stella. The two were married by Bishop Savelli in Cesena, who was delighted to preside over this single joyful occasion during a troubled time.

Perhaps it was this springtime awakening of love, or merely shrewd opportunism, that prompted Antonio Maria Ordelaffi to make an unexpected proposal as well. The oldest of the three brothers who claimed lordship of Forlì left his safe haven of Ravenna to test the waters of the town. With Count Girolamo Riario dead and papal support slow in coming, he hoped the Forlivesi might be ready for the return of the Ordelaffis. Unable to marshal an army himself, Antonio was disappointed by his Venetian protectors, who were not interested enough in the little town to cross their bellicose neighbor Milan. But Antonio Maria, young, handsome, and, as events showed, quite imaginative, hit upon another solution. Approaching the castle in secret, he fired two arrows into the fortress of Ravaldino. These arrows carried letters with the anonymous suggestion that the countess marry Antonio Ordelaffi and restore peace to Forlì. Caterina ignored these advances, audacious in their timing, since a mere week had passed since her husband's murder; yet the proud Antonio Maria informed both Ferrara and Florence of this amorous sally, hoping to garner their support.

Bishop Savelli wisely used the time he bought with his phony papal briefs. While pummeling the fortress walls of Schiavonia with noisy cannon fire, the worldly bishop employed a quieter technique with its castellan: a handsome bribe of twelve hundred ducats. A few days later, the keeper of the outlying fortress of Forlimpopoli gave up his charge for even less. Caterina's position was weakening, but she demonstrated extraordinary endurance while the Orsis were cracking under the strain.

The pope, in his last bid for compromise, wrote to the Forlivesi on April 24, stating that he had appointed a cardinal governor for the city, and he would be arriving soon. The new papal representative was none other than Cardinal Raffaello Riario, the nephew of the deceased count. The papal mandate gave the cardinal authority to intervene to protect the interests and well-being of the Riario children in an attempt to exclude Caterina from serving as regent for the underage Ottaviano. The pope hoped that the Riario name would be enough to appease the family's partisans while still ensuring papal dominion of the city. The elated Forlivesi assumed that together with the cardinal, the pope would send his soldiers to quiet the town. Things looked bleak for Caterina.

The tide turned abruptly on April 29, when a contingent of twelve thousand men, including cavalry, infantry, archers, and artillery, set up camp outside the gates. Trailing in the wake of the soldiers were what all city dwellers feared most: the sackers. These parasites followed the military and then perched like vultures on the sidelines, awaiting the fall of a city. Once it capitulated, they went to work. Taking apart houses with their demolition instruments, they carried away anything, from the valuable to the simply useful. At the sight of even a fragment of the Milanese army, the Forlivesi rued their folly in baiting the duke of Milan and Bentivoglio. Frantic letters from the Orsis, Savelli, and the Council of Eight coursed to Lorenzo de' Medici, whose intervention was limited to annexing the Piancaldoli castle on the Imola-Florence border.

The Milanese forces sent a ducal emissary to demand the restoration of the Riarios. While Savelli reiterated the papal position and the Orsis seethed, town criers suddenly overwhelmed the piazza with shouts of "The church is here! The church is here!" The Council of Eight, believing that the Roman army was fast approaching, put its waning hopes into this one last basket.

The Forlivesi flooded out of the Porta Cotogni just in time to see the arrival of the soldiers. Not the teeming mass of fighting men expected by the townspeople, a mere fifty horsemen came into view. To the chagrin of the Forlivesi, the cavalry rode up to Ravaldino, unrolled the standard of the Riario rose, and rode across the lowered drawbridge to join Caterina's troops in the castle. The long-awaited "papal army" had been sent by the cardinal camerlengo, Raffaello Riario, to aid his aunt Caterina. The Forlivesi now knew all was lost. All they could do was await retribution, in the form of sacking, looting, and executions.

The vengeful Orsis dashed to the Porta San Pietro, now truly intending to kill the Riario children, who were no longer a useful political tool. They hammered at the door, swearing that Bishop Savelli had ordered them to take the children for "safekeeping." The guards refused them, following the bishop's orders. Ronche and the Orsis insisted, alternating curses and pleas, until Savelli's soldiers rained stones from the tower upon the intruders and threatened to call the city with the warning bell.

Caterina heard the shouts and cheers outside the castle walls. Coming out to the ramparts, she no longer heard "Church! Church!" or "Orsi! Orsi!" but now "Duke! Duke!" to hail her uncle's troops. She strained her ears to listen for the word for which she had fought so long and hard. At last, the name "Ottaviano!" rang through the air. She had won. Her son was alive and Forlì was hers.

12

THE SPOILS OF WAR

APRIL 30 MARKED the Feast of Saint Mercuriale, the patron saint of Forlì. And in 1488, the Forlivesi celebrated the holiday in honor of not only their saint but also a living icon, Caterina Riario Sforza. Moments after the Council of Eight capitulated in the face of the Milanese army and returned the town to Riario rule, citizens who had hidden away in their homes since Girolamo's murder poured into the streets, cheering for their indomitable countess. The long stalemate had come to a close. Anxious council members accompanied the Sforza representatives to free nine-year-old Ottaviano from his prison in the Porta San Pietro. They escorted the bewildered boy to the piazza and led his horse three times around the square, as he took symbolic possession of the city.

Hundreds trailed after Ottaviano as he rode out of the square and along the wide road to the Ravaldino fortress. Two long weeks had passed since Caterina had last seen her son. All the Forlivesi remembered the sight of the boy standing at the edge of the moat, with an Orsi dagger pressed to his throat, while Caterina defied his captors. By the time the procession reached the ramparts, thousands of onlookers eagerly awaited their reunion.

The drawbridge lowered, revealing Caterina standing alone in the cavernous entrance. Abandoning her sword and other trappings of war, she wore a simple dress of brown, the color of mourning. Little Ottaviano bolted into his mother's arms as she stepped onto the banks, and the crowd wept as they witnessed their embrace. Ottaviano sobbed openly, but Caterina hid her face against her son's body. After a few moments she raised her head, searching for her other children; Livio, whom she had last seen in the arms of the assassin Ludovico Orsi; Bianca, her precious only girl; Sforzino, a tiny infant; Cesare and Galeazzo, her other sturdy little sons. Noting her concern, the delegates, ambassadors, and townspeople immediately swept her off to the Porta San Pietro, where she was reunited with the rest of the Riario heirs. As she gathered her children into her arms, the horrors of the past weeks were momentarily forgotten, washed away by joyful tears.

Caterina changed into more glorious raiment to make her triumphant entrance into Forlì. The dark colors of widowhood were shelved for the moment as the victorious countess donned sumptuous silk and brocade robes in celebration. Even after two weeks of imprisonment, she looked radiant as she rode through the Porta Cotogni with Ottaviano by her side. Nobles in a rainbow of heraldic colors framed Caterina and her son. Squadrons of Milanese and Bentivoglio soldiers in glittering polished armor escorted the returning rulers. The people of Forlì were elated, a surprising turnaround from the previous day, when they had scoffed at the Milanese envoys. While all the Forlivesi waved banners and shouted, "Riario! Riario!" and "Sforza! Sforza!" Caterina and Ottaviano made the triple circuit around the piazza, side by side, as cheers of allegiance rang out around them. The Riarios had reclaimed Forlì. But Caterina knew better than to relax. The danger was far from over. The next threat would arise not from her enemies, but her allies.

TWENTY THOUSAND MEN, the soldiers of the duke of Milan, were camped outside the gates of Forlì, each eagerly awaiting the signal to begin the sack. The townspeople, for all their apparent jubilation, were dreading the inevitable reprisal. The Forlivesi had looted Caterina's palace, leaving it in shambles. The countess had nothing to lose; once the festivities were over, she and her children would be safely ensconced in the fortress. Every citizen was certain that she would open the gates to her friends and relatives and use the flood of soldiers to purge the town of its guilt for Girolamo's death, her children's abduction, and the people's defection to papal rule.

But Caterina again took the people of Forlì by surprise. After her victory march, Caterina invited the captains of the armies to dine with her in the house of a loyal Forlivese nobleman, Luffo Numai. Amid the toasts and congratulations, Caterina coolly informed them that their services were no longer needed, and ordered that the armies, except for a small Milanese contingent, remain camped outside the gates while preparing for their long march home. The captains were thunderstruck. The rules of war demanded a sack. Their men had seen neither battle nor glory—only long idle days of waiting. The leaders protested that it would be easier to deny the army their wages than refuse them the satisfaction of pillage. Caterina, unruffled, replied that her subjecs had stolen jewels, silver, and other valuables from her house. If the soldiers sacked Forlì, her possessions would end up in their bags, along with everything else, and she would never see them again. Certainly her brother, the duke of Milan, she astutely noted, would not want to see his nephew's inheritance dissipated in this way. The captains cursed and threatened, but Caterina serenely poured more wine and allotted them campsites outside the three gates: San Pietro, Cotogni, and Schiavonia.

Word soon spread through the town: *"Madonna non vuole, Madonna non vuole!"* ("Our Lady doesn't want it [the sack]!"). Leone Cobelli narrated the triumphant return of Caterina with pride and joy. The chronicler also knew that the benevolent countess, hailed by the citizens as the "Savior of Forlì" on April 30, was a far cry from the woman he had seen the night before.

After the Council of Eight had fallen on April 29, several leading Riario partisans had taken over the decision making. Luffo Numai and Tommaso degli Orcioli, friends of Ludovico Ercolani, who had obtained the important messages from Caterina moments before she was captured in the Riario palace, came to Ravaldino that very night to discuss conditions of the surrender. Cobelli, who moved easily and unobtrusively among the coteries of the nobility, managed to introduce himself into the delegation. Inside Ravaldino, he witnessed Caterina's tirade over the wrongs done by the Forlivesi to her family. Her indictment of Forlì was terrible: she mounted accusations of murder, treachery, abduction, desecration, and thievery and she found the town guilty on every score. Giving vent to two weeks of pent-up rage, Caterina exclaimed that the sack was no more than what the citizens deserved.

Cobelli, rapt, then watched the normally reserved countess struggle to master herself. She did not want a sack; the weakest inevitably suffered most when anarchy reigned. She knew well that young women were always the first to be harmed when bloodthirsty soldiers raged through a town. Caterina regained her calm. She would not permit girls to be dishonored because, as Cobelli quoted her, "I care about women."[1] Caterina gave the Forlivesi a chance to redeem themselves. That same night, she ordered archers to pepper the town with written messages curled around arrows: "My people of Forlì, hurry, put to death my enemies! I promise you that if you deliver them to me, I will take you as my dearest brothers. Quickly then! Fear nothing! The Milanese army is at the gate, soon you will be rewarded, and my enemies will have their just deserts!"

As Caterina's messages penetrated every street, Ludovico, Checco, Ronche, and other conspirators were huddled in the Orsi palace. From the first cries of "Duke! Duke!" and "Ottaviano! Ottaviano!" they knew the game had ended. Leaving their wives and children in the care of their aged father, Andrea Orsi, who was too ill to accompany them, the Orsi brothers set off with seventeen of their accomplices toward Ravenna. They did not leave empty-handed. Amid murder and kidnapping, the Orsis had found a little time for looting. Tens of thousands of ducats' worth of silver and jewels were stuffed into their saddlebags, along with cash and valuables stolen from Jewish moneylenders. So laden, the fugitives took to the road, but the Venetians had no intention of harboring fugitives from the duke of Milan and expelled them. They eventually found asylum in the Papal States.

With her realm saved and her enemies on the run, Caterina turned to dealing with her subjects. Edicts flowed down from the walls of Ravaldino, broadcast through the city by the town criers. The exiles who had returned to Forlì upon the death of Girolamo were ordered to leave before sundown. Bishop Savelli and his assistants were detained, not unkindly, but as an insurance policy, should the pope make one last attempt to claim the territory. Finally, Caterina received three soldiers—Capoferri, Serughi, and Denti—into her quarters. She showered the battle-hardened but slightly embarrassed men with praise, thanks, and rich rewards for having refused to give up her children to the murderous Orsis.

That night, while the Forlivesi were feasting and celebrating their good fortune, Caterina sent a few men out to recover her husband's corpse from its pauper's grave at the Church of Saint Francis. Although the cathedral of Forlì had rejected Girolamo's body, Imola, the city the count had always preferred, claimed his remains for their main church. Count Girolamo made one last trip to Imola and was entombed in the cathedral, with an elaborate marble monument to commemorate the man who had given much to the town. Caterina never forgave the Cathedral of the Holy Cross. She would give generously for the rest of her life to many religious institutions, but the cathedral of Forlì was left off the countess's list and she never set foot in it again.

Her devastated palace was no longer habitable, so Caterina stayed in the Ravaldino fortress. There she had both the security of the strong defenses and the comfort of her children all safely asleep nearby. On May 1, she awoke and prepared for the grim task of punishing the conspirators. Girolamo had always made a point of not being in town when public executions took place, leaving the inevitable unpopularity of the event to fall on the governors. Caterina was different. As she had already demonstrated during the Roffi conspiracy, she believed that several exemplary punishments would make it clear to the Forlivesi that she had assumed full control of the city.

During the Renaissance, capital punishment was a public affair. Witnesses formed an essential part of an execution. In cases like this one, the magistrates were seeking the repentance of the whole public, and the prisoner's fear and humiliation were thought to function as a deterrent to future wrongdoing. The people themselves were expected to shout and jeer, expressing their rejection of those who had disobeyed the law. It was believed that "eye for an eye" justice was required to restore order.

Caterina began by summoning a new bailiff to town. Matteo Babone of Castelbolognese instilled fear simply with his appearance. Standing head and shoulders above most Forlivesi, Babone had a hulking frame, and his heavy, irregular features were partially concealed by hanks of filthy, matted black hair. The people recoiled in terror from "the Turk," as they dubbed him; he seemed to be conjured out of a nightmare of an Ottoman invasion. Unlike the unfortunate Barone, who had been co-opted to execute the Roffi conspirators and went running to the nearest shrine to expiate his sins, Babone relished his work; having no ties to the townspeople, he felt no qualms about the grisly job.

At daybreak, while Caterina was kneeling in the Church of Saint Francis, praying for her husband's soul, Babone broke down doors and yanked conspirators, still in their bedclothes, to the gallows. Marco Scocciacaro, who had thrown the body of Girolamo from the window into the square, was the first to pay for his crimes. To make the punishment fit the crime, Babone dangled Scocciacaro on a noose from the window through which he had dropped the count. The executioner swung his victim back and forth above the crowd like a grotesque piñata as the Forlivesi clawed at his body. Scocciacaro was still alive when Babone dropped him into the waiting crowd, who tore him limb from limb.

Next came handsome twenty-nine-year-old Pagliarino, nephew of the assassin Giacomo del Ronche. The young man had been caught in conspiracies before and also was a known thief, but Caterina had always pardoned him out of fondness for his mother. But the young man had initiated the desecration of the count's body, dragging it across the piazza. Caterina could no longer be indulgent; he too was suspended from the window. The crowd, now in a frenzy of blood lust, slit his throat, castrated him, and carved out his heart and intestines. The last man killed on that bloody day was Pietro Albanese. At Ravaldino he had incited the Orsis to murder Caterina's children and hurled verbal abuse at the countess. He was hanged at the gallows and his body left among the soldiers, who hacked at it with spades and lances. At last the sun set on the piazza of Forlì, drawing the day's horrors to a close. As Cobelli looked sadly on his beloved square, usually bright with colorful ceramic wares and fragrant with fresh fruit, he breathed in the reek of rotting flesh and sighed, "Unbelievable! To call this a lake of blood would not be a lie."[2]

Caterina intended to use these deaths as a lesson. As soon as night fell, her town criers communicated her demand that all the belongings stolen from her palace be returned. By daybreak, everything except what had been stolen by the fugitive Orsis was piled outside Ravaldino.

May 2 was the day of reckoning for the Orsi family. Ludovico and Checco had fled, leaving their father, wives, daughters, and grandchildren behind. Babone dragged the eighty-year-old Andrea Orsi out of his hiding place in the Convent of Saint Dominic. After tying a rough rope about the man's wizened neck, Babone hauled him through the streets to his own palace. The beating of drums summoned the citizens to the house, where soldiers, builders, and artisans were waiting with various tools. As Orsi and the Forlivesi watched, the elegant palace was destroyed. Babone loomed over the bent elder, taunting him as each frescoed wall fell to the ground and graceful plaster molding was smashed with a pickax. The remains of the Orsi stronghold were then set alight like a funeral pyre for the family who could no longer call Forlì home. Several excited citizens brought home precious objects looted from the Orsis' home as prize spoils for the countess. Caterina refused them, although the Orsis had made good their escape with jewels stolen from her.

His sons gone, Andrea Orsi knew he would have to bear the punishment for the family. They all had devised the plot together around his kitchen table, and although weak in body, he had always insisted that for the rebellion to succeed, all the Riario family must die. Wheezing and coughing in the dust, Andrea cursed his sons for their stupidity: not for their crimes, but for their failures.

As Babone shoved him onto the executioner's podium, however, the anger of the proud noble dissolved as his hands started to tremble. "People of Forlì!" he called out. "Say a prayer for my soul and remember to be wiser than I have been." The words of the Orsi patriarch closed the rebellion. Now all that awaited was his death.

Andrea Orsi's execution was Babone's masterpiece. The old man was tied to a board, with only his head hanging unsupported off the edge. His feet were raised as the plank was tied to the back of a horse, so that his head lay on the ground. Babone then spurred the horse to a canter, dragging Orsi behind it as the old man's head bounced against the hard cobblestones of the square. Three times around the piazza Orsi was dragged, in a bloody parody of the possession ceremony that the Orsis had coveted, until the skull had fractured and Andrea Orsi's head was reduced to a bloody pulp.

As Andrea Orsi's body lay in the square, Caterina announced a reward of a thousand ducats for the return of the fugitive murderers alive, and five hundred for their corpses.[3] But despite her efforts, the Orsis would elude her for years.

After the execution of Andrea Orsi, Caterina summoned the Orsi women. Seven terrified wives, sisters, and daughters had been left behind, one clutching her infant son. The countess then freed all of them and allowed them either to remain in Forlì or to return to their paternal homes.

Caterina then turned to her rescuers and guests, inviting the Milanese generals and local nobles to lunch in the fortress. The noble generals enjoyed a cheerful banquet with Caterina, who impressed them with her knowledge of strategy and her interest in new developments in artillery. But the meal was more than a pleasant diversion. As evening fell, the head of every family in Forlì was summoned to the Ravaldino fortress. The generals retired to another room while several hundred anxious husbands and fathers gathered at the foot of the castle, the encroaching darkness fueling their fears as to what night might bring. Soldiers sorted the men into groups of twenty-five and led them into the castle. In the main chamber, they saw Caterina sitting upon a high throne, illuminated by torchlight. A large Bible sat on a table in front of her, its parchment pages gaping open to display the sentence "In the beginning was the Word." Each man was called forward by name and read a contract guaranteed by the duke of Milan. The document outlined the duties and privileges of good citizens and the punishments for betrayal. With one hand on the Bible and with eyes fixed on the countess, they vowed fidelity to Ottaviano, lord of Forlì, and to Caterina, the regent. Afterward, the relieved subjects were ushered into the next room, where the famous generals toasted and congratulated them, with warm assurances that under Caterina's rule they would prosper in peace. In lieu of a papal sanction of her regency, Caterina had obtained the authority to rule from her own subjects.

May 4 fell on a Sunday, and after a Mass of thanksgiving, the countess convoked the Council of Eight for one last session. Mindful of the brutal deaths they had witnessed in the piazza, the men trembled as they entered the countess's chambers. They had cooperated willingly with Savelli and the Orsis and had rudely dismissed the envoys of Milan and Bologna who had arrived to aid Caterina; they knew there was much to answer for. But for the most part Caterina administered only verbal lashings, although her words stung like strokes of a whip. Four members of the treacherous council were simply dismissed, since Caterina realized they had acted out of fear rather than conviction.

But Niccolò Pansechi, Girolamo's notary and tax collector, was another matter. After having reaped the profits of persuading Girolamo to reinstall the *dazi*, Niccolò had then turned and joined the murderers of the very man who had made him rich.

Pansechi stood before a stone-faced Caterina, the rope of the penitent dangling from his throat. Aware of the gruesome deaths of the conspirators, the traitorous noble tried to find excuses to save his own neck. Caterina pounced. "Traitor!" she exclaimed. "This is the thanks we get for giving you money and position? Do you remember, traitor, how you told us the best thing would be to bring back the *dazi*?" Caterina continued, raising her voice so everyone from her immediate entourage of nobles and soldiers to the servants listening from the halls could hear. "Did you not, traitor, assure us that the people of Forlì were a vile and cowed mass of fools, and once the taxes were reinstated, they would never mention it again?" She rose to her feet in rage. "You are a disgrace! Get out of my sight."[4] A trembling Pansechi was led off by the soldiers, his possessions confiscated and his house given over as barracks for Caterina's troops.

Simone de' Fiorini stumbled forward next. A huge man with bulging eyes set in a wide face, he towered over Caterina. The countess addressed him in deceptively mild tones, asking, "Oh, Simone, what did you do to my husband? You stabbed his body lying dead in the piazza. You called him a traitor." Her words felled the giant man like an ax. Simone sank to his knees, sobbing his excuses. His bent head shook as he begged forgiveness and protested that "mere curiosity" had spurred him to the piazza. Reaching his arms to Caterina he swore that he had attacked only the body of Antonio da Montecchio, the police chief who had come to Girolamo's aid, whom he hated for personal reasons. He fell silent, looking up at Caterina with his hands clasped. Caterina replied coldly, "I will take the same pity on you that you showed to my husband. I will leave you to be torn apart by the dogs."[5]

Her words were harsh, but Caterina knew the piazza had seen enough blood. She exiled Pansechi, Fiorini, and the remaining two council members who had assisted the Orsis, sending them to Milan, where they were to remain for the rest of their lives. Although the penalty for "breaking confines" was death, Pansechi escaped and went to Cotignola. Caterina was probably counting on his committing such a foolish act. She was immediately notified of his escape and sent out a squad of bounty hunters to bring him to Forlì. The greedy, shortsighted Pansechi disappeared into Ravaldino and was never heard from again. Even the groveling Fiorini made his own daring bid for freedom. Eight years after his exile, he left Milan and returned to Romagna to stir up trouble. Once again alerted, Caterina sent out a team of soldiers to capture him, but Fiorini showed surprising agility for such a large man and nimbly escaped out a back window. Caterina's men would pursue him for years but he would never be caught.

Caterina was ready to close this violent chapter of her life. A few more conspirators were rounded up and executed in the dungeons of Forlì, but it was time to turn the page. Caterina hired a new chief magistrate to prepare the documents retroactively legalizing the executions. After she was able to leave Ravaldino, Caterina ordered four public executions and five additional hangings in the fortress.[6] The sons of Giovanni Nanni, a farmer who had been executed for the conspiracy at the Porta Cotogni with the Roffi family, were those who were hanged. The brothers had eagerly joined the Orsi plot, publicly announcing on several occasions that they relished the idea "of eating the heart of the countess and those of her children." Later biographers universally label Caterina's actions here as stemming from a vendetta, although Cobelli considered her merciful. Crimes against the state called for swift justice. As a point of comparison, almost eighty people had been executed on the same day of the attempt on Lorenzo de' Medici's life.[7] The time would come when Caterina would succumb to blind vengeance, but in this case, she behaved as any ruler of her time would. Her enemies on the run, her adversaries exiled, her people reconciled, Caterina was ready to take the reins of Forlì.

The foreign armies left on May 7, bringing the exiles with them. Ottaviano rode with several Forlì nobles to Imola, where the city waited to affirm its loyalty to him. A contingent of soldiers remained in Forlì under the count of Bergamo, nicknamed "Brambilla," meaning "the war cry." This brave and personable warrior took over as the governor of Forlì in the place of Domenico Ricci, Girolamo's brother-in-law. Caterina also released Bishop Savelli and his assistants against the safe return of her mother and sister in Cesena. With her whole family finally reunited about her, she spent most of her time inside the fortress. To ensure that no outbreaks of violence would perturb the renewed tranquility, Caterina ordered that no citizen could bear arms without authorization and imposed a curfew.

Life slowly returned to normal in Forlì. The market reopened in the piazza and the workers returned to their fields. Caterina did not go back to the palace in the square, however, even though it had been restored after the devastation. She preferred to reside with her family behind the sturdy walls of Ravaldino. Although her rule had the approval of the Forlivesi, Caterina still worried about the pope. She awaited word from Rome that the pontiff had invested Ottaviano with the title of lord of Forlì, naming her as regent, yet none arrived. As May drew to a close, however, Caterina was heartened by an event almost as comforting as a papal confirmation. Cardinal Raffaello Riario arrived in Romagna. Caterina, already grateful for the fifty horsemen he had sent in her hour of need, rode out to meet the twenty-eight-year-old cardinal at Forlimpopoli, with Brambilla and a host of nobles. As he had done six years before, when the Riarios first moved to Forlì after the death of Sixtus, the cardinal brought an impressive entourage. He settled into the fortress of Ravaldino and assisted Caterina in her fledgling steps as sole ruler of two states. Cardinal Riario had grown in importance over the years, and now not only was cardinal camerlengo, in charge of running the conclave after a pope's death, but had gathered further titles and benefices and was even named archbishop of Pisa, although after his capture in the wake of the Pazzi conspiracy, he never set foot in that diocese. Now extremely wealthy, he assisted Caterina in reestablishing her household. Cardinal Riario stayed with the family for several months and Forlì started the summer in the spirit of a joyous family reunion.

Meanwhile, a scandal had developed in nearby Faenza. Delighted chroniclers sped to get the inside story of the most titillating murder of the year. Galeotto Manfredi, ruler of Faenza, who had penned the particularly scabrous account of Caterina's retort at Ravaldino, was murdered on May 31, 1488, by his wife, Francesca Bentivoglio. The daughter of Caterina's close ally Giovanni Bentivoglio, the lord of Bologna, Francesca had married Galeotto Manfredi in 1482. But a few years earlier, during a period of exile in Ferrara, Galeotto had fallen in love with Cassandra, the daughter of a local pharmacist, aptly called "La Pavona" ("the Peacock") by her fellow townspeople. According to rumor, the smitten Galeotto had secretly married the beauty. His official wedding to Francesca Bentivoglio didn't put a damper on Galeotto's affair; he moved Cassandra to Faenza and installed her in a convent where he could visit her regularly. Francesca spent the first few years of marriage ignorant of the affair and even bore Galeotto a son, Astorre, in 1485. But Cassandra's outraged father repeatedly visited Galeotto to complain, and word of this soon reached Francesca. Attempting to confront her husband, she was blocked and beaten by one of his friends, Fra Silvester, a renegade Franciscan brother who lived riotously under the protective wing of Galeotto. Infuriated and also frightened, for wife poisoning was common in Romagna, she returned to her father's fold in Bologna in 1487. Through the intervention of Lorenzo de' Medici, Francesca was persuaded to return to her husband a few months later. They lived separate lives, but Francesca's fury did not abate.

On May 29, 1488, Francesca sent urgent word to her husband that she was deathly ill and begged him to bring her a doctor. But in her semidark room, Francesca was actually quite well, and in the company of three assassins, armed with ropes, swords, and daggers, she awaited Galeotto. Two days and two nights they lay in wait, until he finally arrived with a doctor. Francesca's personal servant, Rigo, detained the doctor outside the door, allowing Galeotto to enter alone. Young, strong, and alert, he sensed danger the instant he crossed the threshold. When the first assassin threw a rope around his neck, Galeotto was quick to react and struggled free, but Francesca did not let her prey escape. Stepping behind her husband, she drove a dagger into his back, and Galeotto fell at her feet, lifeless.[8]

Now the golden nugget of territory between Forlì and Imola shone like a prize, ready for the fastest conqueror to lay claim to it. Giovanni

Bentivoglio immediately sent a force to subdue Faenza. Caterina made a show of solidarity with her sister-in-widowhood, discreetly ignoring the cause of death of Francesca's husband. She sent a sizable contingent under the leadership of Brambilla, the count of Bergamo, who had saved her own lands. At first, the people of Faenza seemed glad to see the Milanese and Bolognese armies and shouted "Duke! Duke!" in the streets, as if to cheer the duke of Milan. But then Lorenzo de' Medici set to work. The last thing the Florentine wanted was a solid block of Romagnol territory under the direct control of the duke of Milan. Lorenzo's agents riled up the citizens against the "murderers of Galeotto" and sent whispers through the countryside about a coup d'état. Even Antonio Maria Ordelaffi appeared in Faenza, perhaps to offer his hand in marriage to Francesca, as he had to Caterina. The temper of the town turned, and suddenly hostility rained down on the joint forces of Milan and Bologna. While dining in the main palace of Faenza, Brambilla and Giovanni Bentivoglio were attacked. Brambilla, the brave soldier and gallant captain who had fought in numerous battles, was killed at the table, while Giovanni Bentivoglio narrowly escaped by climbing out of a window and into the hands of the Florentines. Innocent VIII shot out a papal edict confirming three-year-old Astorre Manfredi as lord of Faenza, putting the boy under the tutelage of a delegation of leading citizens. Caterina received a double disappointment with the dispatch bearing news from Faenza. Her hopes for a unified state were dashed; Faenza would still be controlled by hostile forces. Furthermore, her new friend and protector, Brambilla, was dead. Her first sally as an independent ruler had ended in failure and loss.

JULY BROUGHT THE long-awaited papal confirmation of Caterina's rule. The twelve-page document, dated July 18, 1488, was signed by Pope Innocent VIII and sixteen cardinals, who declared Ottaviano the lord of Forlì and Imola until the end of his family line.[9] Countess Caterina was officially named his regent until the boy came of age. The news was proclaimed to their subjects on July 30 amid tolling bells and banquets. The prominent presence of Cardinal Riario amid the celebrations strongly suggested that he was responsible for the pontiff's change of heart. Together Cardinal Riario and Caterina announced a benevolent change in policy, the first official one by the new rulers of Forlì. They lowered the hated grain *dazi* and decreased taxes on salt and military guards by one third.

When October 19 came and the cardinal took his leave, the citizens of both Forlì and Imola were sad to see him go. His generosity had helped revive the spirits of the tragedy-stricken countess and her subjects. Peace had been restored and the future promised prosperity. Little did Caterina know that the next trauma in her life would arrive soon, and would not be inflicted by troops or revolts, but by Cupid's arrow.

· 13 ·

FANNING THE FLAMES

IN 1489, FORLÌ gossiped about love. Antonio Maria Ordelaffi, the heir of the former ruling family of Forlì, was twenty-nine, four years older than Caterina. Handsome and unmarried, the stateless noble had knocked about Romagna; displaced from the land of his birth, he had nowhere to call home. Many Forlivesi remembered Ordelaffi with open fondness, while others kept their partisanship more secret. During the tumult following Girolamo's murder, Antonio thought he had found the ideal solution to Forlì's political struggles when he proposed to the newly widowed Caterina via two arrows shot over the ramparts of Ravaldino. Later that year, Caterina decided it was time to take a closer look at this tergiversate suitor. She sent him an invitation to Forlì, which he promptly accepted. The Forlivesi, kept well apprised of everything from the proposal to the invitation—most likely by agents of Antonio—began to speculate wildly in the fields, offices, and piazzas. The initial encounter took place in April, the first anniversary of the murder of Girolamo. As spring wore on into summer, Antonio became a regular visitor to the fortress. Caterina seemed very well disposed toward the young noble; they were close in age, and both were attractive. The Forlivesi began to indulge the hope that their political struggles would be resolved with a wedding. When Caterina took a villa four miles outside Imola for the summer and Antonio joined the family, the townspeople assumed that the deal had been worked out.[1] A delegation of Forlivesi went so far as to visit the Ordelaffi family in Ravenna to offer their congratulations.

The chronicler Leone Cobelli delighted in Caterina's newfound romance. As the summer days passed, he noted that the countess had still not returned. He painted banners and standards with their coats of arms intertwined, a gift for the newlyweds, he thought, expecting effusive thanks for his efforts. He was mistaken.

The rumors of the Riario-Ordelaffi wedding escaped the city borders and raced to the ears of Ludovico the Moor, Cardinal Raffaello Riario, Lorenzo de' Medici, and even the pope himself. Irate letters poured into Forlì, criticizing Caterina for her conduct. All the parties were concerned about the consequences of such a marriage. What would happen to the Riario children? After she had fought to save them at Ravaldino, would she be willing to fritter away their inheritance for an Ordelaffi exile? Pope Innocent contemplated using "Caterina's disorderly life"[2] as an excuse to rescind his approval of her regency and turn her state over to his own son Francescetto. Cardinal Riario frantically prepared to ride to Forlì. As relatives of Caterina, Ludovico the Moor and Cardinal Riario were the most concerned by the rumors. They had thrown their weight behind Caterina to win her lands back, but not out of love for kin. Each of her powerful allies planned on controlling her territory through her, viewing Caterina as a pawn on the chessboard of Italian politics. While impressed by her determination to keep her states, they doubted her ability to rule. Each man, in fact, maintained a number of spies in her household to keep abreast of all that happened in Caterina's life. As the duke of Milan explained to his envoy Branda da Castiglione, "Now we shall have to govern Forlì, until the child comes of age."[3] Caterina, however, would prove to be anything but a docile political tool.

In any case, their fears were unfounded. While Caterina may have succumbed to the charms of Antonio Maria Ordelaffi during the summer months of 1489, marriage was not on her mind. Having just defended her state at great risk, she had no intention of handing it over to political rivals.

Caterina returned from her pleasant summer holiday to the pandemonium generated by the Forlivesi gossip mills. Far from pleased by Cobelli's romantic creations, she put the dumbfounded chronicler in prison. Firing off letters to her uncle and to Cardinal Riario, she assured them that there was no marriage in the works. Then she wrote a formal letter to Venice, the official protectors of Antonio, and complained about the inconvenience and embarrassment caused by the presence of Antonio Maria Ordelaffi and the worries of the duke of Milan. She was well aware that several Forlivesi had gone to Ravenna to congratulate the rest of the Ordelaffi clan. The ruling body of Venice, the Signoria, called Antonio back and gave him a military commission with handsome pay in Friuli, a mountainous region in northeast Italy, where he would be safely out of the way.

Caterina rounded up the principal scandalmongers and threw them into prison alongside the miserable Cobelli. The elegant dance teacher was crushed when confronted by the ire of his heroine. He stammered a weak defense, but Caterina knew Cobelli had consorted with the Orsis after her husband's murder, and though she had tolerated his prying for years, enough was enough. She intended to unleash further punishment on the hapless painter, but Tommaso Feo, her trusted castellan and the savior of Ravaldino, intervened.[4] Out of gratitude to Feo, Caterina let the crestfallen chronicler go. Bernardi, who would take over as the principal historian of Forlì, wrote that Cobelli tried to burn the hundreds of pages he had written about Caterina over the years, but his friends stopped him. The book survived, but Cobelli's pleasure in recounting the affairs and events in the life of the countess died in that instant. His accounts would grow more bitter and critical as the years went on.

After the scandal surrounding her purported marriage, Caterina directed her energies toward pious activities. Her own territory of Imola had recently been the scene of a popular miracle. In the spring of 1483, while Caterina and Girolamo had been in Rome attending Mass on Holy Thursday, the day of Christ's Last Supper, a solitary pilgrim named Stefano Manganelli from Cremona was making his way toward the Marian shrine in Loreto, hoping to arrive in time for Easter. The devout man stopped at every image of Mary gracing the Via Emilia, never failing to light a candle to the Madonna. It had been an unusually severe winter, and although the calendar had reached the spring equinox, the weather remained cold. That Thursday, Manganelli arrived three miles from Imola at a locality called Piratello. At the intersection of a small secondary road he saw a rough stone pillar with a niche carved into it. Nestled within this humble setting was a fresco of the Madonna and Child. The pilgrim retrieved a small candle from his sack and lit it, but when he reached to place his offering on the stone ledge of the niche his hand slipped and the candle went out. As Manganelli righted it, the flame returned as if lit by itself. At that moment, the startled pilgrim heard a sweet voice carried on the chilly Romagnol wind. It said, "I am the Immaculate Virgin Mary." Falling to his knees, he asked the Mother of God how he could serve her. She ordered him to go to the next town and tell the people to build her a shrine at Piratello. "If they don't believe you," the voice continued, "show them this." Stefano Manganelli's cape filled with roses, a flower unobtainable in the freezing Romagnol spring.[5]

The bishop of Imola had been delighted by the news of a miracle on his turf, and Caterina and Girolamo had sent funds to arrange a little shrine around the fresco. People crowded the Via Emilia to see the image, while pottery artists kept their kilns filled with ceramic copies of the Madonna di Piratello. In a time when the hard realities of hunger, illness, and death struck early and often, these brushes with the divine reenergized the faithful and gave them hope that their prayers were heard.

In 1489, Caterina renewed her interest in the Madonna di Piratello. Undoubtedly performing a kind of public penance for the summer's scandal, Caterina sought and received permission from Pope Innocent to build a church on the site. Caterina paid for most of the construction, from the church walls to the bronze bell in the tower. The shrine of Piratello still exists and Caterina's bell tower stands over what is now the cemetery of Imola.

Soon after, Caterina returned to the affairs she had overseen before her husband's murder. During the cold winter of 1489, she sent to Mantua for a large quantity of down to replace the bedding lost when her palace was ransacked, in order to render her new home in the castle more comfortable. Always focused on the future of her children, Caterina also began negotiations to affiance her eight-year-old daughter, Bianca, to Astorre Manfredi, the new lord of Faenza, now age four. The marriage, which would ensure a friendly presence in Faenza, sandwiched as it was between the two Riario territories, was heartily supported by the Bentivoglios of Bologna. Lorenzo de' Medici of Florence, on the other hand, hesitated. Caterina had to send him several pointed letters, demanding a "simple yes or no,"[6] before he finally sent his approval. Given that Lorenzo had undone the Sforza-Bentivoglio plan to take Faenza in 1488, his acceptance of the match was considered necessary. Caterina also resumed her exchanges with the duke of Ferrara, still hoping to obtain compensation for her lost *cascina* and livestock, but to little avail. The powerful lord exchanged gifts and pleasantries but refused to take the countess seriously.

Caterina began to realize that even her own retainers were skeptical of her authority. In October, while checking on the work at Piratello, Caterina stopped to visit her fortress in Imola. She called the castellan, Giovanni Andrea de' Gerardi, and told him to let her enter. He refused. De' Gerardi, like many in Caterina's court, was from Savona, the home of the Riario family. Girolamo had brought many of his kinsmen to Romagna during his rule, and they remained loyal to him and his heirs. De' Gerardi claimed that he held the fortress for Lord Ottaviano and would open only to him.

Enraged and humiliated, Caterina stood outside her own fortress, shouting to be allowed in. At length, de' Gerardi allowed her to enter, accompanied by a few female servants. He had heard what happened to the last castellan who had refused entry to Caterina and was taking no chances.

Once inside, she discovered that like Zaccheo, this castellan had loaned money to Girolamo and now wanted the five thousand ducats he claimed to be owed before he would abandon the castle. He had not worked for the Riario family without learning a thing or two. De' Gerardi insisted that the money be deposited outside Caterina's territory and guaranteed by a letter of credit.

Caterina did not have such funds available, nor did she have an inclination to pay them. She wrote immediately to Cardinal Riario in Rome, outlining the problem. The cardinal instantly realized the danger, should open hostility develop between the castellan and the countess. The castellan would be easy prey for a wealthy Riario enemy to manipulate if the matter was left unsettled. On November 2, the cardinal arrived in Imola, having ridden from Rome in only six days. In contrast to his flamboyant earlier appearances, he brought only a small escort of forty men. Moments after his arrival, he accompanied Caterina to the fortress, where he was able to soothe the castellan and negotiate an armistice. They agreed that Caterina would find the money, and the castellan would allow the countess access to her fortress. To all appearances, peace was restored. But Caterina smoldered in resentment at the castellan's defiance.

The Riario family took the opportunity of the cardinal's presence to enjoy a little reunion. Caterina, Ottaviano, and Cardinal Riario all traveled to Forlì, where they enjoyed the first wines of fall with fragrant roasted chestnuts. Led by the illustrious cardinal, Caterina and all her children, barefoot and dressed in the traditional garb of the penitent, even took a little pilgrimage to Piratello during the month of the dead. As the solemn procession of public repentance made its way along the Via Emilia, it seemed as though Caterina had made her peace with the world.

In early 1490, Caterina started to deal with the harsh realities of ruling Forlì. The first item on the agenda that year was how to return a cash flow to the town. Ever since the murder of Girolamo and the public looting that followed it, the Jewish moneylenders of Forlì had stayed away. Poor citizens without land or other holdings always had difficulty raising funds, and the particularly harsh winter of 1489 had resulted in a negligible harvest that summer. Caterina could certainly sympathize. To raise money for herself and her family, she had repeatedly pawned jewels in Genoa, Bologna, and other major centers where large sums could be obtained quickly. After the death of Girolamo, only the timely intervention of the duke of Milan kept her from losing almost twenty-five thousand ducats in jewels to pay back a loan of a few thousand in cash.

Raising money in the Renaissance was a difficult affair. The large banking concerns of Tuscany served businesses and land-rich nobles. The commercial industries of the age had little trouble finding backers as the competing banking families were always looking for new investments. But usury, or lending money at interest to individuals, had always been considered a mortal sin, and therefore, officially it was difficult for a private individual to take out a loan. Furthermore, peasants and artisans had little in the way of collateral—a few trinkets here, or some produce there—and thus were considered a poor risk. Jews, on the other hand, who by law could own no land, amassed wealth in movable goods and so filled this niche. Most cities had Jewish moneylenders whose capital was underwritten by the local government. But political instability always spelled trouble for the Jews. Everyone knew that they kept cash, jewels, and silver plate on hand, and often a random street riot furnished a sufficient excuse to raid their homes. Their departure, however, produced financial difficulties, for the Jewish community served a practical purpose in the economic fabric of society.

In February, representatives from the four quarters of Forlì came to Caterina, requesting that the countess ask some Jews to move to Forlì and reestablish a cash flow there. While Caterina saw the wisdom of the idea, she demurred. Musing aloud, she recalled the days when Girolamo had called these same men together to propose a Monte di Pietà, a group that would lend money against pawned objects with little or no interest. The count, she recollected, had personally offered to put up five hundred ducats of capital and had invited them to do the same, but she seemed to remember that they had scoffed at the very idea. The magistrates squirmed and blushed under her inquisitive gaze. They stammered promises to bring in some experts in establishing a Monte di Pietà, although Girolamo's vision would not be realized until 1527. Caterina, in return, invited Guglielmo d'Alia, a wealthy Bolognese Jew, to set up business in Forlì.

Within a few weeks, Caterina was wrestling with a different problem. An old Imolese rivalry, dating back centuries to the antagonism between the popes and the emperors, reared its head in the normally tranquil town. The Tartagni family, along with their friends the Codronchi and Viani clans (loyal Riario partisans), had sided with the imperial Ghibellines during the long wars of the thirteenth century. The Mercati family, supporters of the pope, belonged to the Guelph faction.

In February Caterina leased a large part of her land in Imola to be worked by Cristoforo Tartagni. The favor conferred on the family, with its accompanying profits, awakened the old family feud, and on February 26, Giulio Mercati attacked Cristoforo, wounding him in the head with a dagger. Within hours, family alliances had brought dozens of angry combatants to the streets. The governor of Imola, Guglielmo da Tedescho, alerted Caterina, who acted at once. Recognizing the type of bitter hatred that had torn apart Rome when the Orsinis and Colonnas clashed, she promptly dispatched eighty cavalry to restore peace. As soon as the city was settled, she exiled the Mercati family for their role as the instigators of the attack.

Caterina's main worry, however, was the control of her fortresses. Her political survival depended on commanding the main defensive structures of her lands. The castellan of Imola had already revealed his untrustworthiness, and she soon began to doubt even the steadfast Tommaso Feo, the backbone of her defense at Ravaldino. Although he had proved himself unshakable, Caterina knew that he, like Girolamo, hailed from Savona and that his tie to the Riario clan was stronger than his bond to her. Tommaso had witnessed her weakest hours and therefore knew her too well. His friendship with Cardinal Riario also concerned Caterina. The cardinal had been a staunch ally up to this point, but she had no illusions about the Riario family.

Caterina put forward this list of practical reasons to justify her removal of Feo, but her real intention was to install a new man in the castle: her lover. Her designs began innocently enough. In June 1489, Caterina had offered Tommaso Feo her sister Bianca in marriage. Not only would the marriage forge a stronger link with Caterina, but it would probably cause Feo to give up his position, since a fortress keeper could never leave his castle. Most women would not want to live inside what was essentially a prison, so Caterina had presented them with land in the territory of Bosco, assuming that they would move there. But Tommaso stayed. Caterina had to find a less subtle means to dispatch him.

One year later, she renewed her efforts by appointing a permanent castellan to the smaller fortress of Forlimpopoli outside the city. Her choice fell on her stepfather, Gian Pietro Landriani, the husband of Lucrezia, Caterina's mother, who had been in Romagna as part of the Milanese contingent since 1488. When he swore loyalty to her on July 30, no one suspected a master plan was underway.

During the sultry days of August, Caterina purged the fortress of Ravaldino of its keeper using no weapon but womanly wiles. The countess came to the Ravaldino keep on August 30, accompanied by her son Ottaviano and Tommaso Feo's younger brother Giacomo. That warm summer morning, Caterina looked more like a young woman out to enjoy the last days of pleasant weather than a head of state. Conversing amiably, the group enjoyed lunch together in the castle. Caterina, always more interested than her son in military matters, drew Tommaso aside to discuss tactical aspects of the fortress. Tommaso noted that Caterina had planted new gardens, and the countess invited him out to see the results of her handiwork. The castellan hesitated. The garden lay outside the walls of the defensive keep and Tommaso was required to remain within it at all times. Caterina gently assured him that Ottaviano, as well as his own brother, would remain in the keep. He could certainly slip away for a few moments of sunshine. Tommaso, bedazzled by the countess, forgot his wife and his duties as he followed Caterina out of Ravaldino. They strolled in the orchard for a time, laughing and chatting in perfect accord. Caterina was dressed in a sheer linen shift covered with a thin cotton smock; the light material revealed her form as she stood in the sunlight. The scorching midday heat obliged them to seek shade under a fig tree, and the pair savored an impromptu snack of the ripe fruit. After a while, Caterina stood, her golden hair glittering, and offered her arm to the castellan, asking if he would escort her to her rooms. Captivated, Tommaso started to walk toward the little palace on the grounds, where Caterina lived. But as he drew closer to this building, Tommaso stopped dead, the memory of his duty jerking him back to reality. He pulled away, trying to think of how to take his leave of the fascinating woman standing before him. Caterina, unperturbed, feigned not to notice his crisis of conscience and continued to walk toward her rooms, stopping, turning, or laughing as her hand rested lightly on his arm. Slowly, the castellan's last reserves crumbled and he stepped over the threshold into Caterina's residence. Through another door he glimpsed Caterina disappearing into the bedroom. Eager to claim his prize, he started forward, but heavy hands pulled him back as a voice said, "You are prisoner of the countess. You will not be harmed." Tommaso, duped, handed over his sword. A moment ago, he had been anticipating Caterina's warm embrace; now cold iron shackles encircled his arms. The terrified castellan bolted, pushing through the guards and running across the grounds to the moat. He swam across but found the gates locked. In a few moments, Tommaso was recaptured by Caterina's captain of the gate. Feo, the loyal defender and foolish brother-in-law, went to inhabit the prison cells he had so jealously guarded. Caterina was quick to alert her more troublesome neighbors that the castle was now back under her complete control. Writing to the duke of Ferrara, she explained that she could "no longer trust Tommaso Feo," and, in view of "his indecent behavior," she had no choice but to dismiss him. Her letter also served to establish her as a figure of moral rectitude after the scandalous rumors regarding Antonio Ordelaffi.[7]

The dismissal of Feo was more of a farce than a serious security issue. No one in Imola or Forlì had fallen for the accusation of indecency. In fact, contemporaries hinted that Caterina had taken the fortress from one Feo to give it to another. Giacomo, Tommaso's twenty-year-old brother, was strikingly handsome and athletic, although he had little education and fewer manners. He had lived in the Riario household as one of Girolamo's stable grooms, a mere boy of fifteen when he first laid eyes on Caterina. His blatant adoration for her likely exhilarated her after years of being chained to a husband who barely appreciated her. She had spent decades keeping her emotions in check; her first great passion had a strong effect.

Power intoxicated Caterina. She had regained two of her fortresses. Now she would recapture the third. Giovanni de' Gerardi, the castellan of Imola, wanted money. Caterina promised him four thousand ducats in cash and silver, almost the entire sum he had demanded, to be deposited with his brother in nearby Modena. On December 16, de' Gerardi left the castle, laden with the treasures he had accumulated from the Riario coffers. He rode at such a hard gallop that the Imolesi wondered what "had frightened him so much." Perhaps he was worried that he might suffer the fate of Caterina's other castellans and be imprisoned or murdered, or maybe he was concerned about getting to his promised payment as soon as possible. The castellan survived the trip out of Imola, but when he arrived in Modena he found only a useless letter of credit. In vain, de' Gerardi complained to the duke of Milan of his mistreatment. Caterina had outfoxed him as well. Her castles free, Caterina now installed castellans who were loyal only to her. Her stepfather, Gian Pietro Landriani, was transferred from Forlimpopoli to Imola while the vacated fortress was taken over by Caterina's stepbrother Pietro Landriani. Her most precious fortress—her own home of Ravaldino—was in the hands of her lover, Giacomo Feo.

In 1491 began the happiest period of Caterina's life thus far. She was in command of her dominions, her children were thriving, and she had discovered an outlet for her passion. As always, money was tight. Her letters to her uncle in Milan usually requested some kind of financial support to pay her soldiers or buy grain after a poor harvest. She even had to endure the humiliation of declining a request to lend her tapestries and silver to the duke of Ferrara for his son's wedding, because she had long since pawned them. But despite financial struggles, Caterina's infatuation kept her spirits high. On January 23, 1491, a delegation from Milan arrived at the fortress to pay their respects to the new castellan. In the high tower of the castle facing the city of Forlì, Giacomo and Caterina, the Milanese ambassador, the Forlivese nobleman Luffo Numai, and a few gentlemen gathered for a special ceremony. To Caterina's intense pride and joy, Giacomo Feo was knighted; the Milanese ambassador fastened a golden spur around his ankle and a sword at his waist. Luffo Numai in turn hung a gold chain of authority around his neck. That Sunday morning, Forlì witnessed the transmogrification of Giacomo Feo from the stable boy at everyone's beck and call to "Sir Giacomo."

Caterina's romance blossomed behind the high walls of Ravaldino. As castellan, Giacomo Feo could not leave the keep, so they spent their days within the fortress and in the expansive grounds Caterina had been cultivating. As a diversion from diplomatic letters and audiences, Caterina enjoyed horticulture. During her time at the courts of Milan and Rome, she had encountered not only kings and artists, but also doctors, botanists, and alchemists. She had loved learning about the properties of plants and how to mix different herbal compounds. Caterina dedicated many hours to her "experiments," as she called them, growing more adept at distilling, sun drying, and concocting every day.[8] Her gardens included orchards full of sweet fruit that she sent as gifts to allies and friends, and her herb garden contained not only fragrant plants for cooking but also ingredients for medicinal potions and beauty emulsions. Although still young herself, Caterina took pains to keep the attention of her youthful lover. She prepared a special blend of saffron, cinnabar, and sulfur, with which she rinsed her hair and then brushed it dry for long hours in the sun, to keep her tresses shining.

The thrill of secrecy electrified Caterina's new romance. Despite his knighthood, Giacomo Feo was a nullity in the Italian political landscape. He brought no military allegiance and no wealth of land; all he had to offer Caterina was his heart. But as regent for her son Ottaviano, she had to be careful. If Caterina happened to die while her Riario children were still underage, it would be messy and costly to dislodge Feo from the lordship of Forlì. The furtive nature of Caterina's relationship culminated in a secret marriage, which would be revealed only on Caterina's deathbed.[9]

Caterina's proud letters recounting the knighthood conferred on Giacomo aroused the suspicions of her uncle Ludovico the Moor, and soon enough he installed a spy in her court. Florence also took an avid interest, sending a representative to evaluate potential weaknesses in Forlì because of Caterina's new attachment. In public, at least at first, Caterina and Giacomo behaved normally, trying not to arouse suspicion. But the Forlivesi knew better. Caterina's subjects prudently held their tongues even when they noticed that Caterina no longer traveled to Imola for the hot summer months, but rather stayed in Forlì to be near Feo, who was obliged to remain in Ravaldino.

This decision to stay near her beloved nearly had disastrous consequences for her children. Summer migration to better-ventilated areas spared delicate constitutions the effects of the "bad air" of an urban center. In the summer of 1491 Ottaviano and Cesare fell ill with tertian fever. In the hot weather mosquitoes infested the stagnant moat around Ravaldino, which only aggravated their discomfort. Caterina wrenched herself away from Feo to accompany her children to the better climate of their country house in Imola. Along the way Caterina herself succumbed to fever. Giacomo, lovelorn and impetuous, quit his post as castellan, handing over the castle to his uncle Cesare Feo, and raced to Imola to be by Caterina's side. There was no doubt in anyone's mind now. Caterina and Giacomo were lovers.

Most of her subjects looked upon the affair with an indulgent eye. Many understood that little love had existed between Count Girolamo and Caterina. They had been allies in their political interests, she had borne him six children, but Girolamo had never showered her with affection. They may have thought that the countess deserved a little passion in her life and hoped that the affair would blow over soon.

In some ways the early stages of the affair were a boon to Forlì. Caterina, desiring more time with her beloved, reconvened the Council of Forty, which had been suspended since Girolamo's murder. She also reconstituted the Council of the Elders. It seemed that the countess was ready to relinquish some of her power. Furthermore, she recognized that the presence of peacekeeping soldiers posed an undue burden on the people. Caterina abolished the tax that paid for their lodging and proposed instead the construction of a military quarter outside the walls to remove the discomfiting presence of the military. To pay for the project, she put a tax on grain, but offered those who couldn't afford the monetary contribution the possibility of carrying lumber or digging foundations in lieu of the fees. In the eyes of the Forlivesi, love had apparently softened the countess.

But a small group of her subjects remained concerned. Caterina and Giacomo's open cohabitation in Imola hinted at a secret marriage, a serious threat to political stability. They saw no good in the groom turned knight. Jealousy grew into deep hostility, and by September plans were afoot to murder the countess and her lover.

Caterina habitually made the rounds of her fortresses both major and minor, ensuring that they were well maintained and that the castellans remained loyal. While in Imola, Caterina and Giacomo planned to travel to nearby Tossignano to pay a visit to one of their minor fortresses. But shortly before their departure, two Imolesi informed Caterina that a trap awaited her at the castle; she and Giacomo would both be killed as soon as they were inside. Caterina sent soldiers in her stead and within hours the culprits were apprehended.

Descending to the interrogation cells, Caterina was surprised by the identity of her would-be assassins. Besides her own castellan of Tossignano, they were Marcantonio and Teseo Tartagni, whose family Caterina had honored with the right to work her land only one year earlier, and Domenico Viani, whose side Caterina had taken in the resulting conflict with the Mercati family. Enea Viani, the head of the family, had escaped and found refuge with the duke of Ferrara. These people only had reason to be grateful to her, for she had made them prosperous and exiled their enemies. What could have spurred them to turn against her?

The answers were blunt and unanimous. They were protecting the rights of Ottaviano. Worried that Caterina's favoritism was undermining the rightful claim of the Riario heir, they had intended to take her prisoner, kill Feo, and, as had been done in Faenza, appoint a regency of leading citizens.

Caterina sentenced the four ringleaders to death but commuted the sentence to imprisonment under one of the towers of the Ravaldino fortress. Buried under the pillar of Caterina's defenses, the conspirators saw their sons brought to the castle as hostages to prevent any further uprising by the network of family clans that dominated Imola. Their houses were razed and their wives, the daughters of a powerful Florentine, Cosimo Pallavicini, were exiled from Imola, with their dowries deposited in Caterina's bank vaults.

Caterina had subdued the conspiracy but could not bear it that Enea Viani had escaped unscathed. That he had been given refuge by the duke of Ferrara was insult upon injury. Relations between Ercole of Ferrara and Caterina had improved little since the death of Girolamo. Although the duke and the countess regularly exchanged gifts at the beginning of Lent, Ercole sending salted eels for the long meatless weeks and Caterina offering candied chestnuts and the first fruits of the Romagnol orchards, most of their correspondence was fraught with hostility. Caterina battled endlessly for restitution from the duke. Border skirmishes destroyed her property and bandits murdered her citizens in the Ferrara woods, but the aloof Ercole rarely responded to her complaints.

Upon discovering that her would-be assassin was safely ensconced in Ferrara, she called a halt to the favors and courtesies customary between courts, and bombarded the city with letters demanding the immediate expulsion of Viani. Although Ercole never responded directly, in the early months of 1492 Viani was finally captured and brought to Forlì, where he joined his fellow conspirators in prison. The dukes of Milan and Ferrara interceded on behalf of the Imolese noble, but to no avail.

The Tossignano conspiracy was a portent of graver things to come, but Caterina remained blind to the problems caused by Giacomo's presence. To complicate matters, she needed to conceal that she was pregnant with his child. Her secluded court life within the castle walls went a long way to veil her expanding silhouette from curious eyes, and large, loose robes did the rest. In the summer of 1492, Caterina disappeared from court for several weeks with a bout of fever. She saw no one except her most immediate circle but continued to send correspondence and conduct business at a brisk rate from her bed. By the time the ambassador to the duke of Milan noticed Caterina's absence, she had already been confined to her bed for eight days, and it was several more weeks until Caterina was up and about again. Most likely this disappearance was connected to the birth of Giacomo and Caterina's son, Bernardino, who would join the Riario children in the castle as Giacomo's illegitimate offspring from an unknown mother. It was probably in this period that Caterina and Feo married in secret to ensure the child's eventual rights, although the actual date of their marriage remains unknown. Everyone took the new addition in stride, especially Cobelli, who knew well the dangers of exposing the countess's indiscretions. One elderly artisan, a certain Sante di Sole, foolishly repeated the rumor, in public, that Caterina was Bernardino's mother. His punishment was exemplary. The irate countess assailed the poor man. "What is this I hear, that you have been running off at the mouth about me?" she demanded angrily. "Have you been saying that Sir Giacomo's son is mine?"[10] The unfortunate man stammered and protested but, implacable, Caterina ordered the poor man beaten so harshly that he died from his injuries. Caterina, certain that she could coerce her people into keeping her secrets, ordered several other similar beatings. In public, Caterina's maternity of Bernardino remained uncertain until her deathbed, when she finally admitted to the child by her clandestine marriage with Feo and made provisions for him in her will.

In 1493, the Florentine ambassador Puccio Pucci arrived in Romagna and paid a visit to Caterina at her home inside Ravaldino. Although he would officially reside in Faenza, a Florentine ally, his real task was to keep an eye on the countess. On May 21 he arrived for an audience with Caterina and left posterity a picturesque description of her domestic life. Entering the throne room, he found Giacomo perched on a windowsill and wearing a fitted crimson silk jacket. His light brown hair fell in soft curls around his face and hung like tendrils over the collar. The sunlight illuminating him from behind bathed him in golden light and sparkled on the brocade mantle thrown carelessly over his shoulders. Caterina sat by him on a throne decorated with broad wings. Dressed in white damask silk, she looked like an angel, the porcelain glow of her face set off by the black scarf around her neck. "They seemed alone in the world,"[11] wrote the startled ambassador, embarrassed by his intrusion upon such an intimate moment. Amid murmurs and caresses, the countess and her beloved Giacomo watched two small children playing. One was the countess's and one was Feo's. Caterina's toddler Sforzino cavorted with their son Bernardino until Sforzino fell and cut his leg and head and was carried away by Lazarus, a Jewish doctor of Caterina's household. The two parents hovered anxiously, no longer concerned about witnesses to their union.

Cobelli was both amazed and disappointed by Caterina's subjugation to Feo. Blaming it on the stars, he observed that "Venus and Mars dominate the skies." The weary chronicler rued the strange transformation of "our countess who we knew as virtuous, wise, and prudent."[12]

14

BLINDED BY LOVE

S CATERINA CONTINUED her affair with Giacomo Feo, the political landscape in Italy was altering dramatically and dangerously. The distractions of her private life would blind her to its implications for her state.

The year 1492 had opened a new era for Italy, as well as for the Western world. In April Lorenzo de' Medici died and was mourned almost universally. Eulogized as "Italy's peacekeeper," Lorenzo the Magnificent was recognized as one of the greatest figures of the Renaissance. Caterina wrote letters of condolence and sincerely grieved for the passing of a man she had admired since she was a child. Yet it seemed that Lorenzo passed little of his "magnificence" on to his heirs. Lorenzo's son, twenty-one-year-old Piero, known as "the Unlucky," was no substitute for his father. Lorenzo had excelled through his bravery, brilliance, and benevolence; Piero embodied mediocrity. He favored recreation over statecraft and preferred hauteur to humility. The golden age of the Medicis was over. Piero's arrogance as well as his lack of interest in affairs of state soon led to widespread discontent among the Florentines. Moreover, the prominent scions of the cadet branch of the family, Giovanni and Lorenzo di Pierfrancesco de' Medici, who had always resented their status as the "lesser Medicis"—less honored, less wealthy, and less powerful—embarked on a subversive campaign to discredit Piero. Florence, once a bastion of stability in Renaissance politics, was developing fissures in its very foundations.

Caterina was focused so intently on her corner of Romagna that she was slow to appreciate the transformative events taking place in Europe. For Spain, 1492 had been a year of triumph. After over a decade of war, the sovereigns Ferdinand and Isabella had retaken Granada, the last Moorish stronghold on the Iberian Peninsula, which had been in Muslim hands for 250 years. The newfound strength of victorious Spain introduced an important new player in the European balance of power. In the same year Pope Innocent VIII Cybo died, which brought a sigh of relief for Caterina, as Innocent had been hostile to the Riario family even as a cardinal. His successor, the Spanish cardinal Roderigo Borgia, was close to Isabella and Ferdinand and seemed, at first, like a godsend to the Riario family. Cardinal Borgia had stood as godfather to Ottaviano and had received Caterina's ambassadors warmly, promising to be like a "father to Ottaviano" while offering assurance that Caterina could "count on him for anything." There was every reason to hope for great things for Forlì during the pontificate of Alexander VI Borgia. Amid the jubilation for a freed Spain and a new pontiff, one momentous undertaking of 1492 passed relatively unnoticed. Isabella and Ferdinand outfitted a small group of ships to search for a safer trade route to the Indies, entrusting them to one Christopher Columbus from Genoa.

In France, 1492 saw twenty-two-year-old King Charles VIII take command of his throne from his sister, Anne of Beaujeu, who had been serving as regent. Described by the Italians as "hunchbacked and hideously ugly," King Charles was rumored to be barely literate, but he had been raised on tales of war and glory. Any lingering hostilities from the Hundred Years' War finally evaporated in November 1492, when Charles VIII and Henry VII Tudor of England signed the Treaty of Étaples, concluding an extended conflict between the two nations. Furthermore, Charles's marriage to Anne of Brittany had united the entire territory of France under one ruler. Like Spain, France was a unified, powerful country in 1492, ready to flex its muscles. With veteran troops at his command, Charles dreamed of an opportunity to show his strength. He cast his gaze across the Alps toward Italy.

Caterina's uncle Ludovico the Moor proved to be the catalyst for the unhappy encroachment of foreign armies on Italian soil. Ludovico, still only the power behind the throne, had long looked to consolidate his authority. In 1489 Caterina's brother Gian Galeazzo Sforza, now twenty years old and the rightful duke of Milan, had married Isabella of Aragon, the daughter of Alfonso, duke of Calabria, and the granddaughter of King Ferrante of Naples. After years of subjugation to his mother, Bona of Savoy, and then Ludovico the Moor, Gian Galeazzo seemed content to leave governing to his uncle and devoted himself instead to hunting, fishing, and other pleasant pastimes. His new bride was not of the same mind. Raised at one of the most powerful and ruthless courts of Italy, Isabella had no intention of taking second place to a usurper. When Ludovico married Beatrice d'Este two years later, sparks began to fly in earnest. Although the two weddings were social and political events of great importance in northern Italy, Caterina attended neither. As a dutiful niece and sister, she sent huge delegations bearing lavish gifts, but in 1489 she was still weathering the aftermath of Girolamo's murder. In 1491, however, she was probably too attached to Feo to be parted from him. That year a third wedding cemented the series of alliances that would ultimately affect Caterina's realm. The heir to the Duchy of Ferrara, Alfonso d'Este, on January 30, 1491, wed Caterina's sister Anna Sforza, reinforcing the bond between Ferrara and Milan.

Isabella had borne a son, Francesco, to Gian Galeazzo, the heir to the throne of Milan. Although her husband was of an age to rule and they had produced a legitimate heir, Isabella nonetheless was relegated to living in Beatrice's shadow. Leonardo da Vinci arranged pageants and decorations in Beatrice's honor, not Isabella's. In 1492 Beatrice traveled to Venice in the glamorous role of ducal ambassador, while the true duchess was confined to the park at Pavia as keeper of a witless husband. It was too much for the pride of the Aragon family. Isabella wrote repeatedly to her father, Duke Alfonso of Calabria, complaining about these insults and referring to herself as "the most unhappily married woman in the world." Outraged, the hot-tempered Alfonso wanted to attack Milan immediately, but his father, King Ferrante of Naples, wiser and more politically astute, counseled patience, warning that if Milan called France to its aid, everyone would lose.

In January 1494, events came to a head. King Ferrante of Naples died, succeeded by his son Alfonso II, Isabella's father, who immediately took a threatening stance toward Milan. The Neapolitan monarchy had strong ties to Spain and Alfonso knew he could request support from Queen Isabella and King Ferdinand if he should need it.

Naples was separated from Milan by three hundred miles and three city-states. As a Spaniard, Pope Alexander was sympathetic to Alfonso and would allow the Neapolitan army passage through papal territory to Tuscany. Had Piero de' Medici maintained his father's alliance with Milan, Duke Alfonso's soldiers would have been halted on those borders. Because of his agreement with the duke of Milan, Lorenzo the Magnificent would never have countenanced a Neapolitan army passing through his lands, and without safe conduct through Florence, the Neapolitan troops would have to fight half the way to Milan. But Lorenzo's craven scion foolishly decided to throw his lot in with Naples, giving the troops access almost to the gates of Milan. The last stretch of land they would need to cover would be Romagna, including Forlì.

Ludovico, now very worried, sought help from beyond the Alps, inviting King Charles VIII into Italy. Milanese agents pressed the French court, reminding Charles that he had an ancient claim to Naples through his grandmother, Marie of Anjou. Cardinal Giuliano della Rovere joined the court as papal legate to France, bearing another reason for Charles to descend into Italy. By this time the criminal excesses of Pope Alexander, especially in favor of his son Cesare Borgia, were crying out for someone to depose the unfit pontiff. The French king was convinced, and he traveled over the Alps and entered Asti in September 1494.

"The snake has its tail in Italy," warned a Florentine ambassador, "and the Italians are pulling it with all their might." Charles VIII was feted in Milan but also made a short trip to Pavia to visit Gian Galeazzo. There, Isabella of Aragon threw herself at the French king's feet, imploring Charles to reconsider the attack on her family, but to no avail. Charles continued his advance. By the time the king reached Piacenza, he learned that Gian Galeazzo had succumbed to a stomach ailment and died. A rumor that the death was caused by poisoning tore through Italy and suspicion fell on Ludovico the Moor. This story gained momentum when Caterina's uncle arrested Isabella and separated the infant Francesco from his mother. Scandals aside, Ludovico succeeded in obtaining what he had long desired: he was proclaimed duke of Milan within the year. Caterina knew enough to conceal any distress she felt about the circumstances of her brother's death.

In 1494, Caterina found herself in an unenviable position. The crossing point for the northern- and southern-bound armies would be Romagna. Forlì was still, technically, under papal control; Caterina's authority as regent stemmed from papal decree, and therefore Caterina was legally bound and loyal to the pope. A Neapolitan ambassador had promptly arrived in Forlì to inform her that the pope was supporting the king of Naples. At the same time, letters poured in from Milan, reminding Caterina of her great debt to Milan and to her own family, who had returned her state to her. In the first weeks of the negotiations, Caterina and Feo, who was privy to every aspect of Caterina's governance, together with Giovanni Bentivoglio of Bologna, tried to maintain a neutral stance to avoid being crushed between these two colliding titans.

Troops were gathering in Bologna for the assault, bringing with them sophisticated artillery. Archers and cavalry cantered down the Via Emilia toward Cesena, neighbor to Forlì, to await the arrival of the king. They were remarkably well behaved—some farmers compared their passage to that of a group of friars—and much to the relief of the terrified denizens of Romagna, they left women, fields, and homes in peace. Charles VIII had brought a new weapon to the field, never before seen in feudal Europe: a standing army. Almost twenty thousand men, in the ranks of infantry, artillery, and cavalry, were perpetually on call and ready for battle; in the past, soldiers were levied from farms or fiefs as the occasion demanded. The expense of maintaining so many men in a foreign country was overwhelming. Charles needed to come, see, and conquer with lightning speed.

Distressed by Caterina's reluctance to assist Naples, Pope Alexander dispatched Cardinal Raffaello Riario to persuade her. Cardinal Riario arrived in Forlimpopoli, where he met a resolutely neutral countess. To his surprise and displeasure, all of his meetings with Caterina took place under the intrusive gaze of Giacomo Feo, who distrusted all of Caterina's family, whether Riario or Sforza. The former stable boy now advised Caterina on all matters of state and in mid-September Giacomo became general in chief and vice lord of her dominions. Caterina had fallen under the shadow of her new husband. On the stormy sea of Italian politics, it was Giacomo Feo who was now navigating amid kings, dukes, and diplomats. He closed the town's gates, allowing no military contingent, not even close friends of the Sforza family, to enter its walls. Requests to house Sforza soldiers were first ignored and eventually refused. Even Caterina would not intervene against Feo's dictums. By now, Feo controlled the fortress of Ravaldino through his uncle the castellan; he also handled all the city revenues. He paid the soldiers and therefore had their loyalty.

Feo's motivation for barring the city gates probably had more to do with self-preservation than international diplomacy. Mingled among the warring armies were several influential people who longed for his demise. Reports from both the ducal court of Milan and the papal court in Rome identified Feo as the biggest impediment to diplomatic relations with Caterina. In a fracas among soldiers, it would be easy to claim that Giacomo had fallen as a casualty of war. Instead of the velvet and brocade finery he usually donned, nowadays Feo prudently wore a metal breastplate both day and night. But Caterina and Feo also demonstrated sincere concern for their citizens. Edicts streamed out of Ravaldino, ordering farmers who lived in the countryside to move within the city walls for protection from the ever more numerous Neapolitan and French soldiers converging on their lands. The couple also saw to reinforcing the fortresses of Imola, Tossignano, and Bubano with toughened veterans.

The two warring states intensified their courtship of Caterina's Forlì. Economic concerns played no small part. Caterina had lamented long and often to Ludovico that her lands suffered from her lack of income. Bologna was loyal to Milan and its readiness to send soldiers and welcome troops was repaid with a yearly stipend, or *condotta*. Feo and Caterina also insisted on compensation for their fealty. Alexander VI, who owed his papacy to a series of well-placed bribes, understood the pathway to Forlì's loyalty. He issued a sixteen-thousand-ducat *condotta* to Caterina in return for support against Milan and the French. As an added bonus, the fief of San Mauro, which had been occupied by the Zampeschi family since 1484, was finally returned to the Riario dominions. Under Feo's influence, Caterina chose the *condotta* over kin and sided with Naples.

The conditions of Caterina's alliance included the promise that Naples would provide men and weapons to protect her territories from the inevitable French reprisals. Forlì kept its side of the bargain, remaining loyal to its new ally, much to the consternation of Ludovico of Milan. Caterina also kept her allies abreast of the movement of the enemy troops, sending out scouts and spies to report on French activities. The night of September 4, she even ordered the bakers of Forlì to stay up all night and prepare bread to feed the Neapolitan soldiers.[1] Of course, this being Italy, her alliance with Naples didn't impede her from attempting to obtain a *condotta* for her son Ottaviano from the French army of Charles VIII.

On October 20, two thousand French and Milanese soldiers approached the gate of Caterina's fortress of Mordano near Imola, calling to the castellan to surrender. Caterina's handpicked guardian staunchly refused, declaring his loyalty to Ottaviano even as the sun glinted off the latest high-powered cannons trained on the castle walls. The captain of the Milanese troops tried to convince him that it would be better for the town to surrender now, to his fellow Italians, than to wait for the French, because they "are mad dogs and will put everyone to the sword." Caterina's soldiers responded in a single voice: "Bring your French! You'll find us ready for them! We are ready to die for the countess and Ottaviano!"[2]

And the French did come. The defense of Mordano did Caterina proud. Although no aid was forthcoming from Caterina's allies, the two hundred defenders held out from 9 A.M. until the late afternoon. When the cannons ripped away the castle walls, the guards stepped into the breaches and fought hand to hand. Attempts to scale the wall were valiantly resisted and the wounded refused treatment so as to remain in the front lines. The heroic band of men fought until a cannonball broke the drawbridge chain and the French were able to swarm the castle and village. They razed every structure there, leaving only the city hall. The surviving soldiers were drawn and quartered. The more fortunate citizens ran into the arms of the Milanese soldiers in surrender, hoping to be spared and detained in prison camps. The women of the city hid in the church, but the French soldiers entered and carried them away. Cobelli refused to discuss what happened to them afterward, so as not to "further dishonor them."[3]

The savagery of the French at Mordano jolted Caterina from her stupor. The moment the alert arrived that it was under siege she wrote to her ally the duke of Calabria, asking him for support. He didn't respond. Caterina summoned her subjects and explained that after the useless alliances with Naples, Florence, and the papacy, which were meant to ensure the protection of her lands and people, she would put the city under the wing of Ludovico and the French. The Neapolitans and Florentines had broken the most important stipulation of their treaty, to help protect tiny Forlì against the enormous French army. "There was no reason to treat me this way," wrote Caterina to Piero de' Medici five days after the sack of Mordano. "I have kept [our treaty] and done more than I was obliged to."[4] Florence realized immediately the danger of Caterina's defection; now the French troops would have a foot on their doorstep. The Florentine ambassador Bernardo Bibbiena tried to persuade Piero de' Medici to mollify Caterina, but his pleas fell on deaf ears. Caterina personally notified the duke of Calabria of her change of heart and soon she was welcomed into the bosom of the Milanese league.

Caterina's change of allegiance turned the tide of battle. The duke of Calabria started to beat a hasty retreat down the peninsula, with Charles's army in hot pursuit. The French king, however, tarried awhile in Tuscany, laying waste to the border towns. Piero the Unlucky, hoping to find the easiest remedy for his mistaken alliance, met with the French king and offered a partial surrender: the king would be given the seaport Pisa and several fortresses, but the city of Florence would remain untouched. Piero returned on November 8, proud of his handiwork, but after hearing of the gallant defense of Mordano, the Florentines were ashamed to have capitulated so easily. Combined with the rancor sown by the Medici brothers Giovanni and Lorenzo di Pierfrancesco, the cowardly submission of the Florentine leader moved the city council to issue a decree of banishment the next day. Piero and his brother Giovanni (the future Pope Leo X) were driven from the city.

Charles VIII obtained Tuscany without a fight and with his lance symbolically lowered he rode through Florence on his way to Naples. On November 23, Forlì and Imola saw the last of the French troops disappear along the Via Emilia. The enormous expedition worked its way down the Italian peninsula with little or no resistance. At Naples, the Battle of Fornovo culminated in Charles's coronation as king of Naples, but the empty title was overturned the moment Charles turned to head north again. Caterina, like most Italians, thought that the arrival of Charles had been an unfortunate hiccup in the history of Italian politics. But opening the door to the French would have dangerous consequences. France could lay sovereign claim to practically every state in Italy. The "eldest daughter of the church," France had been a Christian nation since the reign of King Clovis in the fifth century. After a millennium of marriages and alliances, most ruling families were tinged with a little French blood. France had enjoyed this taste of Italy and soon would be back for more.

By the time King Charles left, it was clear to every state on the Italian peninsula that Caterina's involvement with Giacomo Feo made her a liability. Concluding that she was a puppet in the hands of Feo, who was tied to no political interest but his own, the Florentines, the papacy, and the Milanesi believed that Caterina was becoming a threat to political stability as well as to her own children. The Florentine ambassador Puccio Pucci issued a dire warning that would prove prescient: "The countess will bury her children, her allies, and all her belongings, she will sell her soul to the devil, she will give her state to the Turk, before she gives up Giacomo Feo!"[5]

The only way out of this situation, the prophetic Florentine foresaw, was through death. Ottaviano was coming of age. Feo would have to have Girolamo's heir murdered before he could claim the rule of Imola and Forlì, or Ottaviano would have to kill Feo to claim his birthright.

In 1495 Ottaviano turned sixteen, finally old enough take over his dominions. Forlì and Imola crackled with tension. Who would win this undeclared tug-of-war? How would Caterina choose between her son and her lover? Antonio Ordelaffi, quick to smell a weakness, tried to take advantage of the situation by inciting the Orcioli and Marcobelli families to revolt, but the plot was crushed before it could hatch. Once again Feo shut down the city of Forlì. No one was allowed in or out without his approval.

The first eruption of open hostility came during an argument between Giacomo and Ottaviano. The teenage boy, furious at the smug

Giacomo, usurper of his mother and his lands, gave vent to a tirade. Giacomo halted his venomous accusations with a resounding slap. Caterina sat by silently, torn between her lover and her son.

Shocked, Caterina's own retainers decided to take matters into their own hands. Giovanni Antonio Ghetti, who had helped liberate Ravaldino from Tommaso Feo so that Giacomo could take his place, took the lead in this plot. His wife, Rosa, was Caterina's favorite lady in waiting, and together this couple knew, more than anyone else, how far Caterina had regressed under the influence of Giacomo. They hardly recognized her as the confident woman they had once admired. Ghetti's relative Domenico joined in, along with two priests, one being the unscrupulous Antonio Pavagliotta, who needed money to support his mistress and three children. The other cleric, Domenico da Bagnacavallo, was looking to curry a little favor with the powerful Cardinal Riario, who certainly would not object to the deed the plotters planned to carry out. They rounded out the crew with one of Ghetti's servants, who was particularly skilled with a knife.

On August 27, 1495, Caterina and Giacomo had gone for a picnic in the woods outside Forlì, along with her oldest children, Ottaviano, Cesare, and Bianca. In a rare moment of domestic peace, the whole group was singing merrily together in celebration of a successful day's hunt. Cheeks flushed from the activities, eyelids heavy from the abundant lunch, the family traveled in a pleasant little cavalcade along the road. Caterina sat in a carriage with Bianca, surrounded by brightly clad servants carrying the spoils of the chase, while Giacomo, Cesare, and Ottaviano, on horseback, brought up the rear, together with the usual bodyguards.

They crossed the bridge by the Schiavonia gate of Forlì. As Caterina's cart passed through the gate, Ghetti and his followers stepped out of their hiding places, cutting Giacomo off from the rest of the group. "What brings you here, Gian Antonio?" asked Feo in good humor. "Are you well?"

Ghetti's accomplices casually took the reins of Feo's horse and held them fast. "I'm quite well," responded Ghetti, smiling as his servant came up behind Giacomo and stabbed him in the back.

Feo fell from his horse, into the arms of his killers, able to gasp only "Oh God! Oh my lady! I am dead!"[6] before falling to the ground amid a hail of blows.

Caterina's Sforza reflexes responded instantly. In a flash, she leapt out of the carriage and onto the nearest horse and galloped to the safety of Ravaldino. Ottaviano and Cesare had already raced to the house of Paolo Denti, a local nobleman, while Feo's own bodyguards had scattered at the first sign of trouble. Glancing over her shoulder, Caterina searched through her tears for a glimpse of her beloved. The horrific vision of Feo's mangled body falling lifeless into a ditch was burned into her mind.

15

AVENGING FURY

IN CANTO XXVII of Dante's *Inferno*, as the Florentine poet wends his way through the darkest circles of the damned, one of the suffering souls halts him. From his prison of flames, Guido di Montefeltro, a celebrated *condottiere* who gave many years of service to Forlì, begs to know if his beloved town is at peace or at war.

"That Romagna of yours," Dante sadly replies, "is not and never was without war in the heart of its tyrants."[1] Between the Guelph and Ghibelline contests and power-hungry tyrants ruling its towns, Romagna had rarely known peace and stability since the distant days of the Roman Empire.

In 1495, the furious, grief-stricken Caterina Sforza added her own episode to Forlì's violent history. After the death of young Giacomo Feo, the countess unleashed a torrent of reprisals. The assassin, Giovanni Antonio Ghetti, was the first to pay. Still stained with Feo's blood, he made a boastful entrance into the main piazza of Forlì, accompanied by his cousin Bernardino and his two clerical accomplices. They summoned the Forlivesi to the square with cries of "Caterina! Caterina!" and "Ottaviano! Ottaviano!" The ubiquitous scribe Cobelli led the rush to the piazza, where Ghetti and his co-conspirators were proclaiming that they had liberated the city from the "traitor

Feo." The killers even went so far as to brag that Caterina and Ottaviano had ordered them to do so. Like Cassius and Brutus, they expected to be hailed as liberators for saving the people from tyranny.
Or perhaps they were relying on a desperate gambit: when Caterina
saw her people rejoicing in Feo's death, she would finally realize how
much hostility her lover had engendered over the years and would
find it in herself to treat his assassins with clemency. It was a grave
miscalculation.

Caterina's chief of police came out to investigate the ruckus, and
upon seeing the bloody swords and hearing the braggarts' cries, he
hastened to report to Ravaldino. Moments later, he returned, accompanied by a contingent of soldiers. They seized Ghetti by the shoulders, in the same fashion that Ghetti himself had arrested Tommaso
Feo four years ago in Ravaldino. And just as Tommaso did, Ghetti
struggled free and tried to escape by darting through the crowds.
The other assassins scattered; sympathetic townspeople helped Antonio Pavagliotta and several others to scale the city walls, while Domenico da Bagnacavallo found refuge at his cousin's house by hiding
in a dowry chest.

The police chief sealed Ghetti's fate with one sentence: "One hundred ducats to whoever brings Ghetti to the countess, dead or alive!"
A militiaman by the name of Bernardo chased Ghetti down to the
cemetery of Santa Croce. There, among the tombs, Bernardo and
his accomplice executed him in the manner by which murderers were
punished in Dante's Hell. They cleaved his head from crown to teeth,
then lopped off his fingers and other extremities, scattering them
among the graves.

But Caterina's thirst for revenge was not sated. Summoning Tommaso Feo from his governorship of Imola, she ordered him to sack
and raze Ghetti's house. Tommaso, who had long borne a grudge
against Ghetti for conspiring to remove him from the fortress of Ravaldino, eagerly obliged. Ghetti's wife, Rosa, Caterina's former confi-
dante and friend, was inside the castle with several of their children.
They all were thrown down one of the deep wells of Ravaldino and
left to die. A few days later, the last Ghetti scion was dispatched; soldiers found the five-year-old son in the care of a friend of the family
and slit his throat.

The chronicler Cobelli, despite his ill-treatment by Caterina over the Antonio Maria Ordelaffi affair, took pains in his account to specify that Caterina did not order the murder of the women and children.[2] The letters flying up and down the Italian peninsula told another story. "She has used maximum cruelty against a priest," wrote the Milanese ambassador Francesco Tranchedini to Duke Ludovico, and "that which seems most detestable, she had women killed, the wives of the two Ghetti brothers, the young sons aged three and nine months and even the nurse. All Romagna is crying to the heavens."[3]

Whether or not Caterina gave the order for the murder of innocents, she never intervened to save Ghetti's wife or children. Nor did she call a halt when her soldiers rounded up every family known to be hostile to Feo and threw them into dungeons, hanged them in the square, or drove them into exile. Tranchedini, writing from Bologna, was not an eyewitness, but he informed the duke that the local people were horrified to hear that "the countess had cruelly punished anyone she got her hands on, as accomplices of the two who killed Feo."[4]

The Ghetti family's horrendous deaths marked the beginning of the darkest moment of Caterina's life. She had lost control of her state, her position, and her dignity through her passion for Feo, but in avenging his death she seemed to take leave of her soul.

On the night of the murder, several members of the confraternity of the Battuti Neri retrieved Giacomo's body from the ditch outside the Schiavonia gate, bringing the tattered carcass to the Church of San Girolamo. Cobelli slipped in to see what had happened to Feo. "What shame! What cruelty!" he lamented in his diary. "Such a beautiful face rent like a split pomegranate!"[5] The fine brocade jacket once tightly fitted to his broad shoulders now hung from the corpse in shreds, soaked in blood.

The following morning, hundreds assembled outside Ravaldino wearing the somber colors of mourning. The drawbridge was lowered and a procession slowly crossed toward the city gate. The vicar of the bishop of Forlì, dressed in funerary robes, walked in front, accompanied by Scipione Riario, Girolamo's natural son, now in his twenties, who lived with the family. Caterina came next, holding the hand of little Bernardino, her three-year-old son by Feo. Her pale face bore the signs of a sleepless night, but her expression was unreadable. She looked at no one and acknowledged nothing except the little boy by her side.

The Sforza-Feo household made an impressive sight, with ambassadors, ladies in waiting, and an honor guard in polished armor wending their way across the moat. Three pages, dressed in mourning livery, rode with the group. The first displayed Feo's sword and golden spur, the second his helmet, and the last his cuirass, denoting Giacomo's knightly status. Dozens of nobles, both local and foreign, joined the cortege as they headed into the city. Others poured into Forlì from neighboring towns, gathering in the market square, where a giant catafalque had been prepared during the night. The towering monument was draped in gold cloth and surrounded by torches. At the appointed time, the canons of the cathedral, the parish priests, and the confraternities encircled the platform, bearing aloft thirty-three crosses as they sang psalms and prayers. The air was heavy with the scent of incense; a slowly cadenced chant set a stately pace for the procession that then wound to the Church of San Girolamo. Count Girolamo Riario, lord of Forlì, had not received such elaborate obsequies.

Feo was temporarily laid to rest in the chapel containing the splendid tomb of the unfortunate Barbara Manfredi, the murdered wife of Pino Ordelaffi. Never to be outdone by the former ruling family, Caterina would soon commission a monument to outshine that of the discarded Ordelaffi bride. Although he was almost universally loathed in life, Giacomo Feo drew hundreds to his funeral, many undoubtedly spurred by the fear that Caterina might take vengeance on them if they did not appear.

But Feo's funeral offered only a moment of respite. Soon the countess continued her campaign of retribution, using all means at her disposal. Caterina rounded up the rest of the conspirators and targeted virtually anyone who had resented Giacomo Feo. The Marcobelli family, the Orcioli family, and the delle Selle family saw their houses torn down, their warehouses sacked, and their relatives thrown into the Ravaldino dungeons. An entire neighborhood of Forlì was sacked and destroyed as Caterina tried to eradicate all those hostile to Feo. In Imola, Tommaso Feo also worked ceaselessly to avenge his brother, filling the jail cells and torture chambers. Caterina dispatched agents to hunt down the remaining fugitives.

Informers soon betrayed the hiding place of Domenico da Bagnacavallo, and a squadron retrieved the terrified priest from his refuge inside his cousin's dowry chest. Brought to Ravaldino, he was tortured by fire until he gave up the names of his accomplices. His "confession" poured salt on Caterina's open wounds. He swore that when Giovanni Antonio Ghetti had recruited the priest, the assassination had been approved not only by Cardinal Raffaello Riario but also by Ottaviano, Caterina's own son.

Now Caterina's public cruelty reached its apex. The offending priest was stripped almost nude in the square and tied by his feet to the back of a horse. The executioner drove the animal through the streets to just outside the city walls, until they reached the spot where Bagnacavallo and his co-conspirators had killed Feo. The grisly cavalcade then turned and dragged the battered priest down alleys, through refuse, and over stones, then back to the piazza. Despite his numerous wounds, the man was still alive. A partisan of Feo sliced open the offender's face: vicious revenge for the disfigurement of Giacomo. While Bagnacavallo whispered prayers of penitence, the soldiers beat and stabbed him to death, then dismembered the corpse.

Two days after Feo's funeral, Caterina finally tackled her thorny domestic situation. Ottaviano and Cesare, afraid of their mother's grief and anger, had sought safety in the house of the Denti family. Paolo Denti, head of the household, was the soldier who had stubbornly refused to surrender the Riario children to Girolamo's murderers seven years earlier. Now he was risking his life for the Riario heirs again. Ottaviano's conspicuous absence from the funeral rendered him guilty in Caterina's eyes. The Forlivesi watched in astonishment as armed guards surrounded the Denti palace, issuing a summons for Ottaviano and his brother to appear before their mother at Ravaldino. The rightful heir to the city—who had stood with a knife at his throat after the death of his father—was now under arrest at his mother's behest. Convinced that Caterina had gone too far, an angry crowd followed Ottaviano and his armed escort back to Ravaldino. As the shouting Forlivesi approached the ramparts, cannon fire drowned their objections. The townspeople left Ottaviano to face his mother alone. No witnesses, except for a few tightlipped family intimates and Scipione Riario, Caterina's stepson, were permitted at the interview between the heir to Forlì and his regent. Accusations flew and recriminations resounded as the family members aired their many grievances. Ottaviano was put under house arrest and confined to the fortress under the watchful eye of his mother. Scipione, who had objected to the violence of Caterina's reprisals, was locked in one of the dungeons, where he served a bitter sentence of eighteen months.

Caterina's behavior toward her own children shocked Italy. Letters and reports, written by eyewitnesses or reporting hearsay, recounted the lurid tales of the countess's escalating vengeance. Antonio Pavagliotta's mistress had been captured and, together with their three children, murdered. The priest himself, betrayed and captured outside Ravenna, had fared little better than his colleagues. He was brought to the square on a market day, scorched over hot coals, and then beheaded. The bodies of the assassins hung outside the walls of the city, a macabre warning to those who would betray the countess. The heads were affixed to the municipal bell tower, where they remained for over a year, until February 17, 1497, "when there was a strong wind." Caterina, who had ordered such gruesome ornaments removed after the execution of the Roffi conspirators, remained in stony silence this time. She also allowed her troops to run rampant through the city. In the past, she had invariably intervened to protect Forlì from the rapacious behavior of soldiers. But because none of the people had helped her beloved Giacomo, she would not help them either.

Caterina was in a private hell. Her vendetta had brought her only disgrace. Her disclosure to the Forlivesi that she and Giacomo had been secretly married (although she didn't claim Bernardino as her son) impressed no one as a reasonable excuse for the slaughter. Cobelli, totaling the number of people targeted for revenge in the wake of Feo's murder, listed thirty-eight dead and many others tortured, exiled, or imprisoned.[6] In the reprisals after the murder of Girolamo, nine had died—a pittance, compared to this bloodbath. Pope Alexander VI, the duke of Milan, and the Signoria of Florence recoiled at what the pope described as the "unheard-of bloodthirstiness committed to satisfy her passions."[7]

Overcome with misery, Caterina chose to live among the dead. She ordered a memorial to her beloved cast in bronze, the most precious sculptural material available. The large, finely chased casket rested on four exquisitely modeled lion's paws. Feo's monument rivaled Barbara Manfredi's tomb as Forlì's finest work of sculpture. But no Forlivesi, pilgrims, or tourists would ever see it. Instead of placing it in a church, Caterina erected her shrine to Feo within the walls of Ravaldino, where she could dwell on the loss of her husband every day.

Giacomo was not denied the honor of a public monument, however. Feo's sudden rise in status and wealth had made him eligible to endow a private family chapel in the Church of San Girolamo. To fresco its walls, Caterina and Giacomo had hired Melozzo da Forlì, the former court painter to Pope Sixtus IV who had decorated the Riario palace in Rome and immortalized Girolamo Riario on the walls of the Vatican library. Melozzo replicated the grandeur of his Roman frescoes in this work, *The Stories of Saint Giacomo*, particularly in the martyrdom scene, where the perspective illusion of the deeply vaulted hall employed the same dramatic rendering of space. The mathematician Luca Pacioli lauded the chapel for its "wondrously perfect proportions." Melozzo had died in 1494, much lamented by all of Forlì, especially by his friend Leone Cobelli, who had looked to the older master as his mentor in painting. Caterina now continued the project, hiring Melozzo's best assistant, Marco Palmezzano, to create *The Miracle of the Hanged Man*, which included several portraits of members of Caterina's family. A striking and youthful Giacomo stands at the center, with Melozzo's perfectly ordered world arrayed around him. Girolamo Riario kneels in sharp profile before the figure of Saint Giacomo, who is resurrecting a hanged man. The expressionless face and turned head seem to emphasize his distance from Caterina's affections. By adding a portrait of her first husband in her lover's chapel, Caterina highlighted Giacomo's loyalty to the Riario clan, reminding viewers that he had faithfully served the count for many years. This image would preserve for posterity Giacomo's identity as a noble retainer of the Riario family, not the countess's gigolo. Caterina kneels behind Girolamo, dressed in pilgrim's garb and shrouded in a heavy widow's veil. She too looks ahead with empty eyes. There, represented amid her deceased husbands, Caterina appears devoid of life, oblivious to young Ottaviano, who bows his head, in a cascade of golden ringlets, toward her, begging for her attention. She seems to ignore even Feo, whose adoring gaze tries to direct her to the miracle of the resurrected man. This portrait captures the devastated Caterina, oblivious to the world around her, looking fixedly toward the afterlife.[8]

The winter of 1496 was one of the coldest on record. Sleet, hail, and freezing winds howled around the stone walls of Ravaldino. Apprehensive Forlivesi wondered what the future held. Many had noted ominous portents, such as stones falling from the skies. Famine had struck in Romagna, pushing the price of grain too high for the poor people of the city to afford.

Those icy months were further darkened by the appearance of a new disease. The mysterious genital rashes and swollen lymph nodes baffled local doctors as they plied the usual salt-dried serpent powder or leek paste used to treat leprosy or canker sores. The inflammations disappeared after a few days, which seemed merciful, for it was not known that this was merely the first phase of the affliction. The spread of syphilis had begun. Named the "French disease" for the soldiers of Charles VIII who had disseminated it, the deadly infection had arrived for the first time in this part of Europe. With the Holy Year in the offing, celebrating the fifteen-hundredth anniversary of Christ's birth, the menacing auguries and the new plague seemed to herald the end of the world.

The fortress ramparts had become Caterina's tomb where she mourned Feo and dwelled on the wreckage of her lands caused by the French invasion and her own rage. The woman who had bravely stormed into plague-stricken areas, fought off assassins and usurpers, and survived the delivery of seven children, was paralyzed by sorrow, shame, and disappointment. In a desperate letter to her uncle, she confided thoughts about drowning herself.[9]

But true to Sforza form, Caterina's first steps toward recovery were taken on a battlefield. During the French invasion, Count Guido of Gaggiolo, known as "Guerra" ("War") had profited from the general distraction to capture the town of Castrocaro from the archbishop of Ravenna and that of Cuseroli from his own brother. In November 1495, a Romagnol league of sorts, comprising soldiers from Faenza, Castrocaro, and Forlì, assembled under the command of Achille Tiberti, lord of Cesena. The small but well-trained force marched south to retake these cities and rid Romagna of the bellicose Count Guido. The expedition was successful: Guerra was killed, the castle of Cuseroli was returned to Caterina's friend and ally, and Caterina was given the fortress town of Castrocaro.

But this Pyrrhic victory was short-lived. The archbishop of Ravenna claimed protection from the Republic of Venice, which had been willing to deal with Guerra but would not tolerate Caterina's possession of the town. The military machine of the Most Serene Republic trained its sights on Caterina's tiny garrison. Terrified at the prospect of conflict with his fickle Venetian allies, the duke of Milan implored Caterina to return the town. Caterina dutifully obeyed her uncle, but the taste of battle had revitalized her spirits.

As the winter wore on, Caterina shifted her focus from her own woes to her subjects. Confronting a famine, caused by both the cold weather and the troops' trampling on the fields, she purchased large quantities of grain to sell cheaply to her people. From February to June, five hundred pounds of flour a day were distributed free of charge to the poor of Forlì. Concerned about protecting the destitute from starvation in the future, Caterina and the archbishop of Forlì subsidized the local confraternities to form the Company of Charity, which would guarantee food to deprived families.

The salt shortage of 1496 was only slightly less serious. The wet winter had kept the salt beds in Cervia from drying out, so they could not be harvested, and without the precious mineral people would be unable to cure meats and preserve other foods. Caterina bought four hundred sacks of salt for transport from the Adriatic coast to Forlì. So precious was this shipment that it traveled under the protection of a military detachment. Arriving in big chunks and full of sand, the salt nevertheless allowed Forlì and Imola to stave off famine for a year.

While dedicating time and energy to repairing her relationship with her subjects, Caterina also began to rebuild her personal world. She started by tearing down the palace where she had lived with Girolamo, leaving no beam standing to remind her of "every memory of that place where she had suffered shame and disrespect."[10] The destruction of the house on the piazza where she had lived among the people coincided with the unexpected illness and death of her own twelve-year-old son, Giovanni Livio. This child, born shortly after her arrival in Forlì, had been the symbol of her new life and her role as the wife of Count Girolamo of Forlì. But during the twelve years since that joyous day, Livio's godfather had murdered Girolamo, the city had turned against her, and now she had alienated her citizens. No longer a Forlivesi or a Riario or a Feo, she was all Sforza.

The remains of her old house were reused for new building proj-

ects, the most important being her new home in the fortress of Ravaldino. As a child in Milan, Caterina had flourished within the
confines of family castles. The Sforzas had excelled in construct-
ing strong castles for security but also for pleasure. The high walls
of Ravaldino protected Caterina from the danger of assassination as
well as the critical eyes of the world. During the course of 1496, Caterina transformed part of the dank Ravaldino into a comfortable and
luxurious living space reminiscent of her childhood home. Within
the square belt of the ramparts, Caterina built a palace nestled by
the *maschio*, or keep. High vaulted ceilings—instead of low coffered
wood—displayed Caterina's taste for modern architecture. As in her
former palace in Rome, there were richly carved columns and exquisitely painted walls, punctuated by decorative reliefs, bearing her
coat of arms. Delicately designed ceramic tiles paved the floors in the
warm yellows and reds typical of Romagna. This became her intimate inner sanctum, known as Il Paradiso. Open loggias embellished
with frescoed vines and garlands looked out over a vast park with orchards that supplied her table with fruits; exotic trees, imported for
their height, formed a shield around Caterina's playground. A large
herb garden encircled the little hut Caterina used for her "experiments," the production of formulas for beauty creams and medicinal
remedies. Outside the castle walls, a large forest offered Caterina and
her family quarry for their favorite sport, hunting. The two-mile cir-
cumference was delineated by thick bushes, which contained ample
boar, stag, and hare. Caterina's Paradise was connected to the main
keep by a covered walkway, where a spiral staircase wound up to her
lookout point on the *maschio*. The military portion of the fortress was
never neglected: the barracks, the squares where she could review the
troops, and the dungeons were all repaired and updated. The domestic renovations had simply transformed the gloomy fortress into a
magnificent castle.[11]

The year 1496 held one more tragedy for Caterina. In May, her
half sister Bianca died in childbirth. Caterina joined Bianca's husband, Tommaso Feo, in Imola to mourn. After the death of her husband, sister, and son in a short time, Caterina turned to her family and set about mending fences with her children. She began with
Ottaviano, thinking to arrange a fitting marriage for her firstborn.
She negotiated an engagement to Isotta Bentivoglio, the daughter

of Giovanni Bentivoglio of Bologna. This marriage would cement family alliances, but in the summer of 1496, Isotta surprised everyone by declaring her intention of taking religious vows and joining a convent. The embarrassment caused by her abrupt rejection of Ottaviano increased Caterina's already considerable doubts about Bentivoglio loyalties. In the wake of Feo's death, numerous rumors implicated Giovanni Bentivoglio (among many others) in the murder. Conspirators in the assassination, thieves, and even one of Caterina's more unscrupulous accountants had found refuge with the Bentivoglios. Caterina perceived the refusal of marriage as a betrayal and it nearly drove her into another vengeful fury. Her rapid-fire letters to her uncle insisted that she had been "atrociously provoked." "I tolerated this [Bentivoglio's offenses] with much patience, yet fury often weakens patience, and furthermore, demonstrating that many wrongs and injuries don't have any effect, often encourages the wicked to do even worse." Caterina closed the letter, however, with the promise to "tend toward forgiveness rather than vendetta."[12] Nonetheless, Caterina had already sought revenge by sending assassins into Bologna to murder one of her bitterest enemies, Giovanni Battista Brocchi. They failed and Caterina sheepishly had to admit to her uncle that she had sent the killers. In her defense she wrote, "I have been gravely wronged, and I still want to get my hands on him, to further thwart those who conspire against me . . . I confess, I did not do a good thing, as you said, but there is no need for Mr. Giovanni [Bentivoglio] to act amazed, as I am made of the same stuff as he."[13] In the end Caterina took a more diplomatic revenge, threatening to offer shelter to the Malvezzi clan, implacable enemies of the Bentivoglios. But the rising tide of hostility was weakening the two former allies.

Having failed to unite Ottaviano with the Bentivoglio family, Caterina decided to arrange for him to gain some military experience. From June to September she bombarded Duke Ludovico of Milan with letters asking him to "get sixteen-year-old Ottaviano's career off to a good start."[14] Ludovico, perhaps sensing that in military matters Ottaviano was more of a Riario than a Sforza, responded with a new marriage proposal. The next candidate was a daughter of Marquis Giovanni Francesco Gonzaga of Mantua, a wealthy state traditionally allied with Milan. Caterina's diplomatic refusal cited the "poor and turbulent condition of things in Italy,"[15] but her desire to avoid outside political interference is evident in her letter. Amid complaints regarding Giovanni Bentivoglio, who "wants to govern here as well," Caterina hinted at her doubts about the Gonzaga family's motives for the match. Ottaviano, however, spent no time despairing over his lost fiancées. He was already involved with a carpenter's daughter, who bore him a child in 1497.

The marriage offers continued; in 1497 Lorenzo di Pierfrancesco de' Medici offered his daughter and in 1498 the Gonzaga offer was renewed. But Caterina held out for a military career for her firstborn. In June 1498, Ottaviano's long-awaited *condotta* arrived. He would be employed by Florence in the war against Pisa for the amount of seventeen thousand ducats. The contract had been negotiated by a new friend of the countess, Giovanni de' Medici of Florence. Caterina proudly prepared one hundred light cavalry and one hundred infantrymen to accompany her son on his first steps toward glory. Ottaviano returned in August after a modest success, although reports revealed that he ran a disorderly camp and was incapable of disciplining his soldiers. Nonetheless, the proud mother celebrated her son with a commemorative medal. The papal bull by which Sixtus IV gave Forlì to the Riarios permitted the family to mint their own coins. Girolamo had used this privilege only once or twice during his reign, but Caterina had struck several coins since his death. In the earlier medals, Caterina, invariably represented in profile, wore a low-cut dress and her uncovered hair tied back, with a single loose strand framing her face. A diadem of pearls crowned her brow, indicating her status as sovereign. On the recto of two of the surviving coins the words TIBI ET VIRTUTI, "to you and to virtue," frame a figure of Fortune, while another from 1493 shows winged Victory riding in a two-horse chariot encircled by the motto VICTORIAM FAMA SE- QUETUR, "fame follows victory." In 1496 Caterina minted another set of coins in which the figures of Victory and Fortune made way for mention of Ottaviano. Caterina still appeared on the front, but now tightly cloaked in a widow's veil, older and more sober than in the earlier medals and taking her first steps back from the throne to prepare the way for her son. The medal commemorating Ottaviano's Pisa campaign was designed by Niccolò Fiorentino, who made no attempt to idealize the nineteen-year-old. With an empty expression and heavy jowls, Ottaviano already looked like an old man.[16]

Caterina's maternal attentions were not limited to Ottaviano, the heir to Forlì and Imola. Her second born, Cesare, had been destined for a career in the church since his childhood, and on February 19, 1492, at the age of twelve, he was given his "first tonsure," the shaving of the hair from his crown, leaving only a ring of locks encircling his ears, nape, and forehead. Now Caterina endeavored to ensure that he collected the benefices and titles customary among Renaissance prelates. Her relations with Cardinal Raffaello Riario had soured since the death of Feo because Caterina was certain that Cardinal Riario had encouraged, if not personally sent, the assassins. Despite Cardinal Riario's many displays of assistance through the years, Caterina complained about him ceaselessly to Duke Ludovico in 1496. "I don't know if he thinks he is dealing with a child here or if it is because I am a woman that he thinks he can beat me with his words," she railed in a letter dated April 11, 1496. "If I told you all the anguish and troubles he has made me suffer: I would seem like more than a martyr for his behavior and continual fabrications about me."[17] This time Caterina got her revenge through diplomatic channels. In the fall of 1496, as the cardinal lay seriously ill, Caterina convinced the duke of Milan to transfer his abbeys and benefices in Milan to Cesare upon his death.

Bianca Riario, Caterina's only girl, was growing up to be as lovely as her mother. Fifteen in 1496, Bianca had been intended for Astorre Manfredi of neighboring Faenza since she was eight. The official engagement was several years in the making, as the political consequences were significant for both Florence and Bologna. The Medicis were hesitant to allow Caterina a foothold in Faenza, and Giovanni Bentivoglio of Bologna, Astorre's grandfather, had long dithered about the match, sometimes supporting and sometimes opposing it. In 1495, during those last happy days before Feo was murdered, the engagement was finally made official, and ten-year-old Astorre paid his first visit to Forlì. He rode with an honor guard of thirty men, impressing the townspeople with his horse and handsome clothes. Caterina struck another medal for the occasion, but the festivities were short-lived. In December 1495, Ottaviano Manfredi, Astorre's cousin and pretender to the rule of Faenza, attacked the little town to wrest it from the child Astorre. Caterina joined forces with Giovanni Bentivoglio to subdue the attack, but the scuffles caught the eye of Venice, which was looking for a foothold in the heart of Romagna. Venice offered itself as "protector" of Faenza, openly interfering in local politics. Soon Faenza appeared to be slipping into the hands of Venice and the future rule of Astorre seemed irreparably compromised. Venice worked tirelessly to oust the town's loyal castellan and replace him with one of their own collaborators. Caterina, recognizing the hostile maneuver, immediately warned the duke of Milan. But Milan's lingering fear of the French gave precedence to the duke's tenuous alliance and he remained silent. In the midst of the overbearing Venetian presence in Faenza and Caterina's own misgivings about Giovanni Bentivoglio's intentions, Bianca's wedding was soon called off.

By 1496 the towns of Romagna realized that they had little protection from the nibbles and scratches inflicted by their larger neighbors. Venice raided Caterina's lands with alarming regularity, stealing livestock and ruining crops. Finding her uncle unwilling to assist her in obtaining justice, she assembled her own standing force of eight thousand soldiers ready to deter the Most Serene Republic. Some of the men were her own citizens looking to defend their homes, while others were soldiers of fortune hoping to make a little money in eternally war-torn Romagna. In 1496 only one other large northern state remained hostile to Venice, and so Caterina turned her attention to her neighbor Florence.

With the expulsion of Piero the Unlucky and his family, Florence had appointed more representatives to the governing body, expanding the popular voice in the republic after years of Medici oligarchy. The driving influence behind this reform was a Dominican friar from Ferrara, Girolamo Savonarola. The forty-four-year-old had gaunt features honed by an ascetic life and dark eyes that blazed from under the black hood of his habit; his dynamic preaching had mesmerized the Florentines. His prophecy that Italy's sinful ways would have dire results had presaged the arrival of Charles VIII of France. Nobles and peasants, old and young, and men and women flocked to his sermons and turned their minds to repentance.

Giovanni and Lorenzo di Pierfrancesco of the cadet branch of the Medicis had also reaped immense profits from Piero's disgrace. They had changed their names from Medici to Popolani, meaning "of the people," shamelessly pandering to anti-Medici sentiment while greedily appropriating Medici villas, jewels, and art. Giovanni "Il Popolano" began frequenting Forlì in the summer of 1496. A wealthy businessman, he went there to hire some of Caterina's well-trained troops for an imminent war with Pisa, which had taken advantage of Charles VIII's departure to declare independence from Florence. However, political observers in the know suspected that his real motive was to lure the countess of Forlì to the side of Florence and France in the latest arrangement of Italian political divisions.

The young Medici was thirty when he first met Caterina. With flowing light brown hair, warm eyes, and aristocratic features, Giovanni paired physical beauty with a splendid education. Many a woman in Florence had already succumbed to the boyish charm of this lover of art, literature, and brilliant conversation. At thirty-three, Caterina was still renowned as a beauty, and at long last, her excellent schooling at the Sforza court found an appreciative admirer in Giovanni Popolano.

As an honored guest, the Medici was lodged inside the official residence at Ravaldino, but before long Caterina offered him rooms in Il Paradiso. In mid-October, Francesco Tranchedini, Ludovico the Moor's eyes and ears in Forlì, warned the duke of Milan that Giovanni was living in the fortress and that he had seen Caterina "caressing him." The envoy concluded that Caterina would be "willing to go so far as to marry him to satisfy her lust."[18]

Ostensibly, other business concerns had protracted Giovanni's stay. The winter, a war, and internal disorganization had caught Florence with no stores of food for its people. By contrast, Caterina had reaped a modest harvest in Forlì and had put away huge grain stores to ensure that her people had food throughout the winter. Late in 1496, Giovanni and Caterina officially became business partners. In the spring of 1497, 130,000 bushels of grain were shipped from Forlì to Florence, garnering considerable income for Caterina, food for Florence, and frayed nerves for the duke of Milan.

Duke Ludovico pelted Caterina with endless demands for clarification regarding Giovanni and her position toward Florence, as the rumors increased. Caterina coolly denied any intimate relationship with the Florentine businessman, even going so far as to gently taunt the duke when she was confronted with a recent report that she had tried to obtain permission for the marriage from the king of France. "According to some chatterboxes, I have had any number of husbands," she pointed out before flatly denying a marriage to

Giovanni. "I am no longer at that age when others should think that these youthful appetites reign in me; foremost on my mind is my duty to govern these states."[19] Patently untrue, but Caterina had no intention of being tethered by her uncle. To him, she consistently maintained that she was eternally loyal and grateful to Milan, Giovanni was just a welcome guest, and Ottaviano would be willing to accept his *condotta* to fight for Milan at any moment. The duke, no stranger to political deceptions himself, was not completely fooled, but all that the frustrated Ludovico could do was lament that she sold so much grain to Florence.

Meanwhile, within the walls of Il Paradiso, Caterina had finally found a soul mate. No arriviste like Girolamo or stable boy like Feo, Giovanni was her equal. They shared similar interests: Caterina had remained a voracious reader all her life, and with Giovanni she could discuss literature. Like all Florentines, he had a scientific bent and took an interest in Caterina's botanical experiments, assisting her in obtaining the more exotic ingredients. Despite his reservations about the relationship between Caterina and Giovanni, Tranchedini acknowledged in a letter to the duke of Milan that Caterina's household seemed tranquil and her children appeared to get along well with the Florentine. As a member of a ruling family from a greater state, Giovanni would pose no threat to her sons, and at long last Caterina knew peace with a man whom all her children, from Ottaviano to little Bernardino, respected and admired.

Giovanni's arrival also brought considerable economic improvement. With their grain business flourishing, he helped Caterina to get her jewels out of pawn. He brought exquisite Florentine luxury goods to Caterina and her children. She put aside her widow's wear and soon returned to her stylish ensembles. The Forlivesi were well aware of the relationship between Caterina and the young Medici; loose tongues claimed that the countess was "afraid of a cold bed." Unlike previous occasions, she ordered no beatings for rumormongering.

Happy and confident, Caterina began to find the will to look inward again. Busy months had bolstered her strength, and at last, as the first fruits of June ripened in her orchard, she turned to mending her spiritual troubles. She had heard much about Girolamo Savo-

narola from Giovanni. Caterina's old acquaintance Sandro Botticelli had become one of his followers, known as the *piagnoni*, and had
been renewed through repentance. The friar arranged "bonfires of
the vanities" in Florence, helping citizens rid themselves of the lures
and temptations of the sinful life. Women brought clothes, makeup,
and ribbons; artists brought their more erotic drawings; men brought
cards and dice; they all looked to start anew on a steady path toward
Heaven.

The horrible massacres following Feo's murder weighed heavily
on Caterina's conscience, especially now that she had found a greater,
richer love than her earlier blind passion. The Holy Year was now
only three years away. In 1500 she would be able to travel to Rome to
obtain remission for all of her sins by praying at the shrines to Saint
Peter and Saint Paul. But the troubled times in Italy and the ever-
present specter of death had Caterina concerned about the welfare of
her immortal soul. She wrote to Savonarola in the summer of 1496.
Her letter has been lost, but the friar's response has been preserved.
Savonarola exhorted her, telling to her to pray but also to ensure that
others prayed for her as well. Understanding her active character,
he also counseled her to do good works and to donate generously to
the needy, because "charity extinguishes sins, as water puts out fire.
Above all," Savonarola advised, "employ every care and attention to
dispense justice to your subjects."[20]

Caterina followed the friar's advice and dedicated herself to char-
itable works in Forlì and Imola, supporting shrines and organizing
confraternities. She also took an interest in a Florentine community
of nuns known as the Muratte. The convent, founded in 1424, sat at
the end of the Via Ghibellina, by the city walls. The convent had enjoyed Medici protection for many years and had been substantially
rebuilt by Lorenzo the Magnificent after a fire in 1475 had nearly destroyed the structure. The sisters lived by the rule of Saint Benedict,
dedicating their days to manual labor, which they did while reciting constant prayers. Caterina bestowed generous gifts on the sisters.
Whenever they in turn sent her sweets or other fruits of their labors,
Caterina always thanked them kindly but insisted that they should
not worry about acknowledging her donations. Their holy prayers for
her soul were recompense enough.

It was also probably the friar's influence that persuaded Caterina to grant pardons to her most hated enemies: the Tartagni family and Giovanni Brocchi. As she sought her own forgiveness, it was her duty to offer the same, as Savonarola certainly would have reminded her.[21]

One last item needed to be settled in Caterina's life—her irregular situation with Giovanni. By August 1497, Caterina and Giovanni were expecting a child; in September she married the young Medici in a secret ceremony in the fortress of Castrocaro, far from her uncle and his spies. Concealing her marriage to Feo had been due to his low station, but this time Caterina needed to keep Duke Ludovico in the dark until the complicated web of Italian alliances saw a reflowering of friendship between Milan and Florence. Her realm, life, and soul stood on an even keel for the first time in her life, and Caterina looked forward to the future. Probably in this year, the late summer or fall of 1497, the most famous portrait of Caterina was executed. Today gracing the Pinacoteca Civica, the art museum of Forlì, the image of a lovely young woman seated by a window is attributed to Lorenzo di Credi, the former collaborator of both Leonardo and Botticelli, who ran a flourishing studio in Florence. The painting was executed in the avant-garde style of female portraiture pioneered by Leonardo. Caterina turns her head for a three-quarter view, typically used for men: a bolder image than the modest profile portraits of earlier years. Her long fingers delicately arrange jasmine buds in a bowl. This inclusion of hands was the latest rage in portraits, as they provided a precious clue to the personality of the sitter. Caterina sits tall, with her hair pulled gently back and coiled at the back of her head as a few red-gold tendrils frame her face. Steady brown eyes gaze warmly at the viewer. Behind her head a red curtain hints at the fiery character that fascinated Italy, while her beloved castle of Ravaldino is portrayed outside the window in front of her. Her simple but elegant clothes reflect the Florentine distaste for ostentation, not straitened circumstances. No jewels encircle her fingers or throat; the radiance of her skin provides sheen enough. The thirty-five-year-old newlywed Caterina looks serenely out on the world. She had love and success. And now she was immortalized through art. In May 1497 the first edition of Jacopo Filippo Foresti's *Lives of Illustrious Women*[22] was printed, featuring Caterina's biography.

Caterina's contentment was not shared by the duke of Milan or his envoy. After months of denials, the astounded Tranchedini was bitterly embarrassed by the arrival of a letter from Giovanni Bentivoglio, confirming the marriage. *"Nisi maledictos homo qui confidet in homine et maxime in muliere,"* "Cursed is the man who places his trust in men and even more so he who trusts a woman," wrote the exasperated ambassador. Venice took the opportunity to reprove Duke Ludovico for his inability to control Caterina. The doge was uninterested in the sentimental aspect of her arrangements because, as he wrote, "it is the nature of the female sex." What he found objectionable were "her mistakes in public office." The Venetian ruler insisted that "the duke, her uncle, should make sure she understands her role and duties in the present state of Italy." In short, the crown jewel of Romagna, Forlì, with its strong fortresses, strategic position, and well-trained troops, now shimmered in the palm of Florence.

The spring of 1498 was enlivened by a splendid carnival thrown by Ottaviano while Caterina was in the final months of her pregnancy. Dances, parties, and banquets heralded a golden age of relations between Forlì and its rulers. The new arrival to the Sforza-Medici household, Ludovico Sforza de' Medici, was born on the night of April 6 in the fortress of Ravaldino. Caterina named the boy after her uncle, in the hopes of mending fences, but no Milanese ambassador was present at his baptism. The birth was a joyous event nonetheless, and the fruit of Caterina's most fulfilling relationship.

Soon, however, the celebratory atmosphere was swiftly dispersed by gathering tumult. Girolamo Savonarola, the brilliant preacher who had led cynical Florence to repentance and had directed Caterina toward the road to salvation, was executed in the Piazza della Signoria in Florence on May 23, 1498. The Dominican had gone so far as to criticize Pope Alexander VI himself, insistently calling for church reform. Several pro-Medici supporters had plotted against the friar and in 1497 Savonarola was banned from preaching. The priest continued his work anyway and in April he was imprisoned and tortured to obtain a spurious confession of heresy. He was hanged and burned, and then his ashes were scattered in the Arno to ensure that no relics could be collected to venerate the renegade preacher as a martyr.

Today Savonarola seems an enigmatic figure; some portray him as the Inquisition personified, others as a power-hungry politician, while still others work to have him proclaimed a saint. The Savona-

rola Caterina knew was a stern but supportive adviser who helped
her return from spiritual death. Although Caterina's correspondence
contains no comment on the sad end of Savonarola, her support of the
friar's beloved Muratte continued until the end of her life.

That summer, Ottaviano left with his *condotta* for Pisa, accompanied by Giovanni and a trusted castellan. But the sight of the eldest
Riario taking the field flanked by a Medici brought out the vindictive side of the Most Serene Republic. Caterina found herself under
constant attack, from little turf invasions to full-scale assault on her
castles. The indomitable countess knew it was only a matter of time
before she would find Venetian troops digging under her very walls,
but she responded to her uncle's warning with a valiant reply: "When
Venice attacks, I will have enough spirit to defend myself!"[23] Besides
relying on her own troops and well-built fortresses, Caterina was also
anticipating aid from her new allies and family in Florence to fend
off whatever the Venetians might bring. She expected to meet Venice
head-on in battle, declaring to her uncle, "If I must lose because I am
a woman, I want to lose like a man."[24]

But the mainstay of her alliance and the pillar of her new happy
life was tottering. Giovanni, like many of the Medicis, was cursed
with gout and suffered a serious attack after his return from Pisa. He
spent one romantic week with Caterina in the fortress but then retired to the thermal baths in Bagno in Romagna for treatment. Gout,
an arthritic condition characterized by large amounts of uric acid deposited in the joints, was alleviated by drinking large quantities of water. Sweating in the hot baths also helped eliminate toxins from the
body. Giovanni departed for Bagno on August 28 in hopes that the
waters would relieve his painful and debilitating condition. Caterina's
daughter, Bianca, also unwell, went with him. The first days brought
good results. Giovanni wrote to Caterina on September 2, asking for
hats and cloths to change during his steam baths. The young Medici
was feeling well and felt certain he would be home soon. Urgent political matters occupied most of their correspondence; they both knew
that Venice was on the verge of an attack. Giovanni trusted Caterina's judgment in military matters and reiterated his faith in her wisdom. On September 11, emphasizing the need for secrecy, Giovanni
recommended no longer using the usual secretaries but only direct
correspondence. That businesslike letter was the last between hus-

band and wife. On September 12 Caterina was urgently summoned to Bagno, where Giovanni died that night in her arms. His body was claimed the next day by his brother Lorenzo di Pierfrancesco and brought back to Florence for burial. Caterina was alone once again. The lover who had changed her life, the father of her infant son, her friend and ally had slipped away, taken not by sword or dagger but by a fever. Caterina, heartbroken, rode back to Forlì and into her fortress. She donned mourning clothes and draped the bright walls of Paradise in black, but she could spend little time crying over her lost love. Every bit of her energy was directed toward preparing for the Venetian attack.

The swift and ferocious assault at the end of September probably saved Caterina's sanity. Florence had sent a pitifully small force to prevent the Venetian army from entering Tuscan and Romagnol territory. The mercenary captain Dionigio Naldi, assisted by Caterina's fine troops, held the Apennine Pass into Tuscany. The Florentine Simone Ridolfi, a close friend of Giovanni, and his handful of men were overrun at Marradi on the dividing line between Florence and Romagna. Caterina had long predicted this strategic approach by Venice, but the Florentines had paid no heed. Now it was Caterina's soldiers from Imola who turned the tables and rescued the castle. Caterina had saved the day, Florence reaped the profits, and Venice sharpened its knives against the countess of Forlì.

16

INTRIGUE AND INVASION

I N 1499, TWENTY-NINE-YEAR-OLD Niccolò Machiavelli's romantic conquests far outnumbered his political successes. With chestnut hair cropped tightly around his long thin face and a meticulously barbered beard, he cut a dashing figure in Renaissance courts. His dark, glittering eyes were his most striking feature: quick to appraise a situation, narrow with wry humor, or wink at a pretty serving girl.

Born in 1469, Machiavelli came of age in the golden twilight of Lorenzo the Magnificent's Florence. His father, Bernardo di Niccolò di Buoninsegna, of the old yet impoverished Machiavelli line, had obtained a law degree but could barely scratch out a living for his wife and four children. Niccolò, the oldest, was endowed with a good humanist education but had no training in the practical skills that might make him wealthy. In the spring of 1498, however, the ambitious young man landed a job with the Great Council of Florence, thanks to his public and vocal disapproval of Girolamo Savonarola. As chief of the Second Chancery and secretary of the Ten of Liberty and Peace, Niccolò's task was to keep the governing bodies apprised of potential military and political problems. With a salary of 192 ducats a year and a prestigious position, Machiavelli's prospects were looking very favorable. "Il Machia," as his friends called him, was already a political player, but his second diplomatic commission, in July 1499, would reveal the young man to be less adept than he had imagined. His mission was to persuade Caterina Sforza, the countess of Forlì, to renew the contract with Florence for a contingent of her troops commanded by her son Ottaviano. The tricky part of the negotiations lay in the fact that Florence not only intended to reduce Ottaviano's salary from seventeen thousand to ten thousand ducats but also had never paid him for his earlier service. Nor did the council want an alliance with Forlì whereby Florence would have to guarantee the safety of the town, despite the fact that they wanted Caterina to send them her best soldiers. She had already refused to renew her contract under these insulting conditions in January and showed no sign of changing her mind.

The friends of the rising diplomat, however, were blind to the difficulties of the task. Caterina Sforza, they breathed in awed whispers, the most famous woman in Italy! Didn't she capture the Castel Sant'Angelo while pregnant? Hadn't she outwitted her husband's assassins? Was it true that she was the most beautiful woman in the world? Biagio Buonaccorsi, Machiavelli's closest friend, was green with envy. Three days after Machiavelli's arrival in Forlì Buonaccorsi wrote to him, begging for a portrait of the thirty-six-year-old celebrity by return mail, preferably rolled instead of folded so as not to damage the image.

Men like Machiavelli and his friends were intrigued by Caterina's reputation for boldness, of a sort not limited to the battlefield. She had gone through three husbands and, rumor had it, countless lovers. Whereas Caterina's first husband had been chosen for her, she was the one who decided to enter into her next two marriages. The stories about her, true or false, fueled the fantasies of many star-struck Italians.

Machiavelli set off to visit the countess, looking forward to adventure and success. Probably he thought he would charm the countess into conceding her soldiers immediately and then spend a pleasant interval in Forlì, enjoying her favors. But in 1499, with the death of Giovanni de' Medici, Caterina was fully immersed in the business of taking care of her family. According to reports from Rome, her second son, Cesare, was doing the family proud. Caterina discreetly disclaimed any credit for her son's merits, writing that her nineteen-year-old was "still fresh from the nest, and if he doesn't yet know how to fulfill his offices, Your Excellency will excuse him considering that he was raised by a woman."[1] Meanwhile Caterina, through her agents, convinced Cardinal Raffaello Riario to renounce his title of archbishop of Pisa in favor of his cousin Cesare.

Caterina was also negotiating a military appointment for thirteen-year-old Galeazzo and a marriage, once again, for her only daughter, Bianca. After the failure to wed Bianca to Astorre Manfredi, she had toyed with an offer from the count of Caiazzo, although she eventually demurred because "he was somewhat advanced in age."[2]

Ottaviano remained unmarried as well. In May 1498, Caterina had been surprised to see the bishop of Volterra in her court, proffering an unexpected bride for her eldest son: Lucrezia Borgia, the daughter of Pope Alexander VI. The Borgia pontiff was already Ottaviano's godfather and the proposed match would catapult Ottaviano into the most powerful family in Italy, but Caterina shrewdly read between the lines of the offer. The blandishments included gifts, lands, and titles, but Caterina was not so dazzled that she did not see that the pope expected her to abdicate immediately in favor of Ottaviano, leaving the state in the inexperienced hands of her nineteen-year-old son. Furthermore, Lucrezia had already been married, at age thirteen, to Lord Giovanni Sforza of Pesaro, Caterina's cousin. The marriage had been annulled three years later for alleged impotency on the part of Giovanni Sforza, despite the fact that his first wife had died in childbirth. Caterina knew that the Borgias used marriages as political steppingstones and unscrupulously discarded spouses when they were no longer useful.

Yet Pope Alexander pressured Caterina, deploying her own uncle Cardinal Ascanio Sforza to persuade her, as well as trying to enlist the Medicis. Caterina answered the pope in less than delicate terms, bluntly stating that her son was busy learning the art of war, a warning that she was training him to defend his lands. She also decried the poor treatment of her cousin, claiming that she had no intention of marrying her son to a woman "who had slept for three years in her husband's bed and with one of our own family to boot; for which he could not but derive great shame and infamy from the illustrious lords in many respects."[3] She reproached her own uncle, claiming that she doubted that Cardinal Ascanio could in good conscience ask her to give her son "someone else's wife."[4] In short, Caterina wrote, when she did decide to marry her son, it would be to a person whose family was not actively plotting against her and "contrary to and repelled by her continued well-being."[5] By doing this she well may have saved Ottaviano's life, for Lucrezia's next husband, Alfonso, duke of Calabria, was murdered by her brother Cesare in June 1500. But the countess had made a powerful and ruthless new enemy in Pope Alexander VI.

Caterina had rightly read the papal intent. In 1499 the Borgias were preparing to extend their greedy fingers into Romagna. In May, Pope Alexander VI made his intentions clear with a papal bull in which he declared Caterina *iniquitatis filia*, "a daughter of iniquity."[6] This Old Testament term was used to refer to unjust rulers or tyrants. Even in this case Caterina broke new ground for her era: this was the first time the epithet had ever been used for a woman. The pope, citing tyranny and three years of unpaid tribute, was deposing the Riario rulers in favor of his son Cesare. In response, Caterina immediately dispatched her envoy Giovanni delle Selle to Rome to negotiate and eventually pay the thirty-six hundred ducats owed in tribute, if necessary, but the pope refused to meet with him. It was clear that Caterina could expect to encounter a papal army in the near future.

Caterina would need the friendship of Florence. The king of France was on the move. Now allied with Venice, he was marching toward Milan. Her most powerful ally, Duke Ludovico the Moor, would soon be completely absorbed in repelling this advance and thus unable to come to the aid of Caterina. If the French captured Milan, the city on the Arno would be her only friend. As the French rolled over the Alps and the papal army moved north, the two forces would meet on the strip of the Apennines, the mountains where Tuscany and Romagna were joined. Caterina couldn't afford to antagonize Florence, and Florence couldn't afford to lose Forlì as a friendly neighbor.

Machiavelli arrived at Forlì in the cool morning hours of July 17, but Caterina kept him waiting until the afternoon, when Giovanni da Casale, acting as Caterina's chancellor, received the young diplomat. As the hot summer sun waned, Casale accompanied Machiavelli to the inner sanctum of Ravaldino, Il Paradiso. In the countess's beautifully decorated private apartments overlooking the Apennines,

Niccolò first came face to face with the legendary Caterina. She was simply but elegantly dressed, with the white widow's veil concealing her blond hair. In aspect, she seemed anything but the passionate fire-brand she was reputed to be. Machiavelli began with an eloquent out-pouring of Florence's love for the countess and her family and their appreciation for her loyalty. It was this "affection they had for her and her merits," rather than any real need for her services, that impelled them to offer to renew Ottaviano's contract at a rate of pay applicable to times of peace, ten thousand ducats.

Caterina wryly responded that "the words of Florentines were al-ways so very pleasing to hear."[7] On the other hand, she observed, their actions tended to provoke displeasure. Her "merits," so lauded by the polished phrases of the envoy, had never been recognized in any ma-terial way. Throughout Italy, she said, Florence was reputed to be a grateful republic, one that remembered its friends as well as its ene-mies, but in her case "now showed ingratitude for one who had done more than any other ally."[8] In supporting Florence so staunchly and loyally, Caterina had incurred the wrath of Venice and had been at-tacked for her fidelity. Closing their interview, she promised to think things over; Machiavelli was escorted from Paradise and left to his purgatory of waiting.

While Machiavelli composed his letter to Florence, optimistically recounting the first meeting, Caterina informed Milan of their en-counter. At the same time she enlisted her secretary to entertain Ma-chiavelli and gauge what Florence was really willing to offer.

After two days of waiting, Machiavelli was summoned back to the castle to meet with Caterina. He found the countess at her most charming as she invited him to understand her position. She too loved Florence, and indeed she and her family had been honored with Flor-entine citizenship as of 1498, but she carried a proud family name and had to consider her honor. Indeed, now that she also bore the name of Medici the question of honoring such exalted lineages was foremost in her mind. She explained that the duke of Milan, pressed for rein-forcements against the advancing French, had already offered a con-dotta for Ottaviano at the same pay. Machiavelli parried by turning to another, less pointed subject, a simple purchase of gunpowder, can-nonballs, and potassium nitrate for making explosives for the Flor-entine war against Pisa. Caterina again demurred, apologizing that her supply wasn't sufficient to defend the borders of her own small realm, but she was in the midst of purchasing some from Pesaro that she would be happy to share with Florence. She also had infantry for hire, "well armed, good men and ready immediately," who had been personally trained by her. As the negotiations drew to a close that day, Caterina gently revealed that she would lose face by accepting the dishonorable conditions Florence was proposing, especially if Florence didn't honor the terms of the first contract.

The number of well-placed Florentines in her court, as well as her readiness to offer men and supplies, had convinced the young diplomat that "every day he saw clearly evident signs"[9] of Caterina's friendship toward Florence. As his later treatises would show, he was sensitive to a ruler's fear of losing reputation or face. He recommended that Florence demonstrate its appreciation for the countess in deeds, not words, and championed her request for the back pay due her son and a new *condotta* for Ottaviano at twelve thousand ducats. Machiavelli was hoping that with some cash and an honorable position for her son, Florence could keep Caterina's loyalty without having to formally promise to protect her state, should it be attacked. He suggested a little flattery and a few gifts to woo Caterina as a military bedfellow, but offered no promise of marriage.

The next day Caterina gave the Florentine envoy a glimpse of her dowry. As he watched from the ramparts of Ravaldino, fifty mounted crossbowmen rode in review under the watchful eye of the countess on their way to the duke of Milan. The well-made weapons expertly handled by the crack troops impressed Machiavelli. The following morning, Machiavelli was treated to the sight of five hundred infantrymen marching in perfect formation. These seasoned troops were also on their way to Milan, and Caterina made sure that Machiavelli knew that the duke had already paid for them three days earlier. Machiavelli saw how quickly she could muster her men and how well they were trained, and was duly smitten.

On July 23 Machiavelli hurried to the countess's chambers with the news that Florence was willing to raise Ottaviano's pay to twelve thousand ducats but found Caterina silent and distracted; she abruptly got up to leave five minutes after they had sat down. A perplexed Machiavelli returned to his chambers, confused as to what Caterina had in mind. A messenger arrived shortly after, bearing Caterina's apol-

ogies. She was "worried sick" over the illness of Ludovico, her infant son by Giovanni de' Medici. She would be happy to conclude
the treaty as soon as possible under the stated conditions; the back
pay owed Ottaviano, the new *condotta* at twelve thousand ducats, and
a written statement of Florence's obligation to "defend, protect, and
maintain her state." Machiavelli balked at the last condition, saying
to Caterina's secretary that he could not sign such an agreement without authorization from the Signoria of Florence. He suggested that
he could offer a verbal promise, but nothing written. Caterina's closest adviser, Giovanni da Casale, accepted the terms, promising that
tomorrow all would be concluded. A confident letter then went from
Machiavelli to the Signoria, claiming that the deed was done: Caterina and her state would be at their disposal, but Florence would not
need to offer more than the occasional trinket.

The next morning Machiavelli appeared in the countess's chambers for the signing. Arriving at this fourth meeting, Il Machia
thought all was settled, but Caterina turned the tables. "After sleeping on it," she decided she required the written obligation of Florence
to defend her lands. She was sorry, of course, that she "had indicated
other ideas through Giovanni da Casale," but Machiavelli should not
be surprised, for "the more things are discussed, the better they are
understood."[10] While Machiavelli had thought the seduction of Caterina was complete, she made it clear that the courtship was only
beginning. Stung by his misreading of the situation, he showed his
shock and hurt through both his words and gestures, betraying his
inexperience. Only later would Machiavelli learn to conceal his true
thoughts behind a mask of wit and irony. Caterina remained unmoved
during his protests and Machiavelli had to inform Florence of his failure. Machiavelli soon left Forlì and Giovanni da Casale traveled to
Florence to continue negotiations directly with the Signoria.

Caterina's abrupt about-face was not only a professional embarrassment for Il Machia, but undoubtedly it humiliated him in the eyes
of his friends. Later, Machiavelli would take his revenge by denounc-
ing Caterina in all of his famous treatises: as a tyrant in the *The Prince*
and as the ribald woman on the ramparts who was willing to sacrifice
her own children in both *Florentine Histories* and *Discourses on the First
Ten Books of Titus Livius*. But one can glimpse the Caterina he once
admired—the alert general, worried mother, and charming count-

ess—in the pages of *On the Art of War*, where he describes her defense of Forlì against the French: "She would have the spirit to await an army, as neither the king of Naples nor the duke of Milan had done. And though her efforts did not turn out well, nonetheless she earned the esteem her valor deserved."[11]

When midsummer 1499 arrived, Caterina was hovering over little Ludovico's bedside. The child was burning with malarial fever, and none of Caterina's remedies could halt its advance. By August 3, she was in despair. The year before she had lost Ludovico's father, and the infant was all she had left of her greatest love. Writing to Ludovico's uncle Lorenzo di Pierfrancesco de' Medici, she intimated that the fever had arrived twelve hours earlier than expected and that it was higher than the last time. "I don't know what else to say"[12] are the simple sad words of a mother on the brink of losing her beloved son. Asking for prayers, the only remedy left to her, she returned to her vigil at her son's bedside. Five days later, her prayers were answered. She wrote a few tentative words of hope to Lorenzo in Florence: "He has recovered enough that if nothing else happens, we hope he may be cured of this illness. Thank God for everything."[13]

The boy recovered, and Caterina set about enjoying the waning days of summer. She ordered special sugar confections from Florence and received cases of pomegranates from her friends in the convent of the Muratte. She purchased a new saddle of Florentine leather and began teaching Ludovico her own greatest passion, riding. In these days, Caterina's thoughts rested solely with her family. Her younger sister Chiara arrived in Forlì that summer. Once a cheerful girl lapping up her sister's stories on her bridal route from Milan to Rome, now Chiara was older, sadder, and financially ruined by her husband's mismanagement. Desperate, Chiara had thrown herself on her sister's mercy. The countess interceded with the duke of Milan so that Chiara, who had arrived in Forlì "destitute and derelict," could leave for Milan with the personal assurances from Duke Ludovico that he would see to her needs. Caterina also concerned herself with finding a husband and dowry for Giacomo Feo's sister, who was in her late teens and still unmarried.

Caterina's most serious worry was about the future of her youngest son, Ludovico. Giovanni de' Medici, albeit from the less wealthy cadet branch of the Medici family, had been well-to-do, and as his only son, Ludovico was entitled to his inheritance. As soon as she could leave Ludovico, she traveled with Ottaviano, Luffo Numai, and other important Forlivesi as witnesses to meet with the Medici representatives. Before a notary, she declared the fact that she had hidden so desperately from the duke of Milan. She and Giovanni de' Medici had been married in September 1497, and Ludovico was the child of that marriage. Caterina assumed the guardianship of their son and then gave the equivalent of an exclusive interview with the chronicler Andrea Bernardi, ensuring that her story of the marriage, birth, and guardianship would be recorded. Giovanni's brother Lorenzo di Pierfrancesco, however, was a greedy man, only too happy to take advantage of Caterina's distance from Florence to absorb his brother's inheritance. Lorenzo wanted inventories of the grain business Giovanni had shared with Caterina and the personal possessions left in Forlì. He had already had Giovanni's silver plate packed off to Florence within days of his death. The letters between Lorenzo and Caterina increased in hostility as she took more of an interest in the Medici estate and noted more and more discrepancies in Lorenzo's accounting. The tension would mount for several years until matters finally came to a head in an out-and-out legal battle that would last half a decade.

The arrival of the bubonic plague abruptly halted Caterina's pleasant summer. By the end of August, the illness was raging through Forlì. The bane of the Renaissance era, this terrible disease came from a bacterium hosted by rats, traveling from the infected rodents to humans via fleas. Its onset was marked by a high fever and enlarged lymph nodes, known as buboes, which typically killed victims within three to four days. Europe's first experience of the Black Death had occurred in 1348, when it claimed a third of the population. One hundred and fifty years later, its cause remained a mystery but most well-informed rulers knew of efficacious ways to limit its spread. Caterina had seen the plague before and though she personally feared it little, she knew its capacity for devastation. This time the stakes were much higher. With Cesare Borgia and the French closing in, a plague would weaken the defenses of Romagna; the sickness would have to be defeated in Forlì before it could contaminate other areas. Caterina sealed off her city. No market, no traveling shows, no large assemblies. She brought in special doctors to assist the ill and priests to console the dying. Food and necessities were distributed to the populace free of charge. The city was divided into sectors and subjected to strict rules of hygiene. Those infected were immediately isolated in the Church of San Giovanni while a confraternity of volunteers collected the dead for hasty burial outside the city walls. The clothes, belongings, and even the houses of the incurable were burned, which brought many protests. But these stringent measures saved the region; the casualty count was 179 people, much lower than expected, and the sickness did not reach any of the surrounding countryside.

No sooner had the plague subsided than the mail brought bad news: the French had entered Lombardy. Duke Ludovico had sent his finest *condottiere*, Galeazzo Sanseverino, count of Caiazzo, north to meet the oncoming French, who were led by the Milanese traitor and exile Gian Giacomo Trivulzio, but Sanseverino never intercepted the opposing army. Trivulzio arrived at Alessandria and at Caterina's childhood home of Pavia, both of which had capitulated without a fight. As the Venetians advanced to Lodi, Count Sanseverino was nowhere to be found; sensing certain defeat, he had abandoned the cause. Ludovico the Moor fled Milan on September 2 to seek asylum with the Holy Roman Emperor Maximilian I of Hapsburg, related to the Sforza family through his marriage to Caterina's sister Bianca Maria. On August 31, one of Caterina's trusted agents in Florence, a priest named Francesco Fortunati, sent a hastily scribbled warning to the countess. "These are the times to have both men and money . . . The moment is coming when they will need to be spent."[14] Fortunati was so fearful for his own safety that he also pleaded with her not to show his letters to Giovanni da Casale, Caterina's Milanese chancellor. No alliance was safe, no friendship honored. Each man would have to fend for himself.

Caterina continued her deliberations with Florence through Giovanni da Casale and even succeeded in convincing Niccolò Machiavelli to inform the French king that she was an ally of the Florentine Republic. Meanwhile she kept an agent, Vincenzo Calmeta, to further her suits at the court of King Louis XII, who was now the king of France and claiming the lordship of Milan.

But on October 31, the eve of the Feast of the Dead, Caterina received grave news. A letter from Vincenzo Calmeta informed the countess that he had finally been granted an audience with King

Louis XII to discuss her case. Also present was Gian Giacomo Tri-vulzio. Calmeta swore that he had done everything in his power but that nothing could stop the ax from falling on Forlì. Trivulzio had confided to Calmeta that the French army had little interest in Forlì and that the true enemy of Forlì was the pope. The French had tried to avoid the wearisome campaign in Romagna by protesting to Pope Alexander VI that they had used all their war funds in capturing Milan, but he replied that his needs were minimal: some artillery and the loan of a few soldiers. The pope himself would pay for the siege of Forlì. In short, as Calmeta's blunt message proved, Caterina had been betrayed by all. The Florentines would not object for fear that Alexander would attack Pisa to give it to Cesare. Even Cardinal Riario and Cardinal Giuliano della Rovere had managed to put aside their differences to join the plot against her in Rome. "Everyone is waiting for your undoing and ruin, most of all Rome, from whence comes all this evil."[15] Louis XII dismissed any appeal that Caterina might make with a few words: "We are not the judges of the pope, nor can we forbid that he act as he wishes in his own jurisdiction." The king continued this pious lip service, telling Calmeta that "her captains had the right to defend against any other power; but against the pope who is your overlord it is not lawful."[16] Calmeta then begged the countess not to lose heart and to bolster her courage, for invasion was imminent. The following day, the pope issued his death sentence on Caterina's rule with a note written in his own hand. The Riario family was officially deposed and instructed to surrender Forlì and Imola immediately.

Caterina, always at her best when faced with the worst, immediately began readying her state for attack. On November 1 she called the governing Council of Forty and obtained promises of loyalty to Ottaviano. Starting with her own little farm, she ordered all rural buildings within a quarter mile around the city walls to be razed and gardens and trees cut down. Forlì would offer no food or shelter to her invaders. The bell tower of the city palace was outfitted with a lookout post so that the citizens could be warned instantly when the troops arrived. Rural inhabitants, who lived "three artillery shots away," were ordered to take all their belongings from their houses, harvest all the wheat and hay, and leave the land bare. She leveled all the parks in a mile radius around the city, again commencing with her own. Every citizen was to have rations on hand for four months. Caterina would personally assist those who could not afford to lay down such stores.

She sent some of her finest horses to the marquis of Mantua, who had long been angling for the fine creatures that Caterina bred herself. With her forests razed and her enemies at the gates, there would be no time to hunt and ride, but perhaps she could win back a little friendship. She mentioned the pope's persecution and her intention to resist the oncoming army. "We will not abandon our home, but we will defend our possessions as long as we can, and perhaps they will not find [the conquest] as easy as they think."[17] She readied weapons and medicines and drilled her troops, anticipating the moment of confrontation. Florence, while publicly indifferent to Caterina's plight, sent weapons and supplies to her. Alexander VI, in his continuing effort to isolate Caterina completely, threatened the Signoria in a letter of November 16 with dire consequences should the Florentines continue to assist his enemies.

Aware that the beautiful and brave countess was as legendary as his own son Cesare, Alexander took steps to deflect sympathy from her. To cut off any hope of alliances for Caterina, the crafty pope wrote to the Signoria in Florence on November 21, accusing the countess of attempting to poison him. The story bruited by the papal agents was that these two men of Romagna were sent by Caterina to pretend they had a letter from the people of Forlì and to introduce the poison once they had gained admission to his presence. Here the versions differ, one claiming that the men had been handed a vial prepared by the countess herself, the other stating that she had given them letters that had been enclosed in the grave of a plague victim for two days. One of the two, the story went, decided he could make more money off the affair by telling the pope, informing His Holiness just in the nick of time. As preposterous as it sounded, Cardinal Riario scented imminent danger and fled the same night in disguise. The name had become a death sentence. Cardinal Riario, who had not known such fear since his days as a hostage after the Pazzi conspiracy, first took refuge with the Orsini family, long-standing Riario allies, but then smuggled himself across the Siena border and caught a boat for Savona near Genova, his hometown. Alexander continued to spread his own brand of poison, ensuring that every court in the land was informed about Caterina's attempt to murder the pontiff. It was an old but effective ploy. Twenty years earlier, Caterina's late and unlamented husband Girolamo had tried to lure Lorenzo the Magnificent into a similar trap. The papal claims of foul play achieved their aim; everyone understood that helping the countess would be a very serious offense against a very powerful man. Florence, however, despite all its quibbles with Caterina, proved the most loyal of her friends. They refused to sell gunpowder and ammunition to Cesare Borgia. Taking a leaf from Caterina's book, they claimed that they had run out. Meanwhile they continued to ply the king of France with requests to put Forlì under his protection, warning him that the political ambitions of the Borgias were boundless and that someday soon they would come into conflict with his own. Fearful for their own precarious position, the Florentines secretly aided Caterina, hoping that her defense would buy them enough time to convince the French king to leave Tuscany in peace.

Caterina's last preparations were made in early December. While the rest of Europe was counting off the days of Advent, waiting to celebrate the birth of Jesus, Caterina was waiting for the arrival of the man whom many would dub the "Antichrist," Cesare Borgia. The city of Imola had already surrendered, but the castellan, Dionigio Naldi, was detaining Cesare at the fortress of Imola to gain a few more precious days for the countess. His honorable surrender on December 11 awakened the Forlivesi to the cold reality that there were no more obstacles between Cesare and Forlì. The next day, Caterina sent Ottaviano to Florence, where her other children and her sister had taken refuge. This time, no one would use her loved ones as leverage against her. She would have liked to have her oldest son fight by her side, but having fostered and followed his military career from the beginning, she knew that Ottaviano had inherited more of his father's trepidation toward the battlefield than his mother's boldness.

Caterina called her people together once more. Would they resist the Borgia storm together? The frightened Forlivesi were losing heart. Undecided, they referred the question to the Elders of Forlì, who also wavered. They timidly suggested that although they knew no one could defend the city better than she, perhaps Caterina should emulate the duke of Milan and leave town, so as to minimize the damage to its people. They proposed this weak solution as merely a "temporary retreat," arguing that she could save herself and her citizens and then return when the pope died.

Then, more villainously, on December 14 Luffo Numai, who had consigned the city of Forlì to Caterina after Girolamo's death, and Giovanni delle Selle, who had risen to great heights under her reign, abandoned the countess and the defense of Forlì. Undoubtedly hoping to negotiate even better political positions under Borgia rule, they swayed the people of Forlì to take the state from Caterina and her children and confer it upon the enemy. Crying "The People, the People!" Numai and delle Selle rang Caterina's warning bell in the city palace before riding to Imola to offer the submission of the Forlivesi to Cesare Borgia, who gladly accepted. The Forlivesi raced to the Abbey of San Mercuriale in thanksgiving and took up the statue of Mercuriale, their patron saint, carrying it in procession out to the main square, where they lit candles and made an improvised shrine above the monument to the twelve thousand French soldiers they had repelled and massacred three hundred years earlier. No longer the proud resisters of foreign invaders, the Forlivesi became the shame of Italy. On December 19, 1499, heavy rains extinguished the candles around the statue of Mercuriale. The clatter of hoofbeats grew louder as a white horse carrying the Borgia commander entered the square. The enemy was at the countess's door.

17

ITALY'S IDOL

O N DECEMBER 26, 1499, Caterina awoke in Paradise. Although her beloved Giovanni was no longer by her side and her chambers were devoid of the happy chatter of her children, she still relished her comfortable inner sanctum next to the keep. From her window, Caterina could see the sun glowing along the tip of the Apennines. Cesare Borgia had begun the siege of Forlì a week earlier. The town had capitulated even before Cesare had arrived, leaving only Ravaldino to resist the invaders. So far Caterina had held her own well. She had stopped Cesare's soldiers from looting and pillaging on Christmas Day by distracting them with the threat of a Venetian attack, and her own actions as a warrior were limited to a few well-aimed cannon shots at the palaces of Forlì's foulest traitors.

It was Saint Stephen's Day, the twenty-third anniversary of her father's murder in Milan. As she heard Mass with her commanders, Caterina may have thought of her father, Duke Galeazzo Maria. Never in written, spoken, or recorded word did she show any rancor toward the man who had married her off at age ten to the pope's dissolute nephew; indeed, in her thirty-six years, she had never known among her husbands, lovers, or adversaries anyone who equaled her father's strength of will and love of life. At every confrontation, Caterina always cited her father's "fearlessness" or "strategic brilliance," and she had spent her whole life trying to emulate those qualities, never more so than in her bold defense of her lands. How different she had been at fourteen—so naively excited to be going to Rome despite the hasty departure after her father's death. A lifetime later, Caterina had borne eight children, buried three husbands, and fought off endless plots and intrigues. Most of all, with the help of Savonarola's instruction, she had found spiritual peace. Should she die that day, Caterina was confident that she would find her way to Paradise, while if Cesare Borgia were to be killed, he would have Hell to pay.

Trumpets broke Caterina's reveries and summoned her to the battlefield. She strapped on her cuirass, one of the very few made for a woman in that age. It was as expertly crafted as her luxurious gowns had been in her youth; the steel was shaped to her curves and reinforced to prevent crushing or compressing her breasts. It was also streamlined so that she could wear it underneath her clothes. Tiny plates fit perfectly together to allow for a wide range of movement. The delicate floral pattern lightly incised on the front was the only concession to ornament, and on the upper left plate Saint Catherine of Alexandria, Caterina's patron saint, was etched into the steel.

She raced up the narrow spiral steps that led from her rooms to the lookout point over the bastions, her long skirts rustling. Her men-at-arms were gawking as they peered over the moat. No cannon fire, no projectiles, no billowing acrid smoke greeted her, only the crisp, cold winter wind. Looking down over the low wall, she could clearly see Cesare Borgia, duke of Valentinois, astride his white horse. He was poised at the edge of the moat and surrounded by a small coterie of liveried guards. Cesare had thrown a silver and black cloak over his suit of armor, and instead of a helmet, he sported a black velvet beret adorned with a long white feather. It was hard to tell from his apparel whether he had come to fight or to court. The duke slid easily from his horse and with a polished gesture swept his hat from his head, extending it at arm's length as he made a deep bow toward the lady on the ramparts. Caterina, well versed in courtly manners, returned the greeting with a regal nod.

Hat in hand, Cesare addressed the countess in the most complimentary terms, praising both her education and her wisdom. He observed that states come and they go, assuring her that if she would cede the fortress to him, his father, Pope Alexander VI, would happily give her another. As crafty as he was bold, and aware of Caterina's soft spot for handsome young men, Cesare was flirting.

Without replying, Caterina stood on the rampart, listening. Encouraged, the duke pressed his suit. He offered her land, compensation, and even a home in Rome if that was what she preferred. The promises of the pope and his son would be guaranteed by illustrious witnesses, including one of French royal blood. Cesare's seductive words, however, were laced with unmistakable warnings. Even if the countess remained indifferent to the prospect of horrible bloodshed among her people, certainly she would balk at the idea of all of Italy laughing at her, ridiculing her for the futile and wasteful defense of her tiny dominion.

Caterina's face still gave no indication of her thoughts. She stood erect until Cesare's last pleas were carried off by the wind. She let silence fill the void of his empty promises, and then she spoke.

While gracefully acknowledging Cesare's fulsome compliments, she noted that Cesare had overlooked her greatest quality. She was the daughter of a man who knew no fear, and like her father, she would follow her chosen course to the end. She curtly reminded her antagonist that unlike him, she bore an honorable name. Never would she disgrace her forefathers and the glorious house of Sforza by conceding victory to a lesser house without a fight. Moreover, she added, "all of Italy knows the worth of the Borgia word. The bad faith of the father has removed any credit from the son." It was of no matter whom they brought as witnesses. If "the principal was false," she said, "so would be its satellites."[1] Then she issued a few warnings of her own. The indefatigable countess boasted that the walls of her fortress were holding strong and that word had gone out to the Holy Roman Emperor Maximilian I, husband to her sister Bianca Maria. Reinforcements would arrive at any moment. Having done some military recognizance of her own, Caterina knew Cesare was still waiting for his heavy artillery to arrive, and his troops were restless, awaiting their pay. Finally, she stated that her refusal to accept his ignoble offers, unworthy of her Sforza heritage, would garner only respect throughout the whole world. Even if she should die on this battlefield, her name would live on forever. As her last words rang though the chilly morning air, Caterina saluted the duke, turned on her heel, and disappeared into the keep.

A baffled, angry Cesare rode back to his quarters. This insufferable woman had bested him in front of both armies. Her calm self-assurance remained unmoved by his charm, promises, or threats. The soldiers had heard her call the pope a liar. He would have to show them that this woman could not insult him so blatantly nor dismiss him so easily.

A few hours later, Cesare rode back to the fortress and the trumpeter again gave the signal for a parley. Caterina had used the time to develop a scheme of her own. If the pope's insolent son thought that he was such a magnet for women, let that be his downfall. For this encounter, Caterina put aside the mien of the tough warrior and became the elegant countess who had also broken her share of hearts. Instead of appearing at the ramparts, Caterina ordered the drawbridge to be lowered and walked out to the midpoint.

Cesare dismounted and strode toward the drawbridge, stopping at the edge of the moat. Caterina approached him, coming to the edge of the bridge. The onlookers saw the duke earnestly try to persuade the countess to cede the castle. Caterina looked up at the tall soldier and into his eyes, as if trying to read the sincerity of his offer. A few moments later, her shoulders drooped and her brow furrowed as if reconsidering her position. Cesare, pressing his advantage, reached for her arm. A gesture from Caterina indicated that they should enter the castle to discuss terms, and she walked back toward the fortress. Cesare made to follow suit, but as he stepped onto the drawbridge, it started to rise. Cesare leapt back just in time to escape capture. Enraged, embarrassed, and no doubt frightened by his narrow escape, the pope's son erupted in a flood of obscenities.[2] He walked to the edge of the moat and roared so that everyone in his camp could hear that a reward of a thousand ducats awaited anyone who captured Caterina dead. Caterina, now back on the ramparts, retorted that she would give five thousand ducats for the corpse of the Borgia captain. Caterina enjoyed standing on the ramparts and taunting an enemy. She had outwitted the College of Cardinals on the bastions of the

Castel Sant'Angelo and bested Giralamo Riario's assassins from this very wall a decade earlier. In such verbal jousts, Cesare never stood a chance.

Diarists, ambassadors, and the simply curious flocked to Forlì to witness the most ruthless man in Italy thwarted by this fearless woman. Sadly, Leone Cobelli was not among the onlookers, as he lay dying at the time of the siege. After a lifetime of following Caterina's adventures, Cobelli would not recount her most noble hour; his last written words cursed the French: "those barbarians and people without law." Andrea Bernardi was now the sole local chronicler for the troubled city, but this barber-scribe had found a friend in Cesare, who took an avid interest in how this showdown would be recorded. Flattered by praise and honors, Bernardi allowed the Borgia prince to read and edit his manuscript, leaving future readers to wonder what Cesare may have added or omitted. The other witnesses produced a fast-paced crossfire of letters resembling the fiery exchange of artillery between the two camps, some favoring Caterina, others backing Cesare. Every head of state had eyes and ears at Forlì; the siege of the tiny town potentially held massive ramifications for the other polities.

Time would be a deciding factor for both camps. The political tides were shifting once again, possibly in Caterina's favor. Gian Giacomo Trivulzio, whom Louis XII had left in charge of Milan, had already earned the disapproval of the Milanesi, and Duke Ludovico began to seem preferable to the tyrant. Ludovico had wasted no time while in Germany; there he had recruited an army and soon would be ready to march on Milan. The moment Ludovico began his siege of the city, the king of France would seek to defend it and therefore recall his soldiers employed in Cesare's Romagna campaign. The Borgia commander would be left alone. Adept at intrigue, Duke Ludovico had even devised a strategy to keep Venice at bay. Through various agents at the court of the Holy Roman Emperor, Ludovico had succeeded in stirring up the old Turkish enmity toward Venice. The Turks exploited Venice's distraction with Italian politics to seize several territories in the Adriatic. The ease of their capture emboldened the Ottoman army to venture onto Italian soil and attack Venetian holdings in Friuli. Like the tentative rays of sunshine peeking through the overcast January morning, hope stirred in the hearts of the defenders of Forlì. Well-informed of unfolding events by spies and agents, Caterina understood that she needed to keep her defenses strong and her spirits up.

Many military experts observing the siege of Forlì thought that Caterina's fortress was strong enough to withstand the wait until the French called back their troops. Giovanni Sforza, lord of Pesaro (and the discarded husband of Lucrezia Borgia), wrote encouragingly to the marquis of Mantua, predicting that with her men and her provisions, Caterina could hold out against Cesare for at least four months.

Ravaldino was built along a trapezoidal plan, with long curtain walls anchored by squat towers. The keep stood at the northern short end of the fort, a forty-five-foot square tower with thick walls and rounded corners. The space within the walls had always been used for military exercises and reviews, and during peaceful periods the countess had even beautified it with a garden; now the citadel operated like a well-run factory. Stations for making cannonballs, repairing swords, and delivering medical treatment were lined up in a neat row. A deep moat surrounded the whole structure, with access to it only through drawbridges and tunnels. Opposite the keep and along the western wall, Caterina had constructed *rivellini*, heavily built triangular defensive structures detached from the main curtain walls. These miniature forts, pointing like spearheads at the enemy, presented formidable obstacles to soldiers rushing to surmount the walls. Each narrow opening of a *rivellino* held three cannons, allowing the defenders a wide range of fire.

Until Caterina's time, castles like Ravaldino were considered impregnable. But warfare had changed. Old-fashioned battering rams and fire from low heavy cannons would have glanced off the slanted bastions at the base of the castle, but the new firearms could direct shots at the straight walls above. The moat had kept archers out of range, but the latest projectiles crossed it easily. If the walls gave, Forlì's four months would be reduced to four hours. Taking stock of her situation, Caterina knew Cesare had arrived with almost twelve thousand men. Flemish, German, and Swiss mercenaries comprised the bulk of his infantry, but King Louis had given him two thousand well-trained veteran troops and he commanded two thousand experienced Spanish soldiers as well, who were the backbone of Cesare's army. They seemed inexhaustible compared to the thousand faithful soldiers inside the walls of Ravaldino. Cesare also possessed copious artillery. Seventeen smaller movable guns—"iron mouths" as they were called—were pointed at Caterina's walls. Five big cannons, unwieldy but powerful, were pounding at her fortifications. Cesare also had eleven lithe falconet guns, the latest in artillery. Only about three feet long, they peppered the defenders with two- to three-pound iron balls. The fanciest weapon in Cesare's armory was one he had brought from Rome: the Tiverina, named after the Tiber River. Nine feet in length, it could fire projectiles the size of a soccer ball instead of the usual three- to four-inch shot. Caterina knew her fortress was strong, but these advanced firearms rendered her walls vulnerable.

Likewise, Cesare had problems to contend with. Like Caterina, he demanded discipline from his troops, but it was much harder to control twelve thousand soldiers from numerous countries who were working for a paycheck. The French soldiers from the king's standing army were needed to keep them in line. And not all was well with the Forlivesi who had capitulated to him. Already they were beginning to rue their decision. Forced to billet his soldiers, they soon found themselves turned out of their homes. Artisans could only watch as their shops were taken over by the army's blacksmiths or used as stables; any Forlivesi who hesitated to comply received a savage beating. Looting, rape, and other forms of brutality were common. Even Saint Mercuriale fell victim. Having discovered that the makeshift shrine to the saint rested above the monument to the French soldiers killed by Guido di Montefeltro in 1282, the French contingent among Cesare's troops knocked the statue of the saint into the mud and hacked it to pieces, declaring that the patron saint of Forlì "did not deserve to be above the bones of our dead." The townspeople gathered the pieces and brought them into the church, as they had done with the broken bodies of those murdered and left in the square. To quell any spirit of resistance in Forlì, the Borgia commander made every man, woman, and child, even priests and Jews, wear the white cross of the penitent. Cesare then decreed that anyone carrying weapons would be immediately hanged and any attack against his soldiers would receive an exemplary punishment.

Frustrated by Caterina's resistance, and alarmed by the French soldiers' admiration for her, he had raised the bounty on her head to ten thousand ducats, but still no one was willing to betray her. Cesare then searched for ways to get into the castle. On December 27, he ordered his troops to dig a tunnel under the moat to the castle, a futile exercise that actually benefited the Forlivesi. The energy the soldiers expended digging into the frozen earth meant less time for them to torment the townspeople. Cesare then ordered the falconets to be planted all around the keep, planning to throw all his firepower at Caterina's stronghold and blast her out.

On December 28, Cesare started hammering Ravaldino in earnest. With the morning light reflecting off the muzzles of the falconets, they resembled silver streams feeding into the moat. The bombardment took out one of the defense towers and left Caterina's beloved Paradise a ruin, but she was undaunted. The keep remained intact; she moved in there. Her return fire caused Cesare even greater damage. Borgia's French artillery expert, Costantino da Bologna, was killed. A loud lament went up from the enemy camp, and the French exclaimed that the king would have happily given ten thousand ducats to bring that valuable man back to life again. Caterina had also selected her artillery chief with care. Bartolomeo Bolognesi's cannons responded shot for shot to Cesare attacks, and he remained ever-vigilant to respond to any careless exposure on the part of the enemy. He "never fails to salute any who pass by," wrote an observer to the duke of Milan, recounting that Duke Cesare had grown so exasperated that he was offering a thousand ducats for Bolognesi's corpse and two thousand for him alive.

News of the extraordinary defense on the part of one courageous woman spread like wildfire through Italy. The diarist Antonio Grumello from Pavia wrote at the time, "There has never been seen a woman with so much spirit."[3] "She has shown herself a female of great governance," wrote one commentator from her old enemy Venice. "Certainly this woman could be called a Virago."[4] Virago, derived from *vir*, the Latin word for "man," denoted a woman who possessed qualities that the Renaissance associated with men: strength, standing, and importance. Caterina was one of the few women of her age to be referred to that way. Public opinion, at least, seemed to be in Caterina's favor. Ottaviano was trying to find reinforcements for his mother, and the Florentines secretly promised to send soldiers; the hardest part would be getting them into the fortress. It took a clever ruse to do so.

On one freezing January morning, a group of men came chanting though Cesare's camp. Wearing traveling cloaks and carrying the traditional staff of the pilgrim, they begged safe transit through Forlì on their journey to Rome for the Holy Year. Promising to pray for those who let them pass, the band made its way toward Ravaldino. Suddenly the drawbridge was lowered and they all rushed inside: forty extra men to defend the fortress.

No one knew who sent them; most speculated Florence, although others thought it might have been Ludovico the Moor. But the fact was that it could have been Cardinal Riario from Savona, or Giovanni Bentivoglio from Bologna, for now sympathies were starting to turn toward Caterina.

Cesare knew he was running out of time, he was still waiting for money to pay his troops, and although he knew the funds were forthcoming, he also had been apprised that Giovanni Sforza had almost managed to intercept and seize his precious cash. Cesare's outraged father sputtered tirades against Caterina and the house of Sforza, "the seed of the serpent Satan!"[5] The Borgia's list of enemies was growing and the more time he spent stalled by a woman, the more he would seem weak in the eyes of his adversaries. He could break a lance or straighten a horseshoe in his bare hands. He could kill a bull in a ring, but he couldn't defeat this woman.

He decided to concentrate all his energies on what his experts had discovered to be the weakest section of wall: the southern stretch facing the mountains. For two days he moved his guns to the other side of the fort, digging trenches and building protective ramparts for the gunmen. Most of his soldiers were in the city, celebrating Epiphany, the Feast of the Three Kings who came to see the infant Jesus. Instead of giving gifts, as was traditional in Europe, the soldiers were looting and pillaging and bringing prostitutes to their banqueting table. The local chronicler Bernardi was horrified by their obscene pranks and how they "blessed the table in their own way,"[6] finding it particularly abhorrent that they ate standing up. When the festivities ended, Cesare began the siege again. Day and night he pummeled the southern wall of Ravaldino with cannonballs. The blows began to take effect, ripping holes in the long straight curtain wall. Caterina and her men never showed signs of worry, and as night fell they raced to repair the breaks with sandbags or stones, so that the next morning found the wall whole again. Caterina slyly undermined the morale of Cesare's men; at night as the French soldiers were huddled in frozen ditches with their cannons, they could hear pipes and drums playing inside the fort. While those in the fortress repaired the walls and tended the wounded, Caterina kept up the illusion that they were simply having a merry dance. From time to time, the defenders of Ravaldino would scrawl a gibe onto one of the cannonballs: "Hey, slow down, you'll hit our toilets!"

But as pieces of the Ravaldino wall fell, they began to pile up in the moat, slowly creating a pathway. Cesare, seeing his opportunity, ordered every peasant in Forlì to bring a bundle of logs for his soldiers to build into rafts, and he requisitioned two long flat riverboats from Ravenna. On January 12, three weeks after Cesare had made his entry into Forlì, the Borgia commander threw everything he had at the now fragile castle wall. The extra pay had arrived and he distributed the money liberally, offering incentives for harder work. The efforts paid off, and Cesare's artillery ripped a large breach into Caterina's wall. Fallen debris hindered the defenders' attempts to repair the damage, as did well-aimed shots from the falconets. Cesare's men made the log rafts and anchored them to the rubble in the half-filled moat. The enemy now had a bridge into Caterina's fort. At noon Cesare went to lunch with his commanding officers and boasted, "Today is Sunday; by Tuesday Lady Caterina will be in my hands."[7] The officers protested that he should not cry victory too soon. Undoubtedly the countess would repair to the keep and they would have to besiege the stronghold. A confident Cesare offered a three-hundred-ducat wager on the outcome.

While Cesare was taking bets, Caterina was repositioning her guns. Using the fallen pieces of stone as cover, she aligned all her weapons to fire on the opening in the wall. A French assault through that crevice would be a suicide run. Cesare, having finished his meal, strode back to the moat and issued the order to take the citadel. The soldiers crossed the makeshift bridge in maniples of sixteen, climbing through the breach and pouring into the citadel.

Not one shot greeted them. Caterina's guns remained silent, and none of the defenders met Cesare's soldiers head-on. The desertion of Caterina's camp had begun; the soldiers at the breach had seen a window of freedom and had taken it. A Swiss mercenary named Cupizer climbed unimpeded to the top of the Porta Cotogni and plucked Caterina's standard, the Riario rose and the Sforza viper, from the top. The fortress was taken, and only one question remained: would the last band of defenders put their weapons down quietly or would they fight to the death?

Caterina never hesitated. She strode out of the keep to meet her attackers, followed by Alessandro Sforza, her older brother; Scipione Riario, her stepson; and her few remaining loyal men. She fought in the front ranks, refusing to yield when her officers tried to call for a retreat. The Venetian mercenary Sanuto was already amazed by her spirit, but when he saw that she knew how to handle a sword and "wounded many men,"[8] he was astounded. For two hours she fought side by side with her men through the endless onslaught of Cesare's soldiers. By late afternoon, the defenders were exhausted yet the stream of Cesare's mercenaries seemed endless. Caterina ordered her men to gather ammunition, wood, straw—anything flammable—and make a broad wall of fire. The curtain of smoke slowed the invaders, offering the defenders a moment of respite as the French labored to extinguish the flames. No sooner had the French beaten down the bonfire than Caterina and her soldiers came running toward them to continue the fight. Eyes watering from the smoke and arms aching from the heavy sword, Caterina was the equal of any man on the battlefield. One by one, her weary comrades at arms, aware that they had lost, hoped to escape with their lives by raising the white flag of surrender. But drawing strength from desperation, as the marquis of Mantua wrote, Caterina persisted, with the walls of her Paradise to her back, even as her companions laid down their arms. She had no intention of leaving the battlefield alive. Her captains, her castellan, and her brother were all taken prisoner, but Caterina backed her way into the keep. As she sealed the entry gate, she was already barking orders to the soldiers to prepare for a siege.

Cesare, however, had one last trick up his sleeve. He rode up to the keep, his white horse darkened by soot and grime amid the carnage. The Borgia herald sounded his trumpet and Caterina was called to speak to Cesare for the third and last time. Cesare, feigning solicitous concern, begged Caterina to stop this pointless waste of lives. Caterina replied that if he respected life as much as he claimed, he would show mercy to her townspeople and to her soldiers who had surrendered to him. Before she could utter another word, a heavy hand fell on her shoulder, and she heard a voice in French say, "Madame, you are a prisoner of my lord, the constable of Dijon." Caterina had been betrayed from within the walls of her own castle.

How could it happen that she was surprised within her own stronghold? Many contemporaries pondered the reasons for the sudden fall of the castle. The surprise turn of events implied treachery. Andrea Bernardi, while writing his chronicle under the watchful eye of Cesare Borgia, hinted that the fortress "was taken by things seen and unseen." Cesare himself was the first to admit in a letter to his father that he "never would have taken the castle if all her men had the countess's spirit." Gian Giacomo Trivulzio in Milan, astonished by Caterina's capture, claimed to the ambassador of the duke of Ferrara that "there must have been great cowardice in that castle to be lost so pathetically." As far as he could tell the fortress should have been able to hold out for fifteen more days.

Machiavelli, an open admirer of Cesare Borgia, analyzed the fall of Forlì closely in his book *On the Art of War.* "The fortress was divided in three parts and each part was separated by trenches and water from the others with bridges linking the structures together. Once the duke with his artillery had demolished one of the areas of the fortress and opened a hole in the wall; once Giovanni da Casale who was in charge of guarding it, didn't defend that opening, but retreated to some other part, the duke's troops entered without any conflict through that spot and took everything in a moment."[9] But the Florentine pundit maintained that the true weakness was Caterina, who "had more faith in her fortresses than in conquering the love of her people."[10]

Giovanni da Casale's name soon became synonymous with *traitor.* The Florentine historian Guicciardini, writing a few years later, condemned Casale's men as being of "the same infamy and misery of Giovanni da Casale, their captain."[11] Giovanni had been named as Caterina's latest lover by the Venetian mercenary Sanuto. But in the year after Giovanni de' Medici's death, speculation linked Caterina with every man who came near her. Achille and Polidoro Tiberti, the brothers from Cesena, had each been rumored as paramours despite the fact that they both worked actively against the countess at the behest of Cesare Borgia. Ottaviano Manfredi, the on-again, off-again claimant to Faenza, had also been romantically tied to her, although he had led an attack on Forlì for Venice. Even poor Francesco Fortunati, the priest from Cascina, had been accused of breaking his vows with the beautiful countess. Like an account from tabloid journalism, Giovanni da Casale's supposed betrayal was rendered all the more poignant because he was presumed to be Caterina's lover. His reputation in tatters—a serious problem for a soldier for hire—Casale attempted to refute the accusations, laying the blame on Caterina's brother Alessandro for his cowardice as well as the rivalries and insubordination among his fellow officers. How a French soldier gained access to the sealed keep remains a mystery, but as one modern writer put it, "The castellan was a traitor, a coward, or a fool."[12] Machiavelli best summed up that cold evening of January 12: "The poor defenses of the fortress and the little wisdom of those defending it shamed the great undertaking of the countess."[13]

Contemporaries noticed that Cesare, although eager to claim his prize, took his time entering the keep, waiting for it to be completely subdued. Once inside, he encountered the first of many problems that Caterina would cause for him. The French soldier, a certain Bernard, who had captured the countess, demanded his reward. Cesare ordered that the soldier be paid two thousand ducats. Outraged, Bernard reminded Cesare that he had publicly promised ten thousand ducats for the countess. Cesare's protests were silenced as the soldier pulled out his dagger and held it to Caterina's throat. If Cesare denied him his full prize, threatened Bernard, then all he would get of Caterina was her head. Then the captain of the French forces, Yves D'Allegre, raced to the defense of his officer, Bernard, and soon the keep resounded with shouts in French, Spanish, and Italian. Over the weeks of watching Caterina, D'Allegre had been smitten by her beauty, bravery, and ingenuity. The ancient French sense of chivalry stirred in the soldier, who balked at Caterina's being consigned directly to Cesare. Under French law, no woman could be taken as a prisoner of war; in D'Allegre's hands, she would be in the custody of the king of France. The Borgia family recognized no such niceties. In their clutches, Caterina would meet a brutal end. The negotiations between Bernard, who wanted money, D'Allegre, who desired honor, and Cesare, who ached for revenge, resulted in D'Allegre's successfully declaring Caterina to be under the protection of Louis XII; therefore she could not be tortured, imprisoned, or killed. As a professional soldier, he thought he had secured Caterina's safety. But Cesare had fought too hard for this particular prize to give it up so lightly. He insisted that the countess be entrusted to the Borgias for "safekeeping." Although technically under the jurisdiction of the French and therefore invio- late, she was thereby consigned to Cesare, who, unbeknownst to the French, did not live by a reliable code of ethics.

Well past midnight, Caterina was led out of the keep into the car- nage surrounding her citadel. Seven hundred lay dead, defenders and assailants alike. Caterina stepped over rubble and bodies. Scat- tered fragments of the sumptuous bronze monument she had made in honor of Giacomo Feo lay on the ground; the urn had been smashed and the prized bronze, the best metal for artillery, had been carted away to be melted and made into more weapons. Cesare's soldiers were disappointed with the paltry contents of the treasury; convinced that the defenders had swallowed gold ducats or jewels for safekeep- ing, they slit the bodies open to search the entrails. The acrid smell of gunpowder stung Caterina's eyes and burned in her nose and throat, mercifully covering the stench of death. Caterina had ordered all the ammunition in the fortress burned, to ensure that the fall of her cas- tle would not provision Cesare's attack on his next target. Caterina didn't wince at the horror but commented that the fate of the dead didn't upset her as much as that of the survivors.[14] Death in combat was infinitely more honorable than survival through surrender. The French soldiers sorted their prisoners; those who were Italian were allowed to live, but the foreign mercenaries were put to death. Ca- terina's brother, her secretary, and a priest who had remained to the bitter end to administer the sacraments to Caterina and her men were all apprehended. A large number of women—ladies in waiting and maidservants—who had remained in the fort, loyal to their mistress, were now in the hands of the troops. Several prisoners were killed, in- cluding the unfortunate priest who had stayed by Caterina's side and a young courtier who had gallantly defended the countess. Cesare put ransoms on the noblemen, which were soon paid, but there would be no freedom for Caterina. She was led from the fortress, her home for twelve years, into an uncertain future. As the chronicler Bernardi put it, "Paradise was now governed by devils."[15]

A heavy escort accompanied Caterina to the palace of Luffo Nu- mai, the changeable Forlivese nobleman who had welcomed Cesare into his home. The Borgia captain was happily ensconced in the comfortable house. With his dinner warm on the table and the Sangiovese wine ready to wash away the day's bloodshed, Cesare savored the moment when Caterina's children would be brought to him in chains. With all the heirs present, his victory would be complete. His envoys, however, returned empty-handed. Caterina informed her captor that she had sent her children to Florence before the siege and, as they were all Florentine citizens through her marriage to Giovanni de' Medici, he would be unable to demand their release into his custody. Cesare may have captured her fortress and even her person, but his claim on the cities of Imola and Forlì would remain tenuous as long as the rightful lord was still alive. Once again Cesare had been outwitted; his pretensions to nobility, grace, and chivalry were now smothered by rage. Cesare had never been able to make Caterina fear him, and her taunts had shown the world that she didn't respect him. Borgia would regain his honor by taking hers.

For all the pain, misery, and humiliation that Cesare's rape inflicted on her, he could not get the better of Caterina. Although the next morning he boasted to his men, "She defended her fortresses better than her virtue," few laughed, while the rest of Italy mourned her plight. The duke of Milan received a letter about the fall of Forlì, informing him that "it's believed that he has treated her badly." In the halls of the Vatican, courtiers recounted that when he discovered that the children were safe, the pope's son vented his rage on Caterina, "taking her and subjecting her to cruel torments." Trivulzio, the governor of Milan, crudely stated that "certainly Madame won't lack for sex" during her detention, while Bernardi lamented "the injustices to the body of our poor, unfortunate countess."

Cesare even tried to create the illusion that the countess did not spurn his attentions. He dressed her in a black velvet gown with elegant trim to replace the tattered, bloody clothes she had been arrested in. Cesare himself always wore all black, one of the first in Italy to reject the older fashion of bright fabrics in favor of the dark tones that set off his pale skin and golden hair. Together, the two made a striking pair. He kept Caterina prisoner both day and night in his rooms in the Numai palace, never letting her out of his sight, sharing meals and allowing visitors to see her unshackled and ostensibly unharmed in the bedroom. Corporal violence on a noblewoman was frowned upon in both France and Italy, and by trading on Caterina's reputation as sexually voracious, Borgia tried to pass them off as honeymooners, rather than rapist and victim. A few fell for the dupe, claiming that Cesare seemed quite enamored; others who had caught a glimpse of the countess imprisoned in Cesare's room said that although she spoke very little and often looked as if she had been crying, she still held her head high. For all his attempts to undermine her virtue, Caterina remained more admired than Cesare. Another formidable woman, Isabella d'Este, marquise of Mantua, renowned for her intelligence and determination, admiringly remarked in reference to Caterina, "If the French criticize the cowardliness of our men, at least they should praise the daring and valor of the Italian women."[16] Her words echoed the sentiments of men and women in the streets and piazzas, who coined the saying "When the French deal with Italian men they find women, but when they meet women they find men."

Even the Republic of Venice offered encomium. "Although this woman is an enemy of the Venetian state, she truly deserves infinite praise and immortal memory among the famous and worthy Roman captains."[17] The French soldiers who had lost many men at her hands were able to demonstrate a respect for Caterina that Cesare could not. The troops who had fought at Forlì named their best falconet gun La Madame de Fourly in her honor, while Jehan de Auton, the French biographer of Louis XII, wrote this of the countess: "Under her feminine body she had a masculine courage; she had no fear of danger; no matter how close it approached, she never backed down."[18]

On January 21, nine days after the fall of Ravaldino, Cesare set off to begin the siege of Pesaro, the territory of Giovanni Sforza, Caterina's cousin and his former brother-in-law. Cesare took Caterina with him, relishing the thought that she would witness the fall of another family stronghold. They were traveling by night along the Via Emilia when the horses abruptly stopped. Yves D'Allegre was blocking the path with three hundred infantrymen. The Frenchman's honor was wounded at the idea of Caterina's being held as a prisoner of war when she was rightfully under the protection of King Louis XII. Perhaps fearing that Cesare would kill her en route, D'Allegre claimed custody of the countess with the intention of bringing her to France. The soldiers stood at the ready, their hands on their weapons. Cesare handed over his prisoner and raced off to Cesena. Captain D'Allegre bundled up his precious charge and sent her back to Forlì, to the house of the Paolucci family. As Caterina got into bed alone for the first time since her capture, she dreamed that she might soon be free.

But like the Greek warrior Achilles, Cesare did not take losing his prize lightly. The next morning he returned to Forlì to discuss Caterina's fate by the light of day. Bernard, the soldier who had seized Caterina, D'Allegre, and a few other French captains objected to Caterina's confinement in defiance of French law. Cesare countered by asserting his rights as the supreme commander of the victorious army. The Frenchmen readily responded that they were not fighting for Cesare but for King Louis. Furthermore, they added, without their aid Cesare never would have succeeded in taking the fortress. As voices were raised and soldiers called to arms, the people of Forlì gathered in the piazza to witness another great Sforza spectacle. The French soldiers were lined up with their lances on one side, with Cesare and his men facing them. And then money talked. Cesare offered Bernard and the French soldiers the full reward for Caterina. Ten thousand ducats was a small fortune and the French backed down at once. Only D'Allegre was unmoved by Cesare's largesse and tried to do his best for Caterina by declaring her a French subject, but he could do little against his compliant men. She would be returned to Cesare "in deposit," with the pope as guarantor of her safety. As Machiavelli bluntly put it, "She was sold to the Duke Valentino." The brief window of freedom slammed shut and Caterina was again at Cesare's mercy.

The following morning, Cesare and his soldiers packed up once again to depart. Borgia rounded up his men, and still reeking from the evening's excesses, attended Mass in the cathedral. Luffo Numai led the city elders to the main piazza, where they swore an oath of loyalty to Cesare and the pope. The city was subdued and Ravaldino was repaired, the mended breach in the fortress wall marked with the Borgia symbol, a bull.

Riding between Cesare and D'Allegre, with six hundred cavalry in her wake, Caterina began her long journey toward Rome, where she would be a "guest" of the pope. The people of Forlì lined the streets for one last glimpse of their countess. Her long years of rule ended, Caterina rode bloodied but unbowed. The tragic figure of the proud and beautiful countess inspired epic poems and popular songs, such as

the nobleman Marsilio Compagnon's "Lament of Caterina Sforza."[19]
These mournful verses were sung in soldiers' camps throughout Italy
long after the fall of Forlì.

> *Ah you frightened Italians,*
> *I will stand with my armor.*
> *I'd rather lose in battle*
> *and die with honor.*
>
> *Before I'd be sent to wander*
> *with my children through the world*
> *and sink shamefully into oblivion,*
> *I'd sooner be tortured and killed.*
>
> *Listen to this brokenhearted plea.*
> *I am Caterina of Forlì.*

18

THE LONG NIGHT OF
CASTEL SANT'ANGELO

THE CASTEL SANT'ANGELO may have been named for the archangel Michael, but there was nothing celestial about the dark recesses of its dungeons. Caterina's cramped cell stank of excrement and rot. She had already endured a long and unpleasant trip to Rome, punctuated by episodes of false hope and bitter disappointment. At the town of Pesaro, which Cesare was planning to wrest from Caterina's cousin Giovanni, the Borgia commander had changed his mind and decided to part with his troublesome prize, consigning Caterina to the custody of Yves D'Allegre. At last, Caterina could expect some respite from her captivity and from Cesare's humiliating assaults. But thanks to her uncle Ludovico the Moor that was not to be. The exiled duke of Milan had finally marshaled his army and marched on Milan to recover his duchy from the French king. Too late to assist Caterina at Ravaldino, Ludovico launched a counterattack that served only to deprive her of this protection from Cesare. Captain D'Allegre was abruptly summoned to the front, and with a heavy heart returned Caterina to Cesare before departing at a gallop for Milan. Although Captain D'Allegre's departure destroyed Caterina's dreams of being rid of Cesare, it saved Pesaro. Without the backing of the French army, Cesare had no taste for another fight against the Sforza family. Caterina and Cesare continued on to Rome.

Throughout the voyage, Cesare boastfully planned his triumphal parade in the style of the ancient Roman emperors. He, Cesare, had succeeded where even the emperor Augustus failed. The seductive Egyptian queen Cleopatra had chosen to kill herself rather than be exhibited as the emperor's trophy. Cesare Borgia, on the other hand, had taken his Cleopatra alive: Caterina, as beautiful, proud, and notorious as the Egyptian pharaoh, rode silently next to him. He wanted her clad in golden chains, riding behind his chariot like King Vercingetorix after Caesar's triumph over Gaul.

But it was Cesare's turn for disappointment. On February 26, Caterina arrived in Rome, was discreetly installed in a papal villa by the Vatican hill, and remained in her rooms during Cesare's parade. Not one of the meticulous chronicles that recounted every detail of the spectacle, from Cesare's knee-length black velvet tunic to the sighing girls who admired his passage from their high windows, to Pope Alexander's tears of pride, mentions Caterina. Alexander, aware of his dependence on the French army, prudently avoided antagonizing the French king by exhibiting Caterina as a prisoner.

The long weeks of subjugation to Cesare had not dampened her will. The ambassador of the marquis of Mantua, who saw the countess on February 27, described her as *"indiavolato e forte d'animo,"* "still furious and strong-willed."[1] Although anxious for many reasons during those first months of imprisonment, Caterina had lived in comfort. Lodged in the luxurious recreational palace—known as the Belvedere for its stunning views—Caterina had enjoyed fresh air, the soothing sounds of indoor fountains, and the sweet scent of oranges from the trees in the courtyard. Alexander's predecessor, Innocent VIII, had commissioned the elegant structure for his own enjoyment. Caterina must have been surprised to see the steep tree-lined hill where she had ridden wild during the reign of Sixtus IV tamed to an architectural showplace. The pope permitted her a small coterie of servants, ladies in waiting, plus her Florentine priest and confidant Francesco Fortunati, who acted as her confessor. But as gilded as the cage may have been, Caterina was very much a prisoner. An armed guard of twenty infantrymen surrounded the tiny palace, and letters reached her only sporadically, after being checked by papal agents. The Borgias pressured her daily to sign over her claims to Forlì and Imola, promising her freedom, a new home, and the possibility of being reunited with her children. But Caterina stubbornly refused, day after day. She knew that once she signed away her and Ottaviano's rights, she would be of no further use to them. Like many other Borgia "guests," she would probably succumb to an inexplicable stomach ailment or turn up floating lifeless in the Tiber. Doubting that she would ever be released from captivity, Caterina's only recourse would be escape.

The Borgias found unlikely allies in Caterina's own children. Ottaviano, who had never relished the dangers and responsibilities of ruling a state, had long since set his eye on an ecclesiastical career, while Cesare Riario, her second son, was thriving under Pope Alexander's regime as archbishop of Pisa and hoping for greater church rewards. Neither son cared for the little Romagnol towns their mother had fought so hard to preserve for them. They hoped instead that Caterina would use the leverage of signing away the two territories to gain them further benefices and allow them to live the luxurious life of many Roman prelates. Furthermore, the responsibilities and expenses connected to the guardianship of little Ludovico, their two-year-old stepbrother, were a bother. Their letters to Caterina were startlingly devoid of filial concern over her well-being and were instead packed with lamentation concerning their difficult circumstances. "To my lady dearest mother," begins Ottaviano's epistle of May 11, before launching into an extensive complaint regarding his efforts to secure her freedom. Ottaviano and Cesare were employing an agent, Alexander Bramio, whom Caterina distrusted. "You're wrong to calumnize the people we choose to trust, so you'll see soon enough yourself,"[2] they chastised her in one letter. They rued the depletion of their own funds in seeking her release and resented the burden of their little brother. Ottaviano's closing lines in one letter reveal how little he understood of his mother's suffering. "I am under obligation to take care of little Ludovico, but I would like to be relieved of it and I can't unless you renounce your custody of him. I beg you, if you love me, to renounce him immediately and once I am freed from this obligation procure for me a cardinal's hat."[3]

As was generally the case among the nobility, Caterina had been raised as a pawn in her father's house. Her destiny, whether marriage or religious vows, would be determined by her father in the interests of the family name and future. This sense of filial duty, drummed into Caterina from her infancy, restrained her protests when she was married off at ten. It was her obligation to further the proud name of Sforza. Girolamo Riario, on the other hand, had not been raised with the same long view of family responsibility. As his behavior in Rome showed, time and again, Girolamo put his own interests first—money, titles, privilege; the good name of the della Rovere–Riario papacy was of minimal concern. Ottaviano and Cesare had apparently inherited the self-serving streak of their father, seeking only vain, fleeting enjoyments and uninterested in the future of a dynasty.

Worry over the fate of little Ludovico tormented Caterina during her imprisonment. Greed and envy had caused Giovanni de' Medici's older brother, Lorenzo di Pierfrancesco, to plot against his own cousins, the elder Medici branch. Then Giovanni's premature death had offered Lorenzo an enticing opportunity to absorb his brother's inheritance into his own patrimony. The revelation of Caterina's marriage and the infant heir, Ludovico, had upset his plans to usurp his brother's wealth and threatened a close investigation of Giovanni's accounts, which Lorenzo had already depleted heavily. Caterina's fall and imprisonment had been a godsend for the money-hungry Medici, as was Ottaviano's reluctance to assume guardianship of Ludovico. Using Caterina's imprisonment by the Borgias as an excuse, Lorenzo attempted to have Caterina declared legally unfit to retain custody of the child, so as to seize both Ludovico and his estate. From the high *loggias* of the Belvedere palace, Caterina raged in frustration and began her plan to escape. But it would take one last event in late May to clinch Caterina's resolve to break out of Borgia custody: the defeat and imprisonment of her uncle Duke Ludovico of Milan.

Ludovico the Moor had returned to Milan in January and had reconquered the city by February. Caterina's uncle Ascanio Sforza, the wealthy vice chancellor of the church, had joined him, forming a potent alliance between church and state. Faced with this formidable pair, it behooved the Borgia pope, in the interests of self-preservation, to keep Caterina healthy and comfortable in confinement, so that the Milanese would not be spurred to free her or avenge any action taken against her.

But on April 30, betrayal led Ludovico into the hands of the king of France. By early May, the mighty Sforza duke, who had turned Milan into a glittering magnet for artists like Donato Bramante and Leonardo da Vinci, was languishing in the tower of Loches in France, where he would die after ten years of imprisonment. Shortly thereafter, the Venetians claimed the captured Cardinal Ascanio for their prize, and Alexander VI rejoiced. During a celebration in the papal apartments, Alexander boasted that his triple alliance had yielded the Sforza duke in the hands of the French, the Sforza cardinal in those of the Venetians, and the Sforza countess in the Borgia prison. With her powerful uncles removed from the arena of Italian politics, Caterina had no protection left except the Borgia's vague fear of the French. It was time to take matters into her own hands.

Caterina had a long-standing friend in Milan, Abbot Lauro Bossi. He was closely tied to the Milanese court and related to the same Gian Luigi Bossi who had accompanied Caterina on her very first trip to Rome as the young bride of Girolamo Riario. Although the hows and whys of Bossi's sudden arrival in Rome remain unclear, it appears that before his fall, Duke Ludovico had sent the priest to Rome to assist Caterina in her spiritual needs and any other requirements. As the superior of a monastery, he would be respected among the prelates in Rome and move easily among the Curia. Together, Caterina and the abbot laid the plans for a daring escape.

Although it must have heartened Caterina to find an ally, the messages from her children could only be upsetting. Ottaviano's next letter carried a dull tone of finality. "If His Holiness does not grant our latest petition," it opens brusquely, "then don't expect any more from us. We have impoverished ourselves."[4] Her two eldest scions saw only shame in their mother's stubborn refusals; as they were indifferent to the fate of their cities, they found Caterina's attachment to Imola and Forlì embarrassing and inexplicable. Through their newly acquired Medici relatives they tried to deal directly with Alexander, offering to release all claims for a couple of titles and a little spare cash.

By late May, Caterina was poised for action, preparing to scale the walls of the Belvedere and ride off into the night and freedom. Alexander Bramio, the Florentine agent for the Riarios, went to the Belvedere palace on May 26 to deliver a letter from Ottaviano and Cesare. Instead of ushering him swiftly up to Caterina's rooms, the ashen-faced captain of the guards detained him on the lawn, denying his request to visit the countess, saying she had "not yet got up since she was feeling unwell."⁵ Bramio realized immediately that something had happened but knew better than to interrogate a flustered guard. Returning to the papal palaces, he found one of Alexander VI's secretaries, Messer Adrian, who appeared even more reluctant to talk to him than the prison guard. Bramio followed the discomfited secretary into the papal palace, now asking for an audience with the pope to inform him of developments in the Riario case. Messer Adrian, desperate to get away from Bramio, suggested that it wasn't worth the long wait and elaborate protocol and offered to relay any message Bramio might have; if Bramio was looking for an update on the state of the Riarios' request, everything seemed to be going well. The distressed papal secretary guaranteed him that Ottaviano's requests would soon be fulfilled and that Alexander was delighted to help the Riario family out of his fond memory of Pope Sixtus IV. Amid a steady stream of reassuring phrases, Messer Adrian ushered Bramio to the door, with promises of a meeting the next morning.

Justifiably skeptical, Bramio sent one of his servants the next day to deliver the letter to the Belvedere palace and gauge the atmosphere around the papal court. The prison guard relayed the same tale of Caterina's indisposition, this time with more confidence. As Bramio's envoy crossed the river to return home, however, he was accosted by two men frantically looking for Abbot Lauro. They begged the baffled servant to warn the abbot that Rome was no longer a safe place for him. The two men were employed by a certain Corvarano and his boon companion Giovanbattista da Imola. Corvarano and Giovanbattista, the pair confided, had been with Caterina two nights before and had just been arrested. Racing to the palace where Abbot Lauro was lodged, they discovered that the prelate had been seized from his bed at dawn.

Bramio's loyal servant raced back to the Belvedere, demanding to know what had happened to the countess, but the exasperated custodian yelled for him to "go away, because the devilish affairs of the countess have wrought a huge disgrace."⁶ The guard did, however, confirm that Corvarano and Giovanbattista had been arrested.

Shocked by his servant's report, Bramio returned to Messer Adrian for clarification. The recalcitrant secretary would admit only that there had been some tumult and that the countess had been crying all day and had refused to eat. But as the Florentine agent left the Belvedere, he looked up toward the vineyard, where he saw two figures in the garden. Duke Cesare Borgia was speaking intently to Caterina Sforza.

Bramio slowly gleaned the whole story from the Corvarano family. Abbot Lauro had given a letter to Caterina, which she in turn had handed to Corvarano, who had somehow misplaced the compromising missive, which found its way into the hands of Duke Cesare. Although the letter is not preserved, it certainly contained plans for an escape. Once again, Caterina's little window of freedom had opened briefly and then slammed shut.

Caterina was becoming a liability to the Borgia family. Although not overly reverent about preserving human life (during these same days Cesare was plotting to murder his brother-in-law), Cesare knew that killing Caterina would have several potentially disastrous ramifications. She was a Florentine citizen, related to the powerful Medici family. The republic kept informed of her whereabouts and her well-being. Furthermore, the French army admired her and would be swift to avenge any harm done to her. She had become an international icon, with devotees who continued to seek to liberate her. What was worse, they could not break Caterina's spirit. Despite defeat, rape, the callousness of her children, and the overthrow of her family in Milan, Caterina refused to give in. As long as she remained in the Belvedere, she would be a threat. The Borgias knew she had to be kept alive, but with the minimum expense, trouble, and risk. Caterina's attempted escape gave them the perfect excuse to cast her into the papal dungeon, the Castel Sant'Angelo.

Sixteen years earlier, Caterina had commandeered this same fortress and had held it against the College of Cardinals in 1484, after the death of Sixtus IV. The imposing stone cylinder of Hadrian's mausoleum that formed the castle's core was familiar to her, but little else. The Borgia family had completely transformed the huge mound of masonry into one of the most sophisticated defensive structures in Europe. Similar to that of Ravaldino, a huge moat surrounded the fortress, while a sole drawbridge brought visitors to the heart of the castle. The many circular access slopes of Hadrian's time were closed up, and only one great ramp allowed entrance or exit. Ingeniously, the ramp had gently graded steps to allow horses to climb to the highest part of the fort. The innermost burial chamber, where the ashes of Hadrian had once rested, became the deepest and most frightening cell of the castle, known as the *sammalò*, similar to the French *oubliette*. Borgia enemies were thrown into its depths to await death. The knowledge that they were inside a tomb undoubtedly added an element of psychological torture that made the very mention of the infamous chamber a powerful weapon. The center of the building was crammed with prisons, and the atmosphere was dank with stagnant water from the moat. Grain stores and oil barrels filled some rooms, while other chambers were piled high with ammunition. The fetid halls of interrogation, replete with iron instruments of torture, were feared by all Romans. Atop this harrowing space, the Borgia had built airy papal apartments with vaulted ceilings and windows with panoramic views. Alexander VI had hired Pinturicchio, a talented Umbrian painter, to decorate the rooms; he employed the very latest technique in wall decor, called grotesques, a fanciful type of painting rediscovered in Nero's Golden House, currently all the rage in Rome. Ironically, Alexander, who would be dubbed the "the Christian Nero," chose the mad emperor's favorite type of decoration to adorn his own house of torture. Pinturicchio's masterpiece in the fortress (now lost) was a fresco depicting the encounter between the French king Charles VIII and Pope Alexander. It commemorated the alliance which had brought about the ruin of Milan and Forlì amid portraits of all the Borgia friends, family, and paramours. Ever alert to safety, Alexander's new apartment also contained a secret entrance. Known as the *passetto*, it led to a passageway built into ninth-century Vatican walls to allow the pope to travel from his apartments at the apostolic palace next to Saint Peter's Basilica to the castle, without ever having to step into the street or pass through the gloomy dungeons. The pope organized parties, dinners, and dances in his castle; as prisoners suffered and died below, the Borgia family was literally dancing on their graves. And as of June 1500, Caterina was one of the unfortunate captives.

Caterina had spent most of her life within the walls of a fortress, which probably helped her withstand her imprisonment. Though she was spared the horror of the *sammalò*, Caterina's cell was small and uncomfortable and she was allowed only two serving women to assist her. The cramped quarters and the unpleasant surroundings were less oppressive than the constant fear the Borgias forced her to live in. She ate little, afraid that every meal served to her would be laced with poison. Every night she wondered if she would be quietly smothered in her sleep.

Caterina had one small triumph during the first month of her confinement. The Borgias thrived on elaborate spectacles, and the trial planned for Caterina for the attempted poisoning of Alexander was to be a masterpiece of their style of exhibitionism. Clad in the long white robe of the penitent, with a heavy rope around her neck, Caterina was to kneel before Alexander as he held forth about her crimes. The Borgias had primed "witnesses" for the prosecution, and the two would-be poisoners from November 1499, their bodies contorted by torture, would be on hand to plead for mercy. To set the stage, the papal throne was placed under a fresco of a winged figure cloaked in light, holding a flaming sword and an orb; there Alexander was to appear as the personification of Michael the archangel, dispenser of justice. But Caterina shattered these plans by outlining her defense to the master of ceremonies, should she be dragged into this farce.[7] For every false charge the Borgias might lay at her door, she had a litany of accusations of her own. Her knowledge of Cesare's crimes against her person and others was so extensive that the pope and his son annulled the plans for the great trial without further comment. Caterina and Abbot Lauro were left to die of despair and neglect in the Castel Sant'Angelo.

To add a psychological dimension to their physical agony, Cesare played sadistic pranks on his prisoners. One day at dawn, Caterina was roughly awakened and marched out to the courtyard, where a gallows had been erected. Cesare coolly informed her that this was the day of her execution. As Caterina reeled, the two men accused of poisoning Pope Alexander were brought out and hanged before her eyes. She was returned to her cell and told that her life had been bought by theirs . . . for that day.

Cesare employed Caterina's own children against her by ensuring that their callous letters reached their destination. Having read the contents, he knew that they would inflict more pain than any of his own tortures. The day after her foiled escape, Ottaviano, albeit unaware of the attempt, wrote to plead for a placement as an archbishop if he could not get a cardinal's hat. Essentially washing their hands of their mother's case, the two boys told her she was on her own. Cesare hoped that Caterina, damned to the papal dungeon and abandoned by her children, would be driven to despair.

Don Fortunati, Caterina's loyal Florentine retainer, rallied to Caterina's defense. "The devil must have taken your feelings and your memory,"[8] Caterina's indignant friend fired off to Ottaviano and Cesare. Shocked by the absence of filial piety in Caterina's two eldest, he did not mince words, calling them "petty children," "ignorant fools," and "madmen." The priest's forthright accusations of betrayal and ingratitude had an effect on the two young men. On July 4, Ottaviano assumed a completely different tone as he penned an update on his efforts to free her. They had renounced all claims on Imola and Forlì, having asked for nothing in return. The letter gives off more than a light scent of self-pity as Ottaviano recounts the money and benefices in Romagna that he has sacrificed for her emancipation, but Caterina must have been moved by the transformation of her normally self-seeking son. While Ottaviano still hoped to shirk the responsibility of little Ludovico, in the lengthy conclusion, the Riario sons adopted language more appropriate to the prelates they proposed to be. In homiletic tones, they cautioned her to "not let the devil lead her into despair," reminding her that no matter how bleak things looked, God would always be by her side; her trust in him could not be poorly placed. Let her present suffering "be offered up in expiation of the suffering that she has caused others," they advised, "for one drop of Christ's blood [is] enough to purchase all her sins from Hell."[9] Any renewed motherly affection that Caterina may have felt as she read those words must have been slightly dampened by the closing request: they had included some facsimiles of promissory notes to Lorenzo de' Medici, Caterina's brother-in-law; could she fill them out and send them so the young men could get some money?

By the end of July, the harsh imprisonment, the hot Roman summer, and the pressure from her children took their toll; Caterina became seriously ill. The Mantuan representative in Rome wrote to the marquis that no further negotiations were going on to free her, that Caterina was suffering from a *passion de cuore*, a mixture of depression and debilitating illness, and that she had "released the doctor from her service."[10] It seemed that the Borgias would win, and she would die quietly in the castle, forgotten by all. After the Mantuan letter on July 30, 1500, silence surrounds Caterina. No letters in or out of prison have been preserved, nor were there visitors to offer updates on her condition.

Caterina, however, recovered both her health and her will to live. It would appear that the priests in her life, Don Fortunati and Abbot Lauro, ministered to her ailing spirit. Don Fortunati had ensured that the last written words from her sons offered pious encouragement while Abbot Lauro, sharing her imprisonment, strengthened her faith. Just as physical exercise had once made her strong, so this period of suffering tempered her soul. As she got better, Caterina took a little exercise on the ramparts. Looking over the prison walls, she could see thousands of men and women walking slowly across the Castel Sant'Angelo bridge. Cloaked in threadbare mantles and carrying staffs and pouches, these pilgrims were on their way to Saint Peter's for a once-in-a-lifetime opportunity. Many had made the long, hard journey barefoot as penance for a lifetime of sin, certain that once they reached the basilica and prayed at the grave of Saint Peter, their souls would be cleansed. The Holy Year occurred only once every twenty-five years. While Cesare was bombarding Ravaldino, his father the pope had opened the bricked-up Holy Door in Saint Peter's, the symbol of repentance. In honor of this momentous occasion, the French cardinal Bilhères de Legraulas had commissioned a new statue for the basilica by a twenty-three-year-old Florentine sculptor named Michelangelo Buonarroti. It had been Cardinal Raffaello Riario who had brought the up-and-coming artist to the French cardinal's attention, but unfortunately for him, Riario had fled Rome before the work was done. Caterina herself was imprisoned in the Belvedere when the *Pietà* was placed in its chapel, and thus never got to see the work. She would have particularly appreciated Michelangelo's heroic representation of Mary and found inspiration in Mary's quiet acceptance of divine will. Although she would not cross through the Holy Door or pray before the *Pietà*, the spirit of the Holy Year permeated even the thick walls of the Castel Sant'Angelo. Caterina had been planning since 1498 to come to Rome for forgiveness and a chance to wash away her many sins. Now she was here, a stone's throw from Saint Peter's tomb, yet unable to kneel by the relics of the first pope. In her dark cell, the memory of those she had ordered killed after the death of Feo gnawed at her. Through the offices and counseling of her co-prisoner Abbot Lauro, Caterina found her own way to expiate her sins through acceptance of her own suffering. None of Caterina's letters written during her imprisonment have survived, for Ottaviano destroyed them out of fear and counseled her to do the same with his. But shortly after her transfer to the dungeon, Ottaviano quoted one of her letters, in which kindness and compassion emanate from her every line. "Do not sacrifice everything you have; be careful to not impoverish yourselves to free me from this prison: rather than see you ruined on my account, I am ready and patient to tolerate every discomfort and pain."[11]

For one long silent year, Caterina withstood the desolation of the Castel Sant'Angelo, uniting her pain to that of Christ, a crucifix the only ornament in her small cell. Her prayers bolstered her, sacraments sustained her, and hope buoyed her. In a magnificent paradox, the same pope who so desperately wanted her dead had given her the means to survive.

In the spring of 1501, a new prisoner joined Caterina in the castle. Astorre Manfredi, her would-be son-in-law, had lost the town of Faenza to Cesare after a brave defense. But unlike Caterina, the young nobleman had not earned the admiration of the French and was consigned to the lowest cells. In 1502, the unfortunate boy suffered the fate that Caterina escaped; he was strangled in the prison and his body dumped in the Tiber.

With spring there came a renewed hope of liberty. The French army was on its way south to continue Louis XII's interrupted campaign against Naples. They were expected to pass through Rome and would be angered upon hearing of Caterina's imprisonment. Caterina felt a stirring of anticipation that each day inside those dank walls would be her last. In thanks for Abbot Lauro's extraordinary services and in expectation of their imminent release, Caterina wrote a promissory note for four hundred ducats on May 23, to help the cleric upon his return to the world.[12] The month of June passed slowly, each day bringing the scorching summer heat closer. The Borgias threw parties, executed enemies, and reveled in their good fortune, while Caterina waited for a miracle.

On June 20, Yves D'Allegre rode unannounced into Rome, accompanied by only three horsemen. Dismounting at the Vatican palace, the captain of the French army demanded to be taken immediately to the pope. The chivalrous captain had not forgotten the bold and beautiful countess, and he was furious to find she was being held under considerably worse conditions than when he had left her. Before Pope Alexander, Captain D'Allegre expounded the whole agreement under which Caterina had been released into his custody, every word underlining their affront to the king of France. In vain did the Borgia protest that she had tried to escape and had been accused of attempting to murder the pope. D'Allegre delivered an ultimatum: if she was not liberated immediately, the French soldiers quartered a few miles away at Viterbo would come and do it themselves. Alexander gave in; Caterina would be freed if she would formally renounce any claims on her states of Imola and Forlì. Yves D'Allegre strode out of the papal apartments and took the long *passetto* into the castle. The captain must have been shocked at the sight of Caterina; the stunning warrior had become a pale wraith. No sword and cuirass hung from her shoulders; instead the white robe of the penitent billowed around her wasted form. To Caterina's eyes, the sight of Yves D'Allegre filling the doorway to her cell must have seemed like an archangel arriving to liberate her. With kindness, respect, and a personal guarantee for her safety, D'Allegre accomplished what a year and a half of Borgia torment and imprisonment could not: Caterina renounced her states, agreeing to sign the document once she was safely outside the castle.

On the morning of June 30, while the rest of Rome lay sleeping after a long festive night, the heavy wooden drawbridge to the Castel Sant'Angelo lowered over the moat, and a small group of riders emerged from the dark cavernous opening into the morning light. Seventeen years earlier, Caterina had emerged from this same passage proud and triumphant as she sat high on her horse, radiant in her seventh month of pregnancy and applauded by a crowd of admiring Romans. Now Caterina rode slowly, head high, but her body frail. The little party crossed the small bridge, which had been packed with pilgrims the year before, and then turned right toward the Via dei Pellegrini. Although Caterina happily filled her lungs with the fresh morning air, free from the reek of the castle, every nerve alerted her to the presence of danger. The company of men escorting her was led by the Spaniard Troccio, Cesare's chief assassin. As one of the most intimate members of Alexander's Spanish coterie, he was entrusted with the tasks that required both ruthlessness and discretion. Each time the horses turned down a dark narrow alley, Caterina wondered if this would be the moment she would be strangled and her corpse discarded in the Tiber. She felt no safer as they passed the palaces of her friends and family and traveled past the ghostly ruins of the Coliseum to an unfamiliar door. The coat of arms of Cardinal Giovanni Serra told her that she had been delivered to the home of another of Alexander's Spanish cronies.

Inside the palace, Alexander's notary greeted her with the documents of Caterina's renunciation of Imola and Forlì and a few extra conditions imposed by Pope Alexander VI, but she also found a friendly face in Don Fortunati, her faithful Florentine retainer. Although Caterina was liberated from her prison cell, she could not yet leave Rome. Furthermore, the pope demanded a two-thousand-ducat reimbursement for the expenses of keeping her for the year and a half. Accompanied by Don Fortunati, she signed the papers and sent various letters to gather the funds for the pope. Caterina was gladdened by the release of Abbot Lauro and wrote to the Milanese priest, offering him the permanent position of chaplain in her household.[13]

Once the Borgia demands had been met, Caterina and Fortunati returned to the heart of the city, stopping at the front door of Cardinal Raffaello Riario's house. The cardinal wasn't home; both he and Cardinal Giuliano, as nephews of Sixtus IV, had prudently opted to remain far out of range of the Borgia claws, but Caterina was given a warm welcome. Cardinal Riario lived in one of the most beautiful palaces in Rome, with all the finest amenities of its age. After a hot bath, a good sleep in a comfortable bed, and a hearty meal, Caterina began to resemble her former self. Now looking more like the Italian amazon of legend and song, Caterina was ready to receive her savior, Yves D'Allegre. The contents of the long interview were never revealed, but it seems that the French captain counseled Caterina on her next moves. The Borgia reach was long and their memory longer. At the time, the stories of the Borgia excesses were whispered only among the Italian courts. Many of their misdeeds became public only after their deaths, when the court insiders vented their rage and earned some extra cash by publishing tell-all books. Caterina was a firsthand witness to the corruption in the family; if she chose to recount her story, she warned that she would "shock the world."[14] As long as Troccio dogged her footsteps she would not find safety. Most likely Caterina's French guardian angel helped plan the most secure route for her return to Florence.

Over the next two weeks Caterina regained her strength as a steady flow of well-wishers streamed in and out of the Riario palace. The Orsinis, old allies of the Riarios, stopped by, as well as many who had known her during her happier years as the favorite of Pope Sixtus IV. Outside, Romans gathered in the piazza in front of her house, hoping for a glimpse of one of Italy's most famous daughters. Letters poured in from Florence, containing news of how eagerly her friends awaited her arrival at her new home. Caterina announced that she would soon leave for Florence, taking the Via Flaminia on horseback. Pope Alexander, now all effusive affection, wrote to the Florentines on July 13, committing to their care "his beloved daughter in Christ" whom "he had been forced to detain for reasonable motives."[15]

One warm morning in late July, Caterina took a little boat trip on the Tiber. She sailed down to the sea at Ostia, a frequent pleasurable pastime for Romans. Once at the port, however, Caterina got off the flat-bottomed barge, climbed aboard a seafaring ship, and headed north toward Livorno, at the moment under French control. Besides giving her weakened body a more restful journey than she would have had on horseback, she avoided all papal territory. This escape plan was probably devised during Caterina's long discussions with D'Allegre. At Pisa, she was given a horse and escort and she rode the last fifty miles to Florence. The dramatic Tuscan terrain rose and fell; soft, fertile valleys shot into high craggy mountains that had been split open to quarry the precious marble inside. She picked her way slowly through thick forests where she could barely see a few feet ahead, then galloped across wide plains. At long last, the walls of Florence came into view, surmounted by the high russet dome of Santa Maria del Fiore. From the city gates a group of riders came toward her. The hot July sun formed a haze around them, rendering them unrecognizable. As the riders moved closer she recognized her firstborn, Ottaviano, alongside Cesare and Galeazzo, with Sforzino and nine-year-old Carlo,[16] her son by Giacomo Feo, bringing up the rear. Dismounting, she fell into the embrace of her children. She had found her new home.

19

SLEEP AFTER TOIL

T HE CITY WHOSE wonders had captivated ten-year-old Caterina now welcomed the formidable countess as one of its own. Florence in 1501 was an even greater hub of activity than at the time of her childhood visit. After ousting the Medicis, the republic had been reorganized under a skilled administrator, Piero Soderini. All in all, the city had passed through the political upheavals of the past decade relatively unscathed.

Caterina passed through the municipal gates as a Florentine citizen, surveying the landmarks of her new home as her horse carried her through the narrow, bustling streets. The stern stone blocks of the Palazzo Vecchio, the seat of the Florentine government, loomed above as she crossed the Piazza della Signoria; the dungeons of the Bargello stirred painful memories as she rode along the Via del Proconsolo. At last, the street opened into light and color as the marble-sheathed apse of the cathedral, Santa Maria del Fiore, came into view. Here she turned right toward the road of the Borgo Pinto, where her children had been lodged in the house of a family friend.

There, awaiting her mother's arrival, was Bianca, Caterina's only daughter, holding the sturdy and rambunctious Ludovico. Finally, after almost two years of separation and countless days of worry and fear, she was able to embrace her beloved youngest son. The twenty-year-old Bianca had cared for her brother during her mother's imprisonment, when she and Ludovico were in a similar predicament. Their elder siblings Ottaviano and Cesare had also resented the duty to maintain their unmarried sister and had exploited the Medici influence at court in an effort to unload her, soliciting Cardinal Giovanni de' Medici to help them find a suitable husband for their sister, who was "no longer of an age to be kept at home." Old enough to be mother to her brother, Bianca had remained unmarried, but Caterina would soon put that right.

As soon as he heard of Caterina's return, Lorenzo di Pierfrancesco de' Medici, her brother-in-law, arrived, all welcoming smiles. He arranged for her transfer to the Medici house on the Via Larga, a majestic palace constructed by Michelozzo for Cosimo de' Medici, the founder of the dynasty. The palace was familiar to Caterina, for as a child she had stayed there as a guest of Lorenzo the Magnificent and had since returned on several occasions as the wife of Giovanni de' Medici. Now she would call it home.

The days spent with her children were marked by a constant flow of visitors. Some were old acquaintances, but many were merely curious to meet this notorious woman now living quietly in their midst. If they came for titillating gossip, they were disappointed. Caterina never regaled her visitors with tales of her Borgia capture, nor did she speak against her enemies. The Caterina who returned to Florence was a different woman from the vindictive widow she had been in Forlì.

By August 1501, only months after her arrival, Caterina had already moved out of the house on the Via Larga and into the Medici villa known as Castello. Despite the martial overtones, the villa took its name from the nearby ruins of a Roman aqueduct and the cisterns, *castella*, for water. Originally an austere farmhouse, it had been transformed it into a lovely country estate complete with loggias, courtyards, and stables. Among the jewels of the Medici art collection allocated to this villa was *The Birth of Venus*, Botticelli's stunning rendering of the goddess of love as an ethereal beauty with long, graceful limbs. Instead of gazing every morning at the dark squalor of a prison cell, Caterina now had the soft pastel hues of this remarkable painting to grace the walls. Slowly the eighteen months of torment faded in her memory. She settled in with little Ludovico and prepared to lead a quiet country life.

But political battles and domestic suits seemed to follow her. No sooner had Caterina settled into Castello than her economic situation degenerated from precarious to disastrous. She had no money, and no means of earning it. Yet her children pressed incessantly for financial assistance. Ottaviano and Cesare needed more clothes, more servants, more trips, and more parties. After they had wrung the meager resources out of their mother, and knowing she had jewels in pawn in Venice, they asked her to sell them for whatever ready cash they would bring. The market was bad; Milan was destitute, France would undervalue them, and Genoa would not buy them. Caterina pressed on, trying to raise what little she could. She had known straitened circumstances before, during the years with Girolamo after the death of Pope Sixtus IV. But she had always had land to raise revenue; she merely had to cut down on costs. Now, living in the Medici villa, she had barely enough to survive. Her one remaining resource was her Medici inheritance, the property and income due to her son Ludovico as the sole heir to Giovanni de' Medici's fortune. But Giovanni's brother Lorenzo had no intention of sharing. He had already spent a good deal of the family patrimony and squandered much of Ludovico's inheritance. In July 1502, Lorenzo demanded that Caterina leave the Medici villa. Claiming the grounds and house as his property, he attempted to oust her from her new home. It was as if he had lit a match under a long-forgotten powder keg. Caterina's pugnacious side reemerged for the first time in three years. The more Lorenzo pushed to expel her from the villa, the more Caterina found the spirit to remain. "She is resolved not to leave if not in pieces," wrote the worried Don Fortunati on July 8, 1502, to Ottaviano and Cesare.[1] But if Caterina could withstand the cannons of Cesare Borgia, she could handle the subpoenas of a greedy Medici.

In Florence, however, documents and ducats were more persuasive than artillery. Lorenzo succeeded in convincing the Florentine courts to grant him custody of four-year-old Ludovico. Using Caterina's eighteen-month imprisonment as an excuse, he declared her an unfit mother and took the child away, along with control of his inheritance. The law was intended to protect a child from parents who had committed crimes; yet Caterina had been a prisoner of war and illegally jailed, as the French could not detain female prisoners.

Caterina threw herself into the courtroom with the same intensity she had displayed on the ramparts. Ordering inventories and witnesses, she began the slow and difficult process of reclaiming her son. Lorenzo was no more averse to devious tactics than Cesare Borgia. He employed his own caretaker of Castello, Alberto, to make her life as miserable as possible. Caterina was financially responsible for the care of her family and servants. Yet she had no sheets and no tablecloths, and she was forced to write to her children to plead for six forks. Don Fortunati, her sole loyal supporter, hounded her children for their lack of consideration. Even her brief joy at the arrival of her stepson, Scipione Riario, who had fought valiantly by her side during the siege of Ravaldino, was clouded by the difficulties of feeding and housing his companions, which brought her household number up to "twenty-four mouths, five horses, and three mules."[2]

The battlefield of courts and tribunals was new to her, but Caterina found a new Ravaldino to provide her with a refuge where she could gather strength. No bulwarks or gun lofts graced these high walls, which offered an austere and tranquil respite from the upheavals of the outside world. The convent of the Muratte, meaning the "walled-in ones," was founded in 1424 by Apollonia, a pious lady from Siena. Together with thirteen other women, she had made a home in a small house on a bridge over the Rubicon River. By 1433 the women had formed an order and taken the Benedictine rule, but the local bishop worried that their location on a busy bridge would present too many tempting distractions from the life of prayer and work. Giovanni Benci, the second-richest man in Florence after Cosimo de' Medici, donated to the new order a building on the Via Ghibellina, resting against the city walls. The religious sisters were henceforth known as the Muratte, alluding to their enclosure within the Florentine walls.

Benci beautified the convent over the years. The compound contained a church, choir, common sitting room, and refectory for the community life of the sisters, as well as a scriptorium for copying texts and work rooms for making the embroideries and woven clothes that supported them. The sisters followed the Benedictine rule of *ora et labora*, prayer and work, singing the Divine Office and reciting penitential psalms while doing their handicrafts. The number of women grew and by the end of the fourteenth century the Muratte numbered 170. Five dormitories housed the nuns, and a number of small buildings were added to the complex to allow laywomen to live among the sisters and find peace in their holy way of life.

Caterina had assisted numerous religious communities through her years as countess of Forlì, but she found her spiritual home among the Muratte. The Dominican friar Girolamo Savonarola, who had offered Caterina counsel after her darkest hours, had introduced her to the community. He had preached his first sermon in Florence at their convent and throughout his life maintained an active interest in the well-being of the sisters. As of 1502, Caterina would periodically stay in the convent. Eventually, she would have her own simple cell in the enclosure off the main courtyard. She never took vows but would reside among the Muratte for stretches of time, joining the sisters in prayer and meditation, perhaps even helping them make perfumes and other essences, her own beloved hobby. Caterina, like most noblewomen of her age, frequented spas and thermal baths for her physical health while attending to her spiritual well-being through retreats among these devout women.

The stark convent atmosphere was relieved by several artistic masterpieces. In 1443, Giovanni Benci hired Florence's most sought-after painter, Filippo Lippi, to paint an Annunciation for the high altar of the church. Every time Caterina knelt in the chapel, the luminous pastels and bright flashes of gold leaf brought to life the story of the angel Gabriel and the Virgin Mary. The walled garden in the background resembled the view from the window of her own cell, except that through the magic of Lippi's art, the colors were more limpid and the scenery even more lush. Mary, painted with the ethereal beauty that Filippo conferred on women, bows with eyes cast down in submission to divine will.

Outside the walls of the convent, however, the winds of fortune swirled, waiting to buffet Caterina. On August 18, 1503, Pope Alexander VI died. Not one word of satisfaction has been recorded from Caterina. In what must have seemed like perfect divine retribution, at the exact moment Alexander died, Cesare Borgia also lay deathly ill. A few malicious voices would circulate the rumor that both father and son had accidentally eaten from a dish they had laced with poison, intended for somebody else, but whatever the cause, Cesare could not influence the next election from his sickbed. Pius III Piccolomini was elected a month later, but afflicted with terrible gout, he was ill from the time of his drastically abbreviated coronation ceremony. Less than a month after he was elected, Pius III died. The cardinals returned to the Sistine Chapel, and in one day they unanimously chose his successor, Giuliano della Rovere, who took the name Julius II.

Excitement raced through the Riario family. The nephew of Sixtus IV, Giuliano was cousin to Girolamo Riario. Riario partisans saw the election as an opportunity to return Forlì and Imola to the Riario family, and as a result letters began to fly to and from Caterina's household regarding her eventual return to Forlì. The city was up for grabs. Antonio Maria Ordelaffi had profited from the confusion of two conclaves by claiming the city in a lightning strike. Letters, undoubtedly written by his partisans, sped along the peninsula, claiming that Ordelaffi had been joyfully welcomed by the Forlivesi as their long-awaited rightful ruler. Illness and lack of artillery had prevented him from conquering Ravaldino, stronger than ever after the repairs of Cesare Borgia, but the Ordelaffi supporters lost no time, appearing in Rome within days of the papal coronation with a petition to return Forlì to Antonio Maria. Caterina was apprised immediately that her newly adopted Republic of Florence had abetted Antonio Maria's return to the government. Indignant on her behalf, Caterina's Romagnol supporters urged her to storm the Palazzo Vecchio and to "cry for vengeance until the people were amazed by such ingratitude."[3] Despite Caterina's alliances with Florence and her marriage to a Medici, the people of the city by the Arno thought that the Ordelaffis would make more tranquil neighbors. Julius II, on the other hand, remained unconvinced. He appeared reluctant to accept a return of the Ordelaffis and withheld confirmation of Antonio's rule.

During this stalemate between Pope Julius and Antonio Maria, the fortress of Ravaldino remained in the hands of a castellan who was not only viscerally hostile to Pope Julius II, whom he considered a "traitor," but was also head over heels in love with Caterina, going so far as to call her his wife. The Florentines, always ready to press an advantage, had apparently made advances to the deluded soldier, promising him Caterina in marriage if he would turn the castle over to a guardian of their choosing. This strange hearsay, culled from a dinner conversation with a cousin of the castellan, was picked up by the Venetian diarist Sanuto, who loved nothing more than a tale of intrigue involving Caterina.[4]

The veracity of the story is highly doubtful, but it gives an idea of the effect that Caterina still had upon the popular imagination. Giambattista Tonelli, a long-standing Riario partisan, had already written to Caterina that after the death of Alexander VI, "all the other princes had already returned to their lands" and that he and others were preparing the way for her return to Imola and Forlì. Tonelli's devotion was not spurred by political motives alone. He too had long loved the countess of Forlì. In February 1502 he had expressed his passion, writing, "If I sleep, it seems that I am with you; if I eat, I leave my food and talk to you . . . You are engraved in my heart."[5]

But the very idea of Caterina had the opposite effect among other Romagnoli; Giovanni Maria Ridolfi, a Florentine captain in Romagna, claimed that "if the countess were dead, part of the countryside and the people of Forlì would not be displeased to have Ottaviano, whom they consider a good man."[6] Machiavelli asserted that Caterina had made herself too hated to ever regain her state.

A multitude of extant letters suggests that many in Imola and Forlì were amenable to her return and that she had several sympathizers in Rome who also tried to pave the way for her restoration. Cardinal Raffaello Riario and Cardinal Ascanio Sforza, after a long absence during the reign of Alexander VI, returned to Rome to press for the restitution of the Riario scions. It seemed certain that either mother or son would soon be back in Romagna.

Pope Julius continued to demur. Even when Antonio Maria Ordelaffi, the sometime suitor, frequent troublemaker, and eternal pretender to the throne, died of illness in February 1504, Julius II still did not pronounce in favor of the Riario family. Cesare and Galeazzo were quick to blame their mother, viewing her as a political liability. In a letter to Ottaviano, the two brothers parroted Captain Ridolfi's position (written only three days earlier) that the Romagnoli would "never allow the restoration of the countess if not at her death."[7] The simple truth was that Pope Julius didn't want to give away Forlì, especially to the Riario heirs. Skilled at reading people and a formidable man himself, he took Ottaviano's measure instantly. *"Nel suo gippone c'e poco bambaza,"*[8] said the pope, in his colorful, forthright way, describing the twenty-five-year-old prelate as having little stuffing under his shirt. Julius was looking for strong allies and wanted to bring the entire area of Romagna under direct papal control. Concerned by the open corridor of entry into Italy for the king of France, Julius would end up spending most of his pontificate trying to seal Italy off from another French invasion, ultimately wresting Bologna from the Bentivoglio family and invading Ferrara. The pope intended to sever Rome's relationship with France.

But what did Caterina want? After long years of battles, betrayal, imprisonment, and legal strife, was Caterina really planning to return as countess to rule Forlì? Of all the Riario family members dancing attendance on Pope Julius II, Caterina knew him best. Julius had crossed swords with her late husband Girolamo Riario after the Medici assassination in the Pazzi conspiracy as well as during Girolamo's persecution of the Colonna family. She knew that the pope could not be swayed once he had made up his mind, and despite the exuberant hope of her partisans, she knew he had no reason to favor his Riario cousins. She encouraged her supporters in Romagna, hoping that if she could catapult her family onto the ruler's throne, then Julius might accept it as a fait accompli, but she had few illusions about her allies in Rome. In October 1503, Caterina wrote to Ottaviano, warning him of the treacheries and dangers of the pontifical court. "The iron is hot and it is time to strike it," she advised her son, persuading him to press his suit for Forlì. At the same time she issued a stern warning. "Guard yourself from those you trust and those who offer you advice, know the foul tempers that are all around you; if you allow yourself to be led by others, you will wind up with your cap over your eyes, so wake up!"[9]

Unlike earlier years when she would have leapt on her horse and galloped to the heart of the action, seizing by force what she desired while others hesitated, the older, wiser Caterina sat back in Florence and watched events unfold. After years on the tightrope of Italian politics and in the web of domestic intrigues, Caterina seemed ready to step back from the throne and let her sons take charge.

Her sons, however, were not as popular as Captain Ridolfi seemed to think. Ginevra Bentivoglio, of the ruling house of Bologna, was shocked by the intense dislike Caterina's arrogant sons provoked in the Bolognese and only her respect for Caterina kept her from turning the Bentivoglio house against the Riario family.

The year 1504 brought such a cascade of contradictory and bizarre correspondence that Caterina must have wondered what was in store every time she opened a letter. One report claimed that Imola had cried out for Spanish rule; another declared that the town pined for the Riarios. Venice seemed interested at one point, and then the cities seemed ready to revolt against church rule after the imposition of the *dazi*. This flurry of rumors was interspersed with love letters from her old soldiers, some expressing themselves brusquely, while others penned awkward verses to her.

> *What do you want from me? I've given you my heart!*
> *You have my fidelity, my servitude.*
> *Don't be ruled by ingratitude.*
> *Gentle spirits cannot live without love.*
> *Your favor for me is beatitude.*
> *How can you leave me in solitude?*[10]

By the end of 1504, it became clear that Pope Julius II had no intention of putting Imola and Forlì in Riario hands again. Even Ottaviano had given up and began asking once again for a cardinal's hat in return for any claim on his state.

Although Caterina lost her lands, she regained her youngest son. On June 5, 1505, the lawsuit with Lorenzo di Pierfrancesco de' Medici was resolved and Caterina came into what was left of her Medici husband's wealth. Most important, little Ludovico was returned to her. As Caterina was reestablished as the sole guardian of her son, she legally changed his name. Henceforth he would be known as Giovanni di Giovanni de' Medici to perpetuate the name of his much admired and beloved father. Not even in her wildest dreams could Caterina guess how important that name would one day be to the city of Florence.

As she took her final step back from politics, Caterina focused on her children. She moved back to the Castello villa, which had been returned to her along with custody of her son, intent on raising little Giovanni herself. She had already written to one of her former soldiers to ask him to find a small horse to teach the seven-year-old boy to ride and hunt, as she herself had done years ago on the Sforza estate in Milan.

Caterina's interest in her other children did not diminish. At long last, she had found a husband for her gracious and lovely Bianca. Her first fiancé, Astorre Manfredi, had been deposed and murdered by Cesare Borgia. The passions of a second betrothed, the considerably older count of Caiazzo, had cooled while waiting for Caterina's political troubles to be over. But Triolo de' Rossi, the count of San Secondo in the region of Parma, had brought joyous news during the trying year of 1503 by asking for Bianca's hand. Caterina's twenty-two-year-old daughter was married on July 28, 1503, and Caterina's first legitimate grandchild, Pietro Maria, was born a year later.

Ottaviano likely remained a bitter disappointment to his mother, although she never openly expressed her displeasure with him. By 1503 he had garnered a reputation in Rome as "obese in the body and fat in the head."[11] Still oscillating between his desire for high prelature and a secular life, Ottaviano was considering a marriage proposal with a Venetian noblewoman along with a military *condotta* for Venice in 1503. Ultimately, Ottaviano fell back on the family's ecclesiastical reserves. His uncle, Cardinal Raffaello Riario, ceded the diocese of Viterbo and Volterra to him, and Ottaviano became a bishop in 1507. Unlike his uncles, he would never wear the red hat of the cardinal. Remembering the mistakes his own uncle Sixtus IV had made, Pope Julius avoided appointing the rapacious members of his family to high positions in the church. Although Viterbo had been a papal city for many years and still enjoyed a fair revenue, Ottaviano continued to hound his mother for money and gifts even at the age of thirty. "Could you send a large piece of *ciamellotto* cloth, in either black or purple, because I am with a monsignor every day and don't have the right clothes, imagine how I feel,"[12] he lamented in a letter of June 20, 1507. One month later, he wanted a new mantle and then on August 12 he asked for fifty ducats to buy himself a *gabbano*, a long clerical robe, so he could present himself before the pope as stylishly dressed as the other prelates. In 1508 Ottaviano found himself with clerical duties and no idea how to carry them out. He asked his mother, who spent much of her time in ecclesiastical circles, to send him a "good and honest vicar" to help him, as well as one of his mother's large missals in which all the notes for Holy Week were written, so he would not be lost while presiding over the most solemn Masses of the year.

But Ottaviano's most frequent refrain was to ask that his mother intervene with one of her many relatives to make him a cardinal. Caterina never seemed inclined to pressure her sister who was married to the Holy Roman Emperor to assist Ottaviano. Maximilian I had remained aloof during her defense at Forlì, nor had he intervened in her imprisonment. Completely absorbed in subduing the Netherlands and his unruly German nobles, Maximilian would not meddle in the petty affairs of Italy. Caterina may have also been concerned about the effect of Rome and power on the weak-willed Riario men. It had utterly corrupted Ottaviano's father, Girolamo, and her son had always been more of a Riario than a Sforza. She did, however, take care of Cornelia, Ottaviano's illegitimate daughter, bringing her to live at the convent of the Muratte and ensuring that she was well raised and decorously married.

Cesare, her second oldest, was her most successful son. Named archbishop of Pisa at the age of nineteen, he was well liked in the Curia. But like his older brother, Cesare showed more interest in what he could obtain from his mother than any concern for her wellbeing. More documents testify to his business interests than his pastoral care—not surprising, since it seems that Archbishop Riario preferred to reside in Rome in the splendid palace of his uncle Cardinal Raffaello Riario. After renouncing any claim on Forlì, Ottaviano and Cesare were awarded twenty-five hundred gold ducats a year between them by Julius II for their losses, to be raised by a *dazio* on sheep and supplemented by papal funds.

One of her sons doted on his mother. Galeazzo, named for Caterina's father, was sixteen when his mother was released from the Castel Sant'Angelo. He was the brightest of the Riario boys, and Caterina had always nurtured high hopes for him. When he was only thirteen, she had tried to get him a *condotta*, but ultimately she sent him to Raffaello Riario to complete his education in Rome. At nineteen he married Maria della Rovere, niece of Pope Julius II and sister of the duke of Urbino. One of their daughters would take vows and become a religious sister of Caterina's beloved Muratte. His reputation as a just man and his powerful connections made Galeazzo a favorable candidate as ruler of Forlì and Imola during the years when a Riario return seemed possible. Despite never reclaiming the family throne, Galeazzo lived a successful life and showed a kindness to his mother that his brothers never had. His regular letters express genuine interest in his mother's health and peace of mind; he offered to come to her side at any moment she might need him. Of all her boys sired by Riario, the son bearing the treasured name of her father was her most steadfast.

Her youngest son by Girolamo had been named Francesco but nicknamed "Sforzino." Little information remains about him. Sforzino was fourteen when his mother moved to Florence and he most likely remained in her household for several years beyond that. He too followed an ecclesiastical career, ultimately becoming the bishop of the Tuscan town of Lucca, a few short miles from Pisa, where Cesare was archbishop.

As of 1505, Caterina's energy and drive centered on her beloved Giovanni. Caterina had used her relationship with the marquis of Mantua to influence the Florentine courts, and although she would not exploit her sister Bianca Maria's marriage to Maximilian to obtain Ottaviano's coveted cardinal's hat, she did beg their intervention to retrieve Giovanni from the clutches of his Medici uncle.

Just when Caterina emerged victorious from her custody suit, Florence was entering one of its most glorious artistic zeniths. Michelangelo's *David* had just been hauled into place in front of the Palazzo dei Priori in the center of town, where Caterina would have seen it as she marched to face her opponents in the legal arena. Caterina had much in common with David: like the shepherd boy, she had been thrust into the hard world of politics at a tender age; like the Jewish king, after a long and bitter battle to gain her crown, she had fallen victim to her own lust and cruelty; and like the author of the psalms, she had found solace in adversity through repentance.

Caterina hired tutors to impress reading and writing into the willful head of her spirited son, who cared little for study, preferring swimming and riding. Tutors came and went at the villa. No sooner had one drummed some flowery Latin verses into the child's head than another was on his way from Romagna.

The hours of the day not dedicated to Giovanni were occupied with

Caterina's favorite hobby, botanical experiments—brewing concoctions for everything from antidotes for various ailments to cosmetics. The large garden at Castello offered her possibilities for growing her own herbs, and she corresponded regularly with people all over Italy to obtain ingredients and new recipes. She eagerly awaited shipments of new products from her long-standing friend Anna in Rome, a Jewish woman who prepared the best creams for smoothing unsightly bumps and wrinkles from the skin. Another, Luigi Ciocca of Mantua, could barely contain his excitement as he scribbled across the page that he had obtained a special unguent used by Isabella d'Este, the marquise of Mantua herself. This treasured prize was believed to be the beauty secret of the woman known as the "the First Lady of the Renaissance" and whose likeness would be immortalized by both Leonardo and Titian.

Caterina also gathered remedies and cures. She kept on hand numerous ointments for scrapes and cuts, a necessity with a boisterous boy in the house. Sometimes she used compresses of sage on a skinned knee or elbow; for more serious wounds she prepared a mixture of wax, pine resin, a paste made of milk solids, water and lime powder, and vinegar. Sleeping potions and painkillers were also numerous on her shelves, along with medications for the plague and antidotes to poison. Her labors and discoveries would be posthumously published in her name as *Gli Esperimenti*.

Now in her forties, Caterina still excited the admiration of many, and often a passionate love letter would arrive by post. Warriors fighting at the front dreamed of her; those setting off to seek their fortune wrote to ask for her encouragement. Physically, she kept herself worthy of admiration, drying her hair in the sun to keep it fair and diligently applying preparations to lighten her skin, cover freckles, and wipe away her first wrinkles.

Caterina's household experienced a happy expansion in 1508. Bianca, Caterina's devoted daughter, brought her four-year-old son Pietro Maria and her newborn girl to visit Castello. Caterina doted on them, so much so that Bianca later wrote her mother to thank her for all the attention she had showered on the children. Bianca so appreciated her mother's qualities that she left Pietro Maria in Caterina's care to learn to ride and hunt. Bianca corresponded regularly with her mother, occasionally sending a wheel of Parmesan or a package of candied fruit, Caterina's favorite sweet.

Caterina had found peace at last, preparing the next generation to carry on the Sforza tradition and living in the countryside as she had during her first carefree years of childhood. But as had often happened in her turbulent life, hardship arrived once again. This time danger was not from outside, but from within her own body.

In April 1509, Ottaviano broke a year-long epistolary silence to reprimand Don Fortunati, the faithful parish priest who was always by Caterina's side, that he had not been told that his mother was seriously ill. He complained that he had heard this news from a third party because Don Fortunati's letter of March 14 had not arrived until June 21.

Caterina had suffered a terrible bout of fever, probably the first signs of tuberculosis brought on by the malarial quartan fever that had afflicted her for all of her adult life. She wrestled with the illness for a month and by the time Ottaviano wrote she had already emerged victorious—yet very fragile—from the struggle. Caterina knew it had been a close call. Her first thought upon recovery was to make a pilgrimage to Loreto in thanksgiving. It must have been heartwarming to hear that several of her friends had vowed to make the same trip when they heard of her illness and her recovery, and she was reinvigorated by plans for the trip and seeing old friends.

But just as the May flowers bloomed, Caterina's health started to fail. This time she was gripped by a racking pain in her chest, called *mal di costa*, "rib sickness." The many years of malarial fever had given way to pleurisy and the membranes in her chest cavity were inflamed, making each breath and coughing fit excruciatingly painful. Her two doctors, Giuliano degli Anterigoli and master Giovanni de'Malingegni, hovered at her bedside, using the traditional cure for pleurisy, hot barley cakes applied to the chest and side, but to no avail. Without cortisone to reduce the inflammation or medicines to treat the underlying tuberculosis, there was little to be done but bind her chest tightly, administer narcotics to ease the pain, and wait for the end.

Her saddened friends offered prayers and Masses all over Italy. The religious sisters in the convents that Caterina had long supported recited their rosaries day and night for her. But by May 28, Caterina had been transported from Castello to the Medici house on the Via Larga, where, lucid and in complete possession of her faculties, she asked for a notary to write her will. Surrounded by two priests, two doctors, and three Florentine citizens of the Medici household, Caterina put her worldly affairs in order.[13]

Her first point was to commend her soul to the glory of Heaven, but for her earthly remains Caterina wanted no pomp and expense. Unlike Renaissance rulers who purchased elaborately carved marble coffins and bronze monuments, Caterina asked to be laid to rest without ceremony in the church of the convent of the Muratte.

From her restored fortune, Caterina thanked her new city by leaving a bequest for the care of the Florentine cathedral Santa Maria del Fiore and for the maintenance of the city walls. To her best friend and confessor, Don Fortunati, she allocated the task of organizing one thousand Masses for her soul to be said within two months, and asked the sisters of the convent of the Muratte to offer thirty Masses a year for her soul in perpetuity. She left four gold ducats a year to the convent for the lifetime of the abbess in thanks for this service.

Savonarola had once told her that almsgiving was particularly pleasing to God, so she left a sizable donation to the Dominican convent of Santa Caterina across the street from where the great preacher had once lived. She asked them to construct a room for the use of her son Giovanni, so that his spiritual formation could continue after her death. Caterina also took pains to care for her grandchildren, both legitimate and not. Cornelia, Ottaviano's natural daughter, and Giulia, Galeazzo's daughter by Maria della Rovere, were both left money for their dowries and what remained of Caterina's beautiful clothes and linens. Giulia, the fruit of a successful marriage with a noble family, was given one thousand ducats, while Cornelia, Ottaviano's daughter, was given two thousand. At long last, she acknowledged Carlo Feo as her legitimate son by her marriage to Giacomo Feo and left him two thousand gold ducats.

Her maids were cared for with dowries and new positions, but one in particular, Mora Bona, most likely a freed slave in her retinue, was placed in the service of her son Giovanni. Her other servants were rewarded and her debts paid by Don Fortunati. The kind priest, as executor, was entrusted with Caterina's letters, books, and papers and would become custodian of her literary legacy. That he also received fifteen hundred ducats was revealed to him only a month after her death.

The castle from which Girolamo Riario had first earned his title of count, Castel di Bosco, was left to Galeazzo Riario, who as a noncleric would be able to pass the title down through his line.

Her beloved Giovanni, as she always referred to him, received all the family holdings within the territory of Florence, which were considerable despite his uncle Lorenzo's mismanagement. One third of Caterina's will provided dispositions for Giovanni. The eleven-year-old boy would be raised in the house of Jacopo Salviati, of a noble Florentine family long associated with the Medicis. Don Fortunati would continue to supervise the education of the child. Caterina also imposed a condition on the inheritance: that Giovanni be married as soon as possible. She knew the importance of his lineage and the merging of the Sforza and the Medici families and hoped to ensure a dynasty even after her death. The Riario name had become a curse, but the Medici name was magic.

Ottaviano, Cesare, Galeazzo, and Sforzino, her four sons by Girolamo, would then divide all the holdings and goods outside of Florence plus an inheritance left by their father. The greedy foursome wrote Don Fortunati two weeks after their mother's death, announcing their decision to consider the now wealthy Giovanni their full brother. Four days later Ottaviano wrote again, asking for his mother's dogs and falcons and reminding Don Fortunati to make a perfectly even division of her belongings. Even five years after his mother was dead and buried, Ottaviano still complained to Don Fortunati that he had not had "all that was his."

It might seem strange that Caterina's will makes no mention of her beloved daughter, Bianca, and her two legitimate grandchildren, but as Caterina was dividing properties left in trust by several husbands, it was probably easier to give Bianca her bequest outright, as her daughter would have certainly been by her side from the first illness, thus saving her the difficulties of settling Giovanni's affairs and then receiving the inheritance from him. Caterina had obviously thought out the complexities of her estate beforehand to have made such clear dispositions.

Caterina faced her last hours much as she had confronted other challenges. As she had done in her defense of Ravaldino, she gave orders and organized strategies through her will and then waited for the siege of her illness to end. It didn't take long. Burning the candle at both ends for most of her life as mother, warrior, ruler, lover, extravagant sinner, and meek penitent had taken its toll. Although many noblewomen like Isabella d'Este or Catherine de' Medici lived into their sixties, Caterina's life spark had shone brightly and was extinguished quickly. For the first time in her life, Caterina surrendered. A few hours after she wrote her will, Caterina Riario Sforza died at the age of forty-six.

Condolences poured in from all over Italy, from the brokenhearted laments of those who had long loved her, to fervent promises of prayers from the many priests and nuns who had benefited from her generosity. Michele Marullo of Constantinople, who had been at Caterina's service at Ravaldino during the siege of Cesare Borgia, wrote a long poem in honor of Caterina in measured verse, full of classical allusions.

Her body was placed in a simple tomb in the austere chapel of the Muratte. Fifty years later, Cosimo de' Medici, the first grand duke of Tuscany, placed a marble slab on her grave, crowned with the combined coats of arms of the Sforza and Medici families, to commemorate his celebrated grandmother. It bore the simple inscription CATERINA SFORZA MEDICI. The tombstone was destroyed in 1835 and her remains were lost ten years later; the convent of the Muratte was transformed into a prison. The honors and losses that characterize her gravesite reflect her extraordinary life. From triumph to defeat, notoriety to obscurity, great gain to devastating loss, Caterina remains a woman who will not be forgotten.

Epilogue: Mantua, 1526

THE DOZENS OF candles did nothing to lessen the chill in the room. The oppressive stone walls sealed in the December air, as cold as the lifeless body laid out on the table. A steady stream of people filed through the narrow doorway and, approaching the dais, leaned over to peer at the immobile features of the youthful face. A few glanced surreptitiously to catch sight of the stump of the young man's leg, but the lower body was discreetly covered.

Giovanni di Giovanni de' Medici, the son of Florence's beloved Giovanni de' Medici Il Popolano and Caterina, lay dead in the foreign church of San Francesco in Mantua, struck down at the age of twenty-eight in the midst of a glorious military career. He was soon to be laid to rest in hostile territory.

Caterina's youngest son had shown pure Sforza determination from the beginning. Although he had been raised by the noble and cultured Salviati family, they had never been able to tame his wild streak. Taking no interest in books, art, or math (unlike most other noble Florentines), young Giovanni leaned toward arms, horses, and martial activities. All those who cared for him during his early years concurred that the only person the rebellious child ever obeyed was his mother. After her death, no one could control him. In time, another woman had won him over to some extent, his foster mother, Lucrezia Salviati, who as the daughter of Lorenzo the Magnificent had inherited his charming manner. The rare flashes of courtliness and piety in young Giovanni were no doubt due to her influence.

In 1512, the scions of Lorenzo the Magnificent returned to Florence after a long exile. An exuberant fourteen-year-old Giovanni witnessed the triumphal parade, calling it "a fine sight." Lucrezia's brother Giuliano de' Medici, the duke of Nemours, gathered up the reins of the Florentine government. Crowning the glorious rise of the Medici family, Lucrezia's older brother Giovanni was elected Pope Leo X on March 11, 1513. Although the younger Giovanni belonged to the cadet branch of the Medicis, his foster mother's exalted family connections promised a brilliant career as either a statesman or a prelate.

At seventeen Giovanni was summoned to Rome by Pope Leo and it seemed that the young man's star was on the rise, but he soon earned a reputation for duels and brawls. Ironically, Giovanni's aggressive escapades would reveal his greatest strengths and point the way to his future. The Orsini family, hoping to obtain an important hostage for political leverage, ambushed Giovanni and his ten companions one night in one of the dark alleys near the river. The Orsinis kept a small army of mercenary soldiers in their fortresslike palace, always ready to avenge an insult, bully a lesser family, or simply display their power. In the cramped quarters, weakly lit by a few flickering torches, Giovanni and his little band found themselves surrounded by dozens of professional fighting men.

Giovanni didn't waste time in negotiations. Every bit his mother's son, he pulled his sword and rushed the soldiers. His friends, emboldened by the bravery of their leader, drew their weapons and followed. Giovanni sliced his way through the soldiers, who, shocked by this display of reckless courage, drew away from the fierce young men. Giovanni and his crew fought their way out of the ambush without a casualty. Physical courage, a scarce quality in the political landscape of Italy since Lorenzo the Magnificent's solo foray into Naples and Caterina Sforza's heroic defense of Ravaldino, had returned in the person of this young man.

When the story reached the pope's ears, he finally knew what to do with the teenage dynamo. Giovanni was given command of a hundred men and a job: to capture the town of Urbino under the orders of the papal nephew Lorenzo de' Medici. On this campaign, Giovanni discovered that he had been born for the battlefield.

Giovanni had fulfilled his mother's dreams of a heroic scion of the house of Medici, and at the age of eighteen he complied with the wishes expressed in her will, marrying Maria Salviati, the daughter of Lucrezia and granddaughter of Lorenzo the Magnificent, who loved him deeply but also possessed the clear-eyed political pragmatism of the Medicis. The union of Giovanni and Maria brought together the cadet branch of the Medicis—of which Giovanni was the most important member—and the principal line of Lorenzo the Magnificent. In their son, born in 1519, the two Medici clans, so often at odds, would become one. Pope Leo was so delighted that he stood godfather to the child and suggested the name Cosimo, to revive "the memory of the wisest, bravest, and most prudent man yet born to the house of Medici."

Giovanni's qualities accelerated his military career. By the age of twenty he commanded an army of six thousand infantry. In an Italy where Francis I, the king of France, and the Holy Roman Emperor Charles V were preparing to turn the peninsula into a theater of war, there was plenty of work for Giovanni and his men. Giovanni's soldiers displayed utter loyalty to him, idolizing his decisiveness, his ingenuity, and most of all his indefatigable courage. Undefeated as they battled from one end of the country to the other, Giovanni's army had been dubbed L'Invincibile. Giovanni himself had also earned a new title, L'Italia. The exploits of Caterina's son were uniting the people of Italy. But this very success would be the beginning of Giovanni's undoing.

AROUND THEIR CAPTAIN's bier, Giovanni's soldiers wandered among the mourners, easily recognizable with their close-cropped hair amid the flowing locks of the nobility. Giovanni had shorn his hair early in his military career, claiming that "long hair was good only for housing lice and getting caught by the enemy," and his men had emulated their leader. Their armor also distinguished them, decorated as it was in black bands. At the death of Pope Leo X in 1521, Giovanni donned the bands as a sign of mourning for the pope who gave him his first *condotta*. The army would eventually be known by these black bands, and named for posterity the Bande Nere.

The soldiers eagerly shared anecdotes about his exploits. They boasted that their commander had always fought as one of them. He never wore any recognizable markings that would signal his value alive as a hostage but rather fought side by side with his infantry, risking death equally with them.

Many recalled when, in 1521, Giovanni was charged to wrest Milan, his mother's ancestral home, from the French. Giovanni, stationed to the east on the other side of the river Adda, appeared to be only preventing any further advance by the French army. Suddenly, in full armor and followed by his men, Giovanni swam across the river, surprising the enemy at the gates and successfully regaining the city. This feat had been recounted in every town in Italy and made him a coveted commander among mercenary armies.

Pope Leo sent effusive congratulations to the army, his last letters to them. Giovanni's papal protector died a few weeks later. The death of Leo left Giovanni, close in line for the Medici inheritance, dangerously exposed. Indifferent to politics, he ignored the question. The soldiers never knew anything of the machinations at work to tighten a noose around their beloved commander.

Leo X was succeeded by his cousin Clement VII, the illegitimate son of Guiliano de' Medici, who had been killed in the Pazzi conspiracy in 1478. Clement's entire pontificate was directed toward obtaining the sovereignty of Florence and its territories in order to create the Duchy of Tuscany. Constantly scheming, Clement in 1525 found it expedient to strike an alliance with the French king and sent Giovanni and his Bande Nere to lay siege to Pavia. Ten days before the projected battle, Giovanni was shot in the leg. Once the broken leg was set, the soldier was brought to the safety of Piacenza. King Francis I visited the wounded commander in person and sat by his bedside. Like his mother, Giovanni had also garnered the admiration of the French. Ten days later, after his troops were crushed and the king was led off as a prisoner, he was heard to lament that had Giovanni been present, they would not have lost the day.

AMONG THE MUFFLED conversations in the hushed room, the author Pietro Aretino raised his voice to get the attention of the bereaved guests. Notorious for caustic words, Pietro softened only in the company of his dear friend Giovanni. Aretino had traveled for years with Giovanni, happy to record the exploits of a true hero. In him Aretino had found an antidote to his bitter view of humanity. Pietro had held the young soldier as he drew his last breaths and later penned his eulogy. From one who rarely had a generous comment about anyone, including God, his words about Giovanni are all the more moving: "He gave away to his soldiers more than he ever kept for himself. Fatigue and hardship he endured with the greatest patience. He was the first to mount and the last to dismount. He esteemed men according to their value, not according to their rank and wealth. He was always better than his word in actions, but in council he never traded on his great reputation . . . In short, many may envy him, but none can imitate him."[1]

There in the dark chapel, amid the tales of valor and victory, a nagging question hung in the air. How could it happen that the invincible Giovanni de' Medici, the one man who could have restored peace to Italy, was lying there dead? Could it really be, as Machiavelli suggested, just a cruel trick of fortune, or were darker forces at work? A few eyes came to rest on the papal standard hung over the body in honor of the new incumbent, Pope Clement VII. The more pious offered a quick prayer for the pope, now deprived of his greatest protector; a few others, like Aretino, narrowed their eyes in contempt.

Miles away in Rome, in the opulent papal apartments where Raphael had painted the noble precepts that should inspire rulers, Pope Clement slept fitfully. Plotting for his own illegitimate son, Alexander, to become the first duke of Tuscany, he had to overcome many obstacles. The clever pope had first removed the last Medici of the branch descending from Cosimo the Elder, Ippolito de' Medici, the legitimate son of Giuliano, by naming him, very much against his will, a cardinal. Immediately thereafter, Pope Clement had dispatched him on a diplomatic mission to Hungary, out of the sight of all political players. His role as cardinal would bar him from ever becoming duke. Giovanni was the only obstacle between the dukedom and Alexander de' Medici.

From the beginning of Clement's pontificate, he had made use of Giovanni's talents, sending him from one dangerous situation to the next. Always relishing adventure, Giovanni delighted in the hazardous missions, but his wife, Maria, knew his value to the Medici line and quickly perceived that the pope's reliance on Giovanni actually masked a desire to place him in harm's way. Pope Clement cast Giovanni repeatedly into combat, hoping each time that he would not return.

In his all-consuming desire to obtain Tuscany, Pope Clement had made a devious diplomatic gambit, reconciling with Emperor Charles V after his flirtation with the king of France, pretending to have repudiated Gaulish wiles. But in 1526, Charles V discovered that the pope had again allied himself with the French king Francis I against Charles, and he decided to teach Clement a lesson in loyalty. He dispatched a contingent of sixteen thousand German mercenary soldiers to capture the pope and seize Rome. The Landsknechte swarmed over the Alps, eager to loot the Eternal City. By late October, the troops threatened to engulf Mantua, then wash over the Po River into papal territory. Francesco della Rovere, unable to withstand the mercenaries, had long abandoned his post in Milan. As winter approached, only Giovanni and his Bande Nere stood between the invaders and Rome.

Giovanni engaged the Landsknechte on the banks of the freezing Mincio River on November 21, 1526. In the fierce skirmishes Giovanni managed to defeat the German rear guard, but just as his mother had succumbed to the light mobile artillery at Ravaldino, so Giovanni lost to the falconet, and was hit in the leg on November 25, in the same place where he had been shot a year earlier.

Giovanni was carried to the palace of the marquis of Mantua, who, albeit having treacherously assisted the Landsknechte, immediately offered the best rooms in the palace and called his own doctor to tend the wounded man. This time the leg would not heal. Gangrene soon set in. Aretino took it upon himself to tell his friend that the leg would have to be amputated to save his life. Although it meant the end of his brilliant military career, Giovanni accepted the news with admirable forbearance.

To perform the operation, he would be administered the strongest narcotic available, and ten men were summoned to hold him down, to prevent him from thrashing in pain. Giovanni calmly told Aretino that if he did not choose to be subdued, not even twenty men would be able to contain him. Giovanni then took the candle himself, dismissed his soldiers, and held the light for the surgeon throughout the agonizing operation. He lost his leg, but he won fame as the bravest man in Italy.

For all his stoic suffering, his condition worsened; septicemia began to poison his blood. In his last painful hours, Giovanni, completely lucid, sent affectionate letters to his wife and found the strength to address his soldiers one last time. "Love me when I am dead," he asked of them. The battle-hardened warriors wept as he received last rites. Giovanni struggled to live long enough to see his son, whom he sent for, but he realized death would claim him before he could fulfill that last desire. Asking to be taken from the plush bed of the duke of Mantua and laid in his rough camp cot, Giovanni de' Medici died on November 30, 1526.

The dim skies of the Lombard winter and the heavy snows that had fallen during Giovanni's last days kept the room in semidarkness. The Landsknechte had escaped, leaving a trail of destruction, while Italy's savior lay lifeless in his grave. Aretino, who, like Maria Salviati, had perceived the pope's sinister intentions, commented that one "can hear already the growls of the pope, who will believe that he is better off in having lost such a man."[2]

Pope Clement had gotten his wish, the death of the troublesome heir, but the cost would be staggering. The Landsknechte sacked Rome on May 6, 1527, sending the pope scurrying for Orvieto and claiming the lives of twenty-eight thousand Romans.

A pale ray of sunshine forced its way through the iron-gray clouds, casting a sliver of light into the room. It bathed a tall pale-faced child with chestnut hair cut short like that of the soldiers of the Bande Nere. Seven-year-old Cosimo de' Medici, the only son and heir of Giovanni de' Medici, stood dry-eyed by the window, looking at his father's body.

Cosimo had seen his father little in his short life, his most vivid memory being one brief visit when he was a mere toddler. Giovanni had galloped to the window of the Palazzo Salviati and ordered his nurse to throw the boy out of the window into his waiting arms. The nurse refused at first, but then, frightened by Giovanni's anger, obeyed. The soldier neatly caught Cosimo, delighted to see the child unruffled by the experience. Kissing his son with joy, Giovanni exclaimed, "You'll be a prince. It's your destiny."

Several thoughtful glances were cast at the quiet boy in the corner.

What future awaited this child, the culmination of the two Medici lines? Few could guess the exalted destiny of the taciturn Cosimo on the day of his father's funeral. Pope Clement would succeed in putting his son Alexander on the throne of Florence, but the debauched duke would be so hated that he would be murdered in 1536 after assassinating his own cousin, Cardinal Ippolito. At the age of seventeen, young Cosimo would take his place. Caterina Sforza had left one last great legacy to the world in her grandson, the first Medici head to wear the crown of the grand duke of Tuscany and the beginning of a line that would become synonymous with the great city of Florence.

Notes

1. THE EDUCATION OF AN AMAZON

1. Albeit a century old, Cecilia M. Ady's *A History of Milan Under the Sforza* remains the most comprehensive English-language study of the Sforza reign.
2. Recounted in Luke Syson and Dillian Gordon, *Pisanello: Painter to the Renaissance Court*, p. 40.
3. Ibid., p. 62.
4. Ibid., p. 64.
5. Bibliothèque Nationale, Paris, *Ital.* 1610 f. 22 copy.
6. Niccolò Machiavelli, *Florentine Histories*, p. 307.

2. CHILDHOOD'S END

1. Gregory Lubkin, *A Renaissance Court*, pp. 106–9.
2. Machiavelli, *Florentine Histories*, p. 301.
3. Marquis of Mantua to Gabriella Gonzaga, January 6, 1473. Potenze Estere, Milan State Archives.
4. *Virtue and Beauty*, edited by David Alan, provides details concerning marriage customs as well as objects from the marriage ritual.
5. Lubkin, *A Renaissance Court*, attests to heavy-handed sexual humor in Galeazzo's court, and Philippe Aries, in *Centuries of Childhood: A Social History of Family Life*, chapter 5, discusses adult conversations conducted in front of children.
6. *Archivio Storico Lombardo. Yr XV fasc. III ed P. Ghinzoni.* Milan State Archives.

7. Roma to Giovanni Arcimboldi, "oratore ducale" in Rome, January 23, 1473. Potenze Estere, Milan State Archives.
8. *Ducal register* K. n.1 foglio138t. Milan State Archives.
9. Caterina and Girolamo's marriage arrangements are published in Pier Desiderio Pasolini's *Caterina Sforza*, vol. 3, docs. 54, 59, and 60.

3. THE COUNTESS-IN-WAITING

1. Paul and Lora Merkley, *Music and Patronage in the Sforza Court*, pp. 44–45.
2. Pietro Ghinzoni, *L'inquinto, Ossia una Tassa Odiosa del Secolo XV*, series 2, vol. 1, fasc. 3.
3. Cecilia Ady, *A History of Milan Under the Sforza*, p. 104.
4. Lubkin, *A Renaissance Court*, p. 200.
5. Ibid., p. 198.
6. Story of the death of Galeazzo, studied and documented by Eugenio Casanova, *L'Uccisione di Galeazzo Maria Sforza*, Archivio Storico Lombardo, 1899, and reprinted in Cecilia Ady, *A History of Milan Under the Sforza*, p. 113.
7. From Bibliothèque Nationale, Paris, reprinted in Pasolini, *Caterina Sforza*, vol. 3, n. 70.

4. THE TRIUMPHAL PARADE TO ROME

1. Donne Celebri Caterina to Chiara, April 27, 1477. Milan State Archives.
2. Staccate Bona to Bossi, April 26, 1477. Milan State Archives.
3. Bossi to Bona May 4, 1477, Milan State Archives, reprinted in Pasolini, *Caterina Sforza*, vol. 3, doc. 92.
4. Donne Celebri Caterina to Chiara, May 3, 1477. Milan State Archives.
5. Ibid.
6. Oratore of Milan to Ducal Court, May 11, 1477, Milan State Archives, reprinted in Pasolini, *Caterina Sforza*, vol. 3, docs. 93–94.
7. The events related to the arrival of Caterina in Rome and her encounters with both Girolamo and Pope Sixtus IV were meticulously described by the envoys of the Milanese court accompanying Caterina. The letter, several pages long, is dated May 28, 1477, and is in the Milan State Archives, reprinted in Pasolini, *Caterina Sforza*, vol. 3, doc. 105.

5. COURTIERS AND CONSPIRACIES

1. Lionardo Bruni, *Opere Letterarie*, p. 44.
2. Stefano Infessura, *I Diarii Romani*, Vatican Archives: Registri Garampi 1435–1505, BIIII L89, p. 35.
3. Gregorovius, *History of Rome in the Fifteenth Century*, vol. 7A, p. 243.
4. Registro Ducale N. 123 f. 186, Milan State Archives, reprinted in Pasolini, *Caterina Sforza*, vol. 3, doc. 116.
5. Ibid., vol. 1, p. 81.

6. Gino Capponi, *Confessioni di G.Battista da Montesecco, Relativa alla Congiura dei Pazzi*, in *Storia della reppublica Fiorentina*, vol. 5A, p. 547. The startling confession of Girolamo's personal bodyguard on the eve of the execution clearly implicates Girolamo, while leaving a very small amount of room to claim that Sixtus was unaware of the plot.

6. THE GROWTH OF THE RIARIO DYNASTY

1. Luke Syson and Dora Thornton, *Objects of Virtue: Art in Renaissance Italy*, p. 45.
2. Caterina to Bona of Savoy, September 1, 1479. Potenze Estere Roma, Milan State Archives.
3. Pasolini, *Caterina Sforza*, vol. 1, p. 100.
4. Ibid., vol. 3, doc. 137.
5. Ibid., doc. 140.
6. Edgmont Lee, *Sixtus, His Court, and Rome: Un Pontificato e una Citta*, p. 32.
7. Lisa Passaglia Bauman, *Power and Image: Della Rovere Patronage in Late Quattrocento Rome*, Ph.D. Dissertation, p. 2.
8. Private Archives of the Sforza-Riario families, private writing of the Riario household, fasc. 2, n. 56, Imola and Forlì. Naples State Archives.
9. Pasolini, *Caterina Sforza*, vol. 3, doc. 146.
10. *Diary of Pope Sixtus IV, 1479–1484*, p. 176. Vatican Archives.

7. THE FAIREST IN THE REALM

1. Paola Mettica, "La Societa Forlivese del '400,'" p. 78.
2. Natale Graziani and Gabriella Venturelli, *Caterina Sforza*, p. 46.
3. Stefano Infessura, *Il Diario di Stefano Infessura*, p. 179.
4. Leone Cobelli, *Cronache Forlivesi delle Fondazione della citta fino al 1498*, p. 263.
5. The vivid description of Caterina and Girolamo's entry into Forlì was written by an anonymous eyewitness and is in the Florence National Library, manoscritto 2, f. 368.
6. Antonio Appiani to the duke of Milan, July 15, 1481. Potenze Estere, Milan State Archives.
7. Cobelli, *Cronache Forlivesi*, p. 266.
8. Ibid.
9. Infessura, *Il Diario di Stefano Infessura*, p. 85.
10. Francesco Casati to the duke of Milan, July 18, 1481. Potenze Estere, Milan State Archives, reprinted in Pasolini, *Caterina Sforza*, vol. 3, doc. 165.
11. Antonio Appiani to the duke of Milan, September 7, 1481. Potenze Estere, Milan State Archives, reprinted in Pasolini, *Caterina Sforza*, vol. 3, doc. 182.
12. Med. A. Pr. filza 38. Florence State Archives.
13. Pasolini, *Caterina Sforza*, vol. 1, p. 122.
14. Communi Cotignola, September 22, 1481. Milan State Archives.
15. October 30, 1481, Potenze Estere, Milan State Archives, reprinted in Pasolini, *Caterina Sforza*, vol. 3, doc. 195.

16. Fernand Braudel, *The Structure of Everyday Life*, vol. 1, p. 128, n. 91.
17. Infessura recounts the behavior of Girolamo in *Il Diario di Stefano Infessura*, pp. 40–42.
18. Pasolini, *Caterina Sforza*, vol. 3, doc. 202.
19. Caterina to the Republic of Siena, August 21, 1482, in Pasolini, *Caterina Sforza*, vol. 3, doc. 205.

8. THE BIRTH OF ATHENA

1. Infessura, *Il Diario di Stefano Infessura*, pp. 78–79.
2. Andrea Bernardi, *Cronache Forlivesi dal 1476 al 1517*, p. 294.
3. The statistics here come from Bauman, *Power and Image: Della Rovere Patronage in Late Quattrocento Rome*.
4. Pasolini, *Caterina Sforza*, vol. 3, docs. 174–76.
5. Ludwig van Pastor, *Lives of the Popes*, book 3, chapter 12b, gives an interesting analysis of the fresco cycle.
6. August Schmarsow, *Melozzo da Forlì*, p. 177.
7. Pasolini, *Caterina Sforza*, vol. 1, p. 134.
8. *Diary of Pope Sixtus IV: 1479–1484*, p. 29.
9. Sigismondo dei Conti, quoted in Pastor, *Lives of the Popes*, p. 550.
10. Infessura, *Il Diario di Stefano Infessura*, p. 177.
11. Gregorovius, *History of Rome in the Middle Ages*, vol. 7A, p. 281.
12. Infessura, *Il Diario di Stefano Infessura*, p. 129.
13. Vespucci to Lorenzo de' Medici, August 18, 1484. Florence State Archives, filza 39G.
14. The negotiations between Caterina, Girolamo, and the Curia are recorded in letters by both Pierfilippo Pandolfi and Guidantonio Vespucci to Lorenzo the Magnificent; both are in the Florence State Archives. The Sienese orator Lorenzo Lanti gives a similar version in his letter to the Signoria de Siena, August 26, 1484, available in the Siena Archives.
15. Pasolini, *Caterina Sforza*, vol. 1, p. 150.

9. THE LEAN YEARS

1. Bernardi, *Cronache Forlivesi*, vol. 1, p. 125.
2. Ambassor Vespucci to Lorenzo the Magnificent, Med. A. Pr. filza 39. Florentine State Archives.
3. Cobelli, *Cronache Forlivesi*, vol. 1, p. 28.
4. Ibid.
5. Niccolò Machiavelli, *The Prince*, p. 45.
6. G. F. Oliva to duke of Milan, August 11, 1486, Milan State Archives, in Mario Tabanelli, *Il Biscione e La Rosa: Caterine Sforza, Girolamo Riario, e I loro primi Discendenti*, p. 56. Also, F. Visconti to duke of Milan, November 8, 1486, in ibid., p. 57.
7. F. Visconti to Duke Gian Galeazzo, November 8, 1486. Potenze Estere, Milan State Archives.

8. F. Visconti to Duke Gian Galeazzo, November 26, 1486. Potenze Estere, Milan State Archives.
9. Magdalena Soest's theory was announced first in the German paper *Bild Zeitung* and then recounted in English in "Mona Lisa Revealed as Adventurous Beauty," *The Guardian*, March 14, 2002.

10. TAKING CENTER STAGE

1. Machiavelli, *The Prince*, in *The Portable Machiavelli*, p. 99.
2. In his book *The Courtier*, Baldassare Castiglione describes Duchess Elisabetta Gonzaga of Urbino as the paradigm of feminine virtue. He emphasizes her personal virtue and modesty, which inspired all those in her court to behave with due respect and reverence. Elisabetta, wife of the chronically ill duke of Urbino, did not run her husband's state as Caterina did, but allowed herself to be guided by male counselors and presided over a salon of artists and literati. Personal objects of women, from portraits to their wedding chests, also emphasized the virtue of chastity. See David Alan Brown, *Virtue and Beauty*, and Syson and Thornton, *Objects of Virtue: Art in Renaissance Italy*.
3. Caterina to Duke of Ferrara, July 24, 1487, in Pasolini, *Caterina Sforza*, vol. 3, doc. 249.
4. Andrea Bernardi recounts this story in *Cronache Forlivesi*, p. 135.

11. THE RETORT AT RAVALDINO

1. A. Burriel, *Vita di Caterina Sforza*, vol. 2, p. 260.
2. Cobelli, *Cronache Forlivesi*, p. 119, and Bernardi, *Cronache Forlivesi*, p. 234.
3. Pasolini, *Caterina Sforza*, vol. 1, p. 218.
4. Cobelli, *Cronache Forlivesi*, pp. 320–21.
5. Ibid.
6. Bernardi, *Cronache Forlivesi*, p. 238.
7. The eyewitnesses Cobelli and Bernardi give diverging stories on the whole story of Caterina's behavior at Ravaldino. Bernardi covers it in his *Cronache Forlivesi*, vol. 1, p. 238, and Cobelli in his *Cronache Forlivesi*, p. 322.
8. This, the most famous version of the retort of Ravaldino, was written by Giovanni Corbizi to Lorenzo de' Medici but was sent from Faenza. It is dated April 17, the same day of the event. Med. A. Pr. filza 40-285. Florence State Archives.
9. Lorenzo Giustiniani used the term "tigress" to a Venetian ambassador; it was reprinted in Marino Sanuto, *I Diarii*, vol. 2, p. 60.
10. Med. A. Pr. filza 40-285. Florence State Archives.
11. Niccolò Machiavelli, *Discourses on the First Ten Books of Titus Livius*, book 3, chapter 6.
12. Corbizi to Lorenzo de' Medici, April 17, 1488; Galeotto Manfredi to Lorenzo de' Medici, April 20, 1488; Giovanni Bentivoglio to Lorenzo de' Medici, April 18, 1488; Migliore Cresci to Lorenzo de' Medici, April 17, 1488; and the duke

of Milan to the king of Hungary. Med. A. Pr. filza 40-285, Florence State Archives, reprinted in Pasolini, *Caterina Sforza*, vol. 3, doc. 295.

13. Bernardi, *Cronache Forlivesi*, vol. 1, p. 240.
14. Cobelli, *Cronache Forlivesi*, p. 327.
15. B. Arlotti to the duke of Ferrara, April 30, 1488, reprinted in full in Pasolini, *Caterina Sforza*, vol. 3, doc. 287.
16. Bernardi, *Cronache Forlivesi*, vol. 1, p. 241.
17. Orsi to Medici, April 19, 1488. Florence State Archives.

12. THE SPOILS OF WAR

1. Cobelli, *Cronache Forlivesi*, p. 332.
2. Ibid., p. 336.
3. Milan State Archives, reprinted in Pasolini, *Caterina Sforza*, vol. 3, doc. 294.
4. Cobelli, *Cronache Forlivesi*, p. 339.
5. Ibid., p. 340.
6. Besides the accounts of Cobelli and Bernardi, several letters list those executed by Caterina; the most precise listing is in Giovanni Corbizi to Nicolo Ridolfi, May 7, 1488, reprinted in Pasolini, *Caterina Sforza*, vol. 3, doc. 297.
7. Lauro Martines, *April Blood: Florence and the Plot Against the Medici*, p. 126.
8. The murder of Galeotto Manfredi was first recounted by the Forlivese diarist Andrea Bernardi and confirmed by a letter from Francesco Macchietta to Tomaso Ridolfi of Florence, June 3, 1488, reprinted in Pasolini, *Caterina Sforza*, vol. 3, doc. 302.
9. *Innocentii VIII, Vicariatus*, vol. 98.f.93.b, Vatican Archives.

13. FANNING THE FLAMES

1. Cobelli makes note of the supposed relationship between Antonio Maria and Caterina; see Pasolini, *Caterina Sforza*, vol. 3, p. 319, n. 2. The Cronaca Marconi, an Imolese diarist, said the Forlivesi believed there was an affair, but the Imolesi didn't; see C. Vecchiazzani, *Historia di Forlimpopoli*, vol. 2, pp. 177–78. A letter from the duke of Milan to Branda da Castiglione, September 11, 1489, conveys the fears of her relatives; see Potenze Estere, Milan State Archives.
2. Duke of Milan to Branda da Castiglione, September 11, 1489. Potenze Estere, Milan State Archives.
3. Duke of Milan to Branda da Castiglione, May 13, 1488. Potenze Estere, Milan State Archives.
4. Bernardi, *Cronache Forlivesi*, p. 299.
5. G. F. Cortini, *La Madonna di Piratello presso Imola*, pamphlet.
6. Med. A. Pr. filza 41 n.467. Florence State Archives.
7. Caterina's prim account of Feo's behavior differs from that of the governor of Imola, who refers to how Caterina "got rid of her castellan" in the relative documents of the Imola Archives. Andrea Bernardi provides the most detailed account, with the tale of seduction.

8. Caterina Sforza, *Ricettario di Bellezza*, p. 158.
9. The last will and testament of Caterina specifically states that her son Bernardino, later known as Carlo, was the fruit of a legitimate marriage with Feo, although she does not give the date of the marriage. Med. A. Pr. carte private f. 99 n.12. Florence State Archives.
10. Cobelli, *Cronache Forlivesi*, p. 413.
11. Puccio Pucci to Piero de' Medici. May 21, 1493, carte private filza 54 c.144, Florence State Archives.
12. Cobelli, *Cronache Forlivesi*, p. 415.

14. BLINDED BY LOVE

1. Pasolini, *Caterina Sforza*, vol. 1, p. 340.
2. Burriel, *Vita di Caterina Sforza*, vol. 2, p. 507.
3. Cobelli, *Cronache Forlivesi*, p. 358.
4. Med. A. Pr. filza 54 c.165. Florence State Archives.
5. Ibid.
6. Bernardi, *Cronache Forlivesi*, vol. 1, A2, p. 98, and Cobelli, *Cronache Forlivesi*, p. 394.

15. AVENGING FURY

1. Dante Alighieri, *Inferno*, p. 283.
2. Cobelli, *Cronache Forlivesi*, pp. 383–84.
3. Potenze Estere, Milan State Archives, reprinted in Pasolini, *Caterina Sforza*, vol. 3, doc. 586.
4. Ibid.
5. Cobelli, *Cronache Forlivesi*, p. 384.
6. Cobelli's list is on pp. 390–91; Bernardi also mentions those killed throughout his diary.
7. Cardinal Ascanio Sforza to Duke Ludovico of Milan, Potenze Estere, Milan State Archives, reprinted in Pasolini, *Caterina Sforza*, vol. 3, doc. 634.
8. Tragically, the frescoes were destroyed in World War II; today they are known only through photographs.
9. March 21, 1496. Potenze Estere, Milan State Archives.
10. Bernardi, *Cronache Forlivesi*, vol. 1, A2, p. 129.
11. Attilio Monti, "La Rocca di Ravaldino," *Forum Livii*, pp. 7–21. After Caterina's time, Ravaldino became a prison and is today (much altered) a tourist attraction.
12. Caterina to the duke of Milan, April 14, 1496. Potenze Estere, Milan State Archives.
13. Caterina to the duke of Milan, March 27, 1496. Potenze Estere, Milan State Archives.
14. Caterina to the duke of Milan, September 24, 1496. Potenze Estere, Milan State Archives.

15. Caterina to the duke of Milan, August 22, 1496. Potenze Estere, Milan State Archives.
16. Corrado Ricci, "Il Ritratto di Caterina Sforza," *Forum Livii*, pp. 5–12, and Tabanelli, *Il Biscione e La Rosa*, pp. 97–106. Both discuss Caterina's coins and portraits.
17. Caterina to the duke of Milan, April 11, 1496. Potenze Estere, Milan State Archives.
18. Bologna, Francesco Tranchedini, October 10, 1496. Potenze Estere, Milan State Archives.
19. Caterina to Tranchedini, November 29, 1496. Forlì. Milan State Archives.
20. Med. A. Pr. filza 71 c.27. Florence State Archives.
21. Tranchedini to the duke of Milan, January 28, 1498. Potenze Estere, Milan State Archives.
22. Jacopo Filippo Foresti, *De Plurimis Claris Selectisque Mulieribus.* This work was published in Ferrara in 1497, naming Caterina among the most famous women in history, living or dead. One of the extremely rare originals is kept at Bryn Mawr College.
23. Caterina to the duke of Milan, August 25, 1498. Potenze Estere, Milan State Archives.
24. Ibid.

16. INTRIGUE AND INVASION

1. Caterina to the duke of Milan, January 24, 1499. Potenze Estere, Milan State Archives.
2. Caterina to Lorenzo de' Medici, October 18, 1498. Med. A. Pr. Florence State Archives.
3. Med. A. Pr. filza 79 n.59. Florence State Archives.
4. Ibid.
5. Ibid.
6. Carte di Urbino, cl.I div.F, from *Diversorum, Alexandri VI fol. 132.* Florence State Archives.
7. Machiavelli to Prior Libertà e Gonfaloniere di Giustizia, July 17, 1499, in Pasolini, *Caterina Sforza*, vol. 2.
8. Ibid.
9. Machiavelli to Prior Libertà e Gonfaloniere di Giustizia, July 22, 1499, in Pasolini, *Caterina Sforza*, vol. 2, p. 105.
10. Machiavelli to Prior Libertà e Gonfaloniere di Giustizia, July 24, 1499, in Pasolini, *Caterina Sforza*, vol. 2, p. 108.
11. Niccolò Machiavelli, *On the Art of War*, p. 186.
12. Med. A. Pr. August 3, 1499. Florence State Archives.
13. Med. A. Pr. filza 79. c.2. August 8, 1499. Florence State Archives.
14. Med. A. Pr. August 31, 1499. Florence State Archives.
15. Med. A. Pr. carte private filza 78. Florence State Archives.
16. Ibid.
17. Mantua State Archives, reprinted in Pasolini, *Caterina Sforza*, vol. 3, doc. 1094.

17. ITALY'S IDOL

1. Fabio Oliva, *Caterina Sforza*. Oliva lived only one generation after these events and his account seems to be based on local hearsay, in contrast to that of Bernardi, who was an eyewitness. Oliva's dialogue was expanded by Burriel in *Vita di Caterina Sforza*, pp. 770–73. Bernardi's manuscript, however, was read and edited by Cesare after the fall of Caterina.
2. The story of Caterina's ruse to capture Cesare is told in Vecchiazzani, *Historia di Forlimpopoli*, vol. 2, p. 214.
3. Cronca di Antonio Grumello Pavese dal 1467 al 1529, reprinted in Pasolini, *Caterina Sforza*, vol. 2, p. 188.
4. Sanuto, *I Diarii*, vol. 2, fol. 529.
5. Ibid.
6. Vittorio Mezzamonaco and Sergio Spada, "Gennaio 1500: La fine di una Signoria: Le Ultime Giorni di Caterina Sforza," *Le Pie*.
7. Burriel, *Vita di Caterina Sforza*, vol. 3, pp. 788–89.
8. Sanuto, *I Diarii*, vol. 3, c.57.
9. Machiavelli, *On the Art of War*, p. 186.
10. Machiavelli, *The Prince*, chapter 20.
11. Francesco Guicciardini, *Storie D'Italia*, book 9, chapter 3.
12. Mezzamonaco and Spada, "Gennaio 1500."
13. Machiavelli, *On the Art of War*.
14. Machiavelli, *Letter alle Dieci della Balia*, cited in Pasolini, *Caterina Sforza*, vol. 2, p. 218.
15. Bernardi, *Cronache Forlivesi*, vol. 1, p. 282.
16. Graziani and Venturelli, *Caterina Sforza*, p. 280.
17. Ibid.
18. Ibid., p. 279.
19. Published in Pasolini, *Caterina Sforza*, vol. 2, pp. 270–81. Translation by author.

18. THE LONG NIGHT OF CASTEL SANT'ANGELO

1. Giovanni Lucido to the marquis of Mantua, February 27, 1500, Mantua State Archives, reprinted in Pasolini, *Caterina Sforza*, vol. 3, doc. 1124.
2. Ottaviano to Caterina, May 11, 1500. Med. A. Pr. Florence State Archives.
3. Ibid.
4. Med. A. Pr. filza 85. Florence State Archives.
5. Med. A. Pr. carte private filza 78 c.127. Florence State Archives.
6. Ibid.
7. No record of this intended trial exists anywhere. Pasolini claims to have examined 263 manuscripts (*Caterina Sforza*, vol. 2, p. 266) and enlisted the assistance of Rome's finest archivists with no result; but both her contemporary Bernardi and the later biographer Fabio Oliva claim that Caterina's responses were so shattering as to have silenced the entire process.
8. Piovano to Ottaviano, 1500 (no exact date). Florence State Archives.

9. Ottaviano to Caterina, July 4, 1500. Florence State Archives.
10. Mantua State Archives, reprinted in Pasolini, *Caterina Sforza*, vol. 3, doc. 1138.
11. Ottaviano to Caterina, July 4, 1500. Florence State Archives.
12. Med. A. Pr. filza 72 a.520. Florence State Archives.
13. Francesco Fortunati, July 8, 1501. Florence State Archives.
14. Pasolini, *Caterina Sforza*, vol. 2, p. 304.
15. *Reform. Atti Pubblici*, N.237. Florence State Archives.
16. Caterina's son by Giacomo Feo underwent a mysterious name change during the years between Giacomo's assassination and Caterina's death. He is called Bernardino by all sources in his infancy, but he will be called Carlo in Caterina's will.

19. SLEEP AFTER TOIL

1. Francesco Fortunati to Ottaviano, July 8, 1502. Florence State Archives.
2. Med. A. Pr. July 22, 1502. Florence State Archives.
3. Med. A. Pr. filza 77 n.188. October 23, 1503. Florence State Archives.
4. Sanuto, *I Diarii*, 1.c., cap.V, p. 782.
5. Med. A. Pr. filza 78 c.217. February 21, 1502. Florence State Archives.
6. Dieci di Balia, carteggio, responsive register 74 N.135.
7. Med. A. Pr. filza 77 c.137. Florence State Archives.
8. Sanuto, *I Diarii*, 1.c., cap.V, p. 782.
9. Med. A. Pr. filza 77 c.137. Florence State Archives.
10. Gabriele Piccoli, June 27, 1504. Med. A. Pr. filza 125 c.57. Florence State Archives. Translation by the author.
11. Sanuto, *I Diarii*, 1.c., cap.V, p. 799.
12. Med. A. Pr. July 9, 1507. Florence State Archives.
13. The last will and testament of Caterina was written on May 28, 1509, and is in the Florence State Archives. Med. A. Pr. carte private filza 99 n.12.

EPILOGUE: MANTUA, 1526

1. Pietro Aretino, *The Works of Aretino*, vol. 1, p. 54.
2. Ibid.

Sources

ARCHIVES

All translations of archival documents are by the author.

Florence State Archives: Pre-principality Medici Archive,
    Lorenzo de' Medici, 1474–87
Forlì Archives
Imola Archives
Lombard Historical Archives
Mantua State Archives: Gonzaga Archive
Milan State Archives: Sforza Archive, Potenze Estere
Naples State Archives: Private Archive Sforza Riario
Vatican Archives: Registri Garampi

BOOKS, ARTICLES, AND MANUSCRIPTS

Ackerman, James. *The Villa: Form and Ideology of Country Houses.* London: Thames
    and Hudson, 1990
Acton, Harold. *The Pazzi Conspiracy: The Plot Against the Medici.* London: Thames
    and Hudson, 1979
Ady, Cecilia M. *A History of Milan Under the Sforza*, edited by Edward Armstrong.
    London: Methuen & Co., 1907
Ady, Julia Cartwright. *Isabella D'Este, Marchioness of Mantua, 1473–1530: A Study of
    the Renaissance*, vol. 1. New York: Dutton, 1905

Ajmar-Wollheim, Marta, and Flora Dennis. *At Home in Renaissance Italy*. London: V&A Publications, 2006

Aretino, Pietro. *The Works of Aretino*, vol. 2, translated and edited by Samuel Putnam. Chicago: Pascal Covici, 1926

Aries, Philippe. *Centuries of Childhood: A Social History of Family Life*. New York: Vintage Books, 1962

Aroldi, A. M. *Armi e Armature Italiane*. Milan: Bramante, 1961

Baini, L., and N. Giustozzi. *Guide to the Castel Sant'Angelo*. Milan: Mondadori Electa, 2003

Bassani, Aureliano. *Catharina: Racconto Storico*. Imola (Bologna): La Mandragora, 1994

Bauman, Lisa Passaglia. *Power and Image: Della Rovere Patronage in Late Quattrocento Rome*. Ph.D. dissertation, Northwestern University, June 1990

Bellonci, Maria. *Lucrezia Borgia*. Milan: Mondadori, 1939

Beltrami, Luca. *La Vita nel Castello di Milano al tempo degli Sforza*. Pamphlet. Milan: Tipografia Umberto Allegretti, 1900

Berger, Frederik. *Die Madonna von Forlì*. Berlin: Rütten & Loening, 2002

Bernardi, Andrea. *Cronache Forlivesi dal 1476 al 1517*. Bologna: Deputazione Storia per la Romagna, 1895–97 (Translations by the author)

Beuf, Carlo. *Cesare Borgia: The Machiavellian Prince*. Toronto and New York: Oxford University Press, 1942

Boccaccio, Giovanni. *Famous Women*, edited and translated by Virginia Brown. Cambridge, MA: Harvard University Press, 2001

Bradford, Sarah. *Lucrezia Borgia*. New York: Penguin, 2004

Braschi, Angelo. *Caterina Sforza*. Rocca San Casciano: Cappelli, 1965

Braudel, Fernand. *The Structure of Everyday Life*, vol. 1. New York: Harper & Row, 1985

Breisach, Ernst. *Caterina Sforza: A Renaissance Virago*. Chicago: University of Chicago Press, 1967

Brogi, Cecilia. *Caterina Sforza: La Più Bella, la Più Audace e Fiera, la Più Gloriosa Donna d'Italia, Pari Se Non Superiore ai Grandi Condottieri del Suo Tempo*. Arezzo: Alberti, 1996

Brown, David Alan, ed. *Virtue and Beauty*. Princeton, NJ: Princeton University Press, 2001

Bruni, Lionardo. *History of the Florentine People*, vol. 1, books 1–4, edited and translated by James Hankins. Cambridge, MA: Harvard University Press, 2001

———. *Opere Letterarie*. Torino: Einaudi, 1996

Burchard, Johann. *The Diary of John Burchard of Strasbourg, Bishop of Orta and Civita Castellana: Pontifical Master of Ceremonies to Their Holinesses Sixtus P. P. IV, Innocent P. P. VIII, Alexander P. P. VI, Pius P. P. III, and Julius P. P. II*, A.D. *1483–1506*, translated by Arnold Harris Mathew. London: Francis Griffiths, 1910

Burckhardt, Jacob. *The Civilization of the Renaissance in Italy*. New York and London: Penguin, 1990

Burriel, A. *Vita di Caterina Sforza*. Bologna: San Tomaso D'Aquino, 1795

Capponi, Gino. *Storia della Repubblica di Firenze*, vol. 2A, chap. 5. Florence, 1888

Castiglione, Baldassarre. *The Book of the Courtier: The Singleton Translation*. New York: Norton Critical Editions, 2002

Caterina Sforza: Una Donna del Cinquecento. Catalog of the exhibition, February 5–May 21, 2000. Imola: La Mandragora, 2000

Clark, Kenneth. *Leonardo da Vinci*. London: Penguin, 1988

Clark, Nicholas. *Melozzo da Forlì: Pictor Papalis*. New York: Harper & Row, 1990

Cobelli, Leone. *Cronache Forlivesi delle Fondazione della citta fino al 1498*. Bologna: Regia, 1874 (Translations by the author)

Cole, Alison. *Virtue and Magnificence: Art of the Italian Renaissance Courts*. New York: Harry Abrams, 1995

Cortini, G. F. *La Madonna di Piratello presso Imola*. Pamphlet. Imola: Galeati, 1939

Dante Alighieri. *Inferno*, translated by Robert Pinsky. New York: Farrar, Straus and Giroux, 1994

DeVries, Joyce Carol. *Power, Gender, and Representation in the Italian Renaissance Court: The Cultural Patronage of Caterina Sforza*. Ph.D. dissertation, Harvard University, 2002

Diary of Pope Sixtus IV: 1479–1484. Asque ad Ejus Obit. Vatican Archives: Registri Garampi 1435–1505, BXLVIIII

Durant, Will. *The Renaissance*. New York: Simon and Schuster, 1953

Foresti, Jacopo Filippo. *De Plurimis Claris Selectisque Mulieribus*. Ferrara: Lorenzo de Rubeis, 1497

Frank, Isabelle Jennifer. *Melozzo da Forlì and the Rome of Pope Sixtus IV*. Ph.D. dissertation, Harvard University, 1991

Frick, Carole Collier. *Dressing in Renaissance Florence: Families, Fortunes, and Fine Clothing*. Baltimore and London: Johns Hopkins University Press, 2002

Fusero, Clemente. *The Borgias*. New York: Praeger, 1972

Gherardi, Johannes. *Il Diario Romano*, in L. Muratori, *Rerum Italicorum Scriptores*, N.S. XXIII pt. iii. Citta del Castello: E. Carusi, 1904

Ghinzoni, Pietro. *L'inquinto, Ossia una Tassa Odiosa del Secolo XV*, series 2, vol. 1, fascicolo 3. 1884. Lombard Historical Archives

Giacometti, Massino, ed. *The Sistine Chapel: The Art, the History, and the Restoration*. New York: Harmony, 1986

Gottschewski, Adolf. *Die Porträts der Caterina Sforza*. Strasbourg: J. H. E. Heitz, 1907

———. *Uber die Porträts der Caterina Sforza und über den Bildhauer Vincenzo Onofri*. Strasbourg: J. H. E. Heitz, 1908

Graziani, Natale. *Fra Medioevo ed l'Eta Moderna: li Signoria dei Riario e di Caterina Sforza*, in *Storia di Forli*, vol. 2, pp. 239–61. Bologna: Nuova Alfa Ed., 1990

Graziani, Natale, and Gabriella Venturelli. *Caterina Sforza*. Milan: Mondadori, 2001

Gregorius, Ferdinand. *The History of Rome in the Middle Ages*, translated by Annie Hamilton. London: Bell & Sons, 1894–1906

Guicciardini, Francesco. *Storia d'Italia IV–V, Storie Fiorentine*, ed. Bergamo. Biblioteca Universale Rizzoli, 1998

Hartt, Frederick, and David Wilkins. *The History of Italian Renaissance Art: Painting, Sculpture, and Architecture*. Upper Saddle River, NJ: Pearson, 2002

Hibbert, Christopher. *The House of Medici: Its Rise and Fall*. London: Allen Kane, 1974

Hollingsworth, Mary. *Patronage in Renaissance Italy: From 1400 to the Early Sixteenth Century*. London: John Murray, 1994

Holmes, George, ed. *The Oxford History of Italy*. New York: Oxford University Press, 1997

Holmes, Megan. *Fra Filippo Lippi: The Carmelite Painter*. New Haven, CT: Yale University Press, 1999

Ianziti, Gary. *Humanistic Historiography Under the Sforzas: Politics and Propaganda in Fifteenth-Century Milan*. New York: Oxford University Press, 1988.

Infessura, Stefano. *Il Diario di Stefano Infessura*, ed. Oreste Tommasini. Roma L'Istituto Storico Italiano Palazzo dei Lincei, 1890 (Translations by the author)

——. *I Diarii Romani*. Vatican Archives: Registri Garampi 1435–1505, BIIII L89 (Translations by the author)

Jansen, Sharon. *The Monstrous Regiment of Women: Female Rulers in Early Modern Europe*. New York: Palgrave/Macmillan, 2002

Kelly, John N. D. *Vita dei Papi*. Alessandria: Piemme, 1989

Larner, John. *Italy in the Age of Dante and Petrarch, 1216–1380*. New York: Longman, 1890

Lee, Edgmont. *Sixtus, His Court, and Rome: Un Pontificato e una Citta*, edited by Massimo Miglio. Acts of the conference in Rome, December 3–7, 1984. Vatican City: Vatican School of Paleography and Archives, 1986

Levi, Pisetzky R. *Storia del costume in Italia*, vol. 2. Milan: Istituto Editoriale Italiano, 1965–69

Levy, Allison M. *Widowhood and Visual Culture in Early Modern Europe*. Hampshire, UK, and Burlington, VT: Ashgate, 2003

Lubkin, Gregory. *Florence and Milan: Acts of Two Conferences at Villa I Tatti, 1982–1984*. Florence: Italia Editrice, 1989

——. *A Renaissance Court: Milan Under Galeazzo Maria Sforza*. Berkeley: University of California Press, 1994

——. *Strategic Hospitality: Foreign Dignitaries at the Court of Milan, 1466–1476*. Burnaby, BC: 1986

Machiavelli, Niccolò. *Discourses on the First Ten Books of Titus Livius*, reprinted in *Historical, Political, and Diplomatic Writings of Machiavelli*, translated by Harvey Mansfield. Chicago: University of Chicago Press, 1996

——. *Florentine Histories*, translated by Laura F. Banfield and Harvey C. Mansfield Jr. Princeton, NJ: Princeton University Press, 1988

——. *Legazioni, Commissarie, Scritti di Governo a cura di Fredi Chiappelli*. Bari: G. Laterza, 1971

——. *The Prince*, translated and edited by Peter Bondanella. New York: Oxford University Press, 2005

——. *The Prince*, in *The Portable Machiavelli*, translated by Ellis Farnsworth. Indianapolis: Bobbs-Merrill, 1978

Majanlahti, Anthony. *The Families Who Made Rome*. London: Random House, 2006

Marinelli, Lodovico. "Le Rocche di Imola," in *Atti e memorie della Reale Duputazione di Storia per la Provincia di Romagna*, series 4, vol. 22. Bologna: Luigi Parma, 1931–32

Martines, Lauro. *April Blood: Florence and the Plot Against the Medici*. London: Oxford University Press, 2004

Merkley, Paul and Lora. *Music and Patronage in the Sforza Court*. Turnhout, Belgium: BREPOLS, 1999

Mettica, Paola. "La Societa Forlivese del '400,'" edited by Castrocaro Zauli. Forlì: Camera di Commercio Forlì, March 1983.

Mezzamonaco, Vittorio, and Sergia Spada. "Gennaio 1500: La fine di una Signoria: Le Ultime Giorni di Caterina Sforza," *Le Pie*, 1989, no. 1, pp. 122–41

Milone, Marinella Festa. "Palazzo Riario Altemps," in *Quaderni*, no. 24, 1977–1978, pp. 13–45

Monti, Attilio. "La Rocca di Ravaldino," *Forum Livii*, Anno II n.1–2 gen-apr. 1927, pp. 7–21

——. "Una Visita al castello di Caterina Sforza," *Le Pie*, 1927, vol. 12, pp. 158–61

Murphy, Caroline. *The Pope's Daughter.* New York: Oxford University Press, 2005

Novielli, Valeria. *Caterina Sforza: Una Donna del Cinquecento: Storia e Arte tra Medioevo e Rinascimento.* Imola (Bologna): La Mandragora, 2000

Oliva, Fabio. *Caterina Sforza.* Forlì: Casali Ed., 1821

Pasini, Adamo. *Breve Storia del Madonna del Fuoco.* Forlì: Centro Studi per Il Movimento Cattolico Forlivesi, 1982

Pasolini, Pier Desiderio. *Caterina Sforza.* Three volumes. Rome: Loescher, 1893 (Translations by the author)

——. *Caterina Sforza: Nuovi Documenti.* Bologna: Tipografia A. Garagnani, 1897

Pastor, Ludwig van. *The Lives of the Popes,* vol. 4, edited by Dom Ernest Graf. Farnham, UK: Lund Humphries, 1957

Patridge, Loren. *The Art of Renaissance Rome.* New York: Abrams Perspectives, 1996

Petrassi, Marco. "I Fasti di Sisto IV," *Capitolium*, 1973, vol. 48, n. 1, pp. 13–23

Rachet, Guy. *Catherine Sforza: La Dame de Forlì.* Paris: Denoël, 1987

Ricci, Corrado. "Il Ritratto di Caterina Sforza," *Forum Livii*, 1928, pp. 5–12

Rossi, Gian Giacomo. *Vita di Giovanni dei Medici* (a cura di V. Bramanti). Rome: Salerno Ed., 1996

Rossi, Sergio, and Stefano Valeri, eds. *Le Due Rome del Quattrocento: Melozzo Antonio e la Cultura Artistica del'400 Romano.* International conference, "La Sapienza," University of Rome, February 21–24, 1996. Rome: Lithos Editrice, 1997

Rowdon, Maurice. *Lorenzo the Magnificent.* London: Weidenfeld and Nicolson, 1974

Ruda, Jeffery. *Fra Filippo Lippi: Life and Work.* London: Phaidon, 1993

Santi, Simone. *Fra' Girolamo Savonarola.* Florence: Le Lettere, 2006

Santoro, Caterina. *Gli Sforza.* Milan: Editori Associati, 1994

——. *I Registri delle Lettere Ducali del Periodo Sforzesco.* Forlì: Archivio Storico Civico Castello Sforzesco, 1961

Sanuto, Marino. *I Diarii.* Venice: Marco Visentini, 1903

Schaivo, Armando. "Ritratto di Gerolamo Riario in Vienna," *Studi Romani*, 1969, vol. 17, n. 3, pp. 315–18

Schmarsow, August. *Melozzo da Forlì.* Berlin: HAAC, 1886

Sciafe, Walter. *Florentine Life During the Renaissance.* Honolulu: University Press of the Pacific, 2002

Sforza, Caterina. *Ricettario di Bellezza,* edited by Luigi Pescasio. Castiglione delle Stiviere: Wella Italiana, 1971

Smyth, Craig Hugh, and GianCarlo Garfagnini, eds. *Florence and Milan: Comparisons and Relations.* Acts of two conferences at Villa I Tatti, 1982–1984, organized by Sergio Bertelli, Nicolai Rubinstein, and Craig Hugh Smyth. Florence: La Nuova Italia, 1989

Squadrilli, Tina. *Castel Sant'Angelo: Una Storia Lunga Diciannove secoli*. Rome: Newton and Compton, 2000

Stinger, Charles. *The Renaissance in Rome*. Bloomington: Indiana University Press, 1998

Syson, Luke, and Gordon Dillian. *Pisanello: Painter to the Renaissance Court*. New Haven, CT: Yale University Press, 2001

Syson, Luke, and Dora Thornton. *Objects of Virtue: Art in Renaissance Italy*. London: British Museum Press, 2001

Tabanelli, Mario. *Il Biscione e La Rosa: Caterina Sforza, Girolamo Riario, e I loro primi Discendenti*. Faenza: Fratelli Lega Editori, 1973

Vecchiazzani, C. *Historia di Forlimpopoli*, vol. 2. Rimini, 1647

Viroli, Maurizio. *Niccolò's Smile: A Biography of Machiavelli*. New York: Hill and Wang, 1989

Walsh, Thomas. *The Last Crusader: Isabella of Spain (1452–1503)*. Rockford, IL: TAN Books, 1980

Welch, Evelyn S. *Art and Authority in Renaissance Milan*. New Haven, CT: Yale University Press, 1995

Young, G. F. *The Medici*. New York: Random House, 1930

PHOTO CREDITS

Index